DATE DUE

~~JAN 0 2 1996~~		
		~~OCT 0 4 1996~~

Selections from

SAMUEL JOHNSON

1709–1784

Oxford University Press, Amen House, London E.C. 4

GLASGOW NEW YORK TORONTO MELBOURNE WELLINGTON
BOMBAY CALCUTTA MADRAS KARACHI CAPE TOWN IBADAN

Geoffrey Cumberlege, Publisher to the University

Selections from

SAMUEL JOHNSON

1709–1784

EDITED AND INTRODUCED BY

R. W. CHAPMAN

Geoffrey Cumberlege

OXFORD UNIVERSITY PRESS

London   New York   Toronto

1955

SAMUEL JOHNSON

Born: Lichfield, 18 September 1709
Died: London, 13 December 1784

PRINTED IN GREAT BRITAIN

PREFACE

This anthology is designed to do some justice to the wide
range of Johnson's thought, written and spoken, in prose
and verse, in Greek, Latin, and French as well as in
English. The chronological arrangement shows the de-
velopment of his style to its climax in the *Lives of the
Poets*. The headings are, where possible, his own; but I
have often had to interpolate my own description of a
passage.

As often in the past I have benefited by the wise
counsel of Professor Nichol Smith. In selecting from
the moral essays I have relied on the superior knowledge, and warmer enthusiasm, of Miss Mary Lascelles;
this part of the book is virtually of her choosing. For my
selection from the Lives of Thomson, Watts, and Akenside I am happy to cite the authority of Mr. T. S. Eliot,
who suggested that they would be worthy quarrying.

R. W. C.

1954

CONTENTS

c. 1726
Youthful Verses

Translation of Virgil
Pastoral I

MELIBÆUS.

Now, Tityrus, you, supine and careless laid,
Play on your pipe beneath this beechen shade;
While wretched we about the world must roam,
And leave our pleasing fields and native home,
Here at your ease you sing your amorous flame,
And the wood rings with Amarillis' name.

TITYRUS.

Those blessings, friend, a deity bestow'd,
For I shall never think him less than God;
Oft on his altar shall my firstlings lie,
Their blood the consecrated stones shall dye:
He gave my flocks to graze the flowery meads,
And me to tune at ease th' unequal reeds.

MELIBÆUS.

My admiration only I exprest,
(No spark of envy harbours in my breast)
That when confusion o'er the country reigns,
To you alone this happy state remains.
Here I, though faint myself, must drive my goats,
Far from their antient fields and humble cots.
This scarce I lead, who left on yonder rock
Two tender kids, the hopes of all the flock.
Had we not been perverse and careless grown,
This dire event by omens was foreshown;
Our trees were blasted by the thunder stroke, ⎫
And left-hand crows, from an old hollow oak,   ⎬
Foretold the coming evil by their dismal croak. ⎭

Translation of Horace
Odes, Book II. xiv

Horace. Book 2ᵈ. Ode 14

Alas, dear Friend, the fleeting years
In everlasting Circles run,
In vain you spend your vows and prayers,
They roll, and ever will roll on.

Should Hecatombs each rising Morn
On cruel Pluto's Altar dye,
Should costly Loads of incense burn,
Their fumes ascending to the Skie;

You could not gain a Moments breath,
Or move the haughty King below,
Nor would inexorable Death
Defer an hour the fatal blow.

In vain we shun the Din of war,
And terrours of the Stormy Main,
In vain with anxious breasts we fear
Unwholesome Sirius' sultry reign;

We all must view the Stygian flood
That silent cuts the dreary plains,
And cruel Danaus' bloody Brood
Condemn'd to everduring pains.

Your shady Groves, your pleasing wife,
And fruitfull fields, my dearest Friend,
You'll leave together with your life,
Alone the Cypress shall attend.

After your death, the lavish heir
Will quickly drive away his woe,
The wine you kept with so much care
Along the marble floor shall flow.

1729
Religious Progress

The history of his mind as to religion is an important article. I have mentioned the early impressions made upon his tender imagination by his mother, who continued her pious care with assiduity, but, in his opinion, not with judgement. 'Sunday (said he) was a heavy day to me when I was a boy. My mother confined me on that day, and made me read "The Whole Duty of Man," from a great part of which I could derive no instruction. When, for instance, I had read the chapter on theft, which from my infancy I had been taught was wrong, I was no more convinced that theft was wrong than before; so there was no accession of knowledge. A boy should be introduced to such books, by having his attention directed to the arrangement, to the style, and other excellencies of composition; that the mind being thus engaged by an amusing variety of objects, may not grow weary.'

He communicated to me the following particulars upon the subject of his religious progress. 'I fell into an inattention to religion, or an indifference about it, in my ninth year. The church at Lichfield, in which we had a seat, wanted reparation, so I was to go and find a seat in other churches; and having bad eyes, and being awkward about this, I used to go and read in the fields on Sunday. This habit continued till my fourteenth year; and still I find a great reluctance to go to church. I then became a sort of lax *talker* against religion, for I did not much *think* against it; and this lasted till I went to Oxford, where it would not be *suffered*. When at Oxford, I took up Law's *Serious Call to a Holy Life*, expecting to find it a dull book (as such books generally are), and perhaps to laugh at it. But I found Law quite an overmatch for me; and this was the first occasion of my thinking in earnest of religion, after I became capable of rational inquiry.' From this time forward religion was the predominant object of his thoughts; though, with the just sentiments of

a conscientious Christian, he lamented that his practice
of its duties fell far short of what it ought to be.

Boswell, Life

c. 1730
College Verses

Mea nec Falernæ &c.

Quid mirum Maro quod dignè canit arma Virumque,
    Quid quod putidulùm nostra Camœna sonat?
Limosum nobis Promus dat callidus haustum,
    Virgilio vires Uva Falerna dedit.
Carmina vis nostri scribant meliora Poetæ?
    Ingenium jubeas purior haustus alat.

1731
To Gregory Hickman

Sir

I have so long neglected to return You thanks for the
favours and Assistance I received from you at Stourbridge
that I am afraid You have now done expecting it. I can
indeed make no apology but by assuring you that this
delay, whatever was the cause of it, proceeded neither
from forgetfulness, disrespect, nor Ingratitude; Time has
not made the Sense of the Obligation less warm, nor the
thanks I return less sincere. But while I am acknowledg-
ing one Favour I must beg another, that you would
excuse the omission of the Verses You desired. be pleased
to consider that versifying against ones inclination is the
most disagreable thing in the World, and that ones own
disappointment is no inviting Subject, and that though the
desire of gratifying You might have prevaild over my dislike of it, yet it proves upon reflection so barren that to
attempt to write upon it, is to undertake to build without
materials.

As I am yet unemploy'd, I hope You will, if anything
should offer, remember and recommend

Sir Your humble Servant

Lichfield Oct: 30. 1731   Sam: Johnson

Pope's Messia Translated

Tollite concentrum, *Solymææ* tollite nymphæ!
Nil mortale loquor, cœlum mihi carminis alta
Materies; poscunt gravius cœlestia plectrum.
Muscosi fontes, silvestria tecta, valete,
Aonidesque Deæ, et mendacis somnia *Pindi.*
Tu mihi, qui flammâ movisti pectora sancti
Sidereâ *Isaiæ,* dignos accende furores!
  Immatura calens rapitur per sæcula vates,
Sic orsus—Qualis rerum mihi nascitur ordo!
Virgo! virgo parit! felix radicibus arbor
Jessæis surgit, mulcentesque æthera flores
Cœlestes lambunt animæ; ramisque columba,
Nuncia sacra Dei, plaudentibus insidet alis.
Nectareos rores, alimentaque mitia cœlum
Præbeat, et tacitè fœcundos irriget imbres!
Huc fœdat quos lepra, urit quos febris, adeste!
Dia salutares spirant medicamina rami.
Hic requies fessis; non sacrâ sævit in umbrâ
Vis boreæ gelida, aut rapidi violentia solis.
'Irrita vanescent priscæ vestigia fraudis,'
Justitiæque manus pretio intemerata bilancem
Attollet reducis; bellis prætendet olivas
Compositis Pax alma suas, terrasque revisens
Sedatas niveo Virtus lucebit amictu.
Volvantur celeres anni! Lux purpuret ortum
Expectata diu! Naturæ claustra refringens
Nascere, magne puer! Tibi primas, ecce! corollas
Deproperat tellus, fundit tibi munera, quicquid
Carpit *Arabs,* hortis quicquid frondescit eois.
Altius, en! *Lebanon* gaudentia culmina tollit,
En! summo exultant nutantes vertice silvæ.
Mittit aromaticas vallis *Saronica* nubes,
Et juga *Carmeli* recreant fragrantia cœlum.

Deserti lætâ mollescunt aspera voce,
Auditur Deus! ecce Deus! reboantia circum
Saxa sonant Deus; ecce Deus! deflectitur æther
Demissumque Deum tellus capit; ardua cedrus,
Gloria silvarum, dominum inclinata salutet!
Surgite convalles, tumidi subsidite montes!
Sternite saxa viam, rapidi discedite fluctus!
En! quem turba diu cecinerunt enthea, vates,
En! SALVATOR adest; vultus agnoscite cæci
Divinos, surdas sacra vox permulceat aures!
Ille cutim spissam visus hebetare vetabit,
Reclusisque oculis infundet amabile lumen,
Obstrictasque diu linguas in carmina solvet.
Ille vias vocis pandet, flexusque liquentis
Harmoniæ purgata novos mirabitur auris.

Ye Nymphs of *Solyma!* begin the song:
To heav'nly themes sublimer strains belong.
The mossy fountains and the sylvan shades,
The dreams of *Pindus* and th'*Aonian* maids,
Delight no more—O thou my voice inspire
Who touch'd *Isaiah*'s hallow'd lips with fire!
  Rapt into future times, the Bard begun,
A Virgin shall conceive, a Virgin bear a Son!
From *Jesse*'s root behold a branch arise,
Whose sacred flow'r with fragrance fills the skies.
Th'Æthereal spirit o'er its leaves shall move,
And on its top descends the mystic Dove.
Ye heav'ns! from high the dewy nectar pour,
And in soft silence shed the kindly show'r!
The sick and weak the healing plant shall aid,
From storms a shelter, and from heat a shade.
All crimes shall cease, and ancient fraud shall fail;
Returning Justice lift aloft her scale;
Peace o'er the world her olive wand extend,
And white-rob'd Innocence from heav'n descend.
Swift fly the years, and rise th' expected morn!
Oh spring to light, auspicious Babe, be born!
See Nature hastes her earliest wreaths to bring,
With all the incense of the breathing spring:

See lofty *Lebanon* his head advance,
See nodding forests on the mountains dance,
See spicy clouds from lowly *Saron* rise,
And *Carmel*'s flow'ry top perfumes the skies!
Hark! a glad voice the lonely desart chears;
Prepare the way! a God, a God appears;
A God, a God! the vocal hills reply,
The rocks proclaim th' approaching Deity.
Lo Earth receives him from the bending skies!
Sink down ye mountains, and ye vallies rise:
With heads declin'd, ye Cedars, homage pay;
Be smooth ye rocks, ye rapid floods give way!
The Saviour comes! by ancient bards foretold;
Hear him ye deaf, and all ye blind behold!
He from thick films shall purge the visual ray,
And on the sightless eye-ball pour the day:
'Tis he th' obstructed paths of sound shall clear,
And bid new music charm th' unfolding ear.

1735
Lobo's Abyssinia

Every one acquainted with Johnson's manner will be sensible that there is nothing of it here; but that this sentence[1] might have been composed by any other man.

But, in the Preface, the Johnsonian style begins to appear; and though use had not yet taught his wing a permanent and equable flight, there are parts of it which exhibit his best manner in full vigour. I had once the pleasure of examining it with Mr. Edmund Burke, who confirmed me in this opinion, by his superiour critical sagacity, and was, I remember, much delighted with the following specimen:

'The Portuguese traveller, contrary to the general vein of his countrymen, has amused his reader with no romantick absurdity, or incredible fictions; whatever he relates, whether true or not, is at least probable; and he who tells nothing exceeding the bounds of probability, has a right

[1 Boswell had quoted a specimen of the translation.]

to demand that they should believe him who cannot
contradict him.

'He appears, by his modest and unaffected narration,
to have described things as he saw them, to have copied
nature from the life, and to have consulted his senses, not
his imagination. He meets with no basilisks that destroy
with their eyes, his crocodiles devour their prey without
tears, and his cataracts fall from the rocks without deafen-
ing the neighbouring inhabitants.

'The reader will here find no regions cursed with irre-
mediable barrenness, or blessed with spontaneous fecun-
dity; no perpetual gloom, or unceasing sunshine; nor are
the nations here described either devoid of all sense of
humanity, or consummate in all private or social virtues.
Here are no Hottentots without religious polity or articu-
late language; no Chinese perfectly polite, and completely
skilled in all sciences; he will discover, what will always
be discovered by a diligent and impartial enquirer, that
wherever human nature is to be found, there is a mixture
of vice and virtue, a contest of passion and reason; and
that the Creator doth not appear partial in his distribu-
tions, but has balanced, in most countries, their particular
inconveniences by particular favours.'

Here we have an early example of that brilliant and
energetick expression, which, upon innumerable occasions in his subsequent life, justly impressed the world
with the highest admiration.

Nor can any one, conversant with the writings of Johnson, fail to discern his hand in this passage of the Dedication to John Warren, Esq. of Pembrokeshire, though it is
ascribed to Warren the bookseller:

'A generous and elevated mind is distinguished by
nothing more certainly than an eminent degree of curiosity; nor is that curiosity ever more agreeably or usefully
employed, than in examining the laws and customs of
foreign nations. I hope, therefore, the present I now presume to make, will not be thought improper; which, however, it is not my business as a dedicator to commend, nor
as a bookseller to depreciate.'

                                          Boswell, *Life*

(9)

1737
Harry Hervey

Amidst this cold obscurity, there was one brilliant circumstance to cheer him; he was well acquainted with Mr. Henry Hervey, one of the branches of the noble family of that name, who had been quartered at Lichfield as an officer of the army, and had at this time a house in London, where Johnson was frequently entertained, and had an opportunity of meeting genteel company. Not very long before his death, he mentioned this, among other particulars of his life, which he was kindly communicating to me; and he described this early friend, 'Harry Hervey,' thus: 'He was a vicious man, but very kind to me. If you call a dog HERVEY, I shall love him.'

Boswell, Life

1738
A Birthday Prayer

Sept. 7, 1738.

O God, the Creatour and Preserver of all Mankind, Father of all mercies, I thine unworthy servant do give Thee most humble thanks, for all thy goodness and lovingkindness to me. I bless Thee for my Creation, Preservation, and Redemption, for the knowledge of thy Son Jesus Christ, for the means of Grace and the Hope of Glory. In the days of Childhood and Youth, in the midst of weakness, blindness, and danger, Thou hast protected me; amidst Afflictions of Mind, Body, and Estate, Thou hast supported me; and amidst vanity and Wickedness Thou hast spared me. Grant, O merciful Father, that I may have a lively sense of thy mercies. Create in me a contrite Heart, that I may worthily lament my sins and acknowledge my wickedness, and obtain Remission and forgiveness, through the satisfaction of Jesus Christ. And, O Lord, enable me, by thy Grace, to redeem the time which I have spent in Sloth, Vanity, and wickedness; to make use of thy Gifts to the honour

of thy Name; to lead a new life in thy Faith, Fear, and
Love; and finally to obtain everlasting Life. Grant this,
Almighty Lord, for the merits and through the mediation
of our most holy and blessed Saviour Jesus Christ; to
whom, with Thee and the Holy Ghost, Three Persons
and one God, be all honour and Glory, World without
end. Amen.

Prayers and Meditations, 1785

On Thomas Birch

Εἰς ΒΙΡΧΙΟΝ

Εἶδεν Ἀληθείη πρῴην χαίρουσα γράφοντα
Ἡρώων τε βίους Βίρχιον, ἠδὲ Σοφῶν,
Καὶ βίον, εἶπεν, ὅταν ῥίψῃς θανάτοιο βέλεσσι,
Σοῦ ποτε γραψόμενον Βίρχιον ἄλλον ἔχοις.

London, a Poem

Quis ineptæ
Tam patiens urbis, tam ferreus ut teneat se?
Juv.

Tho' grief and fondness in my breast rebel,
When injur'd THALES bids the town farewell,
Yet still my calmer thoughts his choice commend,
I praise the hermit, but regret the friend,
Resolved at length, from vice and LONDON far,
To breathe in distant fields a purer air,
And, fix'd on Cambria's solitary shore,
Give to St. David one true Briton more.
   For who would leave, unbrib'd, Hibernia's land,
Or change the rocks of Scotland for the Strand?
There none are swept by sudden fate away,
But all whom hunger spares, with age decay:
Here malice, rapine, accident, conspire,
And now a rabble rages, now a fire;
Their ambush here relentless ruffians lay,
And here the fell attorney prowls for prey;
Here falling houses thunder on your head,
And here a female atheist talks you dead.

A transient calm the happy scenes bestow,
And for a moment lull the sense of woe.
At length awaking, with contemptuous frown,
Indignant THALES eyes the neighb'ring town.

Since worth, he cries, in these degen'rate days,
Wants ev'n the cheap reward of empty praise;
In those curs'd walls, devote to vice and gain,
Since unrewarded science toils in vain;
Since hope but sooths to double my distress,
And ev'ry moment leaves my little less;
While yet my steady steps no staff sustains,
And life still vig'rous revels in my veins;
Grant me, kind heaven, to find some happier place,
Where honesty and sense are no disgrace;
Some pleasing bank where verdant osiers play,
Some peaceful vale with nature's paintings gay;
Where once the harrass'd Briton found repose,
And safe in poverty defy'd his foes;
Some secret cell, ye pow'rs, indulgent give.
Let —— live here, for —— has learn'd to live.
Here let those reign, whom pensions can incite
To vote a patriot black, a courtier white;
Explain their country's dear-bought rights away,
And plead for pirates* in the face of day;
With slavish tenets taint our poison'd youth,
And lend a lye the confidence of truth.

Let such raise palaces, and manors buy,
Collect a tax, or farm a lottery,
With warbling eunuchs fill a licens'd stage,
And lull to servitude a thoughtless age.

Prepare for death, if here at night you roam,
And sign your will before you sup from home.
Some fiery fop, with new commission vain,
Who sleeps on brambles till he kills his man;
Some frolick drunkard, reeling from a feast,
Provokes a broil, and stabs you for a jest.
Yet ev'n these heroes, mischievously gay,

* The invasions of the Spaniards were defended in the houses of Parliament.

Lords of the street, and terrors of the way;
Flush'd as they are with folly, youth and wine,
Their prudent insults to the poor confine;
Afar they mark the flambeau's bright approach,
And shun the shining train, and golden coach.
　　In vain, these dangers past, your doors you close,
And hope the balmy blessings of repose:
Cruel with guilt, and daring with despair,
The midnight murd'rer bursts the faithless bar;
Invades the sacred hour of silent rest,
And leaves, unseen, a dagger in your breast.
　　Scarce can our fields, such crowds at Tyburn die,
With hemp the gallows and the fleet supply.
Propose your schemes, ye Senatorian band,
Whose Ways and Means* support the sinking land;
Lest ropes be wanting in the tempting spring,
To rig another convoy for the k——g.
　　A single jail, in ALFRED's golden reign,
Could half the nation's criminals contain;
Fair Justice then, without constraint ador'd,
Held high the steady scale, but deep'd the sword;
No spies were paid, no special juries known,
Blest age! but ah! how diff'rent from our own!
　　Much could I add,—but see the boat at hand,
The tide retiring, calls me from the land:
Farewell!—When youth, and health, and fortune spent,
Thou fly'st for refuge to the wilds of Kent;
And tir'd like me with follies and with crimes,
In angry numbers warn'st succeeding times;
Then shall thy friend, nor thou refuse his aid,
Still foe to vice, forsake his Cambrian shade;
In virtue's cause once more exert his rage,
Thy satire point, and animate thy page.

To a Whig Beauty

Liber ut esse velim, suasisti, pulchra *Maria*:
Ut maneam liber, pulchra *Maria*, vale.

* A cant term in the House of Commons for methods of raising money.

To Edward Cave

Sir   *N⁰ 6, Castle-street, Wednesday Morning.*

When I took the liberty of writing to you a few days ago, I did not expect a repetition of the same pleasure so soon; for a pleasure I shall always think it to converse in any manner with an ingenious and candid man; but having the inclosed poem in my hands to dispose of for the benefit of the author (of whose abilities I shall say nothing, since I send you his performance), I believed I could not procure more advantageous terms from any person than from you, who have so much distinguished yourself by your generous encouragement of poetry; and whose judgement of that art nothing but your commendation of my trifle can give me any occasion to call in question. I do not doubt but you will look over this poem with another eye, and reward it in a different manner, from a mercenary bookseller, who counts the lines he is to purchase, and considers nothing but the bulk. I cannot help taking notice, that, besides what the author may hope for on account of his abilities, he has likewise another claim to your regard, as he lies at present under very disadvantageous circumstances of fortune. I beg therefore that you will favour me with a letter to-morrow, that I may know what you can afford to allow him, that he may either part with it to you, or find out (which I do not expect) some other way more to his satisfaction.

I have only to add, that as I am sensible I have transcribed it very coarsely, which, after having altered it, I was obliged to do, I will, if you please to transmit the sheets from the press, correct it for you; and will take the trouble of altering any stroke of satire which you may dislike.

By exerting on this occasion your usual generosity, you will not only encourage learning, and relieve distress, but (though it be in comparison of the other motives of very small account) oblige in a very sensible manner, Sir,

Your very humble servant, Sam. Johnson.

To Edward Cave

Sir

I am to return you thanks for the present you were so kind as to send by me, and to entreat that you will be pleas'd to inform me by the Penny-post whether you resolve to print the Poem. If you please to send it me by the post with a Note to Dodsley, I will go and read the lines to him, that We may have his Consent to put his name in the Title-page. As to the Printing, if it can be set immediately about, I will be so much the Authours Friend as not to content myself with meer solicitations in his favour. I propose if my calculations be near the truth to engage for the reimbursement of all that you shall lose by an impression of 500 provided, as you very generously propose, that the profit, if any, be set aside for the Authour's use, excepting the present you made, which, if he be a gainer, it is fit he should repay. I beg that you will let one of your servants write an exact account of the expence of such an impression, and send it with the Poem, that I may know what I engage for. I am very sensible from your generosity on this Occasion, of your regard to learning even in its unhappiest State, and cannot but think such a temper deserving of the Gratitude of those who suffer so often from a contrary Disposition.

I am, Sir, Your most humble Servant Sam: Johnson

I beg that you will not   Monday
delay your Answer.   No 6 Castle Street

1740
An Epitaph on Claudy Phillips

Phillips! whose touch harmonious could remove
The pangs of guilty pow'r, and hapless love,
Rest here distrest by poverty no more,
Find here that calm thou gav'st so oft before;
Sleep undisturb'd within this peaceful shrine,
Till angels wake thee with a note like thine.

To Elizabeth Johnson

Dearest Tetty

After hearing that You are in so much danger, as I apprehend from a hurt on a tendon, I shall be very uneasy
till I know that You are recovered, and beg that You will
omit nothing that can contribute to it, nor deny Yourself any thing that may make confinement less melancholy. You have already suffered more than I can bear to
reflect upon, and I hope more than either of us shall suffer
again. One part at least I have often flatterd myself we
shall avoid for the future, our troubles will surely never
separate us more. If M⟨   ⟩ does not easily succeed in
his endeavours, let him not scruple to call in another
Surgeon to consult with him, You may have two or three
visits from Ranby or Shipton, who is said to be the best,
for a Guinea, which You need not fear to part with on so
pressing an occasion, for I can send you twenty pouns
more on Monday, which I have received this night; I
beg therefore that You will more regard my happiness,
than to expose Yourself to any hazards. I still promise
myself many happy years from your tenderness and affection, which I sometimes hope our misfortunes have not
yet deprived me of. David wrote to me this day on the
affair of Irene, who is at last become a kind of Favourite
among the Players, Mr Fletewood promises to give a
promise in writing that it shall be the first next season, if
it cannot be introduced now, and Chetwood the Prompter
is desirous of bargaining for the copy, and offers fifty
Guineas for the right of printing after it shall be played.
I hope it will at length reward me for my perplexities.

Of the time which I have spent from thee, and of my
dear Lucy and other affairs, my heart will be at ease on
Monday to give Thee a particular account, especially if
a Letter should inform me that thy Leg is better, for I
hope You do not think so unkindly of me as to imagine
that I can be at rest while I believe my dear Tetty in pain.

Be assured, my dear Girl, that I have seen nobody in
these rambles upon which I have been forced, that has
not contribute to confirm my esteem and affection for

thee, though that esteem and affection only contributed
to increase my unhappiness when I reflected that the
most amiable woman in the world was exposed by my
means to miseries which I could not relieve.

I am My charming Love Yours

Jan. 31st 1739/40   Sam: Johnson

Lucy always sends her Duty and my Mother her service.

1742

The Use of Catalogues

Nor is the use of catalogues of less importance to those
whom curiosity has engaged in the study of literary history, and who think the intellectual revolutions of the
world more worthy of their attention, than the ravages of
tyrants, the desolation of kingdoms, the rout of armies,
and the fall of empires. Those who are pleased with
observing the first birth of new opinions, their struggles
against opposition, their silent progress under persecution, their general reception, and their gradual decline, or
sudden extinction; those that amuse themselves with remarking the different periods of human knowledge, and
observe how darkness and light succeed each other; by
what accident the most gloomy nights of ignorance have
given way in the dawn of science, and how learning has
languished and decayed, for want of patronage and regard, or been overborn by the prevalence of fashionable
ignorance, or lost amidst the tumults of invasion, and the
storms of violence. All those who desire any knowledge of
the literary transactions of past ages, may find in catalogues, like this at least, such an account as is given by
annalists, and chronologers of civil history.

Account of the Harleian Library

A Speech purporting to be Pitt's[1]

Mr. PITT then spoke to the following purpose:—Sir,
I know not by what fatality the adversaries of the motion

[1 This is the 'Demosthenic oration' that Johnson is reported (inaccurately)
to have declared he wrote 'in a garret in Exeter Street'. See Boswell's *Life*,
ed. Hill–Powell, i. 504.]

are impelled to assist their adversaries, and contribute to their own overthrow, by suggesting, whenever they attempt to oppose it, new arguments against themselves.

It has been long observed, that when men are drawing near to destruction, they are apparently deprived of their understanding, and contribute by their own folly to those calamities with which they are threatened, but which might by a different conduct be sometimes delayed. This has surely now happened to the veteran advocates for an absolute and unaccountable ministry, who have discovered on this occasion, by the weakness of their resistance, that their abilities are declining; and I cannot but hope, that the omen will be fulfilled; and that their infatuation will be quickly followed by their ruin.

To touch in this debate on our domestick affairs, to mention the distribution of the publick money, and to discover their fears, lest the ways in which it has been disbursed, should by this enquiry be discovered, to recal to the minds of their opponents the immense sums which have been annually demanded, and of which no account has been yet given, is surely the lowest degree of weakness and imprudence.

I am so far from being convinced that any danger can arise from this enquiry, that I believe the nation can only be injured by a long neglect of such examinations; and that a minister is easily formidable, when he has exempted himself by a kind of prescription from exposing his accounts, and has long had an opportunity of employing the publick money in multiplying his dependants, enriching his hirelings, enslaving boroughs, and corrupting senates.

That those have been in reality the purposes for which the taxes of many years have been squandered, is sufficiently apparent without an enquiry. We have wasted sums with which the French, in pursuance of their new scheme of encreasing their influence, would have been able to purchase the submission of half the nations of the earth, and with which the monarchs of Europe might have been held dependent on a nod; these they have wasted only to sink our country into disgrace, to heighten the spirit of impotent enemies, to destroy our commerce, and distress our colonies. We have patiently suffered, during a peace of twenty years, those taxes to be extorted from us, by which a war might have been supported against the most powerful nation, and have seen them engulphed in the boundless expences of the government, without being able to discover any other effect from them than the establishment of ministerial tyranny.

There has, indeed, been among the followers of the court a regular subordination, and exact obedience; nor has any man been found hardy enough to reject the dictates of the grand vizier. Every man who has received his pay, has with great cheerfulness complied with his commands; and every man who has held any post or office under the crown, has evidently considered himself as enlisted by the minister.

But the visible influence of places, however destructive to the constitution, is not the chief motive of an enquiry; an enquiry implies something secret, and is intended to discover the private methods of extending dependence, and propagating corruption; the methods by which the people have been influenced to choose those men for representatives whose principles they detest, and whose conduct they condemn; and by which those whom their country has chosen for the guardians of its liberties, have been induced to support in this House measures, which in every other place they have made no scruple to censure.

When we shall examine the distribution of the publick treasure, when we shall enquire by what conduct we have been debarred from the honours of war, and at the same time deprived of the blessings of peace, to what causes it is to be imputed, that our debts have continued during the long-continued tranquillity of Europe, nearly in the state to which they were raised by fighting, at our own expence, the general quarrel of mankind; and why the sinking fund, a kind of inviolable deposit appropriated to the payment of our creditors, and the mitigation of our taxes, has been from year to year diverted to very different uses: we shall find that our treasure has been exhausted, not to humble foreign enemies, or obviate domestick insurrections; not to support our allies, or suppress our factions; but for ends which no man, who feels the love of his country yet unextinguished, can name without horror, the purchase of alliances, and the hire of votes, the corruption of the people, and the exaltation of France.

Such are the discoveries which I am not afraid to declare, that I expect from the enquiry, and therefore I cannot but think it necessary. If those to whom the administration of affairs has been for twenty years committed, have betrayed their trust, if they have invaded the publick rights with the publick treasure, and made use of the dignities which their country has conferred upon them, only to enslave it, who will not confess, that they ought to be delivered up to speedy justice? That they ought to be set as land-marks to posterity, to warn those who shall hereafter launch out on the ocean of affluence and power, not to be too confident of a prosperous gale, but to remember, that there are rocks on which whoever rushes must inevitably perish? If they are innocent, and far be it from me to declare them guilty without examination, whom will this enquiry injure? Or what effects will it produce, but that which every man appears to desire, the re-establishment of the publick tranquillity, a firm confidence in the justice and wisdom of the government, and a general reconciliation of the people to the ministers?

> From *Debates in the Senate of Lilliput*; part of the report of the House of Commons, 9 March 1742, as given in *Gentleman's Magazine*; printed from a later edition, in which the real names of the speakers are substituted for the fictitious names of the *Gent. Mag.*

1744
The Life of Savage

A Foolish Patron

Nor did the kindness of Sir Richard end in common favours. He proposed to have established him in some settled scheme of life, and to have contracted a kind of alliance with him, by marrying him to a natural daughter, on whom he intended to bestow a thousand pounds. But though he was always lavish of future bounties, he conducted his affairs in such a manner that he was very seldom able to keep his promises or execute his own intentions; and, as he was never able to raise the sum which he had offered, the marriage was delayed. In the mean time he was officiously informed that Mr. Savage had ridiculed him; by which he was so much exasperated that he withdrew the allowance which he had paid him, and never afterwards admitted him to his house.

It is not indeed unlikely that Savage might by his imprudence expose himself to the malice of a tale-bearer; for his patron had many follies, which, as his discernment easily discovered, his imagination might sometimes incite him to mention too ludicrously. A little knowledge of the world is sufficient to discover that such weakness is very common, and that there are few who do not sometimes, in the wantonness of thoughtless mirth or the heat of transient resentment, speak of their friends and benefactors with levity and contempt, though in their cooler moments they want neither sense of their kindness nor reverence for their virtue. The fault therefore of Mr. Savage was rather negligence than ingratitude; but Sir Richard must likewise be acquitted of severity, for who is there that can patiently bear contempt from one whom he has relieved and supported, whose establishment he has laboured, and whose interest he has promoted?

Life of Savage

Genius in Affluence

This was the golden part of Mr. Savage's life; and for some time he had no reason to complain of fortune: his appearance was splendid, his expences large, and his acquaintance extensive. He was courted by all who endeavoured to be thought men of genius, and caressed by all who valued themselves upon a refined taste. To admire Mr. Savage was a proof of discernment, and to be acquainted with him was a title to poetical reputation. His presence was sufficient to make any place of publick entertainment popular; and his approbation and example constituted the fashion. So powerful is genius when it is invested with the glitter of affluence! Men willingly pay to fortune that regard which they owe to merit, and are pleased when they have an opportunity at once of gratifying their vanity and practising their duty.

This interval of prosperity furnished him with opportunities of enlarging his knowledge of human nature by contemplating life from its highest gradations to its lowest; and, had he afterwards applied to dramatick poetry, he would perhaps not have had many superiors: for as he never suffered any scene to pass before his eyes without notice, he had treasured in his mind all the different combinations of passions and the innumerable mixtures of vice and virtue, which distinguish one character from another; and, as his conception was strong, his expressions were clear, he easily received impressions from objects, and very forcibly transmitted them to others.

Of his exact observations on human life he has left a proof, which would do honour to the greatest names, in a small pamphlet called *The Author to be let*, where he introduces Iscariot Hackney, a prostitute scribbler, giving an account of his birth, his education, his disposition and morals, habits of life, and maxims of conduct. In the introduction are related many secret histories of the petty writers of that time, but sometimes mixed with ungenerous reflections on their birth, their circumstances, or those of their relations; nor can it be denied that some passages are such as Iscariot Hackney might himself have produced.

Life of Savage

A Superstition

A superstitious regard to the correction of his sheets was one of Mr. Savage's peculiarities: he often altered, revised, recurred to his first reading or punctuation, and again adopted the alteration; he was dubious and irresolute without end, as on a question of the last importance, and at last was seldom satisfied: the intrusion or omission of a comma was sufficient to discompose him, and he would

lament an error of a single letter as a heavy calamity.
In one of his letters relating to an impression of some
verses, he remarks that he had, with regard to the correction of the proof, 'a spell upon him'; and indeed the
anxiety with which he dwelt upon the minutest and most
trifling niceties deserved no other name than that of
fascination.

Life of Savage

Pleasing Intoxication

But though he did not lose the opportunity which success
gave him, of setting a high rate on his abilities, but paid
due deference to the suffrages of mankind when they
were given in his favour, he did not suffer his esteem of
himself to depend upon others, nor found any thing
sacred in the voice of the people when they were inclined
to censure him; he then readily showed the folly of expecting that the publick should judge right, observed how
slowly poetical merit had often forced its way into the
world: he contented himself with the applause of men of
judgement, and was somewhat disposed to exclude all
those from the character of men of judgement who did
not applaud him.

But he was at other times more favourable to mankind
than to think them blind to the beauties of his works, and
imputed the slowness of their sale to other causes; either
they were published at a time when the town was empty,
or when the attention of the publick was engrossed by
some struggle in the parliament, or some other object of
general concern; or they were by the neglect of the
publisher not diligently dispersed, or by his avarice not
advertised with sufficient frequency. Address, or industry,
or liberality, was always wanting; and the blame was
laid rather on any person than the author.

By arts like these, arts which every man practises in
some degree, and to which too much of the little tranquillity of life is to be ascribed, Savage was always able to
live at peace with himself. Had he indeed only made use
of these expedients to alleviate the loss or want of fortune
or reputation, or any other advantages, which it is not

in man's power to bestow upon himself, they might have been justly mentioned as instances of a philosophical mind, and very properly proposed to the imitation of multitudes, who, for want of diverting their imaginations with the same dexterity, languish under afflictions which might be easily removed.

It were doubtless to be wished that truth and reason were universally prevalent; that every thing were esteemed according to its real value; and that men would secure themselves from being disappointed in their endeavours after happiness, by placing it only in virtue, which is always to be obtained: but if adventitious and foreign pleasures must be pursued it would be perhaps of some benefit, since that pursuit must frequently be fruitless, if the practice of Savage could be taught, that folly might be an antidote to folly, and one fallacy be obviated by another.

But the danger of this pleasing intoxication must not be concealed; nor indeed can any one, after having observed the life of Savage, need to be cautioned against it. By imputing none of his miseries to himself he continued to act upon the same principles, and to follow the same path; was never made wiser by his sufferings, nor preserved by one misfortune from falling into another. He proceeded throughout his life to tread the same steps on the same circle; always applauding his past conduct, or at least forgetting it, to amuse himself with phantoms of happiness which were dancing before him, and willingly turned his eyes from the light of reason, when it would have discovered the illusion and shewn him, what he never wished to see, his real state.

Life of Savage

A Noble Parasite

Whoever was acquainted with him was certain to be solicited for small sums, which the frequency of the request made in time considerable, and he was therefore quickly shunned by those who were become familiar enough to be trusted with his necessities; but his rambling manner of life, and constant appearance at houses of

publick resort, always procured him a new succession of
friends, whose kindness had not been exhausted by repeated requests; so that he was seldom absolutely without
resources, but had in his utmost exigences this comfort,
that he always imagined himself sure of speedy relief.

It was observed that he always asked favours of this
kind without the least submission or apparent consciousness of dependence, and that he did not seem to look
upon a compliance with his request as an obligation that
deserved any extraordinary acknowledgements; but a
refusal was resented by him as an affront, or complained
of as an injury: nor did he readily reconcile himself to
those who either denied to lend, or gave him afterwards
any intimation that they expected to be repaid.

He was sometimes so far compassionated by those who
knew both his merit and distresses that they received him
into their families, but they soon discovered him to be a
very incommodious inmate; for, being always accustomed
to an irregular manner of life, he could not confine himself to any stated hours, or pay any regard to the rules of
a family, but would prolong his conversation till midnight,
without considering that business might require his
friend's application in the morning; and, when he had
persuaded himself to retire to bed, was not, without equal
difficulty, called up to dinner: it was therefore impossible
to pay him any distinction without the entire subversion
of all œconomy, a kind of establishment which, wherever
he went, he always appeared ambitious to overthrow.

It must therefore be acknowledged, in justification of
mankind, that it was not always by the negligence or
coldness of his friends that Savage was distressed, but
because it was in reality very difficult to preserve him
long in a state of ease. To supply him with money was a
hopeless attempt, for no sooner did he see himself master
of a sum sufficient to set him free from care for a day,
than he became profuse and luxurious. When once he
had entered a tavern, or engaged in a scheme of pleasure,
he never retired till want of money obliged him to some
new expedient. If he was entertained in a family nothing
was any longer to be regarded there but amusements and

jollity: wherever Savage entered he immediately expected that order and business should fly before him, that all should thenceforward be left to hazard, and that no dull principle of domestick management should be opposed to his inclination, or intrude upon his gaiety.

Life of Savage

Richard Savage

Such were the life and death of Richard Savage, a man equally distinguished by his virtues and vices; and at once remarkable for his weaknesses and abilities.

He was of a middle stature, of a thin habit of body, a long visage, coarse features, and melancholy aspect; of a grave and manly deportment, a solemn dignity of mien, but which, upon a nearer acquaintance, softened into an engaging easiness of manners. His walk was slow, and his voice tremulous and mournful. He was easily excited to smiles, but very seldom provoked to laughter.

His mind was in an uncommon degree vigorous and active. His judgement was accurate, his apprehension quick, and his memory so tenacious that he was frequently observed to know what he had learned from others in a short time, better than those by whom he was informed; and could frequently recollect incidents with all their combination of circumstances, which few would have regarded at the present time, but which the quickness of his apprehension impressed upon him. He had the peculiar felicity that his attention never deserted him: he was present to every object, and regardful of the most trifling occurrences. He had the art of escaping from his own reflections, and accommodating himself to every new scene.

To this quality is to be imputed the extent of his knowledge, compared with the small time which he spent in visible endeavours to acquire it. He mingled in cursory conversation with the same steadiness of attention as others apply to a lecture; and, amidst the appearance of thoughtless gaiety, lost no new idea that was started, nor any hint that could be improved. He had therefore made in coffee-houses the same proficiency as others in their closets; and it is remarkable that the writings of a man of little education and little reading have an air of learning scarcely to be found in any other performances, but which perhaps as often obscures as embellishes them.

His judgement was eminently exact both with regard to writings and to men. The knowledge of life was indeed his chief attainment; and it is not without some satisfaction that I can produce the suffrage of Savage in favour of human nature, of which he never appeared to entertain such odious ideas as some, who perhaps had neither his judgement nor experience, have published, either in ostentation of their sagacity, vindication of their crimes, or gratification of their malice.

His method of life particularly qualified him for conversation, of which he knew how to practise all the graces. He was never vehement or loud, but at once modest and easy, open and respectful; his language was vivacious and elegant, and equally happy upon grave or humourous subjects. He was generally censured for not knowing when to retire, but that was not the defect of his judgement, but of his fortune; when he left his company he was frequently to spend the remaining part of the night in the street, or at least was abandoned to gloomy reflections, which it is not strange that he delayed as long as he could; and sometimes forgot that he gave others pain to avoid it himself.

It cannot be said that he made use of his abilities for the direction of his own conduct: an irregular and dissipated manner of life had made him the slave of every passion that happened to be excited by the presence of its object, and that slavery to his passions reciprocally produced a life irregular and dissipated. He was not master of his own motions, nor could promise any thing for the next day.

With regard to his œconomy nothing can be added to the relation of his life. He appeared to think himself born to be supported by others, and dispensed from all necessity of providing for himself; he therefore never prosecuted any scheme of advantage, nor endeavoured even to secure the profits which his writings might have afforded him. His temper was, in consequence of the dominion of his passions, uncertain and capricious: he was easily engaged, and easily disgusted; but he is accused of retaining his hatred more tenaciously than his benevolence.

He was compassionate both by nature and principle, and always ready to perform offices of humanity; but when he was provoked (and very small offences were sufficient to provoke him), he would prosecute his revenge with the utmost acrimony till his passion had subsided.

His friendship was therefore of little value; for though he was zealous in the support or vindication of those whom he loved, yet it was always dangerous to trust him, because he considered himself as discharged by the first quarrel from all ties of honour or gratitude, and would betray those secrets which, in the warmth of confidence, had been imparted to him. This practice drew upon him an universal accusation of ingratitude: nor can it be denied that he was very ready to set himself free from the load of an obligation, for he could not bear to conceive himself in a state of dependence; his pride being equally powerful with his other passions, and appearing in the form of insolence at one time, and of vanity at another. Vanity, the most innocent species of pride, was most frequently predominant: he could not easily leave off when he had once begun to mention himself or his works; nor ever read his verses without stealing his eyes from the page, to discover, in the faces of his audience, how they were affected with any favourite passage.

A kinder name than that of vanity ought to be given to the delicacy with which he was always careful to separate his own merit from every other man's, and to reject that praise to which he had no claim. He did not forget, in mentioning his performances, to mark every line that had been suggested or amended; and was so accurate as to relate that he owed *three words* in THE WANDERER to the advice of his friends.

His veracity was questioned, but with little reason; his accounts, though not indeed always the same, were generally consistent. When he loved any man he suppressed all his faults; and, when he had been offended by him, concealed all his virtues: but his characters were generally true, so far as he proceeded; though it cannot be denied that his partiality might have sometimes the effect of falsehood.

In cases indifferent he was zealous for virtue, truth, and justice: he knew very well the necessity of goodness to the present and future happiness of mankind; nor is there perhaps any writer who has less endeavoured to please by flattering the appetites or perverting the judgement.

As an author therefore, and he now ceases to influence mankind in any other character, if one piece which he had resolved to suppress be excepted, he has very little to fear from the strictest moral or religious censure. And though he may not be altogether secure against the objections of the critick, it must, however, be acknowledged that his works are the productions of a genius truly poetical, and, what many writers who have been more lavishly applauded cannot boast, that they have an original air, which has no resemblance of any foregoing work; that the versification and sentiments have a cast peculiar to themselves, which no man can imitate with success, because what was nature in Savage would in another be affectation. It must be confessed that his descriptions are striking, his images animated, his fictions justly imagined, and his allegories artfully pursued; that his diction is elevated, though sometimes forced, and his numbers sonorous and majestick, though frequently sluggish and encumbered. Of his style, the general fault is harshness, and its general excellence is dignity; of his sentiments, the prevailing beauty is sublimity, and uniformity the prevailing defect.

For his life or for his writings none, who candidly consider his fortune, will think an apology either necessary or difficult. If he was not always sufficiently instructed in his subject, his knowledge was at least greater than could have been attained by others in the same state. If his works were sometimes unfinished, accuracy cannot reasonably be exacted from a man oppressed with want, which he has no hope of relieving but by a speedy publica-

tion. The insolence and resentment of which he is accused
were not easily to be avoided by a great mind, irritated
by perpetual hardships, and constrained hourly to return
the spurns of contempt and repress the insolence of prosperity; and vanity may surely readily be pardoned in
him, to whom life afforded no other comforts than barren
praises, and the consciousness of deserving them.

Those are no proper judges of his conduct who have
slumbered away their time on the down of plenty, nor
will any wise man presume to say, 'Had I been in
Savage's condition, I should have lived or written better
than Savage.'

This relation will not be wholly without its use if those
who languish under any part of his sufferings shall be
enabled to fortify their patience by reflecting that they
feel only those afflictions from which the abilities of
Savage did not exempt him; or those who, in confidence
of superior capacities or attainments, disregard the common maxims of life, shall be reminded that nothing will
supply the want of prudence, and that negligence and
irregularity long continued will make knowledge useless,
wit ridiculous, and genius contemptible.

Life of Savage

1747–55

THE ENGLISH DICTIONARY

1747

The Germ

The year 1747 is distinguished as the epoch, when Johnson's arduous and important work, his DICTIONARY OF
THE ENGLISH LANGUAGE, was announced to the world,
by the publication of its Plan or *Prospectus*.

How long this immense undertaking had been the
object of his contemplation, I do not know. I once asked
him by what means he had attained to that astonishing
knowledge of our language, by which he was enabled to
realise a design of such extent, and accumulated difficulty.

He told me, that 'it was not the effect of particular study; but that it had grown up in his mind insensibly.' I have been informed by Mr. James Dodsley, that several years before this period, when Johnson was one day sitting in his brother Robert's shop, he heard his brother suggest to him, that a Dictionary of the English Language would be a work that would be well received by the publick; that Johnson seemed at first to catch at the proposition, but, after a pause, said, in his abrupt decisive manner, 'I believe I shall not undertake it.'

Boswell, Life

Plan of the Dictionary

To the Right Honourable
PHILIP DORMER Earl of CHESTERFIELD,
One of his Majesty's Principal Secretaries of State.

MY LORD,

When first I undertook to write an *English* Dictionary, I had no expectation of any higher patronage than that of the proprietors of the copy, nor prospect of any other advantage than the price of my labour. I knew that the work in which I engaged is generally considered as drudgery for the blind, as the proper toil of artless industry; a task that requires neither the light of learning, nor the activity of genius, but may be successfully performed without any higher quality than that of bearing burthens with dull patience, and beating the track of the alphabet with sluggish resolution.

Whether this opinion, so long transmitted, and so widely propagated, had its beginning from truth and nature, or from accident and prejudice; whether it be decreed by the authority of reason, or the tyranny of ignorance, that of all the candidates for literary praise, the unhappy lexicographer holds the lowest place, neither vanity nor interest incited me to inquire. It appeared that the province allotted me was, of all the regions of learning, generally confessed to be the least delightful, that it was believed to produce neither fruits nor flowers; and that, after a long and laborious cultivation, not even the barren laurel had been found upon it.

Yet on this province, my Lord, I entered, with the pleasing hope, that, as it was low, it likewise would be safe. I was drawn forward with the prospect of employment, which, though not splendid, would be useful; and which, though it could not make my life envied, would keep it innocent; which would awaken no passion, engage me in no contention, nor throw in my way any temptation to disturb the quiet of others by censure, or my own by flattery.

I had read indeed of times, in which princes and statesmen thought it part of their honour to promote the improvement of their native tongues; and in which dictionaries were written under the protection of greatness. To the patrons of such undertakings I willingly paid the homage of believing that they, who were thus solicitous for the perpetuity of their language, had reason to expect that their actions would be celebrated by posterity, and that the eloquence which they promoted would be employed in their praise. But I considered such acts of beneficence as prodigies, recorded rather to raise wonder than expectation; and content with the terms that I had stipulated, had not suffered my imagination to flatter me with any other encouragement, when I found that my design had been thought by your Lordship of importance sufficient to attract your favour.

How far this unexpected distinction can be rated among the happy incidents of life, I am not yet able to determine. Its first effect has been to make me anxious lest it should fix the attention of the publick too much upon me, and, as it once happened to an epick poet of France, by raising the reputation of the attempt, obstruct the reception of the work. I imagine what the world will expect from a scheme, prosecuted under your Lordship's influence; and I know that expectation, when her wings are once expanded, easily reaches heights which performance never will attain; and when she has mounted the summit of perfection, derides her follower, who dies in the pursuit.

Not therefore to raise expectation, but to repress it, I here lay before your Lordship the Plan of my under-

taking, that more may not be demanded than I intend;
and that, before it is too far advanced to be thrown into
a new method, I may be advertised of its defects or
superfluities. Such informations I may justly hope, from
the emulation with which those, who desire the praise of
elegance or discernment, must contend in the promotion
of a design that you, my Lord, have not thought unworthy to share your attention with treaties and with
wars.

In the first attempt to methodise my ideas I found a
difficulty, which extended itself to the whole work. It was
not easy to determine by what rule of distinction the
words of this Dictionary were to be chosen. The chief
intent of it is to preserve the purity and ascertain the
meaning of the English idiom; and this seems to require
nothing more than that our language be considered, so
far as it is our own; that the words and phrases used in
the general intercourse of life, or found in the works of
those whom we commonly style polite writers, be selected,
without including the terms of particular professions,
since, with the arts to which they relate, they are generally derived from other nations, and are very often the
same in all the languages of this part of the world.
This is, perhaps, the exact and pure idea of a grammatical
dictionary; but in lexicography, as in other arts, naked
science is too delicate for the purposes of life. The value
of a work must be estimated by its use: it is not enough
that a dictionary delights the critick, unless, at the same
time, it instructs the learner; as it is to little purpose that
an engine amuses the philosopher by the subtilty of its
mechanism, if it requires so much knowledge in its application as to be of no advantage to the common workman.

The title which I prefix to my work has long conveyed
a very miscellaneous idea, and they that take a dictionary
into their hands have been accustomed to expect from it
a solution of almost every difficulty. If foreign words
therefore were rejected, it could be little regarded,
except by criticks, or those who aspire to criticism; and
however it might enlighten those that write, would be
all darkness to them that only read. The unlearned much

oftener consult their dictionaries for the meaning of words, than for their structures or formations; and the words that most want explanation are generally terms of art; which, therefore, experience has taught my predecessors to spread with a kind of pompous luxuriance over their productions.

The academicians of *France*, indeed, rejected terms of science in their first essay, but found afterwards a necessity of relaxing the rigour of their determination; and, though they would not naturalize them at once by a single act, permitted them by degrees to settle themselves among the natives with little opposition; and it would surely be no proof of judgment to imitate them in an errour which they have now retracted, and deprive the book of its chief use by scrupulous distinctions.

Of such words, however, all are not equally to be considered as parts of our language; for some of them are naturalized and incorporated, but others still continue aliens, and are rather auxiliaries than subjects. This naturalization is produced either by an admission into common speech, in some metaphorical signification, which is the acquisition of a kind of property among us; as we say the *zenith* of advancement, the *meridian* of life, the *cynosure* of neighbouring eyes; or it is the consequence of long intermixture and frequent use, by which the ear is accustomed to the sound of words till their original is forgotten, as in *equator, satellites*; or of the change of a foreign to an English termination, and a conformity to the laws of the speech into which they are adopted, as in *category, cachexy, peripneumony*.

Of those which still continue in the state of aliens, and have made no approaches toward assimilation, some seem necessary to be retained, because the purchasers of the Dictionary will expect to find them. Such are many words in the common law, as *capias, habeas corpus, præmunire, nisi prius:* such are some terms of controversial divinity, as *hypostasis:* and of physick, as the names of diseases; and in general, all terms which can be found in books not written professedly upon particular arts, or can be supposed necessary to those who do not regularly study them. Thus, when a reader not skilled in physick happens in Milton upon this line,

> . . . . pining atrophy,
> Marasmus, and wide-wasting pestilence,

he will, with equal expectation, look into his dictionary for the word *marasmus*, as for *atrophy*, or *pestilence*; and will have reason to complain if he does not find it.

It seems necessary to the completion of a dictionary designed not merely for criticks, but for popular use, that it should comprise, in some degree, the peculiar words of every profession; that the terms of war and navigation should be inserted, so far as they can be required by readers of travels, and of history; and those of law, merchandize, and mechanical trades, so far as they can be supposed useful in the occurrences of common life.

But there ought, however, to be some distinction made between the different classes of words; and therefore it will be proper to print those which are incorporated into the language in the usual character, and those which are still to be considered as foreign, in the Italic letter.

Another question may arise with regard to appellatives, or the names of species. It seems of no great use to set down the words *horse*, *dog*, *cat*, *willow*, *alder*, *daisy*, *rose*, and a thousand others, of which it will be hard to give an explanation, not more obscure than the word itself. Yet it is to be considered, that, if the names of animals be inserted, we must admit those which are more known, as well as those with which we are, by accident, less acquainted; and if they are all rejected how will the reader be relieved from difficulties produced by allusions to the crocodile, the chameleon, the ichneumon, and the hyæna? If no plants are to be mentioned, the most pleasing part of nature will be excluded, and many beautiful epithets be unexplained. If only those which are less known are to be mentioned, who shall fix the limits of the reader's learning? The importance of such explications appears from the mistakes which the want of them has occasioned. Had Shakespeare had a dictionary of this kind he had not made the *woodbine* entwine the *honey-suckle;* nor would

Milton, with such assistance, have disposed so improperly of his *ellops* and his *scorpion*.

1754
To Thomas Warton

Sir

It is but an ill return for the book with which you were pleased to favour me, to have delayed my thanks for it till now. I am too apt to be negligent but I can never deliberately show any disrespect to a man of your character, and I now pay you a very honest acknowledgement for the advancement of the literature of our native Country. You have shown to all who shall hereafter attempt the study of our ancient authours the way to success, by directing them to the perusal of the books which those authours had read. Of this method Hughes and Men much greater than Hughes seem never to have thought. The Reason why the authours which are yet read of the sixteenth Century are so little understood is that they are read alone, and no help is borrowed from those who lived with them or before them. Some part of this ignorance I hope to remove by my book which now draws towards its end, but which I cannot finish to my mind without visiting the Libraries of Oxford which I therefore hope to see in about a fortnight. I know not how long I shall stay or where I shall lodge, but shall be sure to look for you at my arrival, and we shall easily settle the rest.

I am Dear Sir Your most obedient and most humble servant

July 16. 1754   Sam: Johnson

1755
To the Earl of Chesterfield

My Lord   February 1755

I have been lately informed by the proprietor of The World that two Papers in which my Dictionary is recommended to the Public were written by your Lordship. To

be so distinguished is an honour which, being very little
accustomed to favours from the Great, I know not well
how to receive, or in what terms to acknowledge.

When upon some slight encouragment I first visited
your Lordship I was overpowered like the rest of Mankind by the enchantment of your adress, and could not
forbear to wish that I might boast myself Le Vainqueur
du Vainqueur de la Terre, that I might obtain that regard
for which I saw the world contending, but I found my
attendance so little incouraged, that neither pride nor
modesty would suffer me to continue it. When I had once
adressed your Lordship in public, I had exhausted all the
art of pleasing which a retired and uncourtly Scholar can
possess. I had done all that I could, and no Man is well
pleased to have his all neglected, be it ever so little.

Seven years, My Lord, have now past since I waited
in your outward Rooms or was repulsed from your Door,
during which time I have been pushing on my work
through difficulties of which it is useless to complain,
and have brought it at last to the verge of Publication
without one Act of assistance, one word of encouragement, or one smile of favour. Such treatment I did not
expect, for I never had a Patron before.

The Shepherd in Virgil grew at last acquainted with
Love, and found him a Native of the Rocks. Is not a
Patron, My Lord, one who looks with unconcern on a
Man struggling for Life in the water and when he has
reached ground encumbers him with help? The notice
which you have been pleased to take of my Labours,
had it been early, had been kind; but it has been delayed till I am indifferent and cannot enjoy it, till I
am solitary and cannot impart it, till I am known and
do not want it.

I hope it is no very cinical asperity not to confess
obligation where no benefit has been received, or to be
unwilling that the Public should consider me as owing
that to a Patron, which Providence has enabled me to do
for myself.

Having carried on my work thus far with so little
obligation to any Favourer of Learning I shall not be

disappointed though I should conclude it, if less be possible, with less, for I have been long wakened from that Dream of hope, in which I once boasted myself with so much exultation, My lord Your Lordship's Most humble Most Obedient Servant,

Sam: Johnson

1755
To the Vice-Chancellor of Oxford

Londini 4to Cal. Mart.
Viro reverendo . . . Huddesford S.T.P. 1755
Universitatis Oxoniensis Vicecancellario dignissimo—
S.P.D.
Sam: Johnson.

Ingratus plane et tibi et mihi videar, nisi quanto me gaudio affecerint, quos nuper mihi honores, te, credo, auctore, decrevit Senatus academicus, literarum, quo tamen nihil levius, officio significem; ingratus etiam nisi comitatem quâ vir eximius mihi vestri testimonium amoris, in manus tradidit, agnoscam et laudem. Si quid est, unde rei tam gratae accedat gratia, hoc ipso magis mihi placet, quod eo tempore in ordines academicos denuò cooptatus sim, quo tuam imminuere auctoritatem, famamque Oxoniensium laedere, omnibus modis conantur homines vafri nec tamen acuti, quibus ego, prout Viro umbratico licuit, semper restiti, semper restiturus. Qui enim, has inter rerum procellas, vel tibi vel Academiae defuerit, illum virtuti et literis, sibique et posteris defuturum existimo. Vale.

To Thomas Warton

Dear Sir
I wrote to You some weeks ago but I believe did not direct accurately, and therefore know not whether you had my Letter. I would likewise write to your Brother but know not where to find him. I now begin to see land, after having wandered, according to Mr Warburton's phrase, in this vast sea of words. What reception I shall

meet with upon the Shore I know not, whether the sound of Bells and acclamations of the People which Ariosto talks of in his last canto or a general murmur of dislike, I know not whether I shall find upon the coast, a Calypso that will court or a Polypheme that will eat me. But if Polypheme comes to me have at his eyes.

I hope however the criticks will let me be at peace for though I do not much fear their skill or strength, I am a little afraid of myself, and would not willingly feel so much ill-will in my bosom as literary quarrels are apt to excite.

Mr Baretti is about a work for which he is in great want of Crescembeni, which you may have again when you please.

There is nothing considerable done or doing among us here, we are not perhaps as innocent as villagers but most of us seem to be as idle. I hope however you are busy, and should be glad to know what you are doing.

I am Dearest Sir, Your most humble servant
Febr. 1, 1755   Sam: Johnson

Orthography

In examining the orthography of any doubtful word, the mode of spelling by which it is inserted in the series of the dictionary, is to be considered as that to which I give, perhaps not often rashly, the preference. I have left, in the examples, to every author his own practice unmolested, that the reader may balance suffrages, and judge between us: but this question is not always to be determined by reputed or by real learning: some men, intent upon greater things, have thought little on sounds and derivations; some, knowing in the ancient tongues, have neglected those in which our words are commonly to be sought. Thus Hammond writes *fecibleness*, for *feasibleness*, because I suppose he imagined it derived immediately from the Latin; and some words, such as *dependant, dependent; dependance, dependence,* vary their final syllable, as one or another language is present to the writer.

In this part of the work, where caprice has long wantoned without control, and vanity sought praise by petty reformation, I have endeavoured to proceed with a scholar's reverence for antiquity, and a grammarian's regard to the genius of our tongue. I have attempted few alterations, and among those few, perhaps the greater part is from the modern to the ancient practice; and I hope I may be allowed to recommend to those whose thoughts have been perhaps employed too anxiously on verbal singularities, not to disturb, upon narrow views, or for minute propriety, the orthography of their fathers. It has been asserted, that for the law to be *known*, is of more importance than to be *right*. 'Change,' says Hooker, 'is not made without inconvenience, even from worse to better.' There is in constancy and stability a general and lasting advantage, which will always overbalance the slow improvements of gradual correction. Much less ought our written language to comply with the corruptions of oral utterance, or copy that which every variation of time or place makes different from itself, and imitate those changes, which will again be changed, while imitation is employed in observing them.

This recommendation of steadiness and uniformity does not proceed from an opinion, that particular combinations of letters have much influence on human happiness; or that truth may not be successfully taught by modes of spelling fanciful and erroneous: I am not yet so lost in lexicography as to forget that *words are the daughters of earth, and that things are the sons of heaven.* Language is only the instrument of science, and words are but the signs of ideas: I wish, however, that the instrument might be less apt to decay, and that signs might be permanent, like the things which they denote.

In settling the orthography, I have not wholly neglected the pronunciation, which I have directed, by printing an accent upon the acute or elevated syllable. It will sometimes be found, that the accent is placed by the author quoted, on a different syllable from that marked in the alphabetical series: it is then to be understood, that custom has varied, or that the author has, in my opinion,

pronounced wrong. Short directions are sometimes given
where the sound of letters is irregular; and if they are
sometimes omitted, defect in such minute observations
will be more easily excused, than superfluity.

Preface to the Dictionary

Definition

That part of my work on which I expect malignity most
frequently to fasten, is the *explanation*; in which I cannot
hope to satisfy those, who are perhaps not inclined to be
pleased, since I have not always been able to satisfy myself. To interpret a language by itself is very difficult;
many words cannot be explained by synonimes, because
the idea signified by them has not more than one appella-
tion; nor by paraphrase, because simple ideas cannot be
described. When the nature of things is unknown, or the
notion unsettled and indefinite, and various in various
minds, the words by which such notions are conveyed,
or such things denoted, will be ambiguous and perplexed.
And such is the fate of hapless lexicography, that not only
darkness, but light, impedes and distresses it; things may
be not only too little, but too much known, to be happily
illustrated. To explain, requires the use of terms less
abstruse than that which is to be explained, and such
terms cannot always be found; for as nothing can be
proved but by supposing something intuitively known,
and evident without proof, so nothing can be defined but
by the use of words too plain to admit a definition.

Other words there are, of which the sense is too subtle
and evanescent to be fixed in a paraphrase; such are all
those which are by the grammarians termed *expletives*,
and, in dead languages, are suffered to pass for empty
sounds, of no other use than to fill a verse or to modulate
a period, but which are easily perceived in living tongues
to have power and emphasis, though it be sometimes such
as no other form of expression can convey.

My labour has likewise been much increased by a class
of verbs too frequent in the English language, of which
the signification is so loose and general, the use so vague

and indeterminate, and the senses detorted so widely from the first idea, that it is hard to trace them through the maze of variation, to catch them on the brink of utter inanity, to circumscribe them by any limitations, or interpret them by any words of distinct and settled meaning; such are *bear, break, come, cast, fall, get, give, do, put, set, go, run, make, take, turn, throw.* If of these the whole power is not accurately delivered, it must be remembered, that while our language is yet living, and variable by the caprice of every one that speaks it, these words are hourly shifting their relations, and can no more be ascertained in a dictionary, than a grove, in the agitation of a storm, can be accurately delineated from its picture in the water.

The rigour of interpretative lexicography requires that *the explanation, and the word explained, should be always reciprocal*; this I have always endeavoured, but could not always attain. Words are seldom exactly synonimous; a new term was not introduced, but because the former was thought inadequate: names, therefore, have often many ideas, but few ideas have many names. It was then necessary to use the proximate word, for the deficiency of single terms can very seldom be supplied by circumlocution; nor is the inconvenience great of such mutilated interpretations, because the sense may easily be collected entire from the examples.

In every word of extensive use, it was requisite to mark the progress of its meaning, and show by what gradations of intermediate sense it has passed from its primitive to its remote and accidental signification; so that every foregoing explanation should tend to that which follows, and the series be regularly concatenated from the first notion to the last.

This is specious, but not always practicable; kindred senses may be so interwoven, that the perplexity cannot be disentangled, nor any reason be assigned why one should be ranged before the other. When the radical idea branches out into parallel ramifications, how can a consecutive series be formed of senses in their nature collateral? The shades of meaning sometimes pass imperceptibly into each other; so that though on one side they apparently differ, yet it is impossible to mark the point of contact. Ideas of the same race, though not exactly alike, are sometimes so little different, that no words can express the dissimilitude, though the mind easily perceives it, when they are exhibited together; and sometimes there is such a confusion of acceptations, that discernment is wearied, and distinction puzzled, and perseverance herself hurries to an end, by crowding together what she cannot separate.

These complaints of difficulty will, by those that have never considered words beyond their popular use, be thought only the jargon of a man willing to magnify his labours, and procure veneration to his studies by involution and obscurity. But every art is obscure to those that have not learned it: this uncertainty of terms, and commixture of ideas, is well known to those who have joined philosophy with grammar; and if I have not expressed them very clearly, it must be remembered that I am speaking of that which words are insufficient to explain.

Preface to the Dictionary

Quotation

When I first collected these authorities, I was desirous that every quotation should be useful to some other end than the illustration of a word; I therefore extracted from philosophers principles of science; from historians remarkable facts; from chymists complete processes; from divines striking exhortations; and from poets beautiful descriptions. Such is design, while it is yet at a distance from execution. When the time called upon me to range this accumulation of elegance and wisdom into an alphabetical series, I soon discovered that the bulk of my volumes would fright away the student, and was forced to depart from my scheme of including all that was pleasing or useful in English literature, and reduce my transcripts very often to clusters of words, in which scarcely any meaning is retained; thus to the weariness

of copying, I was condemned to add the vexation of ex-
punging. Some passages I have yet spared, which may
relieve the labour of verbal searches, and intersperse
with verdure and flowers the dusty desarts of barren
philology.

The examples, thus mutilated, are no longer to be considered as conveying the sentiments or doctrine of their
authors; the word for the sake of which they are inserted,
with all its appendant clauses, has been carefully preserved; but it may sometimes happen, by hasty detrunca-
tion, that the general tendency of the sentence may be
changed: the divine may desert his tenets, or the philosopher his system.

Some of the examples have been taken from writers
who were never mentioned as masters of elegance, or
models of style; but words must be sought where they are
used; and in what pages, eminent for purity, can terms
of manufacture or agriculture be found? Many quotations
serve no other purpose than that of proving the bare
existence of words, and are therefore selected with less
scrupulousness than those which are to teach their structures and relations.

My purpose was to admit no testimony of living
authors, that I might not be misled by partiality, and
that none of my contemporaries might have reason to
complain; nor have I departed from this resolution, but
when some performance of uncommon excellence excited
my veneration, when my memory supplied me, from late
books, with an example that was wanting, or when my
heart, in the tenderness of friendship, solicited admission
for a favourite name.

So far have I been from any care to grace my pages
with modern decorations, that I have studiously endeavoured to collect examples and authorities from the
writers before the restoration, whose works I regard as
the wells of English undefiled, as the pure sources of genuine
diction. Our language, for almost a century, has, by the
concurrence of many causes, been gradually departing
from its original Teutonick character, and deviating toward a Gallick structure and phraseology, from which it

ought to be our endeavour to recal it, by making our ancient volumes the ground work of style, admitting among the additions of later times, only such as may supply real deficiencies, such as are readily adopted by the genius of our tongue, and incorporate easily with our native idioms.

But as every language has a time of rudeness antecedent to perfection, as well as of false refinement and declension, I have been cautious lest my zeal for antiquity might drive me into times too remote, and crowd my book with words now no longer understood. I have fixed Sidney's work for the boundary, beyond which I make few excursions. From the authors which rose in the time of Elizabeth, a speech might be formed adequate to all the purposes of use and elegance. If the language of theology were extracted from Hooker and the translation of the Bible; the terms of natural knowledge from Bacon; the phrases of policy, war, and navigation from Raleigh; the dialect of poetry and fiction from Spenser and Sidney; and the diction of common life from Shakespeare, few ideas would be lost to mankind for want of English words, in which they might be expressed.

Preface to the Dictionary

The Lexicographer Fallible

Thus have I laboured by settling the orthography, displaying the analogy, regulating the structures, and ascertaining the signification of *English* words, to perform all the parts of a faithful lexicographer: but I have not always executed my own scheme, or satisfied my own expectations. The work, whatever proofs of diligence and attention it may exhibit, is yet capable of many improvements: the orthography which I recommend is still controvertible; the etymology which I adopt is uncertain, and perhaps frequently erroneous; the explanations are sometimes too much contracted, and sometimes too much diffused, the significations are distinguished rather with subtilty than skill, and the attention is harassed with unnecessary minuteness.

The examples are too often injudiciously truncated, and perhaps sometimes, I hope very rarely, alleged in a mistaken sense; for in making this collection I trusted more to memory, than, in a state of disquiet and embarrassment, memory can contain, and purposed to supply at the review what was left incomplete in the first transcription.

Many terms appropriated to particular occupations, though necessary and significant, are undoubtedly omitted; and of the words most studiously considered and exemplified, many senses have escaped observation.

Yet these failures, however frequent, may admit extenuation and apology. To have attempted much is always laudable, even when the enterprize is above the strength that undertakes it: To rest below his own aim is incident to every one whose fancy is active, and whose views are comprehensive; nor is any man satisfied with himself because he has done much, but because he can conceive little. When first I engaged in this work, I resolved to leave neither words nor things unexamined, and pleased myself with a prospect of the hours which I should revel away in feasts of literature, the obscure recesses of northern learning which I should enter and ransack, the treasures with which I expected every search into those neglected mines to reward my labour, and the triumph with which I should display my acquisitions to mankind. When I had thus enquired into the original of words, I resolved to show likewise my attention to things; to pierce deep into every science, to enquire the nature of every substance of which I inserted the name, to limit every idea by a definition strictly logical, and exhibit every production of art or nature in an accurate description, that my book might be in place of all other dictionaries whether appellative or technical. But these were the dreams of a poet doomed at last to wake a lexicographer. I soon found that it is too late to look for instruments, when the work calls for execution, and that whatever abilities I have brought to my task, with those I must finally perform it. To deliberate whenever I doubted, to enquire whenever I was ignorant, would

have protracted the undertaking without end, and, perhaps, without much improvement; for I did not find by
my first experiments, that what I had not of my own was
easily to be obtained: I saw that one enquiry only gave
occasion to another, that book referred to book, that to
search was not always to find, and to find was not always
to be informed; and that thus to pursue perfection, was,
like the first inhabitants of Arcadia, to chase the sun,
which, when they had reached the hill where he seemed
to rest, was still beheld at the same distance from them.

I then contracted my design, determining to confide in
myself, and no longer to solicit auxiliaries, which produced more incumbrance than assistance; by this I obtained at least one advantage, that I set limits to my work,
which would in time be ended, though not completed.

Despondency has never so far prevailed as to depress
me to negligence; some faults will at last appear to be
the effects of anxious diligence and persevering activity.
The nice and subtle ramifications of meaning were not
easily avoided by a mind intent upon accuracy, and
convinced of the necessity of disentangling combinations,
and separating similitudes. Many of the distinctions
which to common readers appear useless and idle, will
be found real and important by men versed in the school
philosophy, without which no dictionary can ever be
accurately compiled, or skilfully examined.

Preface to the Dictionary

The Mutability of Language

Of the event of this work, for which, having laboured it
with so much application, I cannot but have some degree
of parental fondness, it is natural to form conjectures.
Those who have been persuaded to think well of my
design, will require that it should fix our language, and
put a stop to those alterations which time and chance
have hitherto been suffered to make in it without opposition. With this consequence I will confess that I flattered
myself for a while; but now begin to fear that I have indulged expectation which neither reason nor experience

can justify. When we see men grow old and die at a certain time one after another, from century to century, we laugh at the elixir that promises to prolong life to a thousand years; and with equal justice may the lexicographer be derided, who being able to produce no example of a nation that has preserved their words and phrases from mutability, shall imagine that his dictionary can embalm his language, and secure it from corruption and decay, that it is in his power to change sublunary nature, and clear the world at once from folly, vanity, and affectation.

With this hope, however, academies have been instituted, to guard the avenues of their languages, to retain fugitives, and repulse intruders; but their vigilance and activity have hitherto been vain; sounds are too volatile and subtile for legal restraints; to enchain syllables, and to lash the wind, are equally the undertakings of pride, unwilling to measure its desires by its strength. The French language has visibly changed under the inspection of the academy; the style of Amelot's translation of father Paul is observed by Le Courayer to be *un peu passé*; and no Italian will maintain, that the diction of any modern writer is not perceptibly different from that of Boccace, Machiavel, or Caro.

Total and sudden transformations of a language seldom happen; conquests and migrations are now very rare: but there are other causes of change, which, though slow in their operation, and invisible in their progress, are perhaps as much superior to human resistance, as the revolutions of the sky, or intumescence of the tide. Commerce, however necessary, however lucrative, as it depraves the manners corrupts the language; they that have frequent intercourse with strangers, to whom they endeavour to accommodate themselves, must in time learn a mingled dialect, like the jargon which serves the traffickers on the Mediterranean and Indian coasts. This will not always be confined to the exchange, the warehouse, or the port, but will be communicated by degrees to other ranks of the people, and be at last incorporated with the current speech.

There are likewise internal causes equally forcible. The language most likely to continue long without altera- tion, would be that of a nation raised a little, and but a little, above barbarity, secluded from strangers, and totally employed in procuring the conveniences of life; either without books, or, like some of the Mahometan countries, with very few: men thus busied and unlearned, having only such words as common use requires, would perhaps long continue to express the same notions by the same signs. But no such constancy can be expected in a people polished by arts, and classed by subordination, where one part of the community is sustained and accom- modated by the labour of the other. Those who have much leisure to think, will always be enlarging the stock of ideas; and every increase of knowledge, whether real or fancied, will produce new words, or combinations of words. When the mind is unchained from necessity, it will range after convenience; when it is left at large in the field of speculation, it will shift opinions; as any custom is disused, the words that expressed it must perish with it; as any opinion grows popular, it will innovate speech in the same proportion as it alters practice.

As by the cultivation of various sciences, a language is amplified, it will be more furnished with words deflected from their original sense; the geometrician will talk of a courtier's zenith, or the eccentric virtue of a wild hero, and the physician of sanguine expectations, and phleg- matic delays. Copiousness of speech will give opportu- nities to capricious choice, by which some words will be preferred, and others degraded; vicissitudes of fashion will enforce the use of new, or extend the signification of known terms. The tropes of poetry will make hourly encroachments, and the metaphorical will become the current sense: pronunciation will be varied by levity or ignorance, and the pen must at length comply with the tongue: illiterate writers will, at one time or other, by public infatuation, rise into renown, who not knowing the original import of words, will use them with collo- quial licentiousness, confound distinction, and forget pro- priety. As politeness increases, some expressions will be considered as too gross and vulgar for the delicate, others as too formal and ceremonious for the gay and airy; new phrases are therefore adopted, which must, for the same reasons, be in time dismissed. Swift, in his petty treatise on the English language, allows that new words must sometimes be introduced, but proposes that none should be suffered to become obsolete. But what makes a word obsolete, more than general agreement to forbear it? and how shall it be continued, when it conveys an offensive idea, or recalled again into the mouths of mankind, when it has once become unfamiliar by disuse, and unpleasing by unfamiliarity?

Preface to the Dictionary

Frigid Tranquillity

In hope of giving longevity to that which its own nature forbids to be immortal, I have devoted this book, the labour of years, to the honour of my country, that we may no longer yield the palm of philology, without a contest, to the nations of the continent. The chief glory of every people arises from its authors: whether I shall add any thing by my own writings to the reputation of English literature, must be left to time: much of my life has been lost under the pressures of disease; much has been trifled away; and much has always been spent in provision for the day that was passing over me; but I shall not think my employment useless or ignoble, if by my assistance foreign nations, and distant ages, gain access to the propagators of knowledge, and understand the teachers of truth; if my labours afford light to the repositories of science, and add celebrity to Bacon, to Hooker, to Milton, and to Boyle.

When I am animated by this wish, I look with pleasure on my book, however defective, and deliver it to the world with the spirit of a man that has endeavoured well. That it will immediately become popular I have not promised to myself: a few wild blunders, and risible absurdities, from which no work of such multiplicity was ever free, may for a time furnish folly with laughter, and harden ignorance in contempt; but useful diligence will at last prevail, and there never can be wanting some who distinguish desert; who will consider that no dictionary of a living tongue ever can be perfect, since, while it is hastening to publication, some words are budding, and some falling away; that a whole life cannot be spent upon syntax and etymology, and that even a whole life would not be sufficient; that he, whose design includes whatever language can express, must often speak of what he does not understand; that a writer will sometimes be hurried by eagerness to the end, and sometimes faint with weariness under a task, which Scaliger compares to the labours of the anvil and the mine; that what is obvious is not always known, and what is known is not always present; that sudden fits of inadvertency will surprise vigilance, slight avocations will seduce attention, and casual eclipses of the mind will darken learning; and that the writer shall often in vain trace his memory at the moment of need, for that which yesterday he knew with intuitive readiness, and which will come uncalled into his thoughts to-morrow.

In this work, when it shall be found that much is omitted, let it not be forgotten that much likewise is performed; and though no book was ever spared out of tenderness to the author, and the world is little solicitous to know whence proceeded the faults of that which it condemns; yet it may gratify curiosity to inform it, that the *English Dictionary* was written with little assistance of the learned, and without any patronage of the great; not in the soft obscurities of retirement, or under the shelter of academick bowers, but amid inconvenience and distraction, in sickness and in sorrow. It may repress the triumph of malignant criticism to observe, that if our language is not here fully displayed, I have only failed in an attempt which no human powers have hitherto completed. If the lexicons of ancient tongues, now immutably fixed, and comprised in a few volumes, be yet, after the toil of successive ages, inadequate and delusive; if the aggregated knowledge, and co-operating diligence of the Italian academicians, did not secure them from the censure of Beni; if the embodied criticks of France, when fifty years had been spent upon their work, were obliged to change its œconomy, and give their second edition another form, I may surely be contented without the praise of perfection, which, if I could obtain, in this gloom of solitude, what would it avail me? I have protracted my work till most of those whom I wished to please have sunk into the grave, and success and miscarriage are empty sounds. I therefore dismiss it with frigid tranquillity, having little to fear or hope from censure or from praise.

Preface to the Dictionary

Specimen Articles

PHILOSOPHY, n.s. [*philosophie*, Fr. *philosophia*, Latin].

1. Knowledge natural or moral.

> I had never read, heard nor seen any thing, I had never any taste of *philosophy* nor inward feeling in myself, which for a while I did not call to my succour. *Sidney.*

> > Hang up *philosophy*;
> > Unless *philosophy* can make a Juliet,
> > Displant a town, rescue a prince's doom,
> > It helps not. *Shakespeare.*

> The progress you have made in *philosophy*, hath enabled you to benefit yourself with what I have written. *Digby.*

2. Hypothesis or system upon which natural effects are explained.

> We shall in vain interpret their words by the notions of our *philosophy*, and the doctrines in our schools. *Locke.*

3. Reasoning; argumentation.

> > Of good and evil much they argu'd then
> > Vain wisdom all and false *philosophy*. *Milton.*

> His decisions are the judgment of his passions not of his reason, the *philosophy* of the sinner not of the man. *Rogers.*

4. The course of the sciences read in the schools.

POESY, n.s. [*poesie*, Fr. *poesis*, Lat. ποίησις].

1. The art of writing poems.

A poem is the work of the poet; *poesy* is his skill or craft of making; the very fiction itself, the reason or form of the work. *Ben Johnson.*

How far have we
Prophan'd thy heav'nly gift of *poesy*?
Made prostitute and profligate the muse,
Whose harmony was first ordained above
For tongues of angels.   *Dryden.*

2. Poem; metrical composition; poetry.

Musick and *poesy* use to quicken you. *Shakespeare.*

There is an hymn, for they have excellent *poesy*; the subject is always the praises of Adam, Noah and Abraham, concluding ever with a thanksgiving for the nativity of our Saviour. *Bacon's New Atlantis.*

They apprehend a veritable history in an emblem or piece of Christian *poesy*. *Brown's Vulgar Errours.*

3. A short conceit engraved on a ring or other thing.

A paltry ring, whose *poesy* was,
For all the world like cutler's poetry
Upon a knife; love me, and leave me not. *Shakespeare.*

ELECTRICAL ⎫
ELECTRICK ⎬ *adj.* [from *electrum.* See ELECTRE].

1. Attractive without magnetism; attractive by a peculiar property, supposed once to belong chiefly to amber.

By *electrick* bodies do I conceive not such only as take up light bodies, in which number the ancients only placed jett and amber; but such as, conveniently placed, attract all bodies palpable. *Brown's Vulgar Errours.*

An *electrick* body can by friction emit an exhalation so subtile, and yet so potent, as by its emission to cause no sensible diminution of the weight of the *electrick* body, and to be expanded through a sphere, whose diameter is above two feet, and yet to be able to carry up lead, copper, or leaf-gold, at a distance of above a foot from the *electrick* body. *Newton.*

2. Produced by an electrick body.

If that attraction were not rather *electrical* than mag-
netical, it was wonderous what Helmont delivereth concerning a glass, wherein the magistery of loadstone was
prepared, which retained an attractive quality. *Brown.*

If a piece of white paper, or a white cloth, or the end
of one's finger, be held at about a quarter of an inch from
the glass, the *electrick* vapour, excited by friction, will, by
dashing against the white paper, cloth, or finger, be put
into such an agitation as to emit light. *Newton's Opt.*

c. 1747

The Winter's Walk

Behold my fair, where-e'er we rove,
  What dreary prospects round us rise,
The naked hills, the leafless grove,
  The hoary ground, the frowning skies.

Nor only through the wasted plain,
  Stern winter, is thy force confest,
Still wider spreads thy horrid reign,
  I feel thy pow'r usurp my breast.

Enliv'ning hope, and fond desire,
  Resign the heart to spleen and care,
Scarce frighted love maintains his fire,
  And rapture saddens to despair.

In groundless hope, and causeless fear,
  Unhappy man! behold thy doom,
Still changing with the changeful year,
  The slave of sunshine and of gloom.

Tir'd with vain joys, and false alarms,
  With mental and corporeal strife,
Snatch me, my *Stella*, to thy arms,
  And screen me from the ills of life.

1747
The Drury Lane Prologue

When Learning's Triumph o'er her barb'rous Foes
First rear'd the Stage, immortal SHAKESPEAR rose;
Each Change of many-colour'd Life he drew,
Exhausted Worlds, and then imagin'd new:
Existence saw him spurn her bounded Reign,
And panting Time toil'd after him in vain:
His pow'rful Strokes presiding Truth impress'd,
And unresisted Passion storm'd the Breast.

Then JOHNSON came, instructed from the School,
To please in Method, and invent by Rule;
His studious Patience, and laborious Art,
By regular Approach essay'd the Heart;
Cold Approbation gave the ling'ring Bays,
For those who durst not censure, scarce cou'd praise.
A Mortal born he met the general Doom,
But left, like *Egypt*'s Kings, a lasting Tomb.

The Wits of *Charles* found easier Ways to Fame,
Nor wish'd for JOHNSON's Art, or SHAKESPEAR's Flame;
Themselves they studied, as they felt, they writ,
Intrigue was Plot, Obscenity was Wit.
Vice always found a sympathetick Friend;
They pleas'd their Age, and did not aim to mend.
Yet Bards like these aspir'd to lasting Praise,
And proudly hop'd to pimp in future Days.
Their Cause was gen'ral, their Supports were strong,
Their Slaves were willing, and their Reign was long;
Till Shame regain'd the Post that Sense betray'd,
And Virtue call'd Oblivion to her Aid.

Then crush'd by Rules, and weaken'd as refin'd,
For Years the Pow'r of Tragedy declin'd;
From Bard, to Bard, the frigid Caution crept,
Till Declamation roar'd, while Passion slept.
Yet still did Virtue deign the Stage to tread,
Philosophy remain'd, though Nature fled.
But forc'd at length her antient Reign to quit,
She saw great *Faustus* lay the Ghost of Wit:

Exulting Folly hail'd the joyful Day,
And Pantomime, and Song, confirm'd her Sway.
    But who the coming Changes can presage,
And mark the future Periods of the Stage?—
Perhaps if Skill could distant Times explore,
New *Behns*, new *Durfeys*, yet remain in Store.
Perhaps, where *Lear* has rav'd, and *Hamlet* dy'd,
On flying Cars new Sorcerers may ride.
Perhaps, for who can guess th' Effects of Chance?
Here *Hunt* may box, or *Mahomet* may dance.
    Hard is his lot, that here by Fortune plac'd,
Must watch the wild Vicissitudes of Taste;
With ev'ry Meteor of Caprice must play,
And chase the new-blown Bubbles of the Day.
Ah! let not Censure term our Fate our Choice,
The Stage but echoes back the publick Voice.
The Drama's Laws the Drama's Patrons give,
For we that live to please, must please to live.
    Then prompt no more the Follies you decry,
As Tyrants doom their Tools of Guilt to die;
'Tis yours this Night to bid the Reign commence
Of rescu'd Nature, and reviving Sense;
To chase the Charms of Sound, the Pomp of Show,
For useful Mirth, and salutary Woe;
Bid scenic Virtue form the rising Age,
And Truth diffuse her Radiance from the Stage.

1748

The Pleasures of Dates

The study of chronology and history seems to be one of
the most natural delights of the human mind. It is not
easy to live without inquiring by what means every thing
was brought into the state in which we now behold it, or
without finding in the mind some desire of being informed concerning the generations of mankind that have
been in possession of the world before us, whether they
were better or worse than ourselves; or what good or evil
has been derived to us from their schemes, practices, and

institutions. These are inquiries which history alone can satisfy; and history can only be made intelligible by some knowledge of chronology, the science by which events are ranged in their order, and the periods of computation are settled; and which therefore assists the memory by method, and enlightens the judgment by showing the dependence of one transaction on another. Accordingly it should be diligently inculcated to the scholar, that unless he fixes in his mind some idea of the time in which each man of eminence lived, and each action was performed, with some part of the contemporary history of the rest of the world, he will consume his life in useless reading, and darken his mind with a crowd of unconnected events; his memory will be perplexed with distant transactions resembling one another, and his reflections be like a dream in a fever, busy and turbulent, but confused and indistinct.

The technical part of chronology, or the art of computing and adjusting time, as it is very difficult, so it is not of absolute necessity, but should however be taught, so far as it can be learned without the loss of those hours which are required for attainments of nearer concern. The student may join with this treatise Le Clerc's *Compendium of History*; and afterwards may, for the historical part of chronology, procure Helvicus's and Isaacson's Tables; and, if he is desirous of attaining the technical part, may first peruse Holder's *Account of Time*, Hearne's *Ductor Historicus*, Strauchius, the first part of Petavius's *Rationarium Temporum;* and at length Scaliger *de Emendatione Temporum.* And for instruction in the method of his historical studies, he may consult Hearne's *Ductor Historicus*, Wheare's Lectures, Rawlinson's *Directions for the Study of History*; and for ecclesiastical history, Cave and Dupin, Baronius and Fleury.

Preface to *The Preceptor*

The Young Idea

Every man, who has been engaged in teaching, knows with how much difficulty youthful minds are confined to close application, and how readily they deviate to any thing, rather than attend to that which is imposed as a task. That this disposition, when it becomes inconsistent with the forms of education, is to be checked, will be readily granted; but since, though it may be in some degree obviated, it cannot wholly be suppressed, it is surely rational to turn it to advantage, by taking care that the mind shall never want objects on which its faculties may be usefully employed. It is not impossible, that this restless desire of novelty, which gives so much trouble to the teacher, may be often the struggle of the understanding starting from that to which it is not by nature adapted, and travelling in search of something on which it may fix with greater satisfaction. For without supposing each man particularly marked out by his genius for particular performances, it may be easily conceived, that when a numerous class of boys is confined indiscriminately to the same forms of composition, the repetition of the same words, or the explication of the same sentiments, the employment must, either by nature or accident, be less suitable to some than others; that the ideas to be contemplated may be too difficult for the apprehension of one, and too obvious for that of another; they may be such as some understandings cannot reach, though others look down upon them as below their regard. Every mind in its progress through the different stages of scholastick learning, must be often in one of these conditions, must either flag with the labour, or grow wanton with the facility of the work assigned; and in either state it naturally turns aside from the track before it. Weariness looks out for relief, and leisure for employment, and surely it is rational to indulge the wanderings of both. For the faculties which are too lightly burthened with the business of the day, may with great propriety add to it some other inquiry: and he that finds himself over wearied by a task, which, perhaps with all his efforts, he is not able to perform, is undoubtedly to be justified in addicting himself rather to easier studies, and endeavouring to quit that which is above his attainment, for that which nature has not made him incapable of pursuing with advantage.

That therefore this roving curiosity may not be unsatisfied, it seems necessary to scatter in its way such
allurements as may withhold it from an useless and un-
bounded dissipation; such as may regulate it without
violence, and direct it without restraint; such as may
suit every inclination, and fit every capacity; may employ
the stronger genius, by operations of reason, and engage
the less active or forcible mind, by supplying it with easy
knowledge, and obviating that despondence, which
quickly prevails, when nothing appears but a succession
of difficulties, and one labour only ceases that another
may be imposed.

Preface to *The Preceptor*

The Vision of Theodore

Son of Perseverance, whoever thou art, whose curiosity
has led thee hither, read and be wise. He that now calls
upon thee is Theodore, the Hermit of Teneriffe, who in
the fifty-seventh year of his retreat left this instruction to
mankind, lest his solitary hours should be spent in vain.

I was once what thou art now, a groveller on the earth,
and a gazer at the sky; I trafficked and heaped wealth
together, I loved and was favoured, I wore the robe of
honour and heard the musick of adulation; I was ambitious, and rose to greatness; I was unhappy, and retired.
I sought for some time what I at length found here, a
place where all real wants might be easily supplied, and
where I might not be under the necessity of purchasing
the assistance of men by the toleration of their follies.
Here I saw fruits and herbs and water, and here determined to wait the hand of death, which I hope, when at
last it comes, will fall lightly upon me.

Forty-eight years had I now passed in forgetfulness of
all mortal cares, and without any inclination to wander
farther than the necessity of procuring sustenance required; but as I stood one day beholding the rock that
overhangs my cell, I found in myself a desire to climb it;
and when I was on its top, was in the same manner determined to scale the next, till by degrees I conceived a wish

to view the summit of the mountain, at the foot of which I had so long resided. This motion of my thoughts I endeavoured to suppress, not because it appeared criminal, but because it was new; and all change, not evidently for the better, alarms a mind taught by experience to distrust itself. I was often afraid that my heart was deceiving me, that my impatience of confinement arose from some earthly passion, and that my ardour to survey the works of nature was only a hidden longing to mingle once again in the scenes of life. I therefore endeavoured to settle my thoughts into their former state, but found their distraction every day greater. I was always reproaching myself with the want of happiness within my reach, and at last began to question whether it was not laziness rather than caution that restrained me from climbing to the summit of Teneriffe.

I rose therefore before the day, and began my journey up the steep of the mountain; but I had not advanced far, old as I was and burthened with provisions, when the day began to shine upon me; the declivities grew more precipitous, and the sand slided from beneath my feet; at last, fainting with labour, I arrived at a small plain almost inclosed by rocks, and open only to the east. I sat down to rest awhile, in full persuasion, that when I had recovered my strength I should proceed on my design; but when once I had tasted ease, I found many reasons against disturbing it. The branches spread a shade over my head, and the gales of spring wafted odours to my bosom.

As I sat thus, forming alternately excuses for delay, and resolutions to go forward, an irresistible heaviness suddenly surprised me; I laid my head upon the bank, and resigned myself to sleep: when methought I heard the sound as of the flight of eagles, and a being of more than human dignity stood before me. While I was deliberating how to address him, he took me by the hand with an air of kindness, and asked me solemnly but without severity, 'Theodore, whither art thou going?' 'I am climbing, answered I, to the top of the mountain, to enjoy a more extensive prospect of the works of nature.'

'Attend first, said he, to the prospect which this place
affords, and what thou dost not understand I will explain. I am one of the benevolent beings who watch over
the children of the dust, to preserve them from those
evils which will not ultimately terminate in good, and
which they do not, by their own faults, bring upon themselves. Look round therefore without fear: observe, contemplate, and be instructed.'

Encouraged by this assurance, I looked and beheld a
mountain higher than Teneriffe, to the summit of which
the human eye could never reach; when I had tired
myself with gazing upon its height, I turned my eyes
towards its foot, which I could easily discover, but was
amazed to find it without foundation, and placed incon-
ceivably in emptiness and darkness. Thus I stood terri-
fied and confused; above were tracks inscrutable, and
below was total vacuity. But my protector, with a voice
of admonition, cried out, Theodore, be not affrighted,
but raise thy eyes again; the Mountain of Existence is
before thee, survey it and be wise.

I then looked with more deliberate attention, and
observed the bottom of the mountain to be a gentle rise,
and overspread with flowers; the middle to be more
steep, embarrassed with crags, and interrupted by precipices, over which hung branches loaded with fruits,
and among which were scattered palaces and bowers.
The tracts which my eye could reach nearest the top
were generally barren; but there were among the clefts of
the rocks a few hardy ever-greens, which though they did
not give much pleasure to the sight or smell, yet seemed to
cheer the labour and facilitate the steps of those who were
clambering among them.

Then, beginning to examine more minutely the different parts, I observed at a great distance a multitude of
both sexes issuing into view from the bottom of the
mountain. Their first actions I could not accurately discern; but, as they every moment approached nearer, I
found that they amused themselves with gathering flowers
under the superintendence of a modest virgin in a white
robe, who seemed not over solicitous to confine them to

any settled place or certain track; for she knew that the whole ground was smooth and solid, and that they could not easily be hurt or bewildered. When, as it often happened, they plucked a thistle for a flower, Innocence, so was she called, would smile at the mistake. Happy, said I, are they who are under so gentle a government, and yet are safe. But I had no opportunity to dwell long on the consideration of their felicity; for I found that Innocence continued her attendance but a little way, and seemed to consider only the flowery bottom of the mountain as her proper province. Those whom she abandoned scarcely knew that they were left, before they perceived themselves in the hands of Education, a nymph more severe in her aspect and imperious in her commands, who confined them to certain paths, in their opinion too narrow and too rough. These they were continually solicited to leave, by Appetite, whom Education could never fright away, though she sometimes awed her to such timidity, that the effects of her presence were scarcely perceptible. Some went back to the first part of the mountain, and seemed desirous of continuing busied in plucking flowers, but were no longer guarded by Innocence; and such as Education could not force back, proceeded up the mountain by some miry road, in which they were seldom seen, and scarcely ever regarded.

As Education led her troop up the mountain, nothing was more observable than that she was frequently giving them cautions to beware of Habits; and was calling out to one or another at every step, that a Habit was ensnaring them; that they would be under the dominion of Habit before they perceived their danger: and that those whom Habit should once subdue, had little hope of regaining their liberty.

Of this caution, so frequently repeated, I was very solicitous to know the reason, when my protector directed my regard to a troop of pygmies, which appeared to walk silently before those that were climbing the mountain, and each to smooth the way before her follower. I found that I had missed the notice of them before, both because they were so minute as not easily to be discerned, and because they grew every moment nearer in their colour to the objects with which they were surrounded. As the followers of Education did not appear to be sensible of the presence of these dangerous associates, or, ridiculing their diminutive size, did not think it possible that human beings should ever be brought into subjection by such feeble enemies, they generally heard her precepts of vigilance with wonder: and, when they thought her eye withdrawn, treated them with contempt. Nor could I myself think her cautions so necessary as her frequent inculcations seemed to suppose, till I observed that each of these petty beings held secretly a chain in her hand, with which she prepared to bind those whom she found within her power. Yet these Habits under the eye of Education went quietly forward, and seemed very little to increase in bulk or strength; for though they were always willing to join with Appetite, yet when Education kept them apart from her, they would very punctually obey command, and make the narrow roads in which they were confined easier and smoother.

It was observable, that their stature was never at a stand, but continually growing or decreasing, yet not always in the same proportions: nor could I forbear to express my admiration, when I saw in how much less time they generally gained than lost bulk. Though they grew slowly in the road of Education, it might however be perceived that they grew; but if they once deviated at the call of Appetite, their stature soon became gigantick; and their strength was such, that Education pointed out to her tribe many that were led in chains by them, whom she could never more rescue from their slavery. She pointed them out, but with little effect; for all her pupils appeared confident of their own superiority to the strongest Habit, and some seemed in secret to regret that they were hindered from following the triumph of Appetite.

It was the peculiar artifice of Habit not to suffer her power to be felt at first. Those whom she led, she had the address of appearing only to attend, but was continually doubling her chains upon her companions; which were so slender in themselves, and so silently fastened, that while the attention was engaged by other objects, they were not easily perceived. Each link grew tighter as it had been longer worn; and when by continual additions they became so heavy as to be felt, they were very frequently too strong to be broken.

When Education had proceeded in this manner to the part of the mountain where the declivity began to grow craggy, she resigned her charge to two powers of superiour aspect. The meaner of them appeared capable of presiding in senates, or governing nations, and yet watched the steps of the other with the most anxious attention, and was visibly confounded and perplexed if ever she suffered her regard to be drawn away. The other seemed to approve her submission as pleasing, but with such a condescension as plainly showed that she claimed it as due; and indeed so great was her dignity and sweetness, that he who would not reverence, must not behold her.

'Theodore,' said my protector, 'be fearless, and be wise; approach these powers, whose dominion extends to all the remaining part of the Mountain of Existence.' I trembled, and ventured to address the inferiour nymph, whose eyes, though piercing and awful, I was not unable to sustain. 'Bright Power,' said I, 'by whatever name it is lawful to address thee, tell me, thou who presidest here, on what condition thy protection will be granted?' 'It will be granted,' said she, 'only to obedience. I am Reason, of all subordinate beings the noblest and the greatest; who, if thou wilt receive my laws, will reward thee like the rest of my votaries, by conducting thee to Religion.'

Charmed by her voice and aspect, I professed my readiness to follow her. She then presented me to her mistress, who looked upon me with tenderness. I bowed before her, and she smiled.

When Education delivered up those for whose happiness she had been so long solicitous, she seemed to expect that they should express some gratitude for her care, or some regret at the loss of that protection which she had hitherto afforded them. But it was easy to discover, by the alacrity which broke out at her departure, that her presence had been long displeasing, and that she had been teaching those who felt in themselves no want of instruction. They all agreed in rejoicing that they should no longer be subject to her caprices, or disturbed by her documents, but should be now under the direction only of Reason, to whom they made no doubt of being able to recommend themselves by a steady adherence to all her precepts. Reason counselled them, at their first entrance upon her province, to inlist themselves among the votaries of Religion; and informed them, that if they trusted to her alone, they would find the same fate with her other admirers, whom she had not been able to secure against Appetites and Passions, and who, having been seized by Habits in the regions of Desire, had been dragged away to the caverns of Despair. Her admonition was vain, the greater number declared against any other direction, and doubted not but by her superintendency they should climb with safety up the Mountain of Existence. 'My power,' said Reason, 'is to advise, not to compel; I have already told you the danger of your choice. The path seems now plain and even, but there are asperities and pitfalls, over which Religion only can conduct you. Look upwards, and you perceive a mist before you settled upon the highest visible part of the mountain; a mist by which my prospect is terminated, and which is pierced only by the eyes of Religion. Beyond it are the temples of Happiness, in which those who climb the precipice by her direction, after the toil of their pilgrimage, repose for ever. I know not the way, and therefore can only conduct you to a better guide. Pride has sometimes reproached me with the narrowness of my view, but, when she endeavoured to extend it, could only show me, below the mist, the bowers of Content; even they vanished as I fixed my eyes upon them; and those whom she persuaded to travel towards them were inclined by Habits, and ingulfed by Despair, a cruel tyrant, whose caverns are beyond the darkness on the right side and on the left, from whose prisons none can escape, and whom I cannot teach you to avoid.'

Such was the declaration of Reason to those who demanded her protection. Some that recollected the dictates of Education, finding them now seconded by another authority, submitted with reluctance to the strict decree, and engaged themselves among the followers of Religion, who were distinguished by the uniformity of their march, though many of them were women, and by their continual endeavours to move upwards without appearing to regard the prospects which at every step courted their attention.

All those who determined to follow either Reason or Religion, were continually importuned to forsake the road, sometimes by Passions, and sometimes by Appetites, of whom both had reason to boast the success of their artifices; for so many were drawn into by-paths, that any way was more populous than the right. The attacks of the Appetites were more impetuous, those of the Passions longer continued. The Appetites turned their followers directly from the true way, but the Passions marched at first in a path nearly in the same direction with that of Reason and Religion; but deviated by slow degrees, till at last they entirely changed their course. Appetite drew aside the dull, and Passion the sprightly. Of the Appetites, Lust was the strongest; and of the Passions, Vanity. The most powerful assault was to be feared, when a Passion and an Appetite joined their enticements; and the path of Reason was best followed, when a Passion called to one side, and an Appetite to the other.

These seducers had the greatest success upon the followers of Reason, over whom they scarcely ever failed to prevail, except when they counteracted one another. They had not the same triumphs over the votaries of Religion; for though they were often led aside for a time, Religion commonly recalled them by her emissary Conscience, before Habit had time to enchain them. But they that professed to obey Reason, if once they forsook her seldom returned; for she had no messenger to summon them but Pride, who generally betrayed her confidence, and employed all her skill to support Passion; and if ever she did her duty, was found unable to prevail, if Habit had interposed.

66   1748

I soon found that the great danger to the followers of Religion was only from Habit; every other power was easily resisted, nor did they find any difficulty when they inadvertently quitted her, to find her again by the direction of Conscience, unless they had given time to Habit to draw her chain behind them, and bar up the way by which they had wandered. Of some of those, the condition was justly to be pitied, who turned at every call of Conscience, and tried, but without effect, to burst the chains of Habit: saw Religion walking forward at a distance, saw her with reverence, and longed to join her; but were, whenever they approached her, withheld by Habit, and languished in sordid bondage, which they could not escape, though they scorned and hated it.

It was evident that the Habits were so far from growing weaker by these repeated contests, that if they were not totally overcome, every struggle enlarged their bulk and increased their strength; and a Habit opposed and victorious was more than twice as strong as before the contest. The manner in which those who were weary of their tyranny endeavoured to escape from them, appeared by the event to be generally wrong; they tried to loose their chains one by one, and to retreat by the same degrees as they advanced; but before the deliverance was completed, Habit always threw new chains upon her fugitive; nor did any escape her but those who, by an effort sudden and violent, burst their shackles at once, and left her at a distance; and even of these, many, rushing too precipitately forward, and hindered by their terrours from stopping where they were safe, were fatigued with their own vehemence, and resigned themselves again to that power from whom an escape must be so dearly bought, and whose tyranny was little felt, except when it was resisted.

Some however there always were, who when they found Habit prevailing over them, called upon Reason or Religion for assistance; each of them willingly came to the succour of her suppliant, but neither with the same strength, nor the same success. Habit, insolent with her power, would often presume to parley with Reason, and

offer to loose some of her chains if the rest might remain.
To this Reason, who was never certain of victory, frequently consented, but always found her concession
destructive, and saw the captive led away by Habit to
his former slavery. Religion never submitted to treaty,
but held out her hand with certainty of conquest; and if
the captive to whom she gave it did not quit his hold,
always led him away in triumph, and placed him in the
direct path to the Temple of Happiness, where Reason
never failed to congratulate his deliverance, and encourage his adherence to that power to whose timely
succour he was indebted for it.

When the traveller was again placed in the road of
Happiness, I saw Habit again gliding before him, but
reduced to the stature of a dwarf, without strength and
without activity; but when the Passions or Appetites,
which had before seduced him, made their approach,
Habit would on a sudden start into size, and with unexpected violence push him towards them. The wretch,
thus impelled on one side, and allured on the other, too
frequently quitted the road of Happiness, to which, after
his second deviation from it, he rarely returned: but, by
a timely call upon Religion, the force of Habit was eluded,
her attacks grew fainter, and at last her correspondence
with the enemy was intirely destroyed. She then began
to employ those restless faculties in compliance with the
power which she could not overcome; and as she grew
again in stature and in strength, cleared away the asperities of the road to Happiness.

From this road I could not easily withdraw my attention, because all who travelled it appeared cheerful and
satisfied; and the farther they proceeded, the greater
appeared their alacrity, and the stronger their conviction
of the wisdom of their guide. Some, who had never deviated but by short excursions, had Habit in the middle
of their passage vigorously supporting them, and driving
off their Appetites and Passions which attempted to interrupt their progress. Others, who had entered this road
late, or had long forsaken it, were toiling on without her
help at least, and commonly against her endeavours.

But I observed, when they approached to the barren top, that few were able to proceed without some support from Habit: and that they, whose Habits were strong, advanced towards the mists with little emotion, and entered them at last with calmness and confidence; after which, they were seen only by the eye of Religion; and though Reason looked after them with the most earnest curiosity, she could only obtain a faint glimpse, when her mistress, to enlarge her prospect, raised her from the ground. Reason, however, discerned that they were safe, but Religion saw that they were happy.

'Now, Theodore,' said my Protector, 'withdraw thy view from the regions of obscurity, and see the fate of those who, when they were dismissed by Education, would admit no direction but that of Reason. Survey their wanderings, and be wise.'

I looked then upon the road of Reason, which was indeed, so far as it reached, the same with that of Religion, nor had Reason discovered it but by her instruction. Yet when she had once been taught it, she clearly saw that it was right; and Pride had sometimes incited her to declare that she discovered it herself, and persuaded her to offer herself as a guide to Religion: whom after many vain experiments she found it her highest privilege to follow. Reason was however at last well instructed in part of the way, and appeared to teach it with some success, when her precepts were not misrepresented by Passion, or her influence overborn by Appetite. But neither of these enemies was she able to resist. When Passion seized upon her votaries, she seldom attempted opposition: she seemed indeed to contend with more vigour against Appetite, but was generally overwearied in the contest; and if either of her opponents had confederated with Habit, her authority was wholly at an end. When Habit endeavoured to captivate the votaries of Religion, she grew by slow degrees, and gave time to escape; but in seizing the unhappy followers of Reason, she proceeded as one that had nothing to fear, and enlarged her size, and doubled her chains without intermission, and without reserve.

Of those who forsook the directions of Reason, some were led aside by the whispers of Ambition, who was perpetually pointing to stately palaces, situated on eminences on either side, recounting the delights of affluence, and boasting the security of power. They were easily persuaded to follow her, and Habit quickly threw her chains upon them; they were soon convinced of the folly of their choice, but few of them attempted to return. Ambition led them forward from precipice to precipice, where many fell and were seen no more. Those that escaped were, after a long series of hazards, generally delivered over to Avarice, and enlisted by her in the service of Tyranny, where they continued to heap up gold till their patrons or their heirs pushed them headlong at last into the caverns of Despair.

Others were inticed by Intemperance to ramble in search of those fruits that hung over the rocks, and filled the air with their fragrance. I observed, that the Habits which hovered about these soon grew to an enormous size, nor were there any who less attempted to return to Reason, or sooner sunk into the gulfs that lay before them. When these first quitted the road, Reason looked after them with a frown of contempt, but had little expectations of being able to reclaim them; for the bowl of intoxication was of such qualities as to make them lose all regard but for the present moment; neither Hope nor Fear could enter their retreats; and Habit had so absolute a power, that even Conscience, if Religion had employed her in their favour, would not have been able to force an entrance.

There were others whose crime it was rather to neglect Reason than to disobey her; and who retreated from the heat and tumult of the way, not to the bowers of Intemperance, but to the maze of Indolence. They had this peculiarity in their condition, that they were always in sight of the road of Reason, always wishing for her presence, and always resolving to return to-morrow. In these was most eminently conspicuous the subtlety of Habit, who hung imperceptible shackles upon them, and was every moment leading them farther from the road, which

they always imagined that they had the power of reaching. They wandered on from one double of the labyrinth
to another with the chains of Habit hanging secretly upon
them, till, as they advanced, the flowers grew paler, and
the scents fainter; they proceeded in their dreary march
without pleasure in their progress, yet without power to
return; and had this aggravation above all others, that
they were criminal but not delighted. The drunkard
for a time laughed over his wine; the ambitious man
triumphed in the miscarriage of his rival; but the captives
of Indolence had neither superiority nor merriment.
Discontent lowered in their looks, and Sadness hovered
round their shades; yet they crawled on reluctant and
gloomy, till they arrived at the depth of the recess, varied
only with poppies and nightshade, where the dominion
of Indolence terminates, and the hopeless wanderer is
delivered up to Melancholy: the chains of Habit are
rivetted for ever; and Melancholy, having tortured her
prisoner for a time, consigns him at last to the cruelty of
Despair.

While I was musing on this miserable scene, my Protector called out to me, 'Remember, Theodore, and be
wise, and let not Habit prevail against thee.' I started,
and beheld myself surrounded by the rocks of Teneriffe;
the birds of light were singing in the trees, and the glances
of the morning darted upon me.

The Preceptor

1749
The Vanity of Human Wishes

Let observation with extensive view,
Survey mankind, from China to Peru;
Remark each anxious toil, each eager strife,
And watch the busy scenes of crouded life;
Then say how hope and fear, desire and hate,
O'erspread with snares the clouded maze of fate,
Where wav'ring man, betray'd by vent'rous pride,
To tread the dreary paths without a guide,

As treach'rous phantoms in the mist delude,
Shuns fancied ills, or chases airy good;
How rarely reason guides the stubborn choice,
Rules the bold hand, or prompts the suppliant voice;
How nations sink, by darling schemes oppress'd,
When vengeance listens to the fool's request.
Fate wings with ev'ry wish th' afflictive dart,
Each gift of nature, and each grace of art,
With fatal heat impetuous courage glows,
With fatal sweetness elocution flows,
Impeachment stops the speaker's pow'rful breath,
And restless fire precipitates on death.

But scarce observ'd, the knowing and the bold
Fall in the gen'ral massacre of gold;
Wide-wasting pest! that rages unconfin'd,
And crouds with crimes the records of mankind;
For gold his sword the hireling ruffian draws,
For gold the hireling judge distorts the laws;
Wealth heap'd on wealth, nor truth nor safety buys,
The dangers gather as the treasures rise.

Let hist'ry tell where rival kings command,
And dubious title shakes the madded land,
When statutes glean the refuse of the sword,
How much more safe the vassal than the lord;
Low skulks the hind beneath the rage of pow'r,
And leaves the wealthy traytor in the Tow'r,
Untouch'd his cottage, and his slumbers sound,
Tho' confiscation's vulturs hover round.

The needy traveller, serene and gay,
Walks the wild heath, and sings his toil away.
Does envy seize thee? crush th' upbraiding joy,
Increase his riches and his peace destroy;
Now fears in dire vicissitude invade,
The rustling brake alarms, and quiv'ring shade,
Nor light nor darkness bring his pain relief,
One shews the plunder, and one hides the thief.

Yet still one gen'ral cry the skies assails,
And gain and grandeur load the tainted gales;
Few know the toiling statesman's fear or care,
Th' insidious rival and the gaping heir.

Once more, Democritus, arise on earth,
With chearful wisdom and instructive mirth,
See motley life in modern trappings dress'd,
And feed with varied fools th' eternal jest:
Thou who couldst laugh where want enchain'd caprice,
Toil crush'd conceit, and man was of a piece;
Where wealth unlov'd without a mourner dy'd,
And scarce a sycophant was fed by pride;
Where ne'er was known the form of mock debate,
Or seen a new-made mayor's unwieldy state;
Where change of fav'rites made no change of laws,
And senates heard before they judg'd a cause;
How wouldst thou shake at Britain's modish tribe,
Dart the quick taunt, and edge the piercing gibe?
Attentive truth and nature to descry,
And pierce each scene with philosophic eye.
To thee were solemn toys or empty shew,
The robes of pleasure and the veils of woe:
All aid the farce, and all thy mirth maintain,
Whose joys are causeless, or whose griefs are vain.

Such was the scorn that fill'd the sage's mind,
Renew'd at ev'ry glance on humankind;
How just that scorn ere yet thy voice declare,
Search every state, and canvass ev'ry pray'r.

Unnumber'd suppliants croud Preferment's gate,
Athirst for wealth, and burning to be great;
Delusive Fortune hears th' incessant call,
They mount, they shine, evaporate, and fall.
On ev'ry stage the foes of peace attend,
Hate dogs their flight, and insult mocks their end.
Love ends with hope, the sinking statesman's door
Pours in the morning worshiper no more;
For growing names the weekly scribbler lies,
To growing wealth the dedicator flies,
From every room descends the painted face,
That hung the bright Palladium of the place,
And smoak'd in kitchens, or in auctions sold,
To better features yields the frame of gold;
For now no more we trace in ev'ry line
Heroic worth, benevolence divine:

The form distorted justifies the fall,
And detestation rids th' indignant wall.
   But will not Britain hear the last appeal,
Sign her foes doom, or guard her fav'rites zeal?
Through Freedom's sons no more remonstrance rings,
Degrading nobles and controuling kings;
Our supple tribes repress their patriot throats,
And ask no questions but the price of votes;
With weekly libels and septennial ale,
Their wish is full to riot and to rail.
   In full-blown dignity, see Wolsey stand,
Law in his voice, and fortune in his hand:
To him the church, the realm, their pow'rs consign,
Thro' him the rays of regal bounty shine,
Turn'd by his nod the stream of honour flows,
His smile alone security bestows:
Still to new heights his restless wishes tow'r,
Claim leads to claim, and pow'r advances pow'r;
Till conquest unresisted ceas'd to please,
And rights submitted, left him none to seize.
At length his sov'reign frowns—the train of state
Mark the keen glance, and watch the sign to hate.
Where-e'er he turns he meets a stranger's eye,
His suppliants scorn him, and his followers fly;
At once is lost the pride of aweful state,
The golden canopy, the glitt'ring plate,
The regal palace, the luxurious board,
The liv'ried army, and the menial lord.
With age, with cares, with maladies oppress'd,
He seeks the refuge of monastic rest.
Grief aids disease, remember'd folly stings,
And his last sighs reproach the faith of kings.
   Speak thou, whose thoughts at humble peace repine
Shall Wolsey's wealth, with Wolsey's end be thine?
Or liv'st thou now, with safer pride content,
The wisest justice on the banks of Trent?
For why did Wolsey near the steeps of fate,
On weak foundations raise th' enormous weight?
Why but to sink beneath misfortune's blow,
With louder ruin to the gulphs below?

What gave great Villiers to th' assassin's knife,
And fixed disease on Harley's closing life?
What murder'd Wentworth, and what exil'd Hyde,
By kings protected, and to kings ally'd?
What but their wish indulg'd in courts to shine,
And pow'r too great to keep, or to resign?
When first the college rolls receive his name,
The young enthusiast quits his ease for fame;
Through all his veins the fever of renown
Burns from the strong contagion of the gown;
O'er Bodley's dome his future labours spread,
And* Bacon's mansion trembles o'er his head.
Are these thy views? proceed, illustrious youth,
And virtue guard thee to the throne of Truth!
Yet should thy soul indulge the gen'rous heat,
Till captive Science yields her last retreat;
Should Reason guide thee with her brighest ray,
And pour on misty Doubt resistless day;
Should no false Kindness lure to loose delight,
Nor Praise relax, nor Difficulty fright;
Should tempting Novelty thy cell refrain,
And Sloth effuse her opiate fumes in vain;
Should Beauty blunt on fops her fatal dart,
Nor claim the triumph of a letter'd heart;
Should no Disease thy torpid veins invade,
Nor Melancholy's phantoms haunt thy shade;
Yet hope not life from grief or danger free,
Nor think the doom of man revers'd for thee:
Deign on the passing world to turn thine eyes,
And pause awhile from letters, to be wise;
There mark what ills the scholar's life assail,
Toil, envy, want, the patron, and the jail.
See nations slowly wise, and meanly just,
To buried merit raise the tardy bust.
If dreams yet flatter, once again attend,
Hear Lydiat's life, and Galileo's end.
Nor deem, when learning her last prize bestows,
The glitt'ring eminence exempt from foes;

* *There is a tradition, that the study of friar Bacon, built on an arch over the bridge, will fall, when a man greater than Bacon shall pass under it.*

See when the vulgar 'scape, despis'd or aw'd,
Rebellion's vengeful talons seize on Laud.
From meaner minds, tho' smaller fines content,
The plunder'd palace or sequester'd rent;
Mark'd out by dangerous parts he meets the shock,
And fatal Learning leads him to the block:
Around his tomb let Art and Genius weep,
But hear his death, ye blockheads, hear and sleep.
    The festal blazes, the triumphal show,
The ravish'd standard, and the captive foe,
The senate's thanks, the gazette's pompous tale,
With force resistless o'er the brave prevail.
Such bribes the rapid Greek o'er Asia whirl'd,
For such the steady Romans shook the world;
For such in distant lands the Britons shine,
And stain with blood the Danube or the Rhine;
This pow'r has praise, that virtue scarce can warm,
Till fame supplies the universal charm.
Yet Reason frowns on War's unequal game,
Where wasted nations raise a single name,
And mortgag'd states their grandsires wreaths regret,
From age to age in everlasting debt;
Wreaths which at last the dear-bought right convey
To rust on medals, or on stones decay.
    On what foundation stands the warrior's pride,
How just his hopes let Swedish Charles decide;
A frame of adamant, a soul of fire,
No dangers fright him, and no labours tire;
O'er love, o'er fear, extends his wide domain,
Unconquer'd lord of pleasure and of pain;
No joys to him pacific scepters yield,
War sounds the trump, he rushes to the field;
Behold surrounding kings their pow'r combine,
And one capitulate, and one resign;
Peace courts his hand, but spreads her charms in vain;
'Think nothing gain'd, he cries, till nought remain,
'On Moscow's walls till Gothic standards fly,
'And all be mine beneath the polar sky.'
The march begins in military state,
And nations on his eye suspended wait;

Stern Famine guards the solitary coast,
And Winter barricades the realms of Frost;
He comes, not want and cold his course delay;—
Hide, blushing Glory, hide Pultowa's day:
The vanquish'd hero leaves his broken bands,
And shews his miseries in distant lands;
Condemn'd a needy supplicant to wait,
While ladies interpose, and slaves debate.
But did not Chance at length her error mend?
Did no subverted empire mark his end?
Did rival monarchs give the fatal wound?
Or hostile millions press him to the ground?
His fall was destin'd to a barren strand,
A petty fortress, and a dubious hand;
He left the name, at which the world grew pale,
To point a moral, or adorn a tale.

    All times their scenes of pompous woes afford,
From Persia's tyrant to Bavaria's lord.
In gay hostility, and barb'rous pride,
With half mankind embattled at his side,
Great Xerxes comes to seize the certain prey,
And starves exhausted regions in his way;
Attendant Flatt'ry counts his myriads o'er,
Till counted myriads sooth his pride no more;
Fresh praise is try'd till madness fires his mind,
The waves he lashes, and enchains the wind;
New pow'rs are claim'd, new pow'rs are still bestow'd,
Till rude resistance lops the spreading god;
The daring Greeks deride the martial show,
And heap their vallies with the gaudy foe;
Th' insulted sea with humbler thoughts he gains,
A single skiff to speed his flight remains;
Th' incumber'd oar scarce leaves the dreaded coast
Through purple billows and a floating host.

    The bold Bavarian, in a luckless hour,
Tries the dread summits of Cesarean pow'r,
With unexpected legions bursts away,
And sees defenceless realms receive his sway;
Short sway! fair Austria spreads her mournful charms,
The queen, the beauty, sets the world in arms;

From hill to hill the beacons rousing blaze
Spreads wide the hope of plunder and of praise;
The fierce Croatian, and the wild Hussar,
And all the sons of ravage croud the war;
The baffled prince in honour's flatt'ring bloom
Of hasty greatness finds the fatal doom,
His foes derision, and his subjects blame,
And steals to death from anguish and from shame.
    Enlarge my life with multitude of days,
In health, in sickness, thus the suppliant prays;
Hides from himself his state, and shuns to know,
That life protracted is protracted woe.
Time hovers o'er, impatient to destroy,
And shuts up all the passages of joy:
In vain their gifts the bounteous seasons pour,
The fruit autumnal, and the vernal flow'r,
With listless eyes the dotard views the store,
He views, and wonders that they please no more;
Now pall the tasteless meats, and joyless wines,
And Luxury with sighs her slave resigns.
Approach, ye minstrels, try the soothing strain,
Diffuse the tuneful lenitives of pain:
No sounds alas would touch th' impervious ear,
Though dancing mountains witness'd Orpheus near;
Nor lute nor lyre his feeble pow'rs attend,
Nor sweeter musick of a virtuous friend,
But everlasting dictates croud his tongue,
Perversely grave, or positively wrong.
The still returning tale, and ling'ring jest,
Perplex the fawning niece and pamper'd guest,
While growing hopes scarce awe the gath'ring sneer,
And scarce a legacy can bribe to hear;
The watchful guests still hint the last offence,
The daughter's petulance, the son's expence,
Improve his heady rage with treach'rous skill,
And mould his passions till they make his will.
    Unnumber'd maladies his joints invade,
Lay siege to life and press the dire blockade;
But unextinguish'd Avarice still remains,
And dreaded losses aggravate his pains;

He turns, with anxious heart and cripled hands,
His bonds of debt, and mortgages of lands;
Or views his coffers with suspicious eyes,
Unlocks his gold, and counts it till he dies.

But grant, the virtues of a temp'rate prime
Bless with an age exempt from scorn or crime;
An age that melts with unperceiv'd decay,
And glides in modest Innocence away;
Whose peaceful day Benevolence endears,
Whose night congratulating Conscience cheers;
The gen'ral fav'rite as the gen'ral friend:
Such age there is, and who shall wish its end?

Yet ev'n on this her load Misfortune flings,
To press the weary minutes flagging wings:
New sorrow rises as the day returns,
A sister sickens, or a daughter mourns.
Now kindred Merit fills the sable bier,
Now lacerated Friendship claims a tear.
Year chases year, decay pursues decay,
Still drops some joy from with'ring life away;
New forms arise, and diff'rent views engage,
Superfluous lags the vet'ran on the stage,
Till pitying Nature signs the last release,
And bids afflicted worth retire to peace.

But few there are whom hours like these await,
Who set unclouded in the gulphs of fate.
From Lydia's monarch should the search descend,
By Solon caution'd to regard his end,
In life's last scene what prodigies surprise,
Fears of the brave, and follies of the wise?
From Marlb'rough's eyes the streams of dotage flow,
And Swift expires a driv'ler and a show.

The teeming mother, anxious for her race,
Begs for each birth the fortune of a face:
Yet Vane could tell what ills from beauty spring;
And Sedley curs'd the form that pleas'd a king.
Ye nymphs of rosy lips and radiant eyes,
Whom Pleasure keeps too busy to be wise,
Whom Joys with soft varieties invite,
By day the frolick, and the dance by night,

Who frown with vanity, who smile with art,
And ask the latest fashion of the heart,
What care, what rules your heedless charms shall save,
Each nymph your rival, and each youth your slave?
Against your fame with fondness hate combines,
The rival batters, and the lover mines.
With distant voice neglected Virtue calls,
Less heard and less, the faint remonstrance falls;
Tir'd with contempt, she quits the slipp'ry reign,
And Pride and Prudence take her seat in vain.
In croud at once, where none the pass defend,
The harmless Freedom, and the private Friend.
The guardians yield, by force superior ply'd;
By Int'rest, Prudence; and by Flatt'ry, Pride.
Now beauty falls betray'd, despis'd, distress'd,
And hissing Infamy proclaims the rest.
    Where then shall Hope and Fear their objects find?
Must dull Suspence corrupt the stagnant mind?
Must helpless man, in ignorance sedate,
Roll darkling down the torrent of his fate?
Must no dislike alarm, no wishes rise,
No cries attempt the mercies of the skies?
Enquirer, cease, petitions yet remain,
Which heav'n may hear, nor deem religion vain.
Still raise for good the supplicating voice,
But leave to heav'n the measure and the choice,
Safe in his pow'r, whose eyes discern afar
The secret ambush of a specious pray'r.
Implore his aid, in his decisions rest,
Secure whate'er he gives, he gives the best.
Yet when the sense of sacred presence fires,
And strong devotion to the skies aspires,
Pour forth thy fervours for a healthful mind,
Obedient passions, and a will resign'd;
For love, which scarce collective man can fill;
For patience sov'reign o'er transmuted ill;
For faith, that panting for a happier seat,
Counts death kind Nature's signal of retreat:
These goods for man the laws of heav'n ordain,
These goods he grants, who grants the pow'r to gain;

With these celestial wisdom calms the mind,
And makes the happiness she does not find.

IRENE

Toryism

Such are the Woes when arbitrary Pow'r,
And lawless Passion, hold the Sword of Justice.
If there be any Land, as Fame reports,
Where common Laws restrain the Prince and Subject,
A happy Land, where circulating Pow'r
Flows through each Member of th' embodied State,
Sure, not unconscious of the mighty Blessing,
Her grateful Sons shine bright with ev'ry Virtue;
Untainted with the Lust of Innovation,
Sure all unite to hold her League of Rule
Unbroken as the sacred Chain of Nature,
That links the jarring Elements in Peace.

Irene: A Tragedy

The Renaissance

The mighty *Tuscan* courts the banish'd Arts
To kind *Italia*'s hospitable Shades;
There shall soft Leisure wing th' excursive Soul,
And Peace propitious smile on fond Desire;
There shall despotick Eloquence resume
Her ancient Empire o'er the yielding Heart;
There Poetry shall tune her sacred Voice,
And wake from Ignorance the Western World.

Irene: A Tragedy

Moonlight

See how the Moon through all th' unclouded Sky
Spreads her mild Radiance, and descending Dews
Revive the languid Flow'rs; thus Nature shone
New from the Maker's Hand, and fair array'd
In the bright Colours of primæval Spring;

When Purity, while Fraud was yet unknown,
Play'd fearless in th' inviolated Shades.
This elemental Joy, this gen'ral Calm,
Is sure the Smile of unoffended Heav'n.

Irene: A Tragedy

1750–2

THE RAMBLER

1750

Romances

Simul et jucunda et idonea dicere vitæ.   HOR.

And join both profit and delight in one.   CREECH.

The works of fiction, with which the present generation
seems more particularly delighted, are such as exhibit
life in its true state, diversified only by accidents that
daily happen in the world, and influenced by passions
and qualities which are really to be found in conversing
with mankind.

This kind of writing may be termed not improperly
the comedy of romance, and is to be conducted nearly by
the rules of comick poetry. Its province is to bring about
natural events by easy means, and to keep up curiosity
without the help of wonder: it is therefore precluded
from the machines and expedients of the heroick romance,
and can neither employ giants to snatch away a lady
from the nuptial rites, nor knights to bring her back from
captivity; it can neither bewilder its personages in deserts,
nor lodge them in imaginary castles.

I remember a remark made by Scaliger upon Ponta-
nus, that all his writings are filled with the same images;
and that if you take from him his lilies and his roses, his
satyrs and his dryads, he will have nothing left that can
be called poetry. In like manner almost all the fictions
of the last age will vanish, if you deprive them of a hermit
and a wood, a battle and a shipwreck.

Why this wild strain of imagination found reception so

long in polite and learned ages, it is not easy to conceive;
but we cannot wonder that while readers could be procured, the authors were willing to continue it; for when a
man had by practice gained some fluency of language, he
had no further care than to retire to his closet, let loose
his invention, and heat his mind with incredibilities; a
book was thus produced without fear of criticism, without
the toil of study, without knowledge of nature, or acquaintance with life.

The task of our present writers is very different; it
requires, together with that learning which is to be gained
from books, that experience which can never be attained
by solitary diligence, but must arise from general converse and accurate observation of the living world. Their
performances have, as Horace expresses it, *plus oneris
quantum veniæ minus*, little indulgence, and therefore more
difficulty. They are engaged in portraits of which every
one knows the original, and can detect any deviation from
exactness of resemblance. Other writings are safe, except
from the malice of learning, but these are in danger from
every common reader: as the slipper ill executed was censured by a shoemaker who happened to stop in his way
at the Venus of Apelles.

But the fear of not being approved as just copiers of
human manners, is not the most important concern that
an author of this sort ought to have before him. These
books are written chiefly to the young, the ignorant, and
the idle, to whom they serve as lectures of conduct, and
introductions into life. They are the entertainment of
minds unfurnished with ideas, and therefore easily susceptible of impressions; not fixed by principles, and therefore easily following the current of fancy; not informed by
experience, and consequently open to every false sugges-
tion and partial account.

That the highest degree of reverence should be paid to
youth, and that nothing indecent should be suffered to
approach their eyes or ears; are precepts extorted by
sense and virtue from an ancient writer, by no means
eminent for chastity of thought.[1] The same kind, though

[1 Juvenal.]

not the same degree of caution, is required in every thing which is laid before them, to secure them from unjust prejudices, perverse opinions, and incongruous combinations of images.

In the romances formerly written, every transaction and sentiment was so remote from all that passes among men, that the reader was in very little danger of making any applications to himself; the virtues and crimes were equally beyond his sphere of activity; and he amused himself with heroes and with traitors, deliverers and persecutors, as with beings of another species, whose actions were regulated upon motives of their own, and who had neither faults nor excellencies in common with himself.

But when an adventurer is levelled with the rest of the world, and acts in such scenes of the universal drama, as may be the lot of any other man; young spectators fix their eyes upon him with closer attention, and hope, by observing his behaviour and success, to regulate their own practices, when they shall be engaged in the like part.

For this reason these familiar histories may perhaps be made of greater use than the solemnities of professed morality, and convey the knowledge of vice and virtue with more efficacy than axioms and definitions. But if the power of example is so great as to take possession of the memory by a kind of violence, and produce effects almost without the intervention of the will, care ought to be taken, that, when the choice is unrestrained, the best examples only should be exhibited; and that which is likely to operate so strongly, should not be mischievous or uncertain in its effects.

The chief advantage which these fictions have over real life is, that their authors are at liberty, though not to invent, yet to select objects, and to cull from the mass of mankind, those individuals upon which the attention ought most to be employed: as a diamond, though it cannot be made, may be polished by art, and placed in such a situation, as to display that lustre which before was buried among common stones.

It is justly considered as the greatest excellency of art, to imitate nature; but it is necessary to distinguish those parts of nature, which are most proper for imitation: greater care is still required in representing life, which is so often discoloured by passion or deformed by wickedness. If the world be promiscuously described, I cannot see of what use it can be to read the account: or why it may not be as safe to turn the eye immediately upon mankind as upon a mirrour which shows all that presents itself without discrimination.

It is therefore not a sufficient vindication of a character, that it is drawn as it appears; for many characters ought never to be drawn: nor of a narrative, that the train of events is agreeable to observation and experience; for that observation which is called knowledge of the world, will be found much more frequently to make men cunning than good. The purpose of these writings is surely not only to show mankind, but to provide that they may be seen hereafter with less hazard; to teach the means of avoiding the snares which are laid by TREACHERY for INNOCENCE, without infusing any wish for that superiority with which the betrayer flatters his vanity; to give the power of counteracting fraud, without the temptation to practise it; to initiate youth by mock encounters in the art of necessary defence, and to increase prudence without impairing virtue.

Many writers, for the sake of following nature, so mingle good and bad qualities in their principal personages, that they are both equally conspicuous; and as we accompany them through their adventures with delight, and are led by degrees to interest ourselves in their favour, we lose the abhorrence of their faults, because they do not hinder our pleasure, or, perhaps, regard them with some kindness, for being united with so much merit.

There have been men indeed splendidly wicked, whose endowments threw a brightness on their crimes, and whom scarce any villany made perfectly detestable, because they never could be wholly divested of their excellencies; but such have been in all ages the great

corrupters of the world, and their resemblance ought no
more to be preserved, than the art of murdering without
pain.

Some have advanced, without due attention to the
consequences of this notion, that certain virtues have
their correspondent faults, and therefore that to exhibit
either apart is to deviate from probability. Thus men are
observed by Swift to be 'grateful in the same degree as
they are resentful.' This principle, with others of the
same kind, supposes man to act from a brute impulse,
and pursue a certain degree of inclination, without any
choice of the object; for, otherwise, though it should be
allowed that gratitude and resentment arise from the
same constitution of the passions, it follows not that they
will be equally indulged when reason is consulted; yet,
unless that consequence be admitted, this sagacious
maxim becomes an empty sound, without any relation
to practice or to life.

Nor is it evident, that even the first motions to these
effects are always in the same proportion. For pride,
which produces quickness of resentment, will obstruct
gratitude, by unwillingness to admit that inferiority which
obligation implies; and it is very unlikely that he who
cannot think he receives a favour, will acknowledge or
repay it.

It is of the utmost importance to mankind, that positions of this tendency should be laid open and confuted;
for while men consider good and evil as springing from
the same root, they will spare the one for the sake of the
other, and in judging, if not of others at least of themselves, will be apt to estimate their virtues by their vices.
To this fatal errour all those will contribute, who confound the colours of right and wrong, and, instead o
helping to settle their boundaries, mix them with so much
art, that no common mind is able to disunite them.

In narratives where historical veracity has no place, I
cannot discover why there should not be exhibited the
most perfect idea of virtue; of virtue not angelical, nor
above probability, for what we cannot credit, we shall
never imitate, but the highest and purest that humanity

can reach, which, exercised in such trials as the various
revolutions of things shall bring upon it, may, by conquering some calamities, and enduring others, teach us
what we may hope, and what we can perform. Vice, for
vice is necessary to be shown, should always disgust; nor
should the graces of gayety, or the dignity of courage,
be so united with it, as to reconcile it to the mind.
Wherever it appears, it should raise hatred by the malignity of its practices, and contempt by the meanness of its
stratagems: for while it is supported by either parts or
spirit, it will be seldom heartily abhorred. The Roman
tyrant was content to be hated, if he was but feared; and
there are thousands of the readers of romances willing
to be thought wicked, if they may be allowed to be wits.
It is therefore to be steadily inculcated, that virtue is the
highest proof of understanding, and the only solid basis
of greatness; and that vice is the natural consequence of
narrow thoughts; that it begins in mistake, and ends in
ignominy.

Rambler, No. 4

Authors

———*Nil fuit unquam*
Sic dispar sibi———   HOR.

Sure such a various creature ne'er was known. FRANCIS.

Among the many inconsistencies which folly produces,
or infirmity suffers, in the human mind, there has often
been observed a manifest and striking contrariety between
the life of an author and his writings; and Milton, in a
letter to a learned stranger, by whom he had been
visited, with great reason congratulates himself upon the
consciousness of being found equal to his own character,
and having preserved, in a private and familiar interview,
that reputation which his works had procured him.

Those whom the appearance of virtue, or the evidence
of genius, have tempted to a nearer knowledge of the
writer in whose performances they may be found, have
indeed had frequent reason to repent their curiosity; the
bubble that sparkled before them has become common

water at the touch; the phantom of perfection has vanished when they wished to press it to their bosom. They have lost the pleasure of imagining how far humanity may be exalted, and, perhaps, felt themselves less inclined to toil up the steeps of virtue, when they observe those who seem best able to point the way, loitering below, as either afraid of the labour, or doubtful of the reward.

It has been long the custom of the oriental monarchs to hide themselves in gardens and palaces, to avoid the conversation of mankind, and to be known to their subjects only by their edicts. The same policy is no less necessary to him that writes, than to him that governs; for men would not more patiently submit to be taught, than commanded, by one known to have the same follies and weaknesses with themselves. A sudden intruder into the closet of an author would perhaps feel equal indignation with the officer, who having long solicited admission into the presence of Sardanapalus, saw him not consulting upon laws, inquiring into grievances, or modelling armies, but employed in feminine amusements, and directing the ladies in their work.

It is not difficult to conceive, however, that for many reasons a man writes much better than he lives. For without entering into refined speculations, it may be shown much easier to design than to perform. A man proposes his schemes of life in a state of abstraction and disengagement, exempt from the enticements of hope, the solicitations of affection, the importunities of appetite, or the depressions of fear, and is in the same state with him that teaches upon land the art of navigation, to whom the sea is always smooth, and the wind always prosperous.

The mathematicians are well acquainted with the difference between pure science, which has to do only with ideas, and the application of its laws to the use of life, in which they are constrained to submit to the imperfection of matter and the influence of accidents. Thus, in moral discussions, it is to be remembered that many impediments obstruct our practice, which very easily give way to theory. The speculatist is only in danger of erroneous reasoning; but the man involved in life, has his

own passions, and those of others, to encounter, and is
embarrassed with a thousand inconveniencies, which
confound him with variety of impulse, and either perplex
or obstruct his way. He is forced to act without deliberation, and obliged to chuse before he can examine; he is
surprised by sudden alterations of the state of things, and
changes his measures according to superficial appearances; he is led by others, either because he is indolent,
or because he is timorous; he is sometimes afraid to know
what is right, and sometimes finds friends or enemies
diligent to deceive him.

We are, therefore, not to wonder that most fail, amidst
tumult, and snares, and danger, in the observance of
those precepts, which they lay down in solitude, safety
and tranquillity, with a mind unbiassed, and with liberty
unobstructed. It is the condition of our present state to
see more than we can attain; the exactest vigilance and
caution can never maintain a single day of unmingled
innocence, much less can the utmost efforts of incorporated mind reach the summits of speculative virtue.

It is, however, necessary for the idea of perfection to be
proposed, that we may have some object to which our
endeavours are to be directed; and he that is most deficient in the duties of life, makes some atonement for his
faults, if he warns others against his own failings, and
hinders, by the salubrity of his admonitions, the contagion
of his example.

Nothing is more unjust, however common, than to
charge with hypocrisy him that expresses zeal for those
virtues which he neglects to practise; since he may be
sincerely convinced of the advantages of conquering his
passions, without having yet obtained the victory, as a
man may be confident of the advantages of a voyage, or
a journey, without having courage or industry to undertake it, and may honestly recommend to others those
attempts which he neglects himself.

The interest which the corrupt part of mankind have
in hardening themselves against every motive to amendment, has disposed them to give to these contradictions,
when they can be produced against the cause of virtue,

that weight which they will not allow them in any other case. They see men act in opposition to their interest, without supposing that they do not know it; those who give way to the sudden violence of passion, and forsake the most important pursuits for petty pleasures, are not supposed to have changed their opinions, or to approve their own conduct. In moral or religious questions alone, they determine the sentiments by the actions, and charge every man with endeavouring to impose upon the world, whose writings are not confirmed by his life. They never consider that themselves neglect or practise something every day inconsistently with their own settled judgment, nor discover that the conduct of the advocates for virtue can little increase, or lessen, the obligations of their dictates; argument is to be invalidated only by argument, and is in itself of the same force, whether or not it convinces him by whom it is proposed.

Yet since this prejudice, however unreasonable, is always likely to have some prevalence, it is the duty of every man to take care lest he should hinder the efficacy of his own instructions. When he desires to gain the belief of others, he should show that he believes himself; and when he teaches the fitness of virtue by his reasonings, he should by his example prove its possibility. Thus much at least may be required of him, that he shall not act worse than others, because he writes better; nor imagine that, by the merit of his genius, he may claim indulgence beyond mortals of the lower classes, and be excused for want of prudence, or neglect of virtue.

Bacon, in his history of the winds, after having offered something to the imagination as desirable, often proposes lower advantages in its place to the reason as attainable. The same method may be sometimes pursued in moral endeavours, which this philosopher has observed in natural inquiries; having first set positive and absolute excellence before us, we may be pardoned though we sink down to humbler virtue, trying, however, to keep our point always in view, and struggling not to lose ground, though we cannot gain it.

It is recorded of Sir Matthew Hale, that he, for a long

time, concealed the consecration of himself to the stricter duties of religion, lest, by some flagitious and shameful action, he should bring piety into disgrace. For the same reason it may be prudent for a writer, who apprehends that he shall not inforce his own maxims by his domestick character, to conceal his name, that he may not injure them.

There are, indeed, a great number whose curiosity to gain a more familiar knowledge of successful writers, is not so much prompted by an opinion of their power to improve as to delight, and who expect from them not arguments against vice, or dissertations on temperance or justice, but flights of wit, and sallies of pleasantry, or, at least, acute remarks, nice distinctions, justness of sentiment, and elegance of diction.

This expectation is, indeed, specious and probable, and yet, such is the fate of all human hopes, that it is very often frustrated, and those who raise admiration by their books, disgust by their company. A man of letters for the most part spends, in the privacies of study, that season of life in which the manners are to be softened into ease, and polished into elegance; and, when he has gained knowledge enough to be respected, has neglected the minuter arts[1] by which he might have pleased. When he enters life, if his temper be soft and timorous, he is diffident and bashful, from the knowledge of his defects; or if he was born with spirit and resolution, he is ferocious and arrogant, from the consciousness of his merit: he is either dissipated by the awe of company, and unable to recollect his reading, and arrange his arguments; or he is hot and dogmatical, quick in opposition, and tenacious in defence, disabled by his own violence, and confused by his haste to triumph.

The graces of writing and conversation are of different kinds, and though he who excels in one might have been with opportunities and application equally successful in the other, yet as many please by extempory talk, though utterly unacquainted with the more accurate

[1 I venture to correct *acts*, the reading of the first edition. The confusion occurs elsewhere in Johnson.]

method, and more laboured beauties, which composition requires; so it is very possible that men, wholly accustomed to works of study, may be without that readiness of conception, and affluence of language, always necessary to colloquial entertainment. They may want address to watch the hints which conversation offers for the display of their particular attainments, or they may be so much unfurnished with matter on common subjects, that discourse not professedly literary glides over them as heterogeneous bodies, without admitting their conceptions to mix in the circulation.

A transition from an author's book to his conversation, is too often like an entrance into a large city, after a distant prospect. Remotely, we see nothing but spires of temples and turrets of palaces, and imagine it the residence of splendour, grandeur, and magnificence; but, when we have passed the gates, we find it perplexed with narrow passages, disgraced with despicable cottages, embarrassed with obstructions, and clouded with smoke.

Rambler, No. 14

Death

——Me non oracula certum,
Sed mors certa facit. LUCAN.

Let those weak minds, who live in doubt and fear,
To juggling priests for oracles repair;
One certain hour of death to each decreed,
My fixt, my certain soul, from doubt has freed. ROWE.

It is recorded of some eastern monarch, that he kept an officer in his house, whose employment it was to remind him of his mortality, by calling out every morning, at a stated hour, *Remember, prince, that thou shalt die!* And the contemplation of the frailness and uncertainty of our present state appeared of so much importance to Solon of Athens, that he left this precept to future ages; *Keep thine eye fixed upon the end of life.*

A frequent and attentive prospect of that moment, which must put a period to all our schemes, and deprive us of all our acquisitions, is indeed of the utmost efficacy to the just and rational regulation of our lives; nor would ever any thing wicked, or often any thing absurd, be undertaken or prosecuted by him who should begin every day with a serious reflection that he is born to die.

The disturbers of our happiness, in this world, are our desires, our griefs, and our fears; and to all these, the consideration of mortality is a certain and adequate remedy. Think, says Epictetus, frequently on poverty, banishment, and death, and thou wilt then never indulge violent desires, or give up thy heart to mean sentiments, οὐδὲν οὐδέποτε ταπεινὸν ἐνθυμήσῃ, οὔτε ἄγαν ἐπιθυμήσεις τινός.

That the maxim of Epictetus is founded on just observation will easily be granted, when we reflect, how that vehemence of eagerness after the common objects of pursuit is kindled in our minds. We represent to ourselves the pleasures of some future possession, and suffer our thoughts to dwell attentively upon it, till it has wholly engrossed the imagination, and permits us not to conceive any happiness but its attainment, or any misery but its loss; every other satisfaction which the bounty of Providence has scattered over life is neglected as inconsiderable, in comparison of the great object which we have placed before us, and is thrown from us as incumbering our activity, or trampled under foot as standing in our way.

Every man has experienced how much of this ardour has been remitted, when a sharp or tedious sickness has set death before his eyes. The extensive influence of greatness, the glitter of wealth, the praises of admirers, and the attendance of supplicants, have appeared vain and empty things, when the last hour seemed to be approaching; and the same appearance they would always have, if the same thought was always predominant. We should then find the absurdity of stretching out our arms incessantly to grasp that which we cannot keep, and wearing out our lives in endeavours to add new turrets to the fabrick of ambition, when the foundation itself is shaking, and the ground on which it stands is mouldering away.

All envy is proportionate to desire; we are uneasy at the attainments of another, according as we think our own happiness would be advanced by the addition of that which he withholds from us; and therefore whatever depresses immoderate wishes, will at the same time set the heart free from the corrosion of envy, and exempt us from that vice which is, above most others, tormenting to ourselves, hateful to the world, and productive of mean artifices, and sordid projects. He that considers how soon he must close his life, will find nothing of so much importance as to close it well; and will, therefore, look with indifference upon whatever is useless to that purpose. Whoever reflects frequently upon the uncertainty of his own duration, will find out, that the state of others is not more permanent, and that what can confer nothing on himself very desirable, cannot so much improve the condition of a rival, as to make him much superior to those from whom he has carried the prize, a prize too mean to deserve a very obstinate opposition.

Even grief, that passion to which the virtuous and tender mind is particularly subject, will be obviated or alleviated by the same thoughts. It will be obviated, if all the blessings of our condition are enjoyed with a constant sense of their uncertain tenure. If we remember, that whatever we possess is to be in our hands but a very little time, and that the little which our most lively hopes can promise us, may be made less by ten thousand accidents; we shall not much repine at a loss, of which we cannot estimate the value, but of which, though we are not able to tell the least amount, we know, with sufficient certainty, the greatest, and are convinced that the greatest is not much to be regretted.

But, if any passion has so much usurped our understanding, as not to suffer us to enjoy advantages with the moderation prescribed by reason, it is not too late to apply this remedy, when we find ourselves sinking under sorrow, and inclined to pine for that which is irrecoverably vanished. We may then usefully revolve the uncertainty of our own condition, and the folly of lamenting that from which, if it had staid a little longer, we should ourselves have been taken away.

With regard to the sharpest and most melting sorrow,

that which arises from the loss of those whom we have loved with tenderness, it may be observed, that friendship between mortals can be contracted on no other terms, than that one must some time mourn for the other's death: And this grief will always yield to the survivor one consolation proportionate to his affliction; for the pain, whatever it be, that he himself feels, his friend has escaped.

Nor is fear, the most overbearing and resistless of all our passions, less to be temperated by this universal medicine of the mind. The frequent contemplation of death, as it shows the vanity of all human good, discovers likewise the lightness of all terrestrial evil, which certainly can last no longer than the subject upon which it acts; and according to the old observation, must be shorter, as it is more violent. The most cruel calamity which misfortune can produce, must, by the necessity of nature, be quickly at an end. The soul cannot long be held in prison, but will fly away, and leave a lifeless body to human malice.

——*Ridetque sui ludibria trunci.*

And soaring mocks the broken frame below.

The utmost that we can threaten to one another is that death, which, indeed, we may precipitate, but cannot retard, and from which, therefore, it cannot become a wise man to buy a reprieve at the expense of virtue, since he knows not how small a portion of time he can purchase, but knows, that whether short or long, it will be made less valuable by the remembrance of the price at which it has been obtained. He is sure that he destroys his happiness, but is not sure that he lengthens his life.

The known shortness of life, as it ought to moderate our passions, may likewise, with equal propriety, contract our designs. There is not time for the most forcible genius, and most active industry, to extend its effects beyond a certain sphere. To project the conquest of the world, is the madness of mighty princes; to hope for excellence in every science, has been the folly of literary heroes; and both have found at last, that they have panted for a height of eminence denied to humanity, and have lost many opportunities of making themselves useful and happy, by a vain ambition of obtaining a species of honour, which the eternal laws of Providence have placed beyond the reach of man.

The miscarriages of the great designs of princes are recorded in the histories of the world, but are of little use to the bulk of mankind, who seem very little interested in admonitions against errours which they cannot commit. But the fate of learned ambition is a proper subject for every scholar to consider; for who has not had occasion to regret the dissipation of great abilities in a boundless multiplicity of pursuits, to lament the sudden desertion of excellent designs, upon the offer of some other subject made inviting by its novelty, and to observe the inaccuracy and deficiencies of works left unfinished by too great an extension of the plan?

It is always pleasing to observe, how much more our minds can conceive, than our bodies can perform; yet it is our duty, while we continue in this complicated state, to regulate one part of our composition by some regard to the other. We are not to indulge our corporeal appetites with pleasures that impair our intellectual vigour, nor gratify our minds with schemes which we know our lives must fail in attempting to execute. The uncertainty of our duration ought at once to set bounds to our designs, and add incitements to our industry; and when we find ourselves inclined either to immensity in our schemes, or sluggishness in our endeavours, we may either check, or animate ourselves, by recollecting, with the father of physick, *that art is long, and life is short.*

Rambler, No. 17

Intellectual Cowardice

Possunt quia posse videntur.   VIRGIL.

For they can conquer who believe they can.   DRYDEN.

There are some vices and errours which, though often fatal to those in whom they are found, have yet, by the

universal consent of mankind, been considered as entitled
to some degree of respect, or have, at least, been exempted
from contemptuous infamy, and condemned by the severest moralists with pity rather than detestation.

A constant and invariable example of this general
partiality will be found in the different regard which has
always been shown to rashness and cowardice, two vices,
of which, though they may be conceived equally distant
from the middle point, where true fortitude is placed,
and may equally injure any publick or private interest,
yet the one is never mentioned without some kind of
veneration, and the other always considered as a topick
of unlimited and licentious censure, on which all the
virulence of reproach may be lawfully exerted.

The same distinction is made, by the common suffrage,
between profusion and avarice, and, perhaps, between
many other opposite vices; and, as I have found reason
to pay regard to the voice of the people, in cases where
knowledge has been forced upon them by experience,
without long deductions or deep researches, I am inclined to believe that this distribution of respect is not
without some agreement with the nature of things; and
that in the faults, which are thus invested with extraordinary privileges, there are generally some latent principles of merit, some possibilities of future virtue, which
may, by degrees, break from obstruction, and by time and
opportunity be brought into act.

It may be laid down as an axiom, that it is more easy
to take away superfluities than to supply defects; and
therefore he that is culpable, because he has passed the
middle point of virtue, is always accounted a fairer object
of hope, than he who fails by falling short. The one has
all that perfection requires, and more, but the excess may
be easily retrenched; the other wants the qualities requisite to excellence, and who can tell how he shall
obtain them? We are certain that the horse may be
taught to keep pace with his fellows, whose fault is that
he leaves them behind. We know that a few strokes of the
axe will lop a cedar; but what arts of cultivation can
elevate a shrub?

To walk with circumspection and steadiness in the right path, at an equal distance between the extremes of errour, ought to be the constant endeavour of every reasonable being; nor can I think those teachers of moral wisdom much to be honoured as benefactors to mankind, who are always enlarging upon the difficulty of our duties, and providing rather excuses for vice, than incentives to virtue.

But, since to most it will happen often, and to all sometimes, that there will be a deviation towards one side or the other, we ought always to employ our vigilance, with most attention, on that enemy from which there is the greatest danger, and to stray, if we must stray, towards those parts from whence we may quickly and easily return.

Among other opposite qualities of the mind, which may become dangerous, though in different degrees, I have often had occasion to consider the contrary effects of presumption and despondency; of heady confidence, which promises victory without contest, and heartless pusillanimity, which shrinks back from the thought of great undertakings, confounds difficulty with impossibility, and considers all advancement towards any new attainment as irreversibly prohibited.

Presumption will be easily corrected. Every experiment will teach caution, and miscarriages will hourly show, that attempts are not always rewarded with success. The most precipitate ardour will, in time, be taught the necessity of methodical gradation and preparatory measures; and the most daring confidence be convinced that neither merit, nor abilities, can command events.

It is the advantage of vehemence and activity, that they are always hastening to their own reformation; because they incite us to try whether our expectations are well grounded, and therefore detect the deceits which they are apt to occasion. But timidity is a disease of the mind more obstinate and fatal; for a man once persuaded that any impediment is insuperable, has given it, with respect to himself, that strength and weight which it had not before. He can scarcely strive with vigour and perseverance, when he has no hope of gaining the victory; and since he never will try his strength, can never discover the unreasonableness of his fears.

There is often to be found in men devoted to literature a kind of intellectual cowardice, which whoever converses much among them, may observe frequently to depress the alacrity of enterprise, and, by consequence, to retard the improvement of science. They have annexed to every species of knowledge some chimerical character of terrour and inhibition, which they transmit, without much reflection, from one to another; they first fright themselves, and then propagate the panick to their scholars and acquaintance. One study is inconsistent with a lively imagination, another with a solid judgment; one is improper in the early parts of life, another requires so much time, that it is not to be attempted at an advanced age; one is dry and contracts the sentiments, another is diffuse and overburdens the memory; one is insufferable to taste and delicacy, and another wears out life in the study of words, and is useless to a wise man, who desires only the knowledge of things.

But of all the bugbears by which the *Infantes barbati*, boys both young and old, have been hitherto frighted from digressing into new tracts of learning, none has been more mischievously efficacious than an opinion that every kind of knowledge requires a peculiar genius, or mental constitution, framed for the reception of some ideas, and the exclusion of others; and that to him whose genius is not adapted to the study which he prosecutes, all labour shall be vain and fruitless, vain as an endeavour to mingle oil and water, or, in the language of chymistry, to amalgamate bodies of heterogeneous principles.

This opinion we may reasonably suspect to have been propagated, by vanity, beyond the truth. It is natural for those who have raised a reputation by any science, to exalt themselves as endowed by heaven with peculiar powers, or marked out by an extraordinary designation for their profession; and to fright competitors away by representing the difficulties with which they must contend, and the necessity of qualities which are supposed to be not generally conferred, and which no man can know, but by experience, whether he enjoys.

To this discouragement it may be possibly answered, that since a genius, whatever it be, is like fire in the flint, only to be produced by collision with a proper subject, it is the business of every man to try whether his faculties may not happily co-operate with his desires; and since they whose proficiency he admires, knew their own force only by the event, he needs but engage in the same undertaking with equal spirit, and may reasonably hope for equal success.

There is another species of false intelligence, given by those who profess to show the way to the summit of knowledge, of equal tendency to depress the mind with false distrust of itself, and weaken it by needless solicitude and dejection. When a scholar whom they desire to animate, consults them at his entrance on some new study, it is common to make flattering representations of its pleasantness and facility. Thus they generally attain one of two ends almost equally desirable; they either incite his industry by elevating his hopes, or produce a high opinion of their own abilities, since they are supposed to relate only what they have found, and to have proceeded with no less ease than they promise to their followers.

The student, inflamed by this encouragement, sets forward in the new path, and proceeds a few steps with great alacrity, but he soon finds asperities and intricacies of which he has not been forewarned, and imagining that none ever were so entangled or fatigued before him, sinks suddenly into despair, and desists as from an expedition in which fate opposes him. Thus his terrours are multiplied by his hopes, and he is defeated without resistance, because he had no expectation of an enemy.

Of these treacherous instructors, the one destroys industry, by declaring that industry is vain, the other by representing it as needless; the one cuts away the root of hope, the other raises it only to be blasted: the one confines his pupil to the shore, by telling him that his wreck is certain, the other sends him to sea, without preparing him for tempests.

False hopes and false terrours are equally to be avoided. Every man who proposes to grow eminent by learning, should carry in his mind, at once, the difficulty of excellence, and the force of industry; and remember that fame is not conferred but as the recompense of labour, and that labour vigorously continued, has not often failed of its reward.

Rambler, No. 25

Stoicism

"Οσσα τε δαιμονίῃσι τύχαις βροτοὶ ἄλγε᾽ ἔχουσιν,
᾽Ων ἂν μοῖραν ἔχῃς, πρᾴως φέρε, μηδ᾽ ἀγανάκτει·
᾽Ιᾶσθαι δὲ πρέπει κάθοσον δύνῃ.   PYTHAG.

Of all the woes that load the mortal state,
Whate'er thy portion, mildly meet thy fate;
But ease it as thou canst——   ELPHINSTON.

So large a part of human life passes in a state contrary to our natural desires, that one of the principal topicks of moral instruction is the art of bearing calamities. And such is the certainty of evil, that it is the duty of every man to furnish his mind with those principles that may enable him to act under it with decency and propriety.

The sect of ancient philosophers, that boasted to have carried this necessary science to the highest perfection, were the stoicks, or scholars of Zeno, whose wild enthusiastick virtue pretended to an exemption from the sensibilities of unenlightened mortals, and who proclaimed themselves exalted, by the doctrines of their sect, above the reach of those miseries which embitter life to the rest of the world. They therefore removed pain, poverty, loss of friends, exile, and violent death, from the catalogue of evils; and passed, in their haughty style, a kind of irreversible decree, by which they forbad them to be counted any longer among the objects of terrour or anxiety, or to give any disturbance to the tranquillity of a wise man.

This edict was, I think, not universally observed; for

though one of the more resolute, when he was tortured by a violent disease, cried out, that let pain harass him to its utmost power, it should never force him to consider it as other than indifferent and neutral; yet all had not stubbornness to hold out against their senses: for a weaker pupil of Zeno is recorded to have confessed in the anguish of the gout, that *he now found pain to be an evil.*

It may however be questioned, whether these philosophers can be very properly numbered among the teachers of patience; for if pain be not an evil, there seems no instruction requisite how it may be born; and therefore, when they endeavour to arm their followers with arguments against it, they may be thought to have given up their first position. But such inconsistencies are to be expected from the greatest understandings, when they endeavour to grow eminent by singularity, and employ their strength in establishing opinions opposite to nature.

The controversy about the reality of external evils is now at an end. That life has many miseries, and that those miseries are, sometimes at least, equal to all the powers of fortitude, is now universally confessed; and therefore it is useful to consider not only how we may escape them, but by what means those which either the accidents of affairs, or the infirmities of nature, must bring upon us, may be mitigated and lightened, and how we may make those hours less wretched, which the condition of our present existence will not allow to be very happy.

The cure for the greatest part of human miseries is not radical, but palliative. Infelicity is involved in corporeal nature, and interwoven with our being; all attempts therefore to decline it wholly are useless and vain: the armies of pain send their arrows against us on every side, the choice is only between those which are more or less sharp, or tinged with poison of greater or less malignity; and the strongest armour which reason can supply, will only blunt their points, but cannot repel them.

The great remedy which heaven has put in our hands is patience, by which, though we cannot lessen the torments of the body, we can in a great measure preserve the peace of the mind, and shall suffer only the natural and genuine force of an evil, without heightening its acrimony, or prolonging its effects.

There is indeed nothing more unsuitable to the nature of man in any calamity than rage and turbulence, which, without examining whether they are not sometimes impious, are at least always offensive, and incline others rather to hate and despise than to pity and assist us. If what we suffer has been brought upon us by ourselves, it is observed by an ancient poet, that patience is eminently our duty, since no one should be angry at feeling that which he has deserved.

> *Leniter ex merito quicquid patiare ferendum est,*
>
> Let pain deserv'd without complaint be borne.

And surely, if we are conscious that we have not contributed to our own sufferings, if punishment falls upon innocence, or disappointment happens to industry and prudence, patience, whether more necessary or not, is much easier, since our pain is then without aggravation, and we have not the bitterness of remorse to add to the asperity of misfortune.

In those evils which are allotted to us by Providence, such as deformity, privation of any of the senses, or old age, it is always to be remembered, that impatience can have no present effect, but to deprive us of the consolations which our condition admits, by driving away from us those by whose conversation or advice we might be amused or helped; and that with regard to futurity it is yet less to be justified, since, without lessening the pain, it cuts off the hope of that reward which he, by whom it is inflicted, will confer upon them that bear it well.

In all evils which admit a remedy, impatience is to be avoided, because it wastes that time and attention in complaints, that, if properly applied, might remove the cause. Turenne, among the acknowledgments which he used to pay in conversation to the memory of those by whom he had been instructed in the art of war, mentioned one with honour, who taught him not to spend his time in regretting any mistake which he had made, but to set himself immediately and vigorously to repair it.

Patience and submission are very carefully to be distinguished from cowardice and indolence. We are not to repine, but we may lawfully struggle; for the calamities of life, like the necessities of nature, are calls to labour and exercises of diligence. When we feel any pressure of distress, we are not to conclude that we can only obey the will of heaven by languishing under it, any more than when we perceive the pain of thirst, we are to imagine that water is prohibited. Of misfortune it never can be certainly known whether, as proceeding from the hand of God, it is an act of favour or of punishment: but since all the ordinary dispensations of Providence are to be interpreted according to the general analogy of things, we may conclude that we have a right to remove one inconvenience as well as another; that we are only to take care lest we purchase ease with guilt; and that our Maker's purpose, whether of reward or severity, will be answered by the labours which he lays us under the necessity of performing.

This duty is not more difficult in any state than in diseases intensely painful, which may indeed suffer such exacerbations as seem to strain the powers of life to their utmost stretch, and leave very little of the attention vacant to precept or reproof. In this state the nature of man requires some indulgence, and every extravagance but impiety may be easily forgiven him. Yet, lest we should think ourselves too soon entitled to the mournful privileges of irresistible misery, it is proper to reflect, that the utmost anguish which human wit can contrive, or human malice can inflict, has been born with constancy; and that if the pains of disease be, as I believe they are, sometimes greater than those of artificial torture, they are therefore in their own nature shorter: the vital frame is quickly broken, or the union between soul and body is for a time suspended by insensibility, and we soon cease to feel our maladies when they once become too violent to be born. I think there is some reason for questioning whether the body and mind are not so

proportioned, that the one can bear all that can be inflicted on the other, whether virtue cannot stand its
ground as long as life, and whether a soul well principled
will not be separated sooner than subdued.

In calamities which operate chiefly on our passions,
such as diminution of fortune, loss of friends, or declension of character, the chief danger of impatience is upon
the first attack, and many expedients have been contrived,
by which the blow may be broken. Of these the most
general precept is, not to take pleasure in any thing, of
which it is not in our power to secure the possession to
ourselves. This counsel, when we consider the enjoyment
of any terrestrial advantage, as opposite to a constant
and habitual solicitude for future felicity, is undoubtedly
just, and delivered by that authority which cannot be
disputed, but in any other sense, is it not like advice, not
to walk lest we should stumble, or not to see lest our eyes
should light upon deformity? It seems to be reasonable
to enjoy blessings with confidence, as well as to resign
them with submission, and to hope for the continuance
of good which we possess without insolence or volup-
tuousness, as for the restitution of that which we lose
without despondency or murmurs.

The chief security against the fruitless anguish of
impatience, must arise from frequent reflection on the
wisdom and goodness of the GOD of nature, in whose
hands are riches and poverty, honour and disgrace,
pleasure and pain, and life and death. A settled conviction of the tendency of every thing to our good, and of
the possibility of turning miseries into happiness, by
receiving them rightly, will incline us to *bless the name of
the* LORD, *whether he gives or takes away*.

Rambler, No. 32

Biography

Quid sit pulchrum, quid turpe, quid utile, quid non,
Plenius et melius Chrysippo et Crantore dicit.[1]   HOR.

Whose works the beautiful and base contain,
Of vice and virtue more instructive rules,
Than all the sober sages of the schools.   FRANCIS

All joy or sorrow for the happiness or calamities of others is produced by an act of the imagination, that realizes the event however fictitious, or approximates it however remote, by placing us, for a time, in the condition of him whose fortune we contemplate; so that we feel, while the deception lasts, whatever motions would be excited by the same good or evil happening to ourselves.

Our passions are therefore more strongly moved, in proportion as we can more readily adopt the pains or pleasure proposed to our minds, by recognizing them as once our own, or considering them as naturally incident to our state of life. It is not easy for the most artful writer to give us an interest in happiness or misery, which we think ourselves never likely to feel, and with which we have never yet been made acquainted. Histories of the downfal of kingdoms, and revolutions of empires, are read with great tranquillity; the imperial tragedy pleases common auditors only by its pomp of ornament, and grandeur of ideas; and the man whose faculties have been engrossed by business, and whose heart never fluttered but at the rise or fall of the stocks, wonders how the attention can be seized, or the affection agitated, by a tale of love.

Those parallel circumstances and kindred images, to which we readily conform our minds, are, above all other writings, to be found in narratives of the lives of particular persons; and therefore no species of writing seems more worthy of cultivation than biography, since none can be more delightful or more useful, none can more certainly enchain the heart by irresistible interest, or more widely diffuse instruction to every diversity of condition.

[1 Horace praises Homer.]

The general and rapid narratives of history, which involve a thousand fortunes in the business of a day, and complicate innumerable incidents in one great transaction, afford few lessons applicable to private life, which derives its comforts and its wretchedness from the right or wrong management of things, which nothing but their frequency makes considerable, *Parva si non fiunt quotidie*, says Pliny, and which can have no place in those relations which never descend below the consultation of senates, the motions of armies, and the schemes of conspirators.

I have often thought that there has rarely passed a life of which a judicious and faithful narrative would not be useful. For, not only every man has, in the mighty mass of the world, great numbers in the same condition with himself, to whom his mistakes and miscarriages, escapes and expedients, would be of immediate and apparent use; but there is such an uniformity in the state of man, considered apart from adventitious and separable decorations and disguises, that there is scarce any possibility of good or ill, but is common to human kind. A great part of the time of those who are placed at the greatest distances by fortune, or by temper, must unavoidably pass in the same manner, and though, when the claims of nature are satisfied, caprice, and vanity, and accident, begin to produce discriminations and peculiarities, yet the eye is not very heedful or quick, which cannot discover the same causes still terminating their influence in the same effects, though sometimes accelerated, sometimes retarded, or perplexed by multiplied combinations. We are all prompted by the same motives, all deceived by the same fallacies, all animated by hope, obstructed by danger, entangled by desire, and seduced by pleasure.

It is frequently objected to relations of particular lives, that they are not distinguished by any striking or wonderful vicissitudes. The scholar who passed his life among his books, the merchant who conducted only his own affairs, the priest, whose sphere of action was not extended beyond that of his duty, are considered as no proper objects of publick regard, however they might have excelled in their several stations, whatever might have been their learning, integrity, and piety. But this notion arises from false measures of excellence and dignity, and must be eradicated by considering, that in the esteem of uncorrupted reason, what is of most use is of most value.

It is, indeed, not improper to take honest advantages of prejudice, and to gain attention by a celebrated name; but the business of the biographer is often to pass slightly over those performances and incidents, which produce vulgar greatness, to lead the thoughts into domestick privacies, and display the minute details of daily life, where exterior appendages are cast aside, and men excel each other only by prudence and by virtue. The account of Thuanus is, with great propriety, said by its author to have been written, that it might lay open to posterity the private and familiar character of that man, *cujus ingenium et candorem ex ipsius scriptis sunt olim semper miraturi*, whose candour and genius will to the end of time be by his writings preserved in admiration.

There are many invisible circumstances which, whether we read as inquirers after natural or moral knowledge, whether we intend to enlarge our science, or increase our virtue, are more important than publick occurrences. Thus Sallust, the great master of nature, has not forgot, in his account of Catiline, to remark that *his walk was now quick, and again slow*, as an indication of a mind revolving something with violent commotion. Thus the story of Melancthon affords a striking lecture on the value of time, by informing us, that when he made an appointment, he expected not only the hour, but the minute to be fixed, that the day might not run out in the idleness of suspense: and all the plans and enterprises of De Witt are now of less importance to the world, than that part of his personal character, which represents him as *careful of his health, and negligent of his life*.

But biography has often been allotted to writers who seem very little acquainted with the nature of their task, or very negligent about the performance. They rarely afford any other account than might be collected from publick papers, but imagine themselves writing a life when they exhibit a chronological series of actions or preferments; and so little regard the manners or behaviour of their heroes, that more knowledge may be gained of a man's real character, by a short conversation with one of his servants, than from a formal and studied narrative, begun with his pedigree, and ended with his funeral.

If now and then they condescend to inform the world of particular facts, they are not always so happy as to select the most important. I know not well what advantage posterity can receive from the only circumstance by which Tickell has distinguished Addison from the rest of mankind, *the irregularity of his pulse*: nor can I think myself overpaid for the time spent in reading the life of Malherb, by being enabled to relate after the learned biographer, that Malherb had two predominant opinions; one, that the looseness of a single woman might destroy all her boast of ancient descent; the other, that the French beggars made use very improperly and barbarously of the phrase *noble Gentleman*, because either word included the sense of both.

There are, indeed, some natural reasons why these narratives are often written by such as were not likely to give much instruction or delight, and why most accounts of particular persons are barren and useless. If a life be delayed till interest and envy are at an end, we may hope for impartiality, but must expect little intelligence; for the incidents which give excellence to biography are of a volatile and evanescent kind, such as soon escape the memory, and are rarely transmitted by tradition. We know how few can portray a living acquaintance, except by his most prominent and observable particularities, and the grosser features of his mind; and it may be easily imagined how much of this little knowledge may be lost in imparting it, and how soon a succession of copies will lose all resemblance of the original.

If the biographer writes from personal knowledge, and makes haste to gratify the publick curiosity, there is danger lest his interest, his fear, his gratitude, or his tenderness, overpower his fidelity, and tempt him to conceal, if not to invent. There are many who think it an act of piety to hide the faults or failings of their friends, even when they can no longer suffer by their detection; we therefore see whole ranks of characters adorned with uniform panegyrick, and not to be known from one another, but by extrinsick and casual circumstances. 'Let me remember,' says Hale, 'when I find myself inclined to pity a criminal, that there is likewise a pity due to the country.' If we owe regard to the memory of the dead, there is yet more respect to be paid to knowledge, to virtue, and to truth.

Rambler, No. 60

1751

Vain Imagination

Dulce est desipere in loco.   HOR.
Wisdom at proper times is well forgot.

Locke, whom there is no reason to suspect of being a favourer of idleness or libertinism, has advanced, that whoever hopes to employ any part of his time with efficacy and vigour, must allow some of it to pass in trifles. It is beyond the powers of humanity to spend a whole life in profound study and intense meditation, and the most rigorous exacters of industry and seriousness have appointed hours for relaxation and amusement.

It is certain, that, with or without our consent, many of the few moments allotted us will slide imperceptibly away, and that the mind will break, from confinement to its stated task, into sudden excursions. Severe and connected attention is preserved but for a short time, and when a man shuts himself up in his closet, and bends his thoughts to the discussion of any abstruse question, he will find his faculties continually stealing away to more pleasing entertainments. He often perceives himself transported, he knows not how, to distant tracts of thought, and returns to his first object as from a dream, without knowing when he forsook it, or how long he has been abstracted from it.

It has been observed that the most studious are not always the most learned. There is, indeed, no great difficulty in discovering that this difference of proficiency may arise from the difference of intellectual powers, of the choice of books, or the convenience of information. But I believe it likewise frequently happens that the most recluse are not the most vigorous prosecutors of study. Many impose upon the world, and many upon themselves, by an appearance of severe and exemplary diligence, when they, in reality, give themselves up to the luxury of fancy, please their minds with regulating the past, or planning out the future; place themselves at will in varied situations of happiness, and slumber away their days in voluntary visions. In the journey of life some are left behind, because they are naturally feeble and slow; some because they miss the way, and many because they leave it by choice, and, instead of pressing onward with a steady pace, delight themselves with momentary deviations, turn aside to pluck every flower, and repose in every shade.

There is nothing more fatal to a man whose business is to think, than to have learned the art of regaling his mind with those airy gratifications. Other vices or follies are restrained by fear, reformed by admonition, or rejected by the conviction which the comparison of our conduct with that of others may in time produce. But this invisible riot of the mind, this secret prodigality of being, is secure from detection, and fearless of reproach. The dreamer retires to his apartments, shuts out the cares and interruptions of mankind, and abandons himself to his own fancy; new worlds rise up before him, one image is followed by another, and a long succession of delights dances round him. He is at last called back to life by nature, or by custom, and enters peevish into society, because he cannot model it to his own will. He returns from his idle excursions with the asperity, though not with the knowledge of a student, and hastens again to the same felicity with the eagerness of a man bent upon the advancement of some favourite science. The infatuation strengthens by degrees, and, like the poison of opiates, weakens his powers, without any external symptom of malignity.

It happens, indeed, that these hypocrites of learning are in time detected, and convinced by disgrace and disappointment of the difference between the labour of thought, and the sport of musing. But this discovery is often not made till it is too late to recover the time that has been fooled away. A thousand accidents may, indeed, awaken drones to a more early sense of their danger and their shame. But they who are convinced of the necessity of breaking from this habitual drowsiness, too often relapse in spite of their resolution; for these ideal seducers are always near, and neither any particularity of time nor place is necessary to their influence; they invade the soul without warning, and have often charmed down resistance before their approach is perceived or suspected.

This captivity, however, it is necessary for every man to break, who has any desire to be wise or useful, to pass his life with the esteem of others, or to look back with satisfaction from his old age upon his earlier years. In order to regain liberty, he must find the means of flying from himself; he must, in opposition to the *Stoick* precept, teach his desires to fix upon external things; he must adopt the joys and the pains of others, and excite in his mind the want of social pleasures and amicable communication.

It is, perhaps, not impossible to promote the cure of this mental malady, by close application to some new study, which may pour in fresh ideas, and keep curiosity in perpetual motion. But study requires solitude, and solitude is a state dangerous to those who are too much accustomed to sink into themselves. Active employment or publick pleasure is generally a necessary part of this intellectual regimen, without which, though some remission may be obtained, a complete cure will scarcely be effected.

This is a formidable and obstinate disease of the intellect, of which, when it has once become radicated by time, the remedy is one of the hardest tasks of reason and of virtue. Its slightest attacks, therefore, should be

watchfully opposed; and he that finds the frigid and
narcotick infection beginning to seize him, should turn
his whole attention against it, and check it at the first
discovery by proper counteraction.

The great resolution to be formed, when happiness
and virtue are thus formidably invaded, is, that no part
of life be spent in a state of neutrality or indifference; but
that some pleasure be found for every moment that is not
devoted to labour; and that whenever the necessary business of life grows irksome or disgusting, an immediate
transition be made to diversion and gayety.

After the exercises which the health of the body requires, and which have themselves a natural tendency to
actuate and invigorate the mind, the most eligible amusement of a rational being seems to be that interchange of
thoughts which is practised in free and easy conversation;
where suspicion is banished by experience, and emulation
by benevolence; where every man speaks with no other
restraint than unwillingness to offend, and hears with no
other disposition than desire to be pleased.

There must be a time in which every man trifles; and
the only choice that nature offers us, is, to trifle in company or alone. To join profit with pleasure, has been an
old precept among men who have had very different
conceptions of profit. All have agreed that our amusements should not terminate wholly in the present moment,
but contribute more or less to future advantage. He that
amuses himself among well-chosen companions, can
scarcely fail to receive, from the most careless and ob-
streperous merriment which virtue can allow, some useful hints; nor can converse on the most familiar topicks,
without some casual information. The loose sparkles of
thoughtless wit may give new light to the mind, and the
gay contention for paradoxical positions rectify the
opinions.

This is the time in which those friendships that give
happiness or consolation, relief or security, are generally
formed. A wise and good man is never so amiable as in
his unbended and familiar intervals. Heroick generosity,
or philosophical discoveries, may compel veneration and

respect, but love always implies some kind of natural or voluntary equality, and is only to be excited by that levity and cheerfulness which disencumber all minds from awe and solitude, invite the modest to freedom, and exalt the timorous to confidence. This easy gayety is certain to please, whatever be the character of him that exerts it; if our superiours descend from their elevation, we love them for lessening the distance at which we are placed below them; and inferiours, from whom we can receive no lasting advantage, will always keep our affections while their sprightliness and mirth contribute to our pleasure.

Every man finds himself differently affected by the sight of fortresses of war, and palaces of pleasure; we look on the height and strength of the bulwarks with a kind of gloomy satisfaction, for we cannot think of defence without admitting images of danger; but we range delighted and jocund through the gay apartments of the palace, because nothing is impressed by them on the mind but joy and festivity. Such is the difference between great and amiable characters; with protectors we are safe, with companions we are happy.

Rambler, No. 89

Friendship

Scilicet ingeniis aliqua est concordia junctis,
Et servat studii fœdera quisque sui,
Rusticus agricolam, miles fera bella gerentem,
Rectorem dubiæ navita puppis amat.　　　　Ovid.

Congenial passions souls together bind,
And ev'ry calling mingles with its kind;
Soldier unites with soldier, swain with swain,
The mariner with him that roves the main.

F. Lewis.

It has been ordained by Providence, for the conservation of order in the immense variety of nature, and for the regular propagation of the several classes of life with which the elements are peopled, that every creature should be drawn by some secret attraction to those of his own kind; and that not only the gentle and domestick animals which naturally unite into companies, or cohabit by pairs, should continue faithful to their species; but even those ravenous and ferocious savages which Aristotle observes never to be gregarious, should range mountains and deserts in search of one another, rather than pollute the world with a monstrous birth.

As the perpetuity and distinction of the lower tribes of the creation require that they should be determined to proper mates by some uniform motive of choice, or some cogent principle of instinct; it is necessary likewise, that man, whose wider capacity demands more gratifications, and who feels in himself innumerable wants, which a life of solitude cannot supply, and innumerable powers to which it cannot give employment, should be led to suitable companions by particular influence; and, among many beings of the same nature with himself, he may select some for intimacy and tenderness, and improve the condition of his existence, by superadding friendship to humanity, and the love of individuals to that of the species.

Other animals are so formed, that they seem to contribute very little to the happiness of each other, and know neither joy, nor grief, nor love, nor hatred, but as they are urged by some desire immediately subservient either to the support of their own lives, or to the continuation of their race; they therefore seldom appear to regard any of the minuter discriminations which distinguish creatures of the same kind from one another.

But if man were to feel no incentives to kindness, more than his general tendency to congenial nature, Babylon or London, with all their multitudes, would have to him the desolation of a wilderness; his affections, not compressed into a narrower compass, would vanish, like elemental fire, in boundless evaporation; he would languish in perpetual insensibility; and though he might, perhaps, in the first vigour of youth, amuse himself with the fresh enjoyments of life, yet, when curiosity should cease, and alacrity subside, he would abandon himself to the fluctuations of chance, without expecting help against any calamity, or feeling any wish for the happiness of others.

To love all men is our duty, so far as it includes a general habit of benevolence, and readiness of occasional kindness; but to love all equally is impossible; at least impossible without the extinction of those passions which now produce all our pains and all our pleasures; without the disuse, if not the abolition, of some of our faculties, and the suppression of all our hopes and fears in apathy and indifference.

The necessities of our condition require a thousand offices of tenderness, which mere regard for the species will never dictate. Every man has frequent grievances which only the solicitude of friendship will discover and remedy, and which would remain for ever unheeded in the mighty heap of human calamity, were it only surveyed by the eye of general benevolence equally attentive to every misery.

The great community of mankind is, therefore, necessarily broken into smaller independent societies; these form distinct interests, which are too frequently opposed to each other, and which they who have entered into the league of particular governments falsely think it virtue to promote, however destructive to the happiness of the rest of the world.

Such unions are again separated into subordinate classes and combinations, and social life is perpetually branched out into minuter subdivisions, till it terminates in the last ramifications of private friendship.

That friendship may at once be fond and lasting, it has been already observed in these papers, that a conformity of inclinations is necessary. No man can have much kindness for him by whom he does not believe himself esteemed, and nothing so evidently proves esteem as imitation.

That benevolence is always strongest which arises from participation of the same pleasures, since we are naturally most willing to revive in our minds the memory of persons, with whom the idea of enjoyment is connected.

It is commonly, therefore, to little purpose, that any one endeavours to ingratiate himself with such as he cannot accompany in their amusements and diversions. Men have been known to rise to favour and to fortune, only by being skilful in the sports with which their patron happened to be delighted, by concurring with his taste for some particular species of curiosities, by relishing the same wine, or applauding the same cookery.

Even those whom wisdom or virtue have placed above regard to such petty recommendations, must nevertheless be gained by similitude of manners. The highest and noblest enjoyment of familiar life, the communication of knowledge and reciprocation of sentiments, must always presuppose a disposition to the same inquiry, and delight in the same discoveries.

With what satisfaction could the politician lay his schemes for the reformation of laws, or his comparisons of different forms of government, before the chymist, who has never accustomed his thoughts to any other object than salt and sulphur; or how could the astronomer, in explaining his calculations and conjectures, endure the coldness of a grammarian, who would lose sight of Jupiter and all his satellites, for a happy etymology of an obscure word, or a better explication of a controverted line?

Every man loves merit of the same kind with his own, when it is not likely to hinder his advancement or his reputation; for he not only best understands the worth of those qualities which he labours to cultivate, or the usefulness of the art which he practises with success, but always feels a reflected pleasure from the praises, which, though given to another, belong equally to himself.

There is indeed no need of research and refinement to discover that men must generally select their companions from their own state of life, since there are not many minds furnished for great variety of conversation, or adapted to multiplicity of intellectual entertainments.

The sailor, the academick, the lawyer, the mechanick, and the courtier, have all a cast of talk peculiar to their own fraternity, have fixed their attention upon the same events, have been engaged in affairs of the same sort, and made use of allusions and illustrations which themselves only can understand.

To be infected with the jargon of a particular profession, and to know only the language of a single rank of mortals, is indeed sufficiently despicable. But as limits must be always set to the excursions of the human mind, there will be some study which every man more zealously prosecutes, some darling subject on which he is principally pleased to converse; and he that can most inform or best understand him, will certainly be welcomed with particular regard.

Such partiality is not wholly to be avoided, nor is it culpable, unless suffered so far to predominate as to produce aversion from every other kind of excellence, and to shade the lustre of dissimilar virtues. Those, therefore, whom the lot of life has conjoined, should endeavour constantly to approach towards the inclination of each other, invigorate every motion of concurrent desire, and fan every spark of kindred curiosity.

It has been justly observed, that discord generally operates in little things; it is inflamed to its utmost vehemence by contrariety of taste, oftener than of principles; and might therefore commonly be avoided by innocent conformity, which, if it was not at first the motive, ought always to be the consequence, of indissoluble union.

Rambler, No. 99

Repentance

At nobis vitæ dominum quærentibus unum
Lux iter est, et clara dies, et gratia simplex.
Spem sequimur, gradimurque fide, fruimurque futuris,
Ad quæ non veniunt præsentis gaudia vitæ,
Nec currunt pariter capta, et capienda voluptas.

PRUDENTIUS.[1]

[1 *Contra Orationes Symmachi*, ii. 905.]

We thro' this maze of life one Lord obey;
Whose light and grace unerring, lead the way.
By hope and faith secure of future bliss,
Gladly the joys of present life we miss:
For baffled mortals still attempt in vain,
Present and future bliss at once to gain.

F. LEWIS.

That to please the Lord and Father of the universe, is
the supreme interest of created and dependent beings, as
it is easily proved, has been universally confessed; and,
since all rational agents are conscious of having neglected
or violated the duties prescribed to them, the fear of being
rejected, or punished by God, has always burdened the
human mind. The expiation of crimes, and renovation
of the forfeited hopes of divine favour, therefore constitute
a large part of every religion.

The various methods of propitiation and atonement
which fear and folly have dictated, or artifice and interest
tolerated in the different parts of the world, however they
may sometimes reproach or degrade humanity, at least
show the general consent of all ages and nations in their
opinion of the placability of the divine nature. That God
will forgive, may, indeed, be established as the first and
fundamental truth of religion; for, though the knowledge of
his existence is the origin of philosophy, yet, without the
belief of his mercy, it would have little influence upon our
moral conduct. There could be no prospect of enjoying
the protection or regard of him, whom the least deviation
from rectitude made inexorable for ever; and every man
would naturally withdraw his thoughts from the contemplation of a Creator, whom he must consider as a
governor too pure to be pleased, and too severe to be
pacified; as an enemy infinitely wise, and infinitely
powerful, whom he could neither deceive, escape, nor
resist.

Where there is no hope, there can be no endeavour. A
constant and unfailing obedience is above the reach of
terrestrial diligence; and therefore the progress of life could
only have been the natural descent of negligent despair
from crime to crime, had not the universal persuasion

of forgiveness, to be obtained by proper means of reconciliation, recalled those to the paths of virtue whom
their passions had solicited aside; and animated to new
attempts, and firmer perseverance, those whom difficulty
had discouraged, or negligence surprised.

In times and regions so disjointed from each other, that
there can scarcely be imagined any communication of
sentiments either by commerce or tradition, has prevailed
a general and uniform expectation of propitiating God
by corporal austerities, of anticipating his vengeance by
voluntary inflictions, and appeasing his justice by a speedy
and cheerful submission to a less penalty, when a greater
is incurred.

Incorporated minds will always feel some inclination
towards exterior acts and ritual observances. Ideas not
represented by sensible objects are fleeting, variable, and
evanescent. We are not able to judge of the degree of
conviction which operated at any particular time upon
our own thoughts, but as it is recorded by some certain
and definite effect. He that reviews his life in order to
determine the probability of his acceptance with God, if
he could once establish the necessary proportion between
crimes and sufferings, might securely rest upon his performance of the expiation; but, while safety remains the
reward only of mental purity, he is always afraid lest
he should decide too soon in his own favour, lest he
should not have felt the pangs of true contrition; lest
he should mistake satiety for detestation, or imagine that
his passions are subdued when they are only sleeping.

From this natural and reasonable diffidence arose, in
humble and timorous piety, a disposition to confound
penance with repentance, to repose on human determinations, and to receive from some judicial sentence the
stated and regular assignment of reconciliatory pain. We
are never willing to be without resource; we seek in the
knowledge of others a succour for our own ignorance,
and are ready to trust any that will undertake to direct us
when we have no confidence in ourselves.

This desire to ascertain by some outward marks the
state of the soul, and this willingness to calm the conscience

by some settled method, have produced, as they are
diversified in their effects by various tempers and principles, most of the disquisitions and rules, the doubts
and solutions, that have embarrassed the doctrine of repentance, and perplexed tender and flexible minds with
innumerable scruples concerning the necessary measures
of sorrow, and adequate degrees of self-abhorrence; and
these rules, corrupted by fraud, or debased by credulity,
have, by the common resiliency of the mind from one
extreme to another, incited others to an open contempt
of all subsidiary ordinances, all prudential caution, and
the whole discipline of regulated piety.

Repentance, however difficult to be practised, is, if it
be explained without superstition, easily understood.
*Repentance is the relinquishment of any practice, from the con-
viction that it has offended God.* Sorrow, and fear, and anxiety,
are properly not parts, but adjuncts of repentance; yet
they are too closely connected with it to be easily separated; for they not only mark its sincerity, but promote
its efficacy.

No man commits any act of negligence or obstinacy,
by which his safety or happiness in this world is endangered, without feeling the pungency of remorse. He
who is fully convinced, that he suffers by his own failure,
can never forbear to trace back his miscarriage to its first
cause, to image to himself a contrary behaviour, and to
form involuntary resolutions against the like fault, even
when he knows that he shall never again have the
power of committing it. Danger, considered as imminent,
naturally produces such trepidations of impatience as
leave all human means of safety behind them: he that has
once caught an alarm of terrour, is every moment seized
with useless anxieties, adding one security to another,
trembling with sudden doubts, and distracted by the
perpetual occurrence of new expedients. If, therefore,
he whose crimes have deprived him of the favour of God,
can reflect upon his conduct without disturbance, or can
at will banish the reflection; if he who considers himself
as suspended over the abyss of eternal perdition only by
the thread of life, which must soon part by its own weak-

ness, and which the wing of every minute may divide, can cast his eyes round him without shuddering with horrour, or panting for security; what can he judge of himself, but that he is not yet awakened to sufficient conviction, since every loss is more lamented than the loss of the divine favour, and every danger more dreadful than the danger of final condemnation?

Retirement from the cares and pleasures of the world has been often recommended as useful to repentance. This at least is evident, that every one retires, whenever ratiocination and recollection are required on other occasions; and surely the retrospect of life, the disentanglement of actions complicated with innumerable circumstances, and diffused in various relations, the discovery of the primary movements of the heart, and the extirpation of lusts and appetites deeply rooted and widely spread, may be allowed to demand some secession from sport and noise, and business and folly. Some suspension of common affairs, some pause of temporal pain and pleasure, is doubtless necessary to him that deliberates for eternity, who is forming the only plan in which miscarriage cannot be repaired, and examining the only question in which mistake cannot be rectified.

Austerities and mortifications are means by which the mind is invigorated and roused, by which the attractions of pleasure are interrupted, and the chains of sensuality are broken. It is observed by one of the fathers, that *he who restrains himself in the use of things lawful, will never encroach upon things forbidden.* Abstinence, if nothing more, is, at least, a cautious retreat from the utmost verge of permission, and confers that security which cannot be reasonably hoped by him that dares always to hover over the precipice of destruction, or delights to approach the pleasures which he knows it fatal to partake. Austerity is the proper antidote to indulgence; the diseases of mind as well as body are cured by contraries, and to contraries we should readily have recourse, if we dreaded guilt as we dread pain.

The completion and sum of repentance is a change of life. That sorrow which dictates no caution, that fear which does not quicken our escape, that austerity which fails to rectify our affections, are vain and unavailing. But sorrow and terrour must naturally precede reformation; for what other cause can produce it? He, therefore, that feels himself alarmed by his conscience, anxious for the attainment of a better state, and afflicted by the memory of his past faults, may justly conclude, that the great work of repentance is begun, and hope by retirement and prayer, the natural and religious means of strengthening his conviction, to impress upon his mind such a sense of the divine presence, as may overpower the blandishments of secular delights, and enable him to advance from one degree of holiness to another, till death shall set him free from doubt and contest, misery and temptation.

> What better can we do than prostrate fall
> Before him reverent; and there confess
> Humbly our faults, and pardon beg, with tears
> Wat'ring the ground, and with our sighs the air
> Frequenting, sent from hearts contrite, in sign
> Of sorrow unfeign'd, and humiliation meek?[1]

Rambler, No. 110.

Capital Punishment

——*Audi,*
Nulla unquam de morte hominis cunctatio longa est. JUV.

——When man's life is in debate,
The judge can ne'er too long deliberate.   DRYDEN.

Power and superiority are so flattering and delightful, that, fraught with temptation and exposed to danger as they are, scarcely any virtue is so cautious, or any prudence so timorous, as to decline them. Even those that have most reverence for the laws of right, are pleased with showing that not fear, but choice, regulates their behaviour; and would be thought to comply, rather than obey. We love to overlook the boundaries which we do not wish to pass; and, as the Roman satirist remarks, he that has no design to take the life of another, is yet glad to have it in his hands.

[1 *Paradise Lost*, x. 1086.]

From the same principle, tending yet more to degeneracy and corruption, proceeds the desire of investing lawful authority with terrour, and governing by force rather than persuasion. Pride is unwilling to believe the necessity of assigning any other reason than her own will; and would rather maintain the most equitable claims by violence and penalties, than descend from the dignity of command to dispute and expostulation.

It may, I think, be suspected, that this political arrogance has sometimes found its way into legislative assemblies, and mingled with deliberations upon property and life. A slight perusal of the laws by which the measures of vindictive and coërcive justice are established, will discover so many disproportions between crimes and punishments, such capricious distinctions of guilt, and such confusion of remissness and severity, as can scarcely be believed to have been produced by publick wisdom, sincerely and calmly studious of publick happiness.

The learned, the judicious, the pious *Boerhaave* relates, that he never saw a criminal dragged to execution without asking himself, 'Who knows whether this man is not less culpable than me?' On the days when the prisons of this city are emptied into the grave, let every spectator of the dreadful procession put the same question to his own heart. Few among those that crowd in thousands to the legal massacre, and look with carelessness, perhaps with triumph, on the utmost exacerbations of human misery, would then be able to return without horrour and dejection. For, who can congratulate himself upon a life passed without some act more mischievous to the peace or prosperity of others, than the theft of a piece of money?

It has been always the practice, when any particular species of robbery becomes prevalent and common, to endeavour its suppression by capital denunciations. Thus, one generation of malefactors is commonly cut off, and their successors are frighted into new expedients; the art of thievery is augmented with greater variety of fraud, and subtilized to higher degrees of dexterity, and more occult methods of conveyance. The law then renews the pursuit in the heat of anger, and overtakes the offender again with death. By this practice capital inflictions are multiplied, and crimes, very different in their degrees of enormity, are equally subjected to the severest punishment that man has the power of exercising upon man.

The lawgiver is undoubtedly allowed to estimate the malignity of an offence, not merely by the loss or pain which single acts may produce, but by the general alarm and anxiety arising from the fear of mischief, and insecurity of possession: he therefore exercises the right which societies are supposed to have over the lives of those that compose them, not simply to punish a transgression, but to maintain order, and preserve quiet; he enforces those laws with severity that are most in danger of violation, as the commander of a garrison doubles the guard on that side which is threatened by the enemy.

This method has been long tried, but tried with so little success, that rapine and violence are hourly increasing, yet few seem willing to despair of its efficacy, and of those who employ their speculations upon the present corruption of the people, some propose the introduction of more horrid, lingering, and terrifick punishments; some are inclined to accelerate the executions; some to discourage pardons; and all seem to think that lenity has given confidence to wickedness, and that we can only be rescued from the talons of robbery by inflexible rigour and sanguinary justice.

Yet since the right of setting an uncertain and arbitrary value upon life has been disputed, and since experience of past times gives us little reason to hope that any reformation will be effected by a periodical havock of our fellow-beings, perhaps it will not be useless to consider what consequences might arise from relaxations of the law, and a more rational and equitable adaptation of penalties to offences.

Death is, as one of the ancients observes, τὸ τῶν φοβερῶν φοβερώτατον, *of dreadful things the most dreadful*; an evil, beyond which nothing can be threatened by sublunary power, or feared from human enmity or vengeance. This terrour should, therefore, be reserved as the last resort of authority, as the strongest and most operative of prohibitory sanctions, and placed before the treasure of life, to guard from invasion what cannot be restored. To equal robbery with murder is to reduce murder to robbery, to confound in common minds the gradations of iniquity, and incite the commission of a greater crime to prevent the detection of a less. If only murder were punished with death, very few robbers would stain their hands in blood; but when, by the last act of cruelty, no new danger is incurred, and greater security may be obtained, upon what principle shall we bid them forbear?

It may be urged, that the sentence is often mitigated to simple robbery; but surely this is to confess that our laws are unreasonable in our own opinion; and, indeed, it may be observed, that all but murderers have, at their last hour, the common sensations of mankind pleading in their favour.

From this conviction of the inequality of the punishment to the offence, proceeds the frequent solicitation of pardons. They who would rejoice at the correction of a thief, are yet shocked at the thought of destroying him. His crime shrinks to nothing, compared with his misery; and severity defeats itself by exciting pity.

The gibbet, indeed, certainly disables those who die upon it from infesting the community; but their death seems not to contribute more to the reformation of their associates, than any other method of separation. A thief seldom passes much of his time in recollection or anticipation, but from robbery hastens to riot, and from riot to robbery; nor, when the grave closes upon his companion, has any other care than to find another.

The frequency of capital punishments, therefore, rarely hinders the commission of a crime, but naturally and commonly prevents its detection, and is, if we proceed only upon prudential principles, chiefly for that reason to be avoided. Whatever may be urged by casuists or politicians, the greater part of mankind, as they can never think that to pick the pocket and to pierce the heart is equally criminal, will scarcely believe that two malefactors so different in guilt can be justly doomed to the same punishment; nor is the necessity of submitting the conscience to human laws so plainly evinced, so clearly stated, or so generally allowed, but that the pious, the tender, and the just, will always scruple to concur with the community in an act which their private judgment cannot approve.

He who knows not how often rigorous laws produce total impunity, and how many crimes are concealed and forgotten for fear of hurrying the offender to that state in which there is no repentance, has conversed very little with mankind. And whatever epithets of reproach or contempt this compassion may incur from those who confound cruelty with firmness, I know not whether any wise man would wish it less powerful, or less extensive.

If those whom the wisdom of our laws has condemned to die, had been detected in their rudiments of robbery, they might, by proper discipline and useful labour, have been disentangled from their habits, they might have escaped all the temptation to subsequent crimes, and passed their days in reparation and penitence, and detected they might all have been, had the prosecutors been certain that their lives would have been spared. I believe, every thief will confess, that he has been more than once seized and dismissed; and that he has sometimes ventured upon capital crimes, because he knew, that those whom he injured would rather connive at his escape, than cloud their minds with the horrours of his death.

All laws against wickedness are ineffectual, unless some will inform, and some will prosecute; but till we mitigate the penalties for mere violations of property, information will always be hated, and prosecution dreaded. The heart of a good man cannot but recoil at the thought of punishing a slight injury with death; especially when he remembers, that the thief might have procured safety by another crime, from which he was restrained only by his remaining virtue.

The obligations to assist the exercise of publick justice are indeed strong; but they will certainly be overpowered by tenderness for life. What is punished with severity contrary to our ideas of adequate retribution, will be seldom discovered; and multitudes will be suffered to advance from crime to crime, till they deserve death, because, if they had been sooner prosecuted, they would have suffered death before they deserved it.

This scheme of invigorating the laws by relaxation, and extirpating wickedness by lenity, is so remote from common practice, that I might reasonably fear to expose it to the publick, could it be supported only by my own observations: I shall, therefore, by ascribing it to its author, Sir Thomas More, endeavour to procure it that attention, which I wish always paid to prudence, to justice, and to mercy.

Rambler, No. 114

Courage and Enterprise

> ——*Nunc, o nunc, Dædale, dixit,*
> *Materiam, qua sis ingeniosus, habes.*
> *Possidet en terras, et possidet æquora, Minos:*
> *Nec tellus nostræ, nec patet unda fugæ.*
> *Restat iter cælo: cælo tentabimus ire.*
> *Da venium cæpto, Jupiter alte, meo.*   OVID.

> Now, Dædalus, behold, by fate assign'd,
> A task proportion'd to thy mighty mind!
> Unconquer'd bars on earth and sea withstand;
> Thine, Minos, is the main, and thine the land.
> The skies are open—let us try the skies:
> Forgive, great Jove, the daring enterprise.

Moralists, like other writers, instead of casting their eyes abroad in the living world, and endeavouring to form maxims of practice and new hints of theory, content their curiosity with that secondary knowledge which books afford, and think themselves entitled to reverence by a new arrangement of an ancient system, or new illustration of established principles. The sage precepts of the first instructors of the world are transmitted from age to age with little variation, and echoed from one author to another, not perhaps without some loss of their original force at every repercussion.

I know not whether any other reason than this idleness of imitation can be assigned for that uniform and constant partiality, by which some vices have hitherto escaped censure, and some virtues wanted recommendation; nor can I discover why else we have been warned only against part of our enemies, while the rest have been suffered to steal upon us without notice; why the heart has on one side been doubly fortified, and laid open on the other to the incursions of errour, and the ravages of vice.

Among the favourite topicks of moral declamation, may be numbered the miscarriages of imprudent boldness, and the folly of attempts beyond our power. Every page of every philosopher is crowded with examples of temerity that sunk under burdens which she laid upon herself, and called out enemies to battle by whom she was destroyed.

Their remarks are too just to be disputed, and too salutary to be rejected; but there is likewise some danger lest timorous prudence should be inculcated, till courage and enterprise are wholly repressed, and the mind congealed in perpetual inactivity by the fatal influence of frigorifick wisdom.

Every man should, indeed, carefully compare his force with his undertaking; for though we ought not to live only for our own sakes, and though therefore danger or difficulty should not be avoided merely because we may expose ourselves to misery or disgrace; yet it may be justly required of us, not to throw away our lives upon inadequate and hopeless designs, since we might, by a just estimate of our abilities, become more useful to mankind.

There is an irrational contempt of danger, which approaches nearly to the folly, if not the guilt, of suicide; there is a ridiculous perseverance in impracticable schemes, which is justly punished with ignominy and reproach. But in the wide regions of probability, which are the proper province of prudence and election, there is always room to deviate on either side of rectitude without rushing against apparent absurdity; and, according to the inclinations of nature, or the impressions of precept, the daring and the cautious may move in different directions without touching upon rashness or cowardice.

That there is a middle path which it is every man's duty to find, and to keep, is unanimously confessed: but it is likewise acknowledged that this middle path is so narrow, that it cannot easily be discovered, and so little beaten, that there are no certain marks by which it can be followed: the care therefore of all those who conduct others has been, that whenever they decline into obliquities, they should tend towards the side of safety.

It can, indeed, raise no wonder that temerity has been generally censured; for it is one of the vices with which few can be charged, and which therefore great numbers are ready to condemn. It is the vice of noble and generous minds, the exuberance of magnanimity, and the ebullition of genius; and is therefore not regarded with much tenderness, because it never flatters us by that appearance of softness and imbecility which is commonly necessary to conciliate compassion. But if the same attention had been applied to the search of arguments against the folly of presupposing impossibilities and anticipating frustration, I know not whether many would not have been roused to usefulness, who, having been taught to confound prudence with timidity, never ventured to excel, lest they should unfortunately fail.

It is necessary to distinguish our own interest from that of others, and that distinction will perhaps assist us in fixing the just limits of caution and adventurousness. In an undertaking that involves the happiness or the safety of many, we have certainly no right to hazard more than is allowed by those who partake the danger; but where only ourselves can suffer by miscarriage, we are not confined within such narrow limits; and still less is the reproach of temerity, when numbers will receive advantage by success, and only one be incommoded by failure.

Men are generally willing to hear precepts by which ease is favoured; and as no resentment is raised by general representations of human folly, even in those who are most eminently jealous of comparative reputation, we confess, without reluctance, that vain man is ignorant of his own weakness, and therefore frequently presumes to attempt what he can never accomplish; but it ought likewise to be remembered, that man is no less ignorant of his own powers, and might perhaps have accomplished a thousand designs, which the prejudices of cowardice restrained him from attempting.

It is observed in the golden verses of Pythagoras, that *Power is never far from necessity*. The vigour of the human mind quickly appears, when there is no longer any place for doubt and hesitation, when diffidence is absorbed in the sense of danger, or overwhelmed by some resistless passion. We then soon discover, that difficulty is, for the most part, the daughter of idleness, that the obstacles with which our way seemed to be obstructed were only phantoms, which we believed real, because we durst not advance to a close examination; and we learn that it is impossible to determine without experience how much constancy may endure, or perseverance perform.

But, whatever pleasure may be found in the review of distresses when art or courage has surmounted them, few will be persuaded to wish that they may be awakened by want or terrour to the conviction of their own abilities. Every one should therefore endeavour to invigorate himself by reason and reflection, and determine to exert the latent force that nature may have reposed in him, before the hour of exigence comes upon him, and compulsion shall torture him to diligence. It is below the dignity of a reasonable being to owe that strength to necessity which ought always to act at the call of choice, or to need any other motive to industry than the desire of performing his duty.

Reflections that may drive away despair, cannot be wanting to him who considers how much life is now advanced beyond the state of naked, undisciplined, un-instructed nature. Whatever has been effected for convenience or elegance, while it was yet unknown, was believed impossible; and therefore would never have been attempted, had not some, more daring than the rest, adventured to bid defiance to prejudice and censure. Nor is there yet any reason to doubt that the same labour would be rewarded with the same success. There are qualities in the products of nature yet undiscovered, and combinations in the powers of art yet untried. It is the duty of every man to endeavour that something may be added by his industry to the hereditary aggregate of knowledge and happiness. To add much can indeed be the lot of few, but to add something, however little, every one may hope; and of every honest endeavour, it is certain, that, however unsuccessful, it will be at last rewarded.

Rambler, No. 129

Pedantry

Quo virtus, quo ferat error? HOR.

Now say, where virtue stops, and vice begins?

As any action or posture, long continued, will distort and disfigure the limbs; so the mind likewise is crippled and contracted by perpetual application to the same set of ideas. It is easy to guess the trade of an artisan by his knees, his fingers, or his shoulders: and there are few among men of the more liberal professions, whose minds do not carry the brand of their calling, or whose conversation does not quickly discover to what class of the community they belong.

These peculiarities have been of great use, in the general hostility which every part of mankind exercises against the rest, to furnish insults and sarcasms. Every art has its dialect, uncouth and ungrateful to all whom custom has not reconciled to its sound, and which therefore becomes ridiculous by a slight misapplication, or unnecessary repetition.

The general reproach with which ignorance revenges the superciliousness of learning, is that of pedantry; a censure which every man incurs, who has at any time the misfortune to talk to those who cannot understand him, and by which the modest and timorous are sometimes frighted from the display of their acquisitions, and the exertion of their powers.

The name of a pedant is so formidable to young men when they first sally from their colleges, and is so liberally scattered by those who mean to boast their elegance of education, easiness of manners, and knowledge of the world, that it seems to require particular consideration; since, perhaps, if it were once understood, many a heart might be freed from painful apprehensions, and many a tongue delivered from restraint.

Pedantry is the unseasonable ostentation of learning. It may be discovered either in the choice of a subject, or in the manner of treating it. He is undoubtedly guilty of pedantry, who, when he has made himself master of some abstruse and uncultivated part of knowledge, obtrudes his remarks and discoveries upon those whom he believes unable to judge of his proficiency, and from whom, as he cannot fear contradiction, he cannot properly expect applause.

To this errour the student is sometimes betrayed by the natural recurrence of the mind to its common employment, by the pleasure which every man receives from the recollection of pleasing images, and the desire of dwelling upon topicks, on which he knows himself able to speak with justness. But because we are seldom so far prejudiced in favour of each other, as to search out for palliations, this failure of politeness is imputed always to vanity; and the harmless collegiate, who, perhaps, intended entertainment and instruction, or at worst only spoke without sufficient reflection upon the character of his hearers, is censured as arrogant or overbearing, and eager to extend his renown, in contempt of the convenience of society, and the laws of conversation.

All discourse of which others cannot partake, is not only an irksome usurpation of the time devoted to pleasure and entertainment, but, what never fails to excite very keen resentment, an insolent assertion of superiority, and a triumph over less enlightened understandings. The pedant is, therefore, not only heard with weariness, but malignity; and those who conceive themselves insulted by his knowledge, never fail to tell with acrimony how injudiciously it was exerted.

To avoid this dangerous imputation, scholars sometimes divest themselves with too much haste of their academical formality, and in their endeavours to accommodate their notions and their style to common conceptions, talk rather of any thing than of that which they understand, and sink into insipidity of sentiment and meanness of expression.

There prevails among men of letters an opinion, that all appearance of science is particularly hateful to women; and that therefore, whoever desires to be well received in female assemblies, must qualify himself by a total rejection of all that is serious, rational, or important; must consider argument or criticism, as perpetually interdicted; and devote all his attention to trifles, and all his eloquence to compliment.

Students often form their notions of the present generation from the writings of the past, and are not very early informed of those changes which the gradual diffusion of knowledge, or the sudden caprice of fashion, produces in the world. Whatever might be the state of female literature in the last century, there is now no longer any danger lest the scholar should want an adequate audience at the tea-table; and whoever thinks it necessary to regulate his conversation by antiquated rules, will be rather despised for his futility than caressed for his politeness.

To talk intentionally in a manner above the comprehension of those whom we address, is unquestionable pedantry; but surely complaisance requires, that no man should, without proof, conclude his company incapable of following him to the highest elevation of his fancy, or the utmost extent of his knowledge. It is always safer to err in favour of others than of ourselves, and therefore we seldom hazard much by endeavouring to excel.

It ought at least to be the care of learning, when she quits her exaltation, to descend with dignity. Nothing is more despicable than the airiness and jocularity of a man bred to severe science, and solitary meditation. To trifle agreeably is a secret which schools cannot impart; that gay negligence and vivacious levity, which charm down resistance wherever they appear, are never attainable by him who, having spent his first years among the dust of

libraries, enters late into the gay world with an unpliant
attention and established habits.

It is observed in the panegyrick on Fabricius the
mechanist, that, though forced by publick employments
into mingled conversation, he never lost the modesty
and seriousness of the convent, nor drew ridicule upon
himself by an affected imitation of fashionable life. To
the same praise every man devoted to learning ought to
aspire. If he attempts the softer arts of pleasing, and
endeavours to learn the graceful bow and the familiar
embrace, the insinuating accent and the general smile,
he will lose the respect due to the character of learning,
without arriving at the envied honour of doing any thing
with elegance and facility.

Theophrastus was discovered not to be a native of
Athens, by so strict an adherence to the Attic dialect,
as showed that he had learned it not by custom, but
by rule. A man not early formed to habitual elegance,
betrays in like manner the effects of his education, by
an unnecessary anxiety of behaviour. It is as possible to
become pedantick by fear of pedantry, as to be troublesome by ill-timed civility. There is no kind of impertinence more justly censurable, than his who is always
labouring to level thoughts to intellects higher than his
own; who apologizes for every word which his own
narrowness of converse inclines him to think unusual;
keeps the exuberance of his faculties under visible restraint; is solicitous to anticipate inquiries by needless
explanations; and endeavours to shade his own abilities,
lest weak eyes should be dazzled with their lustre.

Rambler, No. 173

Life and Letters

Ταῦτ᾽εἰδὼς σοφὸς ἴσθι, μάτην δ᾽ Ἐπίκουρον ἔασον
Ποῦ το κενὸν ζητεῖν, καὶ τίνες αἱ μονάδες.   AUTOMEDON.

On life, on morals, be thy thoughts employ'd;
Leave to the schools their atoms and their void.

It is somewhere related by Le Clerc, that a wealthy trader
of good understanding, having the common ambition to

breed his son a scholar, carried him to an university, resolving to use his own judgment in the choice of a tutor. He had been taught, by whatever intelligence, the nearest way to the heart of an academick, and at his arrival entertained all who came about him with such profusion, that the professors were lured by the smell of his table from their books, and flocked round him with all the cringes of awkward complaisance. This eagerness answered the merchant's purpose: he glutted them with delicacies and softened them with caresses, till he prevailed upon one after another to open his bosom, and make a discovery of his competitions, jealousies, and resentments. Having thus learned each man's character, partly from himself, and partly from his acquaintances, he resolved to find some other education for his son, and went away convinced, that a scholastick life has no other tendency than to vitiate the morals and contract the understanding: nor would he afterwards hear with patience the praises of the ancient authors, being persuaded that scholars of all ages must have been the same, and that Xenophon and Cicero were professors of some former university, and therefore mean and selfish, ignorant and servile, like those whom he had lately visited and forsaken.

Envy, curiosity, and a sense of the imperfection of our present state, incline us to estimate the advantages which are in the possession of others above their real value. Every one must have remarked, what powers and prerogatives the vulgar imagine to be conferred by learning. A man of science is expected to excel the unlettered and unenlightened even on occasions where literature is of no use, and among weak minds, loses part of his reverence, by discovering no superiority in those parts of life, in which all are unavoidably equal; as when a monarch makes a progress to the remoter provinces, the rusticks are said sometimes to wonder that they find him of the same size with themselves.

These demands of prejudice and folly can never be satisfied; and therefore many of the imputations which learning suffers from disappointed ignorance, are without reproach. But there are some failures, to which men of study are peculiarly exposed. Every condition has its disadvantages. The circle of knowledge is too wide for the most active and diligent intellect, and while science is pursued, other accomplishments are neglected; as a small garrison must leave one part of an extensive fortress naked, when an alarm calls them to another.

The learned, however, might generally support their dignity with more success, if they suffered not themselves to be misled by the desire of superfluous attainments. Raphael, in return to Adam's inquiries into the courses of the stars, and the revolutions of heaven, counsels him to withdraw his mind from idle speculations, and employ his faculties upon nearer and more interesting objects, the survey of his own life, the subjection of his passions, the knowledge of duties which must daily be performed, and the detection of dangers which must daily be incurred?

This angelick counsel every man of letters should always have before him. He that devotes himself to retired study naturally sinks from omission to forgetfulness of social duties; he must be therefore sometimes awakened and recalled to the general condition of mankind.

I am far from any intention to limit curiosity, or confine the labours of learning to arts of immediate and necessary use. It is only from the various essays of experimental industry, and the vague excursions of minds sent out upon discovery, that any advancement of knowledge can be expected; and, though many must be disappointed in their labours, yet they are not to be charged with having spent their time in vain; their example contributed to inspire emulation, and their miscarriages taught others the way to success.

But the distant hope of being one day useful or eminent, ought not to mislead us too far from that study, which is equally requisite to the great and mean, to the celebrated and obscure; the art of moderating the desires, of repressing the appetites, and of conciliating or retaining the favour of mankind.

No man can imagine the course of his own life, or the

conduct of the world around him, unworthy his attention; yet, among the sons of learning, many seem to have thought of every thing rather than of themselves, and to have observed every thing but what passes before their eyes: Many who toil through the intricacy of complicated systems, are insuperably embarrassed with the least perplexity in common affairs; many who compare the actions, and ascertain the characters of ancient heroes, let their own days glide away without examination, and suffer vitious habits to encroach upon their minds without resistance or detection.

The most frequent reproach of the scholastick race is the want of fortitude, not martial but philosophick. Men bred in shades and silence, taught to immure themselves at sunset, and accustomed to no other weapon than syllogism, may be allowed to feel terrour at personal danger, and to be disconcerted by tumult and alarm. But why should he whose life is spent in contemplation, and whose business is only to discover truth, be unable to rectify the fallacies of imagination, or contend successfully against prejudice and passion? To what end has he read and meditated, if he gives up his understanding to false appearances, and suffers himself to be enslaved by fear of evils to which only folly or vanity can expose him, or elated by advantages to which, as they are equally conferred upon the good and bad, no real dignity is annexed?

Such, however, is the state of the world, that the most obsequious of the slaves of pride, the most rapturous of the gazers upon wealth, the most officious of the whisperers of greatness, are collected from seminaries appropriated to the study of wisdom and of virtue, where it was intended that appetite should learn to be content with little, and that hope should aspire only to honours which no human power can give or take away.

The student, when he comes forth into the world, instead of congratulating himself upon his exemption from the errours of those whose opinions have been formed by accident or custom, and who live without any certain principles of conduct, is commonly in haste to mingle with the multitude, and show his sprightliness and ductility by an expeditious compliance with fashions or vices. The first smile of a man, whose fortune gives him power to reward his dependants, commonly enchants him beyond resistance; the glare of equipage, the sweets of luxury, the liberality of general promises, the softness of habitual affability, fill his imagination; and he soon ceases to have any other wish than to be well received, or any measure of right and wrong, but the opinion of his patron.

A man flattered and obeyed, learns to exact grosser adulation, and enjoin lower submission. Neither our virtues nor vices are all our own. If there were no cowardice, there would be little insolence; pride cannot rise to any great degree, but by the concurrence of blandishment or the sufferance of tameness. The wretch who would shrink and crouch before one that should dart his eyes upon him with the spirit of natural equality, becomes capricious and tyrannical when he sees himself approached with a downcast look, and hears the soft address of awe and servility. To those who are willing to purchase favour by cringes and compliance, is to be imputed the haughtiness that leaves nothing to be hoped by firmness and integrity.

If, instead of wandering after the meteors of philosophy, which fill the world with splendour for a while, and then sink and are forgotten, the candidates of learning fixed their eyes upon the permanent lustre of moral and religious truth, they would find a more certain direction to happiness. A little plausibility of discourse, and acquaintance with unnecessary speculations, is dearly purchased, when it excludes those instructions which fortify the heart with resolution, and exalt the spirit to independence.

Rambler, No. 180

1752

Too Long upon the Stage

Solve senescentem mature sanus equum, ne
Peccet ad extremum ridendus.   HOR.

The voice of reason cries with winning force,
Loose from the rapid car your aged horse,
Lest, in the race derided, left behind,
He drag his jaded limbs and burst his wind.   FRANCIS.

Such is the emptiness of human enjoyment, that we are always impatient of the present. Attainment is followed by neglect, and possession by disgust; and the malicious remark of the Greek epigrammatist on marriage may be applied to every other course of life, that its two days of happiness are the first and the last.

Few moments are more pleasing than those in which the mind is concerting measures for a new undertaking. From the first hint that wakens the fancy till the hour of actual execution, all is improvement and progress, triumph and felicity. Every hour brings additions to the original scheme, suggests some new expedient to secure success, or discovers consequential advantages not hitherto foreseen. While preparations are made, and materials accumulated, day glides after day through elysian prospects, and the heart dances to the song of hope.

Such is the pleasure of projecting, that many content themselves with a succession of visionary schemes, and wear out their allotted time in the calm amusement of contriving what they never attempt or hope to execute.

Others, not able to feast their imagination with pure ideas, advance somewhat nearer to the grossness of action, with great diligence collect whatever is requisite to their design, and, after a thousand researches and consultations, are snatched away by death, as they stand *in procinctu*[1] waiting for a proper opportunity to begin.

If there were no other end of life, than to find some adequate solace for every day, I know not whether any condition could be preferred to that of the man who

[1 Ready for action.]

involves himself in his own thoughts, and never suffers experience to show him the vanity of speculation; for no sooner are notions reduced to practice, than tranquillity and confidence forsake the breast; every day brings its task, and often without bringing abilities to perform it: difficulties embarrass, uncertainty perplexes, opposition retards, censure exasperates, or neglect depresses. We proceed because we have begun; we complete our design that the labour already spent may not be vain: but, as expectation gradually dies away, the gay smile of alacrity disappears, we are compelled to implore severer powers, and trust the event to patience and constancy.

When once our labour has begun, the comfort that enables us to endure it is the prospect of its end; for though in every long work there are some joyous intervals of self-applause, when the attention is recreated by unexpected facility, and the imagination soothed by incidental excellencies; yet the toil with which performance struggles after idea, is so irksome and disgusting, and so frequent is the necessity of resting below that perfection which we imagined within our reach, that seldom any man obtains more from his endeavours than a painful conviction of his defects, and a continual resuscitation of desires which he feels himself unable to gratify.

So certainly is weariness the concomitant of our undertakings, that every man, in whatever he is engaged, consoles himself with the hope of change; if he has made his way by assiduity to publick employment, he talks among his friends of the delight of retreat; if, by the necessity of solitary application, he is secluded from the world, he listens with a beating heart to distant noises, longs to mingle with living beings, and resolves to take hereafter his fill of diversions, or display his abilities on the universal theatre, and enjoy the pleasure of distinction and applause.

Every desire, however innocent, grows dangerous, as by long indulgence it becomes ascendant in the mind. When we have been much accustomed to consider any thing as capable of giving happiness, it is not easy to restrain our ardour, or to forbear some precipitation in our advances, and irregularity in our pursuits. He that has cultivated the tree, watched the swelling bud and opening blossom, and pleased himself with computing how much every sun and shower add to its growth, scarcely stays till the fruit has obtained its maturity, but defeats his own cares by eagerness to reward them. When we have diligently laboured for any purpose, we are willing to believe that we have attained it, and, because we have already done much, too suddenly conclude that no more is to be done.

All attraction is increased by the approach of the attracting body. We never find ourselves so desirous to finish, as in the latter part of our work, or so impatient of delay, as when we know that delay cannot be long. This unseasonable importunity of discontent may be partly imputed to languor and weariness, which must always oppress those more whose toil has been longer continued; but the greater part usually proceeds from frequent contemplation of that ease which is now considered as within reach, and which, when it has once flattered our hopes, we cannot suffer to be withheld.

In some of the noblest compositions of wit, the conclusion falls below the vigour and spirit of the first books; and as a genius is not to be degraded by the imputation of human failings, the cause of this declension is commonly sought in the structure of the work, and plausible reasons are given why in the defective part less ornament was necessary, or less could be admitted. But, perhaps, the author would have confessed, that his fancy was tired, and his perseverance broken; that he knew his design to be unfinished, but that, when he saw the end so near, he could no longer refuse to be at rest.

Against the instillations of this frigid opiate, the heart should be secured by all the considerations which once concurred to kindle the ardour of enterprise. Whatever motive first incited action, has still greater force to stimulate perseverance; since he that might have lain still at first in blameless obscurity, cannot afterwards desist but with infamy and reproach. He, whom a doubtful promise of distant good could encourage to set difficulties at defiance, ought not to remit his vigour, when he has almost obtained his recompense. To faint or loiter, when only the last efforts are required, is to steer the ship through tempests, and abandon it to the winds in sight of land; it is to break the ground and scatter the seed, and at last to neglect the harvest.

The masters of rhetorick direct, that the most forcible arguments be produced in the latter part of an oration, lest they should be effaced or perplexed by supervenient images. This precept may be justly extended to the series of life: Nothing is ended with honour, which does not conclude better than it began. It is not sufficient to maintain the first vigour; for excellence loses its effect upon the mind by custom, as light after a time ceases to dazzle. Admiration must be continued by that novelty which first produced it, and how much soever is given, there must always be reason to imagine that more remains.

We not only are most sensible to the last impressions, but such is the unwillingness of mankind to admit transcendent merit, that, though it be difficult to obliterate the reproach of miscarriages by any subsequent achievement, however illustrious, yet the reputation raised by a long train of success may be finally ruined by a single failure; for weakness or errour will be always remembered by that malice and envy which it gratifies.

For the prevention of that disgrace, which lassitude and negligence may bring at last upon the greatest performances, it is necessary to proportion carefully our labour to our strength. If the design comprises many parts, equally essential, and therefore not to be separated, the only time for caution is before we engage; the powers of the mind must be then impartially estimated, and it must be remembered that, not to complete the plan, is not to have begun it; and that nothing is done, while any thing is omitted.

But, if the task consists in the repetition of single acts, no one of which derives its efficacy from the rest, it may be attempted with less scruple, because there is always opportunity to retreat with honour. The danger is only, lest we expect from the world the indulgence with which most are disposed to treat themselves; and in the hour of listlessness imagine, that the diligence of one day will atone for the idleness of another, and that applause begun by approbation will be continued by habit.

He that is himself weary will soon weary the publick. Let him therefore lay down his employment, whatever it be, who can no longer exert his former activity or attention; let him not endeavour to struggle with censure, or obstinately infest the stage till a general hiss commands him to depart.

Rambler, No. 207

1750

Milton

The Making of Paradise Lost

It is now more than half a century since the Paradise Lost, having broke through the clouds with which the unpopularity of the author, for a time, obscured it, has attracted the general admiration of mankind; who have endeavoured to compensate the errour of their first neglect, by lavish praises and boundless veneration. There seems to have arisen a contest, among men of genius and literature, who should most advance its honour, or best distinguish its beauties. Some have revised editions, other have published commentaries, and all have endeavoured to make their particular studies, in some degree, subservient to this general emulation.

Among the inquiries to which this ardour of criticism has naturally given occasion, none is more obscure in itself, or more worthy of rational curiosity, than a retrospection of the progress of this mighty genius, in the construction of his work; a view of the fabrick gradually rising, perhaps from small beginnings, till its foundation rests in the centre, and its turrets sparkle in the skies; to trace back the structure, through all its varieties, to the simplicity of its first plan; to find what was first projected, whence the scheme was taken, how it was improved, by what assistance it was executed, and from

what stores the materials were collected, whether its
founder dug them from the quarries of nature, or demolished other buildings to embellish his own.

Preface to Lauder's *Essay on Milton's*
Use and Imitation of the Moderns

Milton's Memory

'Such is the caprice of fortune, this grand-daughter of a
man, who will be an everlasting glory to the nation, has
now for some years, with her husband, kept a little
chandler's or grocer's shop, for their subsistence, lately
at the lower Holloway, in the road between Highgate
and London, and at present in Cocklane, not far from
Shoreditch church.'[1]

That this relation is true cannot be questioned: but,
surely, the honour of letters, the dignity of sacred poetry,
the spirit of the English nation, and the glory of human
nature, require—that it should be true no longer.—In
an age, in which statues are erected to the honour of this
great writer, in which his effigy has been diffused on
medals, and his work propagated by translations, and
illustrated by commentaries; in an age, which amidst all
its vices, and all its follies, has not become infamous for
want of charity: it may be, surely, allowed to hope, that
the living remains of Milton will be no longer suffered
to languish in distress. It is yet in the power of a great
people, to reward the poet whose name they boast, and
from their alliance to whose genius, they claim some kind
of superiority to every other nation of the earth; that
poet, whose works may possibly be read when every
other monument of British greatness shall be obliterated;
to reward him—not with pictures, or with medals, which,
if he sees, he sees with contempt, but—with tokens of
gratitude, which he, perhaps, may even now consider as
not unworthy the regard of an immortal spirit. And
surely, to those, who refuse their names to no other
scheme of expense, it will not be unwelcome, that a
SUBSCRIPTION is proposed, for relieving, in the languor of

[1 Quoted from Newton's *Paradise Lost*.]

age, the pains of disease, and the contempt of poverty, the grand-daughter of the author of *Paradise Lost*. Nor can it be questioned, that if I, who have been marked out as the Zoilus of Milton, think this regard due to his posterity, the design will be warmly seconded by those, whose lives have been employed in discovering his excellencies, and extending his reputation.

Postscript to the above

Prologue to Comus

Ye patriot Crouds, who burn for *England*'s Fame,
Ye Nymphs, whose Bosoms beat at MILTON's Name,
Whose gen'rous Zeal, unbought by flatt'ring Rhimes,
Shames the mean Pensions of *Augustan* Times;
Immortal Patrons of succeeding Days,
Attend this Prelude of perpetual Praise!
Let Wit, condemn'd the feeble War to wage
With close Malevolence, or public Rage;
Let Study, worn with Virtue's fruitless Lore,
Behold this Theatre, and grieve no more.
This Night, distinguish'd by your Smile, shall tell,
That never BRITON can in vain excel;
The slighted Arts Futurity shall trust,
And rising Ages hasten to be just.
At length our mighty Bard's victorious Lays
Fill the loud Voice of universal Praise,
And baffled Spite, with hopeless Anguish dumb,
Yields to Renown the Centuries to come.
With ardent Haste, each Candidate of Fame
Ambitious catches at his tow'ring Name:
He sees, and pitying sees, vain Wealth bestow
Those pageant Honours which he scorn'd below:
While Crowds aloft the laureat Bust behold,
Or trace his Form on circulating Gold,
Unknown, unheeded, long his Offspring lay,
And Want hung threat'ning o'er her slow Decay.
What tho' she shine with no MILTONIAN Fire,
No fav'ring Muse her morning Dreams inspire;

Yet softer Claims the melting Heart engage,
Her Youth laborious, and her blameless Age:
Hers the mild Merits of domestic Life,
The patient Suff'rer, and the faithful Wife.
Thus grac'd with humble Virtue's native Charms
Her Grandsire leaves her in *Britannia*'s Arms,
Secure with Peace, with Competence, to dwell,
While tutelary Nations guard her Cell.
Yours is the Charge, ye Fair, ye Wise, ye Brave!
'Tis yours to crown Desert—beyond the Grave!

To James Elphinston

Dear Sir

You have, as I find by every kind of evidence, lost an excellent mother; and I hope you will not think me incapable of partaking of your grief. I have a mother now eighty-two years of age, whom therefore I must soon lose, unless it please God that she rather should mourn for me. I read the letters in which you relate your mother's death to Mrs. Strahan; and think I do myself honour when I tell you that I read them with tears; but tears are neither to me nor to you of any farther use, when once the tribute of nature has been paid. The business of life summons us away from useless grief, and calls us to the exercise of those virtues of which we are lamenting our deprivation. The greatest benefit which one friend can confer upon another, is to guard, and incite, and elevate his virtues. This your mother will still perform, if you diligently preserve the memory of her life, and of her death: a life, so far as I can learn, useful, wise, and innocent; and a death resigned, peaceful, and holy. I cannot forbear to mention, that neither reason nor revelation denies you to hope, that you may encrease her happiness by obeying her precepts; and that she may, in her present state, look with pleasure, upon every act of virtue to which her instructions or example have contributed. Whether this be more than a pleasing dream, or a just opinion of separate spirits, is indeed of no great importance to us, when we consider ourselves as acting under the eye of God: yet surely there is something pleasing in the belief, that our separation from those whom we love is merely corporeal; and it may be a great incitement to virtuous friendship, if it can be made probable, that that union which has received the divine approbation, shall continue to eternity.

There is one expedient, by which you may, in some degree, continue her presence. If you write down minutely what you remember of her from your earliest years, you will read it with great pleasure, and receive from it many hints of soothing recollection, when time shall remove her yet farther from you, and your grief shall be matured to veneration. To this, however painful for the present, I cannot but advise you, as to a source of comfort and satisfaction in the time to come; for all comfort and all satisfaction, is sincerely wished you by, Dear Sir, Your most obliged, most obedient, and most humble servant, Sam. Johnson.

Sept. 25, 1750.

Prayer on The Rambler

Almighty God, the giver of all good things, without whose help all Labour is ineffectual, and without whose grace all wisdom is folly, grant, I beseech Thee, that in this my undertaking, thy Holy Spirit may not be withheld from me, but that I may promote thy glory, and the Salvation both of myself and others; grant this, O Lord, for the sake of Jesus Christ. Amen.

Prayers and Meditations, 1785

1751
To Samuel Richardson

Dear Sir

Though Clarissa wants no help from external Splendour I was glad to see her improved in her appearance but more glad to find that she was now got above all fears of prolixity, and confident enough of success, to supply whatever had been hitherto suppressed. I never indeed found a hint of any such defalcation, but I fretted: for though the Story is long, every letter is short.

I wish you would add an *Index Rerum*, that when the reader recollects any incident he may easily find it, which at present he cannot do, unless he knows in which volume it is told; For Clarissa is not a performance to be read with eagerness and laid aside for ever, but will be occasionally consulted by the busy, the aged, and the studious, and therefore I beg that this Edition by which I suppose Posterity is to abide, may want nothing that can facilitate its use.

          I am Sir Your obliged humble Servant
March 9th 1750/51   Sam: Johnson

1752
Johnson's Wife's Death

'Jesus said unto her, I am the resurrection and the life: he that believeth in me, though he were dead, yet shall he live, And whosoever liveth, and believeth in me, shall never die.' JOHN xi. 25, 26, former part.

To afford adequate consolations to the last hour, to cheer the gloomy passage through the valley of the shadow of death, and to ease that anxiety, to which beings, prescient of their own dissolution, and conscious of their own danger, must be necessarily exposed, is the privilege only of revealed religion. All those, to whom the supernatural light of heavenly doctrine has never been imparted, however formidable for power, or illustrious for wisdom, have wanted that knowledge of their future state which alone can give comfort to misery, or security to enjoyment; and have been forced to rush forwards to the grave, through the darkness of ignorance; or, if they happened to be more refined and inquisitive, to solace their passage with the fallacious and uncertain glimmer of philosophy.

There were, doubtless, at all times, as there are now, many who lived with very little thought concerning their end; many whose time was wholly filled up by publick or domestick business, by the pursuits of ambition, or the

desire of riches; many who dissolved themselves in luxurious enjoyment, and, when they could lull their minds
by any present pleasure, had no regard to distant events,
but withheld their imagination from sallying out into
futurity, or catching any terrour that might interrupt
their quiet; and there were many who rose so little above
animal life, that they were completely engrossed by the
objects about them, and had their views extended no
further than to the next hour; in whom the ray of reason
was half extinct, and had neither hopes nor fears, but of
some near advantage, or some pressing danger.

But multitudes there must always be, and greater multitudes as arts and civility prevail, who cannot wholly
withdraw their thoughts from death. All cannot be distracted with business, or stunned with the clamours of
assemblies, or the shouts of armies. All cannot live in the
perpetual dissipation of successive diversions, nor will
all enslave their understandings to their senses, and seek
felicity in the gross gratifications of appetite. Some must
always keep their reason and their fancy in action, and
seek either honour or pleasure from intellectual operations; and from them, others, more negligent or sluggish,
will be in time fixed or awakened; knowledge will be
perpetually diffused, and curiosity hourly enlarged.

But, when the faculties were once put in motion, when
the mind had broken loose from the shackles of sense, and
made excursions to remote consequences, the first consideration that would stop her course must be incessant
waste of life, the approach of age, and the certainty of
death; the approach of that time, in which strength must
fail, and pleasure fly away, and the certainty of that dissolution which shall put an end to all the prospects of this
world. It is impossible to think, and not sometimes to
think on death. Hope, indeed, has many powers of delu-
sion; whatever is possible, however unlikely, it will teach
us to promise ourselves; but death no man has escaped,
and, therefore, no man can hope to escape it. From this
dreadful expectation no shelter or refuge can be found.
Whatever we see, forces it upon us; whatever is, new or
old, flourishing or declining, either directly, or by very

short deduction, leads man to the consideration of his end;
and accordingly we find, that the fear of death has always
been considered as the great enemy of human quiet, the
polluter of the feast of happiness, and embitterer of the cup
of joy. The young man who rejoiceth in his youth, amidst
his musick and his gaiety, has always been disturbed with
the thought, that his youth will be quickly at an end. The
monarch, to whom it is said that he is a God, has always
been reminded by his own heart, that he shall die like
man.

This unwelcome conviction, which is thus continually
pressed upon the mind, every art has been employed to
oppose. The general remedy, in all ages, has been to chase
it away from the present moment, and to gain a suspense
of the pain that could not be cured. In the ancient
writings, we, therefore, find the shortness of life frequently
mentioned as an excitement to jollity and pleasure; and
may plainly discover, that the authors had no other
means of relieving that gloom with which the uncertainty
of human life clouded their conceptions. Some of the
philosophers, indeed, appear to have sought a nobler, and
a more certain remedy, and to have endeavoured to overpower the force of death by arguments, and to dispel the
gloom by the light of reason. They inquired into the
nature of the soul of man, and showed, at least probably,
that it is a substance distinct from matter, and, therefore,
independent on the body, and exempt from dissolution
and corruption. The arguments, whether physical or
moral, upon which they established this doctrine, it is not
necessary to recount to a Christian audience, by whom
it is believed upon more certain proofs, and higher
authority; since though they were such as might determine the calm mind of a philosopher, inquisitive only
after truth, and uninfluenced by external objects; yet they
were such as required leisure and capacity, not allowed
in general to mankind; they were such as many could
never understand, and of which, therefore, the efficacy
and comfort were confined to a small number, without
any benefit to the unenlightened multitude.

Such has been hitherto the nature of philosophical

arguments, and such it must probably for ever remain; for, though, perhaps, the successive industry of the studious may increase the number, or advance the probability, of arguments; and, though continual contemplation of matter will, I believe, show it, at length, wholly incapable of motion, sensation, or order, by any powers of its own, and, therefore, necessarily establish the immateriality, and, probably, the immortality of the soul; yet there never can be expected a time, in which the gross body of mankind can attend to such speculations, or can comprehend them; and, therefore, there never can be a time, in which this knowledge can be taught in such a manner, as to be generally conducive to virtue, or happiness, but by a messenger from God, from the Creator of the world, and the Father of spirits.

To persuade common and uninstructed minds to the belief of any fact, we may every day perceive, that the testimony of one man, whom they think worthy of credit, has more force than the arguments of a thousand reasoners, even when the arguments are such as they may be imagined completely qualified to comprehend. Hence it is plain, that the constitution of mankind is such, that abstruse and intellectual truths can be taught no otherwise than by positive assertion, supported by some sensible evidence, by which the assertor is secured from the suspicion of falsehood; and that if it should please God to inspire a teacher with some demonstration of the immortality of the soul, it would far less avail him for general instruction, than the power of working a miracle in its vindication, unless God should, at the same time, inspire all the hearers with docility and apprehension, and turn, at once, all the sensual, the giddy, the lazy, the busy, the corrupt, and the proud, into humble, abstracted, and diligent philosophers.

To bring life and immortality to light; to give such proofs of our future existence, as may influence the most narrow mind, and fill the most capacious intellect; to open prospects beyond the grave, in which the thought may expatiate without obstruction; and to supply a refuge and support to the mind amidst all the miseries of decaying nature, is the peculiar excellence of the gospel of Christ. Without this heavenly Instructor, he who feels himself sinking under the weight of years, or melting away by the slow waste of a lingering disease, has no other remedy than obdurate patience, a gloomy resignation to that which cannot be avoided; and he who follows his friend, or whoever there is yet dearer than a friend, to the grave, can have no other consolation than that which he derives from the general misery; the reflection, that he suffers only what the rest of mankind must suffer; a poor consideration, which rather awes us to silence, than sooths us to quiet, and which does not abate the sense of our calamity, though it may sometimes make us ashamed to complain.

But so much is our condition improved by the gospel, so much is the sting of death rebated, that we may now be invited to the contemplation of our mortality, as to a pleasing employment of the mind, to an exercise delightful and recreative, not only when calamity and persecution drive us out from the assemblies of men, and sorrow and woe represent the grave as a refuge and an asylum, but even in the hours of the highest earthly prosperity, when our cup is full, and when we have laid up stores for ourselves; for, in him who believes the promise of the Saviour of the world, it can cause no disturbance to remember, that this night his soul may be required of him; and he who suffers one of the sharpest evils which this life can show, amidst all its varieties of misery; he that has lately been separated from the person whom a long participation of good and evil had endeared to him; he who has seen kindness snatched from his arms, and fidelity torn from his bosom; he whose ear is no more to be delighted with tender instruction, and whose virtue shall be no more awakened by the seasonable whispers of mild reproof, may yet look, without horrour, on the tomb which encloses the remains of what he loved and honoured, as upon a place which, if it revives the sense of his loss, may calm him with the hope of that state in which there shall be no more grief or separation.

To Christians the celebration of a funeral is by no

means a solemnity of barren and unavailing sorrow, but
established by the church for other purposes.

First, for the consolation of sorrow. Secondly, for the
enforcement of piety. The mournful solemnity of the
burial of the dead is instituted, first, for the consolation
of that grief to which the best minds, if not supported and
regulated by religion, are most liable. They who most
endeavour the happiness of others, who devote their
thoughts to tenderness and pity, and studiously maintain the reciprocation of kindness, by degrees mingle
their souls, in such a manner, as to feel, from separation,
a total destitution of happiness, a sudden abruption of
all their prospects, a cessation of all their hopes, schemes,
and desires. The whole mind becomes a gloomy vacuity,
without any image or form of pleasure, a chaos of confused wishes, directed to no particular end, or to that
which, while we wish, we cannot hope to obtain; for the
dead will not revive; those whom God has called away
from the present state of existence, can be seen no more
in it; we must go to them; but they cannot return to us.

Yet, to show that grief is vain, is to afford very little
comfort; yet this is all that reason can afford; but religion,
our only friend in the moment of distress, in the moment
when the help of man is vain, when fortitude and
cowardice sink down together, and the sage and the
virgin mingle their lamentations; religion will inform us,
that sorrow and complaint are not only vain, but unreasonable and erroneous. The voice of God, speaking
by his Son, and his apostles, will instruct us, that she,
whose departure we now mourn, is not dead, but sleepeth;
that only her body is committed to the ground, but that
the soul is returned to God, who gave it; that God, who
is infinitely merciful, who hateth nothing that he has
made, who desireth not the death of a sinner; to that God,
who only can compare performance with ability, who
alone knows how far the heart has been pure, or corrupted, how inadvertency has surprised, fear has betrayed, or weakness has impeded; to that God, who
marks every aspiration after a better state, who hears the
prayer which the voice cannot utter, records the purpose

that perished without opportunity of action, the wish
that vanished away without attainment, who is always
ready to receive the penitent, to whom sincere contrition
is never late, and who will accept the tears of a returning
sinner.

Such are the reflections to which we are called by the
voice of Truth; and from these we shall find that comfort which philosophy cannot supply, and that peace
which the world cannot give. The contemplation of the
mercy of God may justly afford some consolation, even
when the office of burial is performed to those who have
been snatched away without visible amendment of their
lives: for, who shall presume to determine the state of
departed souls, to lay open what God hath concealed,
and to search the counsels of the Most Highest?—But,
with more confident hope of pardon and acceptance,
may we commit those to the receptacles of mortality,
who have lived without any open or enormous crimes; who
have endeavoured to propitiate God by repentance,
and have died, at last, with hope and resignation. Among
these she surely may be remembered whom we have
followed hither to the tomb, to pay her the last honours,
and to resign her to the grave: she, whom many, who
now hear me, have known, and whom none, who were
capable of distinguishing either moral or intellectual
excellence, could know, without esteem, or tenderness.
To praise the extent of her knowledge, the acuteness of
her wit, the accuracy of her judgment, the force of her
sentiments, or the elegance of her expression, would ill
suit with the occasion.

Such praise would little profit the living, and as little
gratify the dead, who is now in a place where vanity and
competition are forgotten for ever; where she finds a cup
of water given for the relief of a poor brother, a prayer
uttered for the mercy of God to those whom she wanted
power to relieve, a word of instruction to ignorance, a
smile of comfort to misery, of more avail than all those
accomplishments which confer honour and distinction
among the sons of folly. Yet, let it be remembered, that
her wit was never employed to scoff at goodness, nor her

reason to dispute against truth. In this age of wild opinions, she was as free from skepticism as the cloistered virgin. She never wished to signalize herself by the singularity of paradox. She had a just diffidence of her own reason, and desired to practise rather than dispute. Her practice was such as her opinions naturally produced. She was exact and regular in her devotions, full of confidence in the Divine mercy, submissive to the dispensations of providence, extensively charitable in her judgments and opinions, grateful for every kindness that she received, and willing to impart assistance of every kind to all whom her little power enabled her to benefit. She passed through many months of languor, weakness, and decay, without a single murmur of impatience, and often expressed her adoration of that mercy which granted her so long time for recollection and penitence. That she had no failings cannot be supposed: but she has now appeared before the Almighty Judge; and it would ill become beings like us, weak and sinful as herself, to remember those faults which, we trust, Eternal Purity has pardoned.

Let us, therefore, preserve her memory for no other end but to imitate her virtues; and let us add her example to the motives to piety which this solemnity was, secondly, instituted to enforce.

It would not, indeed, be reasonable to expect, did we not know the inattention and perverseness of mankind, that any one who had followed a funeral, could fail to return home without new resolutions of a holy life: for, who can see the final period of all human schemes and undertakings, without conviction of the vanity of all that terminates in the present state? For, who can see the wise, the brave, the powerful, or the beauteous, carried to the grave, without reflection on the emptiness of all those distinctions, which set us here in opposition to each other? And who, when he sees the vanity of all terrestrial advantages, can forbear to wish for a more permanent and certain happiness? Such wishes, perhaps, often arise, and such resolutions are often formed; but, before the resolution can be exerted, before the wish can regulate the conduct, new prospects open before us, new impressions are received; the temptations of the world solicit, the passions of the heart are put into commotion; we plunge again into the tumult, engage again in the contest, and forget that what we gain cannot be kept, and that the life, for which we are thus busy to provide, must be quickly at an end.

But, let us not be thus shamefully deluded! Let us not thus idly perish in our folly, by neglecting the loudest call of providence; nor, when we have followed our friends, and our enemies to the tomb, suffer ourselves to be surprised by the dreadful summons, and die, at last, amazed, and unprepared! Let every one whose eye glances on this bier, examine what would have been his condition, if the same hour had called him to judgment, and remember, that, though he is now spared, he may, perhaps, be tomorrow among separate spirits. The present moment is in our power: let us, therefore, from the present moment, begin our repentance! Let us not, any longer, harden our hearts, but hear, this day, the voice of our Saviour and our God, and begin to do, with all our powers, whatever we shall wish to have done, when the grave shall open before us! Let those, who came hither weeping and lamenting, reflect, that they have not time for useless sorrow; that their own salvation is to be secured, and that 'the day is far spent, and the night cometh, when no man can work;' that tears are of no value to the dead, and that their own danger may justly claim their whole attention! Let those who entered this place unaffected and indifferent, and whose only purpose was to behold this funeral spectacle, consider, that she, whom they thus behold with negligence, and pass by, was lately partaker of the same nature with themselves; and that they likewise are hastening to their end, and must soon, by others equally negligent, be buried and forgotten! Let all remember, that the day of life is short, and that the day of grace may be much shorter; that this may be the last warning which God will grant us, and that, perhaps, he, who looks on this grave unalarmed, may sink unreformed into his own.

Let it, therefore, be our care, when we retire from this

solemnity, that we immediately turn from our wickedness, and do that which is lawful and right; that, whenever disease, or violence, shall dissolve our bodies, our
souls may be saved alive, and received into everlasting
habitations; where, with angels and archangels, and all
the glorious host of heaven, they shall sing glory to God
on high, and the Lamb, for ever and ever.

A Sermon . . . 1788

1753–4

THE ADVENTURER

1753
Fallacies of Co-operation

Nulla fides regni sociis, omnisque potestas
Impatiens consortis erit.   LUCAN.

No faith of partnership dominion owns:
Still discord hovers o'er divided thrones.

It is well known, that many things appear plausible in
speculation, which can never be reduced to practice; and
that of the numberless projects that have flattered mankind with theoretical speciousness, few have served any
other purpose than to show the ingenuity of their contrivers. A voyage to the moon, however romantick and
absurd the scheme may now appear, since the properties
of air have been better understood, seemed highly probable to many of the aspiring wits in the last century, who
began to doat upon their glossy plumes, and fluttered
with impatience for the hour of their departure:

——*Pereunt vestigia mille*
Ante fugam, absentemque ferit gravis ungula campum.

Hills, vales, and floods appear already crost;
And, ere he starts, a thousand steps are lost.   POPE.

Among the fallacies which only experience can detect,
there are some, of which scarcely experience itself can
destroy the influence; some which, by a captivating show

of indubitable certainty, are perpetually gaining upon the human mind; and which, though every trial ends in disappointment, obtain new credit as the sense of miscarriage wears gradually away, persuade us to try again what we have tried already, and expose us by the same failure to double vexation.

Of this tempting, this delusive kind, is the expectation of great performances by confederated strength. The speculatist, when he has carefully observed how much may be performed by a single band, calculates by a very easy operation the force of thousands, and goes on accumulating power till resistance vanishes before it; then rejoices in the success of his new scheme, and wonders at the folly or idleness of former ages, who have lived in want of what might so readily be procured, and suffered themselves to be debarred from happiness by obstacles which one united effort would have so easily surmounted.

But this gigantick phantom of collective power vanishes at once into air and emptiness, at the first attempt to put it into action. The different apprehensions, the discordant passions, the jarring interests of men, will scarcely permit that many should unite in one undertaking.

Of a great and complicated design, some will never be brought to discern the end; and of the several means by which it may be accomplished, the choice will be a perpetual subject of debate, as every man is swayed in his determination by his own knowledge or convenience. In a long series of action some will languish with fatigue, and some be drawn off by present gratifications; some will loiter because others labour, and some will cease to labour because others loiter: and if once they come within prospect of success and profit, some will be greedy and others envious; some will undertake more than they can perform, to enlarge their claims of advantage; some will perform less than they undertake, lest their labours should chiefly turn to the benefit of others.

The history of mankind informs us that a single power is very seldom broken by a confederacy. States of different interests, and aspects malevolent to each other, may be united for a time by common distress; and in the ardour of self-preservation fall unanimously upon an enemy, by whom they are all equally endangered. But if their first attack can be withstood, time will never fail to dissolve their union: success and miscarriage will be equally destructive: after the conquest of a province, they will quarrel in the division; after the loss of a battle, all will be endeavouring to secure themselves by abandoning the rest.

From the impossibility of confining numbers to the constant and uniform prosecution of a common interest, arises the difficulty of securing subjects against the encroachment of governours. Power is always gradually stealing away from the many to the few, because the few are more vigilant and consistent; it still contracts to a smaller number, till in time it centers in a single person.

Thus all the forms of governments instituted among mankind, perpetually tend toward monarchy; and power, however diffused through the whole community, is by negligence or corruption, commotion or distress, reposed at last in the chief magistrate.

'There never appear,' says Swift, 'more than five or six men of genius in an age; but if they were united, the world could not stand before them.' It is happy, therefore, for mankind, that of this union there is no probability. As men take in a wider compass of intellectual survey, they are more likely to chuse different objects of pursuit; as they see more ways to the same end, they will be less easily persuaded to travel together; as each is better qualified to form an independent scheme of private greatness, he will reject with greater obstinacy the project of another; as each is more able to distinguish himself as the head of a party, he will less readily be made a follower or an associate.

The reigning philosophy informs us, that the vast bodies which constitute the universe, are regulated in their progress through the ethereal spaces, by the perpetual agency of contrary forces; by one of which they are restrained from deserting their orbits, and losing themselves in the immensity of heaven; and held off by

the other from rushing together, and clustering round
their center with everlasting cohesion.

The same contrariety of impulse may be perhaps discovered in the motions of men: we are formed for society,
not for combination; we are equally unqualified to live
in a close connexion with our fellow-beings, and in total
separation from them; we are attracted towards each
other by general sympathy, but kept back from contact
by private interests.

Some philosophers have been foolish enough to imagine,
that improvements might be made in the system of the universe, by a different arrangement of the orbs of heaven;
and politicians, equally ignorant and equally presump-
tuous, may easily be led to suppose, that the happiness of
our world would be promoted by a different tendency of
the human mind. It appears, indeed, to a slight and
superficial observer, that many things impracticable in
our present state, might be easily effected, if mankind
were better disposed to union and co-operation: but a
little reflection will discover, that if confederacies were
easily formed, they would lose their efficacy, since
numbers would be opposed to numbers, and unanimity
to unanimity; and instead of the present petty competitions of individuals or single families, multitudes would
be supplanting multitudes, and thousands plotting against
thousands.

There is no class of the human species, of which the
union seems to have been more expected, than of the
learned: the rest of the world have almost always agreed
to shut scholars up together in colleges and cloisters;
surely not without hope, that they would look for that
happiness in concord, which they were debarred from
finding in variety; and that such conjunctions of intellect
would recompense the munificence of founders and
patrons, by performances above the reach of any single
mind.

But discord, who found means to roll her apple into
the banqueting chamber of the goddesses, has had the
address to scatter her laurels in the seminaries of learning.
The friendship of students and of beauties is for the most

part equally sincere, and equally durable: as both depend for happiness on the regard of others, on that of which the value arises merely from comparison, they are both exposed to perpetual jealousies, and both incessantly employed in schemes to intercept the praises of each other.

I am, however, far from intending to inculcate that this confinement of the studious to studious companions, has been wholly without advantage to the publick: neighbourhood, where it does not conciliate friendship, incites competition; and he that would contentedly rest in a lower degree of excellence, where he had no rival to dread, will be urged by his impatience of inferiority to incessant endeavours after great attainments.

These stimulations of honest rivalry are, perhaps, the chief effects of academies and societies; for whatever be the bulk of their joint labours, every single piece is always the production of an individual, that owes nothing to his colleagues but the contagion of diligence, a resolution to write, because the rest are writing, and the scorn of obscurity while the rest are illustrious.

Adventurer, No. 45

Books and Talk

Qui cupit optatam cursu contingere metam,
Multa tulit fecitque puer. HOR.

The youth, who hopes th' Olympick prize to gain,
All arts must try, and every toil sustain. FRANCIS.

It is observed by Bacon, that 'reading makes a full man, conversation a ready man, and writing an exact man.'

As Bacon attained to degrees of knowledge scarcely ever reached by any other man, the directions which he gives for study have certainly a just claim to our regard; for who can teach an art with so great authority, as he that has practised it with undisputed success?

Under the protection of so great a name, I shall, therefore, venture to inculcate to my ingenious contemporaries, the necessity of reading, the fitness of consulting other understandings than their own, and of considering the sentiments and opinions of those who, however neglected in the present age, had in their own times, and many of them a long time afterwards, such reputation for knowledge and acuteness as will scarcely ever be attained by those that despise them.

An opinion has of late been, I know not how, propagated among us, that libraries are filled only with useless lumber; that men of parts stand in need of no assistance; and that to spend life in poring upon books, is only to imbibe prejudices, to obstruct and embarrass the powers of nature, to cultivate memory at the expense of judgment, and to bury reason under a chaos of indigested learning.

Such is the talk of many who think themselves wise, and of some who are thought wise by others; of whom part probably believe their own tenets, and part may be justly suspected of endeavouring to shelter their ignorance in multitudes, and of wishing to destroy that reputation which they have no hopes to share. It will, I believe, be found invariably true, that learning was never decried by any learned man; and what credit can be given to those, who venture to condemn that which they do not know?

If reason has the power ascribed to it by its advocates, if so much is to be discovered by attention and meditation, it is hard to believe, that so many millions, equally participating of the bounties of nature with ourselves, have been for ages upon ages meditating in vain: if the wits of the present time expect the regard of posterity, which will then inherit the reason which is now thought superiour to instruction, surely they may allow themselves to be instructed by the reason of former generations. When, therefore, an author declares, that he has been able to learn nothing from the writings of his predecessors, and such a declaration has been lately made, nothing but a degree of arrogance unpardonable in the greatest human understanding, can hinder him from perceiving that he is raising prejudices against his own performance; for with what hopes of success can he attempt that in which greater abilities have hitherto miscarried? or with what peculiar force does he suppose himself invigorated, that difficulties hitherto invincible should give way before him?

Of those whom Providence has qualified to make any additions to human knowledge, the number is extremely small; and what can be added by each single mind, even of this superiour class, is very little: the greatest part of mankind must owe all their knowledge, and all must owe far the larger part of it, to the information of others. To understand the works of celebrated authors, to comprehend their systems, and retain their reasonings, is a task more than equal to common intellects; and he is by no means to be accounted useless or idle, who has stored his mind with acquired knowledge, and can detail it occasionally to others who have less leisure or weaker abilities.

Persius has justly observed, that knowledge is nothing to him who is not known by others to possess it; to the scholar himself it is nothing with respect either to honour or advantage, for the world cannot reward those qualities which are concealed from it; with respect to others it is nothing, because it affords no help to ignorance or errour.

It is with justice, therefore, that in an accomplished character, Horace unites just sentiments with the power of expressing them; and he that has once accumulated learning, is next to consider, how he shall most widely diffuse and most agreeably impart it.

A ready man is made by conversation. He that buries himself among his manuscripts, 'besprent,' as Pope expresses it, 'with learned dust,' and wears out his days and nights in perpetual research and solitary meditation, is too apt to lose in his elocution what he adds to his wisdom; and when he comes into the world, to appear overloaded with his own notions, like a man armed with weapons which he cannot wield. He has no facility of inculcating his speculations, of adapting himself to the various degrees of intellect which the accidents of conversation will present; but will talk to most unintelligibly, and to all unpleasantly.

I was once present at the lectures of a profound philosopher, a man really skilled in the science which he professed, who having occasion to explain the terms *opacum* and *pellucidum*, told us, after some hesitation, that *opacum* was, as one might say, *opake*, and that *pellucidum* signified *pellucid*. Such was the dexterity with which this learned reader facilitated to his auditors the intricacies of science; and so true is it, that a man may know what he cannot teach.

Boerhaave complains, that the writers who have treated of chymistry before him, are useless to the greater part of students, because they presuppose their readers to have such degrees of skill as are not often to be found. Into the same errour are all men apt to fall, who have familiarized any subject to themselves in solitude: they discourse, as if they thought every other man had been employed in the same inquiries; and expect that short hints and obscure allusions will produce in others the same train of ideas which they excite in themselves.

Nor is this the only inconvenience which the man of study suffers from a recluse life. When he meets with an opinion that pleases him, he catches it up with eagerness; looks only after such arguments as tend to his confirmation; or spares himself the trouble of discussion, and adopts it with very little proof; indulges it long without suspicion, and in time unites it to the general body of his knowledge, and treasures it up among incontestible truths: but when he comes into the world among men who, arguing upon dissimilar principles, have been led to different conclusions, and being placed in various situations, view the same object on many sides; he finds his darling position attacked, and himself in no condition to defend it: having thought always in one train, he is in the state of a man who having fenced always with the same master, is perplexed and amazed by a new posture of his antagonist; he is entangled in unexpected difficulties, he is harassed by sudden objections, he is unprovided with solutions or replies; his surprise impedes his natural powers of reasoning, his thoughts are scattered and confounded, and he gratifies the pride of airy petulance with an easy victory.

It is difficult to imagine, with what obstinacy truths which one mind perceives almost by intuition, will be rejected by another; and how many artifices must be practised, to procure admission for the most evident propositions into understandings frighted by their novelty, or hardened against them by accidental prejudice; it can scarcely be conceived, how frequently, in these extemporaneous controversies, the dull will be subtle, and the acute absurd; how often stupidity will elude the force of argument, by involving itself in its own gloom; and mistaken ingenuity will weave artful fallacies, which reason can scarcely find means to disentangle.

In these encounters the learning of the recluse usually fails him: nothing but long habit and frequent experiments can confer the power of changing a position into various forms, presenting it in different points of view, connecting it with known and granted truths, fortifying it with intelligible arguments, and illustrating it by apt similitudes; and he, therefore, that has collected his knowledge in solitude, must learn its application by mixing with mankind.

But while the various opportunities of conversation invite us to try every mode of argument, and every art of recommending our sentiments, we are frequently betrayed to the use of such as are not in themselves strictly defensible: a man heated in talk, and eager of victory, takes advantage of the mistakes or ignorance of his adversary, lays hold of concessions to which he knows he has no right, and urges proofs likely to prevail in his opponent, though he knows himself that they have no force: thus the severity of reason is relaxed, many topicks are accumulated, but without just arrangement or distinction; we learn to satisfy ourselves with such ratiocination as silences others; and seldom recal to a close examination, that discourse which has gratified our vanity with victory and applause.

Some caution therefore must be used, lest copiousness and facility be made less valuable by inaccuracy and confusion. To fix the thoughts by writing, and subject them to frequent examinations and reviews, is the best method of enabling the mind to detect its own sophisms, and keep it on guard against the fallacies which it practises on others: in conversation we naturally diffuse our thoughts, and in writing we contract them; method is the excellence of writing, and unconstraint the grace of conversation.

To read, write, and converse in due proportions, is therefore the business of a man of letters. For all these there is not often equal opportunity; excellence, therefore, is not often attainable; and most men fail in one or other of the ends proposed, and are full without readiness, or ready without exactness. Some deficiency must be forgiven all, because all are men; and more must be allowed to pass uncensured in the greater part of the world, because none can confer upon himself abilities, and few have the choice of situations proper for the improvement of those which nature has bestowed: it is however reasonable, to have *perfection* in our eye; that we may always advance towards it, though we know it never can be reached.

Adventurer, No. 85

Projectors

———*Magnis tamen excidit ausis.*   OVID.

But in the glorious enterprize he dy'd.   ADDISON.

It has always been the practice of mankind, to judge of actions by the event. The same attempts, conducted in the same manner, but terminated by different success, produce different judgments: they who attain their wishes, never want celebrators of their wisdom and their virtue; and they that miscarry, are quickly discovered to have been defective not only in mental but in moral qualities. The world will never be long without some good reason to hate the unhappy: their real faults are immediately detected; and if those are not sufficient to sink them into infamy, an additional weight of calumny will be superadded: he that fails in his endeavours after wealth or power, will not long retain either honesty or courage.

This species of injustice has so long prevailed in universal practice, that it seems likewise to have infected speculation: so few minds are able to separate the ideas of greatness and prosperity, that even Sir William Temple has determined, 'that he who can deserve the name of a hero, must not only be virtuous but fortunate.'

By this unreasonable distribution of praise and blame, none have suffered oftener than projectors, whose rapidity of imagination and vastness of design raise such envy in their fellow mortals, that every eye watches for their fall, and every heart exults at their distresses: yet even a projector may gain favour by success; and the tongue that was prepared to hiss, then endeavours to excel others in loudness of applause.

When Coriolanus, in Shakespeare, deserted to Aufidius, the Volscian servants at first insulted him, even while he stood under the protection of the household gods; but when they saw that the project took effect, and the stranger was seated at the head of the table, one of them very judiciously observes, 'that he always thought there was more in him than he could think.'

Machiavel has justly animadverted on the different notice taken by all succeeding times, of the two great projectors, Catiline and Cæsar. Both formed the same project, and intended to raise themselves to power, by subverting the commonwealth: they pursued their design, perhaps, with equal abilities and with equal virtue; but Catiline perished in the field, and Cæsar returned from Pharsalia with unlimited authority: and from that time, every monarch of the earth has thought himself honoured by a comparison with Cæsar; and Catiline has been never mentioned, but that his name might be applied to traitors and incendiaries.

In an age more remote, Xerxes projected the conquest of Greece, and brought down the power of Asia against it: but after the world had been filled with expectation and terrour, his army was beaten, his fleet was destroyed, and Xerxes has been never mentioned without contempt.

A few years afterwards, Greece likewise had her turn of giving birth to a projector; who invading Asia with a small army, went forward in search of adventures, and by his escape from one danger, gained only more rashness to rush into another: he stormed city after city, overran kingdom after kingdom, fought battles only for barren victory, and invaded nations only that he might make his way through them to new invasions: but having been fortunate in the execution of his projects, he died with the name of Alexander the Great.

These are, indeed, events of ancient times; but human nature is always the same, and every age will afford us instances of publick censures influenced by events. The great business of the middle centuries, was the holy war; which undoubtedly was a noble project, and was for a long time prosecuted with a spirit equal to that with which it had been contrived: but the ardour of the European heroes only hurried them to destruction; for a long time they could not gain the territories for which they fought, and, when at last gained, they could not keep them: their expeditions, therefore, have been the scoff of idleness and ignorance, their understanding and their virtue have been equally vilified, their conduct has been ridiculed, and their cause has been defamed.

When Columbus had engaged king Ferdinand in the discovery of the other hemisphere, the sailors, with whom he embarked in the expedition, had so little confidence in their commander, that after having been long at sea looking for coasts which they expected never to find, they raised a general mutiny, and demanded to return. He found means to sooth them into a permission to continue the same course three days longer, and on the evening of the third day descried land. Had the impatience of his crew denied him a few hours of the time requested, what had been his fate but to have come back with the infamy of a vain projector, who had betrayed the king's credulity to useless expenses, and risked his life in seeking countries that had no existence? how would those that had rejected his proposals have triumphed in their acuteness? and when would his name have been mentioned, but with the makers of potable gold and malleable glass?

The last royal projectors with whom the world has been troubled, were Charles of Sweden and the Czar of Muscovy. Charles, if any judgment may be formed of his

designs by his measures and his inquiries, had purposed
first to dethrone the Czar, then to lead his army through
pathless deserts into China, thence to make his way by the
sword through the whole circuit of Asia, and by the conquest of Turkey to unite Sweden with his new dominions:
but this mighty project was crushed at Pultowa; and
Charles has since been considered as a madman by those
powers, who sent their ambassadors to solicit his friendship, and their generals 'to learn under him the art of war.'

The Czar found employment sufficient in his own
dominions, and amused himself in digging canals, and
building cities; murdering his subjects with insufferable
fatigues, and transplanting nations from one corner of
his dominions to another, without regretting the thousands that perished on the way: but he attained his end,
he made his people formidable, and is numbered by fame
among the demi-gods.

I am far from intending to vindicate the sanguinary
projects of heroes and conquerors, and would wish rather
to diminish the reputation of their success, than the
infamy of their miscarriages: for I cannot conceive, why
he that has burnt cities, wasted nations, and filled the
world with horrour and desolation, should be more
kindly regarded by mankind, than he that died in the
rudiments of wickedness; why he that accomplished mischief should be glorious, and he that only endeavoured
it should be criminal. I would wish Cæsar and Catiline,
Xerxes and Alexander, Charles and Peter, huddled together in obscurity or detestation.

But there is another species of projectors, to whom
I would willingly conciliate mankind; whose ends are
generally laudable, and whose labours are innocent; who
are searching out new powers of nature, or contriving
new works of art; but who are yet persecuted with incessant obloquy, and whom the universal contempt with
which they are treated, often debars from that success
which their industry would obtain, if it were permitted
to act without opposition.

They who find themselves inclined to censure new
undertakings, only because they are new, should consider,

that the folly of projection is very seldom the folly of a fool; it is commonly the ebullition of a capacious mind, crowded with variety of knowledge, and heated with intenseness of thought; it proceeds often from the consciousness of uncommon powers, from the confidence of those, who having already done much, are easily persuaded that they can do more. When Rowley had completed the orrery, he attempted the perpetual motion; when Boyle had exhausted the secrets of vulgar chymistry, he turned his thoughts to the work of transmutation.

A projector generally unites those qualities which have the fairest claim to veneration, extent of knowledge, and greatness of design: it was said of Catiline, 'immoderata, incredibilia, nimis alta semper cupiebat.' Projectors of all kinds agree in their intellects, though they differ in their morals; they all fail by attempting things beyond their power, by despising vulgar attainments, and aspiring to performances to which perhaps nature has not proportioned the force of man: when they fail, therefore, they fail not by idleness or timidity, but by rash adventure and fruitless diligence.

That the attempts of such men will often miscarry, we may reasonably expect; yet from such men, and such only, are we to hope for the cultivation of those parts of nature which lie yet waste, and the invention of those arts which are yet wanting to the felicity of life. If they are, therefore, universally discouraged, art and discovery can make no advances. Whatever is attempted without previous certainty of success, may be considered as a project, and amongst narrow minds may, therefore, expose its author to censure and contempt; and if the liberty of laughing be once indulged, every man will laugh at what he does not understand, every project will be considered as madness, and every great or new design will be censured as a project. Men, unaccustomed to reason and researches, think every enterprise impracticable which is extended beyond common effects, or comprises many intermediate operations. Many that presume to laugh at projectors, would consider a flight through the air in a winged chariot, and the movement of a mighty engine by the stream of water, as equally the dreams of mechanic lunacy; and would hear, with equal negligence, of the union of the Thames and Severn by a canal, and the scheme of Albuquerque, the Viceroy of the Indies, who in the rage of hostility had contrived to make Egypt a barren desert, by turning the Nile into the Red Sea.

Those who have attempted much, have seldom failed to perform more than those who never deviate from the common roads of action: many valuable preparations of chymistry are supposed to have risen from unsuccessful inquiries after the grand elixir: it is, therefore, just to encourage those who endeavour to enlarge the power of art, since they often succeed beyond expectation; and when they fail, may sometimes benefit the world even by their miscarriages.

Adventurer, No. 99

The Miseries of Life

———*Ultima semper*
Expectanda dies homini, dicique beatus
Ante obitum nemo supremaque funera debet. Ovid.

But no frail man, however great or high,
Can be concluded blest before he die. Addison.

The numerous miseries of human life have extorted in all ages an universal complaint. The wisest of men terminated all his experiments in search of happiness, by the mournful confession, that 'all is vanity;' and the ancient patriarchs lamented, that 'the days of their pilgrimage were few and evil.'

There is, indeed, no topick on which it is more superfluous to accumulate authorities, nor any assertion of which our own eyes will more easily discover, or our sensations more frequently impress the truth, than, that misery is the lot of man, that our present state is a state of danger and infelicity.

When we take the most distant prospect of life, what does it present us but a chaos of unhappiness, a confused and tumultuous scene of labour and contest, disappointment and defeat? If we view past ages in the reflection

of history, what do they offer to our meditation but
crimes and calamities? One year is distinguished by a
famine, another by an earthquake; kingdoms are made
desolate, sometimes by wars, and sometimes by pestilence;
the peace of the world is interrupted at one time by the
caprices of a tyrant, at another by the rage of a con-
queror. The memory is stored only with vicissitudes of
evil; and the happiness, such as it is, of one part of mankind, is found to arise commonly from sanguinary success,
from victories which confer upon them the power, not so
much of improving life by any new enjoyment, as of inflicting misery on others, and gratifying their own pride
by comparative greatness.

But by him that examines life with a more close attention, the happiness of the world will be found still less
than it appears. In some intervals of publick prosperity,
or to use terms more proper, in some intermissions of
calamity, a general diffusion of happiness may seem to
overspread a people; all is triumph and exultation,
jollity and plenty; there are no publick fears and dangers,
and 'no complainings in the streets.' But the condition
of individuals is very little mended by this general calm:
pain and malice and discontent still continue their
havock; the silent depredation goes incessantly forward;
and the grave continues to be filled by the victims of
sorrow.

He that enters a gay assembly, beholds the cheerfulness
displayed in every countenance, and finds all sitting
vacant and disengaged, with no other attention than to
give or to receive pleasure; would naturally imagine, that
he had reached at last the metropolis of felicity, the place
sacred to gladness of heart, from whence all fear and
anxiety were irreversibly excluded. Such, indeed, we may
often find to be the opinion of those, who from a lower
station look up to the pomp and gayety which they
cannot reach: but who is there of those who frequent
these luxurious assemblies, that will not confess his own
uneasiness, or cannot recount the vexations and distresses
that prey upon the lives of his gay companions?

The world, in its best state, is nothing more than a

larger assembly of beings, combining to counterfeit happiness which they do not feel, employing every art and contrivance to embellish life, and to hide their real condition from the eyes of one another.

The species of happiness most obvious to the observation of others, is that which depends upon the goods of fortune; yet even this is often fictitious. There is in the world more poverty than is generally imagined; not only because many whose possessions are large have desires still larger, and many measure their wants by the gratifications which others enjoy: but great numbers are pressed by real necessities which it is their chief ambition to conceal, and are forced to purchase the appearance of competence and cheerfulness at the expense of many comforts and conveniencies of life.

Many, however, are confessedly rich, and many more are sufficiently removed from all danger of real poverty: but it has been long ago remarked, that money cannot purchase quiet; the highest of mankind can promise themselves no exemption from that discord or suspicion, by which the sweetness of domestick retirement is destroyed; and must always be even more exposed, in the same degree as they are elevated above others, to the treachery of dependents, the calumny of defamers and the violence of opponents.

Affliction is inseparable from our present state; it adheres to all the inhabitants of this world, in different proportions indeed, but with an allotment which seems very little regulated by our own conduct. It has been the boast of some swelling moralists, that every man's fortune was in his own power, that prudence supplied the place of all other divinities, and that happiness is the unfailing consequence of virtue. But, surely, the quiver of Omnipotence is stored with arrows, against which the shield of human virtue, however adamantine it has been boasted, is held up in vain: we do not always suffer by our crimes; we are not always protected by our innocence.

A good man is by no means exempt from the danger of suffering by the crimes of others; even his goodness may raise him enemies of implacable malice and restless perseverance: the good man has never been warranted by Heaven from the treachery of friends, the disobedience of children, or the dishonesty of a wife; he may see his cares made useless by profusion, his instructions defeated by perverseness, and his kindness rejected by ingratitude; he may languish under the infamy of false accusations, or perish reproachfully by an unjust sentence.

A good man is subject, like other mortals, to all the influences of natural evil; his harvest is not spared by the tempest, nor his cattle by the murrain; his house flames like others in a conflagration; nor have his ships any peculiar power of resisting hurricanes: his mind, however elevated, inhabits a body subject to innumerable casualties, of which he must always share the dangers and the pains; he bears about him the seeds of disease, and may linger away a great part of his life under the tortures of the gout or stone; at one time groaning with insufferable anguish, at another dissolved in listlessness and languor.

From this general and indiscriminate distribution of misery, the moralists have always derived one of their strongest moral arguments for a future state; for since the common events of the present life happen alike to the good and bad, it follows from the justice of the Supreme Being, that there must be another state of existence, in which a just retribution shall be made, and every man shall be happy and miserable according to his works.

The miseries of life may, perhaps, afford some proof of a future state, compared as well with the mercy as the justice of God. It is scarcely to be imagined that Infinite Benevolence would create a being capable of enjoying so much more than is here to be enjoyed, and qualified by nature to prolong pain by remembrance, and anticipate it by terrour, if he was not designed for something nobler and better than a state, in which many of his faculties can serve only for his torment; in which he is to be importuned by desires that never can be satisfied, to feel many evils which he had no power to avoid, and to fear many which he shall never feel: there will surely come a time, when every capacity of happiness shall be filled, and none shall be wretched but by his own fault.

In the mean time, it is by affliction chiefly that the heart of man is purified, and that the thoughts are fixed upon a better state. Prosperity, allayed and imperfect as it is, has power to intoxicate the imagination, to fix the mind upon the present scene, to produce confidence and elation, and to make him who enjoys affluence and honours forget the hand by which they were bestowed. It is seldom that we are otherwise, than by affliction, awakened to a sense of our own imbecility, or taught to know how little all our acquisitions can conduce to safety or to quiet; and how justly we may ascribe to the superintendence of a higher Power, those blessings which in the wantonness of success we considered as the attainments of our policy or courage.

Nothing confers so much ability to resist the temptations that perpetually surround us, as an habitual consideration of the shortness of life, and the uncertainty of those pleasures that solicit our pursuit; and this consideration can be inculcated only by affliction. 'O Death! how bitter is the remembrance of thee, to a man that lives at ease in his possessions!' If our present state were one continued succession of delights, or one uniform flow of calmness and tranquillity, we should never willingly think upon its end; death would then surely surprise us as 'a thief in the night;' and our task of duty would remain unfinished, till 'the night came when no man can work.'

While affliction thus prepares us for felicity, we may console ourselves under its pressures, by remembering, that they are no particular marks of divine displeasure; since all the distresses of persecution have been suffered by those, 'of whom the world was not worthy;' and the Redeemer of Mankind himself was 'a man of sorrows and acquainted with grief.'

Adventurer, No. 120

1754

The Adventurer's Usefulness

Τί δ' ἔρεξα.   PYTH.

What have I been doing?

As man is a being very sparingly furnished with the power of prescience, he can provide for the future only by considering the past; and as futurity is all in which he has any real interest, he ought very diligently to use the only means by which he can be enabled to enjoy it, and frequently to revolve the experiments which he has hitherto made upon life, that he may gain wisdom from his mistakes, and caution from his miscarriages.

Though I do not so exactly conform to the precepts of Pythagoras, as to practise every night this solemn recollection, yet I am not so lost in dissipation as wholly to omit it; not can I forbear sometimes to inquire of myself, in what employment my life has passed away. Much of my time has sunk into nothing, and left no trace by which it can be distinguished; and of this I now only know, that it was once in my power, and might once have been improved.

Of other parts of life, memory can give some account; at some hours I have been gay, and at others serious; I have sometimes mingled in conversation, and sometimes meditated in solitude; one day has been spent in consulting the ancient sages, and another in writing *Adventurers*.

At the conclusion of any undertaking, it is usual to compute the loss and profit. As I shall soon cease to write *Adventurers*, I could not forbear lately to consider what has been the consequence of my labours; and whether I am to reckon the hours laid out in these compositions, as applied to a good and laudable purpose, or suffered to fume away in useless evaporations.

That I have intended well, I have the attestation of my own heart: but good intentions may be frustrated when they are executed without suitable skill, or directed to an end unattainable in itself.

Some there are, who leave writers very little room for self-congratulation; some who affirm, that books have no influence upon the publick, that no age was ever made better by its authors, and that to call upon mankind to correct their manners, is like Xerxes, to scourge the wind, or shackle the torrent.

This opinion they pretend to support by unfailing experience. The world is full of fraud and corruption, rapine or malignity; interest is the ruling motive of mankind, and every one is endeavouring to increase his own stores of happiness by perpetual accumulation, without reflecting upon the numbers whom his superfluity condemns to want: in this state of things a book of morality is published, in which charity and benevolence are strongly enforced; and it is proved beyond opposition, that men are happy in proportion as they are virtuous, and rich as they are liberal. The book is applauded, and the author is preferred; he imagines his applause deserved, and receives less pleasure from the acquisition of reward than the consciousness of merit. Let us look again upon mankind: interest is still the ruling motive, and the world is yet full of fraud and corruption, malevolence and rapine.

The difficulty of confuting this assertion, arises merely from its generality and comprehension: to overthrow it by a detail of distinct facts, requires a wider survey of the world than human eyes can take; the progress of reformation is gradual and silent, as the extension of evening shadows; we know that they were short at noon, and are long at sunset, but our senses were not able to discern their increase: we know of every civil nation, that it was once savage, and how was it reclaimed but by precept and admonition?

Mankind are universally corrupt, but corrupt in different degrees; as they are universally ignorant, yet with greater or less irradiations of knowledge. How has knowledge or virtue been increased and preserved in one place beyond another, but by diligent inculcation and rational inforcement?

Books of morality are daily written, yet its influence is still little in the world; so the ground is annually ploughed, and yet multitudes are in want of bread. But, surely, neither the labours of the moralist nor of the husbandman are vain: let them for a while neglect their tasks, and their usefulness will be known; the wickedness that is now frequent would become universal, the bread that is now scarce would wholly fail.

The power, indeed, of every individual is small, and the consequence of his endeavours imperceptible, in a general prospect of the world. Providence has given no man ability to do much, that something might be left for every man to do. The business of life is carried on by a general cooperation; in which the part of any single man can be no more distinguished, than the effect of a particular drop when the meadows are floated by a summer shower: yet every drop increases the inundation, and every hand adds to the happiness or misery of mankind.

That a writer, however zealous or eloquent, seldom works a visible effect upon cities or nations, will readily be granted. The book which is read most, is read by few, compared with those that read it not; and of those few, the greater part peruse it with dispositions that very little favour their own improvement.

It is difficult to enumerate the several motives which procure to books the honour of perusal: spite, vanity, and curiosity, hope and fear, love and hatred, every passion which incites to any other action, serves at one time or other to stimulate a reader.

Some are fond to take a celebrated volume into their hands, because they hope to distinguish their penetration, by finding faults which have escaped the publick; others eagerly buy it in the first bloom of reputation, that they may join the chorus of praise, and not lag, as Falstaff terms it, in 'the rearward of the fashion.'

Some read for style, and some for argument: one has little care about the sentiment, he observes only how it is expressed; another regards not the conclusion, but is diligent to mark how it is inferred: they read for other purposes than the attainment of practical knowledge; and are no more likely to grow wise by an examination of a treatise of moral prudence, than an architect to inflame his devotion by considering attentively the proportions of a temple.

Some read that they may embellish their conversation, or shine in dispute; some that they may not be detected in ignorance, or want the reputation of literary accomplishments: but the most general and prevalent reason of study is the impossibility of finding another amusement equally cheap or constant, equally independent on the hour or the weather. He that wants money to follow the chase of pleasure through her yearly circuit, and is left at home when the gay world rolls to Bath or Tunbridge; he whose gout compels him to hear from his chamber the rattle of chariots transporting happier beings to plays and assemblies, will be forced to seek in books a refuge from himself.

The author is not wholly useless, who provides innocent amusements for minds like these. There are, in the present state of things, so many more instigations to evil, than incitements to good, that he who keeps men in a neutral state, may be justly considered as a benefactor to life.

But, perhaps, it seldom happens, that study terminates in mere pastime. Books have always a secret influence on the understanding; we cannot at pleasure obliterate ideas: he that reads books of science, though without any fixed desire of improvement, will grow more knowing; he that entertains himself with moral or religious treatises, will imperceptibly advance in goodness; the ideas which are often offered to the mind, will at last find a lucky moment when it is disposed to receive them.

It is, therefore, urged without reason, as a discouragement to writers, that there are already books sufficient in the world; that all the topicks of persuasion have been discussed, and every important question clearly stated and justly decided; and that, therefore, there is no room to hope, that pigmies should conquer where heroes have been defeated, or that the petty copiers of the present time should advance the great work of reformation, which their predecessors were forced to leave unfinished.

Whatever be the present extent of human knowledge, it is not only finite, and therefore in its own nature capable of increase; but so narrow, that almost every understanding may, by a diligent application of its powers, hope to enlarge it. It is, however, not necessary, that a man should forbear to write, till he has discovered some truth unknown before; he may be sufficiently useful, by only diversifying the surface of knowledge, and luring the mind by a new appearance to a second view of those beauties which it had passed over inattentively before. Every writer may find intellects correspondent to his own, to whom his expressions are familiar and his thoughts congenial; and, perhaps, truth is often more successfully propagated by men of moderate abilities, who, adopting the opinions of others, have no care but to explain them clearly, than by subtle speculatists and curious searchers, who exact from their readers powers equal to their own, and if their fabricks of science be strong, take no care to render them accessible.

For my part, I do not regret the hours which I have laid out in these little compositions. That the world has grown apparently better, since the publication of the *Adventurer*, I have not observed; but am willing to think, that many have been affected by single sentiments, of which it is their business to renew the impression; that many have caught hints of truth, which it is now their duty to pursue; and that those who have received no improvement, have wanted not opportunity but intention to improve.

Adventurer, No. 137

1754
To Joseph Warton

Dear Sir   March 8th, 1754.

I cannot but congratulate you upon the conclusion of a work in which you have borne so great a part with so much reputation. I immediately determined that your name should be mentioned, but the paper having been some time written, Mr. Hawkesworth, I suppose, did not care to disorder its text, and therefore put your eulogy in a note. He and every other man mention your papers of Criticism with great commendation, though not with greater than they deserve.

But how little can we venture to exult in any intellectual powers or literary attainments, when we consider the condition of poor Collins. I knew him a few years ago full of hopes and full of projects, versed in many languages, high in fancy, and strong in retention. This busy and forcible mind is now under the government of those who lately would not have been able to comprehend the least and most narrow of its designs. What do you hear of him? are there hopes of his recovery? or is he to pass the remainder of his life in misery and degradation? perhaps with complete consciousness of his calamity.

You have flatter'd us, dear Sir, for some time with hopes of seeing you; when you come you will find your reputation encreased, and with it the kindness of those friends who do not envy you; for success always produces either love or hatred. I enter my name among those that love, and that love you more and more in proportion as by writing more you are more known; and believe that as you continue to diffuse among us your integrity and learning, I shall be still with greater esteem and affection,

Dear Sir, Your most obedient and most humble servant
Sam. Johnson.

1755

Sunday Observance

July 13, 1755. Having lived not without an habitual reverence for the Sabbath, yet without that attention to its religious duties which Christianity requires, I resolve

1. To rise early, and in order to it, to go to sleep early on Saturday.

2. To use some extraordinary devotion in the morning.

3. To examine the tenour of my life, and particularly the last week; and to mark my advances in religion, or recession from it.

4. To read the Scripture methodically with such helps as are at hand.

5. To go to church twice.

6. To read books of Divinity, either speculative or practical.

7. To instruct my family.

8. To wear off by meditation any worldly soil contracted in the week.

Prayers and Meditations, 1785

To Bennet Langton

Sir

It has been long observed that men do not suspect faults which they do not commit; your own Elegance of manners and punctuality of complaisance did not suffer you to impute to me that negligence of which I was guilty, and which I have not since attoned. I received both your Letters and received them with pleasure proportionate to the esteem which so short an acquaintance strongly impressed, and which I hope to confirm by nearer knowledge, though I am afraid that gratification will be for a time witheld.

I have indeed published my Book, of which I beg to know your Father's judgement and yours, and I have now staid long enough to watch its progress into the world. It has you see, no patrons, and I think has yet had no opponents except the Criticks of the coffeehouse, whose outcries are soon dispersed into the air, and are thought on no more: from this therefore I am at liberty, and think of taking the opportunity of this interval to make an excursion, and why not then into Lincolnshire, or to mention a stronger attraction why not to dear Mr. Langton? I will give the true reason which I know you will approve. I have a Mother more than eighty years old, who has counted the days to the publication of my book in hopes of seeing me, and to her, if I can disengage myself here, I resolve to go.

As I know, dear Sir, that to delay my visit for a reason like this will not deprive me of your esteem, I beg it may not lessen your kindness. I have very seldom received an offer of Friendship which I so earnestly desire to cultivate and mature. I shall rejoice to hear from you till I can see you, and will see you as soon as I can, for when the duty that calls me to Lichfield is discharged, my inclination will hurry me to Langton. I shall delight to hear the ocean roar or see the stars twinkle, in the company of men to whom nature does not spread her volumes or utter her voice in vain.

Do not, dear Sir, make the slowness of this letter a precedent for delay, or imagine that I approved the incivility that I have committed, for I have known you enough to love you, and sincerely to wish a further knowledge, and I assure you once more that to live in a House which contains such a Father and such a Son will be accounted a very uncommon degree of pleasure by, Dear Sir, Your most obliged and most humble Servant

May 6, 1755.   Sam: Johnson

To Charlotte Cotterell

Madam

I know not how liberally your Generosity would reward those who should do you any service, when you can so kindly acknowledge a favour which I intended only to myself. That accidentally hearing that you were in town I made haste to enjoy an interval of pleasure which I feared would be short, was the natural consequence of that self-love which is always busy in quest of happiness, of that happiness which we often miss when we think it near, and sometimes find when we imagine it lost. When I had missed you I went away disappointed, and did not know that my vexation would be so amply repaid by so kind a letter. A letter indeed can but imperfectly supply the place of its writer, at least of such a writer as Miss Cotterel, and a letter which makes me still more desire your presence is but a weak consolation under the necessity of living longer without you, with this however I must be for a time content, as much content at least as discontent will suffer me, for Mr Baretti being a single

Being in this part of the world, and entirely clear from all engagements, takes the advantage of his independence and will come before me, for which if I could blame him, I should punish him, but my own heart tells me that he only does to me, what, if I could, I should do to him.

I hope Mrs Porter when she came to her favourite place, found her house dry, and her woods growing, and the breeze whistling, and the birds singing, and her own heart dancing. And for you, Madam, whose heart cannot yet dance to such musick, I know not what to hope, indeed I could hope everything that would please you, except that perhaps the absence of higher pleasures is necessary to keep some little place vacant in your remembrance for

Madam, your most obliged most obedient and most humble servant

July 19. 1755.   Sam: Johnson

1756
To John Taylor
'The Best Letter in the World'

Dear Sir

You have no great title to a very speedy answer yet I did not intend to have delayed so long. I am now in doubt whether you are not come to town, if you are double postage is a proper fine.

There is one honest reason why those things are most subject to delays which we most desire to do. What we think of importance we wish to do well, to do any thing well, requires time, and what requires time commonly finds us too idle or too busy to undertake it. To be idle is not the best excuse, though if a man studies his own reformation it is the best reason he can allege to himself, both because it is commonly true, and because it contains no fallacy, for every man that thinks he is idle condemns himself and has therefore a chance to endeavour amendment, but the busy mortal has often his own commendation, even when his very business is the consequence of Idleness, when he engages himself in trifles only to put the thoughts of more important duties out of his mind, or to gain an excuse to his own heart for omitting them.

I am glad however that while you forgot me you were gaining upon the affections of other people. It is in your power to be very useful as a neighbour, a magistrate, and a Clergyman, and he that is useful, must conduct his life very imprudently not to be beloved. If Mousley makes advances I would wish you not to reject them. You once esteemed him and the quarrel between you arose from misinformation, and ought to be forgotten.

When you come to town let us contrive to see one another more frequently at least once a week. We have both lived long enough to bury many friends, and have therefore learned to set a value on those who are left. Neither of us now can find many whom he has known so long as we have known each other. Do not let us lose our intimacy at a time when we ought rather to think of encreasing it. We both stand almost single in the world, I have no brother, and with your sister you have little correspondence. But if you will take my advice, you will make some overtures of reconciliation to her. If you have been to blame, you know it is your duty first to seek a renewal of kindness. If she has been faulty, you have an opportunity to exercise the virtue of forgiveness. You must consider that of her faults and follies no very great part is her own. Much has been the consequence of her education, and part may be imputed to the neglect with which you have sometimes treated her. Had you endeavoured to gain her kindness and her confidence you would have had more influence over her. I hope that, before I shall see you, she will have had a visit or a letter from you. The longer you delay the more you will sometime repent. When I am musing alone, I feel a pang for every moment that any human being has by my peevishness or obstinacy spent in uneasiness. I know not how I have fallen upon this, I had no thought of it, when I began the letter, yet am glad that I have written it.

I am, Dearest Sir, Your most affectionate

Novr 18 1756   Saml: Johnson

[The title is Taylor's.]

Great and Little Things

To the Right Hon. WILLIAM HENRY Earl of
ROCHFORD, &c.

My Lord,

When I take the liberty of addressing to your lordship
A Treatise on the Game of Draughts, I easily foresee that I
shall be in danger of suffering ridicule on one part, while
I am gaining honour on the other, and that many who
may envy me the distinction of approaching you, will
deride the present I presume to offer.

Had I considered this little volume as having no purpose beyond that of teaching a game, I should indeed
have left it to take its fate without a patron. Triflers may
find or make any thing a trifle; but since it is the great
characteristic of a wise man to see events in their causes,
to obviate consequences, and ascertain contingencies,
your lordship will think nothing a trifle by which the
mind is inured to caution, foresight, and circumspection.
The same skill, and often the same degree of skill, is exerted
in great and little things, and your lordship may sometimes exercise, on a harmless game, those abilities which
have been so happily employed in the service of your
country.

I am, my Lord,
Your Lordship's most obliged, most obedient,
and most humble Servant,
WILLIAM PAYNE.
Dedication of Payne's *Introduction to the Game of Draughts*

1757
On Tea

We have already given in our collections one of the
letters, in which Mr. Hanway endeavours to show, that
the consumption of Tea is injurious to the interest of
our country. We shall now endeavour to follow him
regularly through all his observations on this modern
luxury; but it can scarcely be candid, not to make a

previous declaration, that he is to expect little justice from the author of this extract, a hardened and shameless Tea-drinker, who has for twenty years diluted his meals with only the infusion of this fascinating plant, whose kettle has scarcely time to cool, who with Tea amuses the evening, with Tea solaces the midnight, and with Tea welcomes the morning.

Review (in *Literary Magazine*) of Hanway's *Journal of Eight Days Journey*

The Origin of Evil

Having thus dispatched the consideration of particular evils, he comes at last to a general reason for which *Evil* may be said to be *our Good*. He is of opinion that there is some inconceivable benefit in pain abstractedly considered; that pain however inflicted, or wherever felt, communicates some good to the general system of being, and that every animal is some way or other the better for the pain of every other animal. This opinion he carries so far as to suppose that there passes some principle of union through all animal life, as attraction is communicated to all corporeal nature; and that the Evils suffered on this globe, may by some inconceivable means contribute to the felicity of the inhabitants of the remotest planet.

How the Origin of Evil is brought nearer to human conception by any *inconceivable* means, I am not able to discover. We believed that the present system of creation was right, though we could not explain the adaptation of one part to the other, or for the whole succession of causes and consequences. Where has this enquirer added to the little knowledge that we had before? He has told us of the benefits of Evil, which no man feels, and relations between distant parts of the universe, which he cannot himself conceive. There was enough in this question inconceivable before, and we have little advantage from a new inconceivable solution.

I do not mean to reproach this author for not knowing what is equally hidden from learning and from ignorance.

The shame is to impose words for ideas upon ourselves or others. To imagine that we are going forward when we are only turning round. To think that there is any difference between him that gives no reason, and him that gives a reason, which by his own confession cannot be conceived.

But that he may not be thought to conceive nothing but things inconceivable, he has at last thought on a way by which human sufferings may produce good effects. He imagines that as we have not only animals for food, but choose some for our diversion, the same privilege may be allowed to some beings above us, *who may deceive, torment, or destroy us for the ends only of their own pleasure or utility*. This he again finds impossible to be conceived, *but that impossibility lessens not the probability of the conjecture, which by analogy is so strongly confirmed.*

I cannot resist the temptation of contemplating this analogy, which I think he might have carried further, very much to the advantage of his argument. He might have shown that these *hunters, whose game is man,* have many sports analogous to our own. As we drown whelps and kittens, they amuse themselves now and then with sinking a ship, and stand round the fields of Blenheim or the walls of Prague, as we encircle a cock-pit. As we shoot a bird flying, they take a man in the midst of his business or pleasure, and knock him down with an apoplexy. Some of them, perhaps, are virtuosi, and delight in the operations of an asthma, as a human philosopher in the effects of the air-pump. To swell a man with a tympany is as good sport as to blow a frog. Many a merry bout have these frolick beings at the vicissitudes of an ague, and good sport it is to see a man tumble with an epilepsy, and revive and tumble again, and all this he knows not why. As they are wiser and more powerful than we, they have more exquisite diversions, for we have no way of procuring any sport so brisk and so lasting, as the paroxysms of the gout and stone, which undoubtedly must make high mirth, especially if the play be a little diversified with the blunders and puzzles of the blind and deaf. We know not how far their sphere of observation may extend. Perhaps now and then a merry being may place himself in such a situation as to enjoy at once all the varieties of an epidemical disease, or amuse his leisure with the tossings and contortions of every possible pain exhibited together.

One sport the merry malice of these beings has found means of enjoying, to which we have nothing equal or similar. They now and then catch a mortal proud of his parts, and flattered either by the submission of those who court his kindness, or the notice of those who suffer him to court theirs. A head thus prepared for the reception of false opinions, and the projection of vain designs, they easily fill with idle notions, till in time they make their plaything an author: their first diversion commonly begins with an ode or an epistle, then rises perhaps to a political irony, and is at last brought to its height, by a treatise of philosophy. Then begins the poor animal to entangle himself in sophisms, and flounder in absurdity, to talk confidently of the scale of being, and to give solutions which himself confesses impossible to be under-stood. Sometimes, however, it happens that their pleasure is without much mischief. The author feels no pain, but while they are wondering at the extravagance of his opinion, and pointing him out to one another as a new example of human folly, he is enjoying his own applause, and that of his companions, and perhaps is elevated with the hope of standing at the head of a new sect.

Review (*Literary Magazine*) of Jenyns's *A Free Inquiry
into the Nature and Origin of Evil*

To Charles O'Conor

Sir,
    I have lately by the favour of Mr. Faulkner seen your account of Ireland, and cannot forbear to solicit a pro-secution of your design. Sir William Temple complains that Ireland is less known than any other country as to its ancient state. The natives have had little leisure and little encouragement for enquiry, and strangers not know-ing the language have had no ability.

I have long wished that the Irish literature were cultivated. Ireland is known by tradition to have been once
the seat of Piety and Learning, and surely it would be
very acceptable to all those who are curious either in the
original of nations or the affinities of languages, to be
further informed of the revolutions of a people so ancient
and once so illustrious.

What relation there is between the Welsh and Irish
languages, or between the Languages of Ireland and that
of Biscay deserves enquiry. Of these provincial and un-
extended tongues it seldom happens that more than one
are understood by any one Man, and therefore it seldom
happens that a fair comparison can be made. I hope you
will continue to cultivate this kind of learning, which has
lain too long neglected and which if it be suffered to remain in oblivion for another century, may perhaps never
be retrieved. As I wish well to all useful undertakings, I
would not forbear to let you know, how much you deserve,
in my opinion, from all lovers of Study, and how much
pleasure your work has given to, Sir, Your most obliged
and most humble servant Sam: Johnson

London, Apr. 9. 1757

1759
To Sarah Johnson

Honoured Madam,

The account which Miss gives me of your health pierces
my heart. God comfort and preserve you and save you,
for the sake of Jesus Christ.

I would have Miss read to you from time to time the
Passion of our Saviour, and sometimes the sentences in
the Communion Service, beginning 'Come unto me, all ye
that travel and are heavy laden, and I will give you rest'.

I have just now read a physical book, which inclines
me to think that a strong infusion of the bark would do
you good. Do, dear mother, try it.

Pray, send me your blessing, and forgive all that I have
done amiss to you. And whatever you would have done,

and what debts you would have paid first, or anything else that you would direct, let Miss put it down; I shall endeavour to obey you.

I have got twelve guineas to send you, but unhappily am at a loss how to send it to-night. If I cannot send it to-night, it will come by the next post.

Pray, do not omit any thing mentioned in this letter: God bless you for ever and ever.

I am your dutiful son

Jan. 13, 1758   Sam: Johnson

Dear honoured Mother

Neither your condition nor your character make it fit for me to say much. You have been the best mother, and I believe the best woman in the world. I thank you for your indulgence to me, and beg forgiveness of all that I have done ill, and all that I have omitted to do well. God grant you his Holy Spirit, and receive you to everlasting happiness, for Jesus Christ's sake. Amen. Lord Jesus receive your spirit. Amen.

I am, dear, dear mother, Your dutiful son,

Jan. 20, 1759.   Sam: Johnson

Rasselas, Prince of Abissinia

Chap. I

Description of a palace in a valley.

Ye who listen with credulity to the whispers of fancy, and persue with eagerness the phantoms of hope; who expect that age will perform the promises of youth, and that the deficiencies of the present day will be supplied by the morrow; attend to the history of Rasselas prince of Abissinia.

Rasselas was the fourth son of the mighty emperour, in whose dominions the Father of waters begins his course; whose bounty pours down the streams of plenty, and scatters over half the world the harvests of Egypt.

According to the custom which has descended from age to age among the monarchs of the torrid zone, Rasselas was confined in a private palace, with the other sons and daughters of Abissinian royalty, till the order of succession should call him to the throne.

The place, which the wisdom or policy of antiquity had destined for the residence of the Abissinian princes, was a spacious valley in the kingdom of Amhara, surrounded on every side by mountains, of which the summits overhang the middle part. The only passage, by which it could be entered, was a cavern that passed under a rock, of which it has long been disputed whether it was the work of nature or of human industry. The outlet of the cavern was concealed by a thick wood, and the mouth which opened into the valley was closed with gates of iron, forged by the artificers of ancient days, so massy that no man could, without the help of engines, open or shut them.

From the mountains on every side, rivulets descended that filled all the valley with verdure and fertility, and formed a lake in the middle inhabited by fish of every species, and frequented by every fowl whom nature has taught to dip the wing in water. This lake discharged its superfluities by a stream which entered a dark cleft of the mountain on the northern side, and fell with dreadful noise from precipice to precipice till it was heard no more.

The sides of the mountains were covered with trees, the banks of the brooks were diversified with flowers; every blast shook spices from the rocks, and every month dropped fruits upon the ground. All animals that bite the grass, or brouse the shrub, whether wild or tame, wandered in this extensive circuit, secured from beasts of prey by the mountains which confined them. On one part were flocks and herds feeding in the pastures, on another all the beasts of chase frisking in the lawns; the sprightly kid was bounding on the rocks, the subtle monkey frolicking in the trees, and the solemn elephant reposing in the shade. All the diversities of the world were brought together, the blessings of nature were collected, and its evils extracted and excluded.

The valley, wide and fruitful, supplied its inhabitants with the necessaries of life, and all delights and super-

fluities were added at the annual visit which the emperour paid his children, when the iron gate was opened
to the sound of musick; and during eight days every one
that resided in the valley was required to propose whatever might contribute to make seclusion pleasant, to fill
up the vacancies of attention, and lessen the tediousness
of time. Every desire was immediately granted. All the
artificers of pleasure were called to gladden the festivity;
the musicians exerted the power of harmony, and the
dancers shewed their activity before the princes, in hope
that they should pass their lives in this blissful captivity,
to which those only were admitted whose performance
was thought able to add novelty to luxury. Such was
the appearance of security and delight which this retirement afforded, that they to whom it was new always
desired that it might be perpetual; and as those, on whom
the iron gate had once closed, were never suffered to
return, the effect of longer experience could not be
known. Thus every year produced new schemes of delight, and new competitors for imprisonment.

The palace stood on an eminence raised about thirty
paces above the surface of the lake. It was divided into
many squares or courts, built with greater or less magnificence according to the rank of those for whom they were
designed. The roofs were turned into arches of massy
stone joined with a cement that grew harder by time, and
the building stood from century to century, deriding the
solstitial rains and equinoctial hurricanes, without need
of reparation.

This house, which was so large as to be fully known to
none but some ancient officers who successively inherited
the secrets of the place, was built as if suspicion herself
had dictated the plan. To every room there was an open
and secret passage, every square had a communication
with the rest, either from the upper stories by private
galleries, or by subterranean passages from the lower
apartments. Many of the columns had unsuspected
cavities, in which a long race of monarchs had reposited
their treasures. They then closed up the opening with
marble, which was never to be removed but in the utmost

exigencies of the kingdom; and recorded their accumulations in a book which was itself concealed in a tower not entered but by the emperour, attended by the prince who stood next in succession.

Chap. II

The discontent of Rasselas in the happy valley.

Here the sons and daughters of Abissinia lived only to know the soft vicissitudes of pleasure and repose, attended by all that were skilful to delight, and gratified with whatever the senses can enjoy. They wandered in gardens of fragrance, and slept in the fortresses of security. Every art was practised to make them pleased with their own condition. The sages who instructed them, told them of nothing but the miseries of publick life, and described all beyond the mountains as regions of calamity, where discord was always raging, and where man preyed upon man.

To heighten their opinion of their own felicity, they were daily entertained with songs, the subject of which was the *happy valley*. Their appetites were excited by frequent enumerations of different enjoyments, and revelry and merriment was the business of every hour from the dawn of morning to the close of even.

These methods were generally successful; few of the Princes had ever wished to enlarge their bounds, but passed their lives in full conviction that they had all within their reach that art or nature could bestow, and pitied those whom fate had excluded from this seat of tranquility, as the sport of chance, and the slaves of misery.

Thus they rose in the morning, and lay down at night, pleased with each other and with themselves, all but Rasselas, who, in the twenty-sixth year of his age, began to withdraw himself from their pastimes and assemblies, and to delight in solitary walks and silent meditation. He often sat before tables covered with luxury, and forgot to taste the dainties that were placed before him: he rose abruptly in the midst of the song, and hastily retired beyond the sound of musick. His attendants observed the change and endeavoured to renew his love of pleasure: he neglected their officiousness, repulsed their invitations, and spent day after day on the banks of rivulets sheltered with trees, where he sometimes listened to the birds in the branches, sometimes observed the fish playing in the stream, and anon cast his eyes upon the pastures and mountains filled with animals, of which some were biting the herbage, and some sleeping among the bushes.

This singularity of his humour made him much observed. One of the Sages, in whose conversation he had formerly delighted, followed him secretly, in hope of discovering the cause of his disquiet. Rasselas, who knew not that any one was near him, having for some time fixed his eyes upon the goats that were brousing among the rocks, began to compare their condition with his own.

'What,' said he, 'makes the difference between man and all the rest of the animal creation? Every beast that strays beside me has the same corporal necessities with myself; he is hungry and crops the grass, he is thirsty and drinks the stream, his thirst and hunger are appeased, he is satisfied and sleeps; he rises again and is hungry, he is again fed and is at rest. I am hungry and thirsty like him, but when thirst and hunger cease I am not at rest; I am, like him, pained with want, but am not, like him, satisfied with fulness. The intermediate hours are tedious and gloomy; I long again to be hungry that I may again quicken my attention. The birds peck the berries or the corn, and fly away to the groves where they sit in seeming happiness on the branches, and waste their lives in tuning one unvaried series of sounds. I likewise can call the lutanist and the singer, but the sounds that pleased me yesterday weary me to day, and will grow yet more wearisome to morrow. I can discover within me no power of perception which is not glutted with its proper pleasure, yet I do not feel myself delighted. Man has surely some latent sense for which this place affords no gratification, or he has some desires distinct from sense which must be satisfied before he can be happy.'

After this he lifted up his head, and seeing the moon

rising, walked towards the palace. As he passed through the fields, and saw the animals around him, 'Ye, said he, are happy, and need not envy me that walk thus among you, burthened with myself; nor do I, ye gentle beings, envy your felicity; for it is not the felicity of man. I have many distresses from which ye are free; I fear pain when I do not feel it; I sometimes shrink at evils recollected, and sometimes start at evils anticipated: surely the equity of providence has ballanced peculiar sufferings with peculiar enjoyments.'

With observations like these the prince amused himself as he returned, uttering them with a plaintive voice, yet with a look that discovered him to feel some complacence in his own perspicacity, and to receive some solace of the miseries of life, from consciousness of the delicacy with which he felt, and the eloquence with which he bewailed them. He mingled cheerfully in the diversions of the evening, and all rejoiced to find that his heart was lightened.

CHAP. VI

A dissertation on the art of flying.

Among the artists that had been allured into the happy valley, to labour for the accommodation and pleasure of its inhabitants, was a man eminent for his knowledge of the mechanick powers, who had contrived many engines both of use and recreation. By a wheel, which the stream turned, he forced the water into a tower, whence it was distributed to all the apartments of the palace. He erected a pavillion in the garden, around which he kept the air always cool by artificial showers. One of the groves, appropriated to the ladies, was ventilated by fans, to which the rivulet that run through it gave a constant motion; and instruments of soft musick were placed at proper distances, of which some played by the impulse of the wind, and some by the power of the stream.

This artist was sometimes visited by Rasselas, who was pleased with every kind of knowledge, imagining that the time would come when all his acquisitions should be of use to him in the open world. He came one day to amuse himself in his usual manner, and found the master busy in building a sailing chariot: he saw that the design was practicable upon a level surface, and with expressions of great esteem solicited its completion. The workman was pleased to find himself so much regarded by the prince, and resolved to gain yet higher honours. 'Sir, said he, you have seen but a small part of what the mechanick sciences can perform. I have been long of opinion, that, instead of the tardy conveyance of ships and chariots, man might use the swifter migration of wings; that the fields of air are open to knowledge, and that only ignorance and idleness need crawl upon the ground.'

This hint rekindled the prince's desire of passing the mountains; having seen what the mechanist had already performed, he was willing to fancy that he could do more; yet resolved to enquire further before he suffered hope to afflict him by disappointment. 'I am afraid, said he to the artist, that your imagination prevails over your skill, and that you now tell me rather what you wish than what you know. Every animal has his element assigned him; the birds have the air, and man and beasts the earth.' 'So, replied the mechanist, fishes have the water, in which yet beasts can swim by nature, and men by art. He that can swim needs not despair to fly: to swim is to fly in a grosser fluid, and to fly is to swim in a subtler. We are only to proportion our power of resistance to the different density of the matter through which we are to pass. You will be necessarily upborn by the air, if you can renew any impulse upon it, faster than the air can recede from the pressure.'

'But the exercise of swimming, said the prince, is very laborious; the strongest limbs are soon wearied; I am afraid the act of flying will be yet more violent, and wings will be of no great use, unless we can fly further than we can swim.'

'The labour of rising from the ground, said the artist, will be great, as we see it in the heavier domestick fowls; but, as we mount higher, the earth's attraction, and the body's gravity, will be gradually diminished, till we shall arrive at a region where the man will float in the air without any tendency to fall: no care will then be necessary, but to move forwards, which the gentlest impulse will effect. You, Sir, whose curiosity is so extensive, will easily conceive with what pleasure a philosopher, furnished with wings, and hovering in the sky, would see the earth, and all it's inhabitants, rolling beneath him, and presenting to him successively, by it's diurnal motion, all the countries within the same parallel. How must it amuse the pendent spectator to see the moving scene of land and ocean, cities and desarts! To survey with equal security the marts of trade, and the fields of battle; mountains infested by barbarians, and fruitful regions gladdened by plenty, and lulled by peace! How easily shall we then trace the Nile through all his passage; pass over to distant regions, and examine the face of nature from one extremity of the earth to the other!'

'All this, said the prince, is much to be desired, but I am afraid that no man will be able to breathe in these regions of speculation and tranquility. I have been told, that respiration is difficult upon lofty mountains, yet from these precipices, though so high as to produce great tenuity of the air, it is very easy to fall: therefore I suspect, that from any height, where life can be supported, there may be danger of too quick descent.'

'Nothing, replied the artist, will ever be attempted, if all possible objections must be first overcome. If you will favour my project I will try the first flight at my own hazard. I have considered the structure of all volant animals, and find the folding continuity of the bat's wings most easily accommodated to the human form. Upon this model I shall begin my task to morrow, and in a year expect to tower into the air beyond the malice or persuit of man. But I will work only on this condition, that the art shall not be divulged, and that you shall not require me to make wings for any but ourselves.'

'Why, said Rasselas, should you envy others so great an advantage? All skill ought to be exerted for universal good; every man has owed much to others, and ought to repay the kindness that he has received.'

'If men were all virtuous, returned the artist, I should

with great alacrity teach them all to fly. But what would
be the security of the good, if the bad could at pleasure
invade them from the sky? Against an army sailing
through the clouds neither walls, nor mountains, nor
seas, could afford any security. A flight of northern
savages might hover in the wind, and light at once with
irresistible violence upon the capital of a fruitful region
that was rolling under them. Even this valley, the retreat
of princes, the abode of happiness, might be violated by
the sudden descent of some of the naked nations that
swarm on the coast of the southern sea.'

The prince promised secrecy, and waited for the performance, not wholly hopeless of success. He visited the
work from time to time, observed its progress, and remarked many ingenious contrivances to facilitate motion,
and unite levity with strength. The artist was every day
more certain that he should leave vultures and eagles
behind him, and the contagion of his confidence seized
upon the prince.

In a year the wings were finished, and, on a morning
appointed, the maker appeared furnished for flight on a
little promontory: he waved his pinions a while to gather
air, then leaped from his stand, and in an instant dropped
into the lake. His wings, which were of no use in the air,
sustained him in the water, and the prince drew him to
land, half dead with terrour and vexation.

Chap. X

*Imlac's history continued. A dissertation
upon poetry.*

Wherever I went, I found that Poetry was considered as
the highest learning, and regarded with a veneration
somewhat approaching to that which man would pay to
the Angelick Nature. And it yet fills me with wonder,
that, in almost all countries, the most ancient poets are
considered as the best: whether it be that every other kind
of knowledge is an acquisition gradually attained, and
poetry is a gift conferred at once; or that the first poetry
of every nation surprised them as a novelty, and retained

the credit by consent which it received by accident at first: or whether, as the province of poetry is to describe Nature and Passion, which are always the same, the first writers took possession of the most striking objects for description, and the most probable occurrences for fiction, and left nothing to those that followed them, but transcription of the same events, and new combinations of the same images. Whatever be the reason, it is commonly observed that the early writers are in possession of nature, and their followers of art: that the first excel in strength and invention, and the latter in elegance and refinement.

'I was desirous to add my name to this illustrious fraternity. I read all the poets of Persia and Arabia, and was able to repeat by memory the volumes that are suspended in the mosque of Mecca. But I soon found that no man was ever great by imitation. My desire of excellence impelled me to transfer my attention to nature and to life. Nature was to be my subject, and men to be my auditors: I could never describe what I had not seen: I could not hope to move those with delight or terrour, whose interests and opinions I did not understand.

'Being now resolved to be a poet, I saw every thing with a new purpose; my sphere of attention was suddenly magnified: no kind of knowledge was to be overlooked. I ranged mountains and deserts for images and resemblances, and pictured upon my mind every tree of the forest and flower of the valley. I observed with equal care the crags of the rock and the pinnacles of the palace. Sometimes I wandered along the mazes of the rivulet, and sometimes watched the changes of the summer clouds. To a poet nothing can be useless. Whatever is beautiful, and whatever is dreadful, must be familiar to his imagination: he must be conversant with all that is awfully vast or elegantly little. The plants of the garden, the animals of the wood, the minerals of the earth, and meteors of the sky, must all concur to store his mind with inexhaustible variety: for every idea is useful for the inforcement or decoration of moral or religious truth; and he, who knows most, will have most power of diversifying his scenes, and of gratifying his reader with remote allusions and unexpected instruction.

'All the appearances of nature I was therefore careful to study, and every country which I have surveyed has contributed something to my poetical powers.'

'In so wide a survey, said the prince, you must surely have left much unobserved. I have lived, till now, within the circuit of these mountains, and yet cannot walk abroad without the sight of something which I had never beheld before, or never heeded.'

'The business of a poet, said Imlac, is to examine, not the individual, but the species; to remark general proper- ties and large appearances: he does not number the streaks of the tulip, or describe the different shades in the verdure of the forest. He is to exhibit in his portraits of nature such prominent and striking features, as recal the original to every mind; and must neglect the minuter discriminations, which one may have remarked, and another have neglected, for those characteristicks which are alike obvious to vigilance and carelessness.

'But the knowledge of nature is only half the task of a poet; he must be acquainted likewise with all the modes of life. His character requires that he estimate the happi- ness and misery of every condition; observe the power of all the passions in all their combinations, and trace the changes of the human mind as they are modified by various institutions and accidental influences of climate or custom, from the spriteliness of infancy to the despon- dence of decrepitude. He must divest himself of the pre- judices of his age or country; he must consider right and wrong in their abstracted and invariable state; he must disregard present laws and opinions, and rise to general and transcendental truths, which will always be the same: he must therefore content himself with the slow progress of his name; contemn the applause of his own time, and commit his claims to the justice of posterity. He must write as the interpreter of nature, and the legislator of mankind, and consider himself as presiding over the thoughts and manners of future generations; as a being superiour to time and place.

'His labour is not yet at an end: he must know many languages and many sciences; and, that his stile may be worthy of his thoughts, must, by incessant practice, familiarize to himself every delicacy of speech and grace of harmony.'

Chap. XXII

The happiness of a life led according to nature.

Rasselas went often to an assembly of learned men, who met at stated times to unbend their minds, and compare their opinions. Their manners were somewhat coarse, but their conversation was instructive, and their disputations acute, though sometimes too violent, and often continued till neither controvertist remembered upon what question they began. Some faults were almost general among them: every one was desirous to dictate to the rest, and every one was pleased to hear the genius or knowledge of another depreciated.

In the assembly Rasselas was relating his interview with the hermit, and the wonder with which he heard him censure a course of life which he had so deliberately chosen, and so laudably followed. The sentiments of the hearers were various. Some were of opinion, that the folly of his choice had been justly punished by condemnation to perpetual perseverance. One of the youngest among them, with great vehemence, pronounced him an hypocrite. Some talked of the right of society to the labour of individuals, and considered retirement as a desertion of duty. Others readily allowed, that there was a time when the claims of the publick were satisfied, and when a man might properly sequester himself, to review his life, and purify his heart.

One, who appeared more affected with the narrative than the rest, thought it likely, that the hermit would, in a few years, go back to his retreat, and, perhaps, if shame did not restrain, or death intercept him, return once more from his retreat into the world: 'For the hope of happiness, said he, is so strongly impressed, that the longest experience is not able to efface it. Of the present state, whatever it be, we feel, and are forced to confess, the misery, yet, when the same state is again at a distance, imagination paints it as desirable. But the time will surely come, when desire will be no longer our torment, and no man shall be wretched but by his own fault.'

'This, said a philosopher, who had heard him with tokens of great impatience, is the present condition of a wise man. The time is already come, when none are wretched but by their own fault. Nothing is more idle, than to inquire after happiness, which nature has kindly placed within our reach. The way to be happy is to live according to nature, in obedience to that universal and unalterable law with which every heart is originally impressed; which is not written on it by precept, but engraven by destiny, not instilled by education, but infused at our nativity. He that lives according to nature will suffer nothing from the delusions of hope, or importunities of desire: he will receive and reject with equability of temper; and act or suffer as the reason of things shall alternately prescribe. Other men may amuse themselves with subtle definitions, or intricate raciocination. Let them learn to be wise by easier means: let them observe the hind of the forest, and the linnet of the grove: let them consider the life of animals, whose motions are regulated by instinct; they obey their guide and are happy. Let us therefore, at length, cease to dispute, and learn to live; throw away the incumbrance of precepts, which they who utter them with so much pride and pomp do not understand, and carry with us this simple and intelligible maxim, That deviation from nature is deviation from happiness.'

When he had spoken, he looked round him with a placid air, and enjoyed the consciousness of his own beneficence. 'Sir, said the prince, with great modesty, as I, like all the rest of mankind, am desirous of felicity, my closest attention has been fixed upon your discourse: I doubt not the truth of a position which a man so learned has so confidently advanced. Let me only know what it is to live according to nature.'

'When I find young men so humble and so docile, said the philosopher, I can deny them no information which my studies have enabled me to afford. To live according to nature, is to act always with due regard to the fitness arising from the relations and qualities of causes and effects; to concur with the great and unchangeable scheme of universal felicity; to co-operate with the general disposition and tendency of the present system of things.'

The prince soon found that this was one of the sages whom he should understand less as he heard him longer. He therefore bowed and was silent, and the philosopher, supposing him satisfied, and the rest vanquished, rose up and departed with the air of a man that had co-operated with the present system.

Chap. XXVIII

Rasselas and Nekayah continue their conversation.

'Dear princess, said Rasselas, you fall into the common errours of exaggeratory declamation, by producing, in a familiar disquisition, examples of national calamities, and scenes of extensive misery, which are found in books rather than in the world, and which, as they are horrid, are ordained to be rare. Let us not imagine evils which we do not feel, nor injure life by misrepresentations. I cannot bear that querelous eloquence which threatens every city with a siege like that of Jerusalem, that makes famine attend on every flight of locusts, and suspends pestilence on the wing of every blast that issues from the south.

'On necessary and inevitable evils, which overwhelm kingdoms at once, all disputation is vain: when they happen they must be endured. But it is evident, that these bursts of universal distress are more dreaded than felt: thousands and ten thousands flourish in youth, and wither in age, without the knowledge of any other than domestick evils, and share the same pleasures and vexations whether their kings are mild or cruel, whether the armies of their country persue their enemies, or retreat before them. While courts are disturbed with intestine competitions, and ambassadours are negotiating in foreign countries, the smith still plies his anvil, and the husbandman drives his plow forward; the necessaries of life are required and obtained, and the successive business of the seasons continues to make its wonted revolutions.

'Let us cease to consider what, perhaps, may never happen, and what, when it shall happen, will laugh at human speculation. We will not endeavour to modify the motions of the elements, or to fix the destiny of kingdoms. It is our business to consider what beings like us may perform; each labouring for his own happiness, by promoting within his circle, however narrow, the happiness of others.

'Marriage is evidently the dictate of nature; men and women were made to be companions of each other, and therefore I cannot be persuaded but that marriage is one of the means of happiness.'

'I know not, said the princess, whether marriage be more than one of the innumerable modes of human misery. When I see and reckon the various forms of connubial infelicity, the unexpected causes of lasting discord, the diversities of temper, the oppositions of opinion, the rude collisions of contrary desire where both are urged by violent impulses, the obstinate contests of disagreeing virtues, where both are supported by consciousness of good intention, I am sometimes disposed to think with the severer casuists of most nations, that marriage is rather permitted than approved, and that none, but by the instigation of a passion too much indulged, entangle themselves with indissoluble compacts.'

'You seem to forget, replied Rasselas, that you have, even now, represented celibacy as less happy than marriage. Both conditions may be bad, but they cannot both be worst. Thus it happens when wrong opinions are entertained, that they mutually destroy each other, and leave the mind open to truth.'

'I did not expect, answered the princess, to hear that imputed to falshood which is the consequence only of frailty. To the mind, as to the eye, it is difficult to compare with exactness objects vast in their extent, and various in their parts. Where we see or conceive the whole at once we readily note the discriminations and decide the preference: but of two systems, of which neither can be surveyed by any human being in its full compass of magnitude and multiplicity of complication, where is the wonder, that judging of the whole by parts, I am alternately affected by one and the other as either presses on my memory or fancy? We differ from ourselves just as we differ from each other, when we see only part of the question, as in the multifarious relations of politicks and morality: but when we perceive the whole at once, as in numerical computations, all agree in one judgment, and none ever varies his opinion.'

'Let us not add, said the prince, to the other evils of life, the bitterness of controversy, nor endeavour to vie with each other in subtilties of argument. We are employed in a search, of which both are equally to enjoy the success, or suffer by the miscarriage. It is therefore fit that we assist each other. You surely conclude too hastily from the infelicity of marriage against its institution; will not the misery of life prove equally that life cannot be the gift of heaven? The world must be peopled by marriage, or peopled without it.'

'How the world is to be peopled, returned Nekayah, is not my care, and needs not be yours. I see no danger that the present generation should omit to leave successors behind them: we are not now enquiring for the world, but for ourselves.'

Chap. XXIX

The debate on marriage continued.

'The good of the whole, says Rasselas, is the same with the good of all its parts. If marriage be best for mankind it must be evidently best for individuals, or a permanent and necessary duty must be the cause of evil, and some must be inevitably sacrificed to the convenience of others. In the estimate which you have made of the two states, it appears that the incommodities of a single life are, in a great measure, necessary and certain, but those of the conjugal state accidental and avoidable.

'I cannot forbear to flatter myself that prudence and benevolence will make marriage happy. The general folly of mankind is the cause of general complaint. What can be expected but disappointment and repentance from a choice made in the immaturity of youth, in the ardour of desire, without judgment, without foresight, without enquiry after conformity of opinions, similarity of manners, rectitude of judgment, or purity of sentiment.

'Such is the common process of marriage. A youth and maiden meeting by chance, or brought together by artifice, exchange glances, reciprocate civilities, go home, and dream of one another. Having little to divert attention, or diversify thought, they find themselves uneasy when they are apart, and therefore conclude that they shall be happy together. They marry, and discover what nothing but voluntary blindness had before concealed; they wear out life in altercations, and charge nature with cruelty.

'From those early marriages proceeds likewise the rivalry of parents and children: the son is eager to enjoy the world before the father is willing to forsake it, and there is hardly room at once for two generations. The daughter begins to bloom before the mother can be content to fade, and neither can forbear to wish for the absence of the other.

'Surely all these evils may be avoided by that deliberation and delay which prudence prescribes to irrevocable choice. In the variety and jollity of youthful pleasures life may be well enough supported without the help of a partner. Longer time will increase experience, and wider views will allow better opportunities of enquiry and selection: one advantage, at least, will be certain; the parents will be visibly older than their children.'

'What reason cannot collect, said Nekayah, and what experiment has not yet taught, can be known only from the report of others. I have been told that late marriages are not eminently happy. This is a question too important to be neglected, and I have often proposed it to those, whose accuracy of remark, and comprehensiveness of knowledge, made their suffrages worthy of regard. They have generally determined, that it is dangerous for a man and woman to suspend their fate upon each other, at a time when opinions are fixed, and habits are established; when friendships have been contracted on both sides, when life has been planned into method, and the mind has long enjoyed the contemplation of its own prospects.

'It is scarcely possible that two travelling through the world under the conduct of chance, should have been both directed to the same path, and it will not often happen that either will quit the track which custom has made pleasing. When the desultory levity of youth has settled into regularity, it is soon succeeded by pride ashamed to yield, or obstinacy delighting to contend. And even though mutual esteem produces mutual desire to please, time itself, as it modifies unchangeably the external mien, determines likewise the direction of the passions, and gives an inflexible rigidity to the manners. Long customs are not easily broken: he that attempts to change the course of his own life, very often labours in vain; and how shall we do that for others which we are seldom able to do for ourselves?'

'But surely, interposed the prince, you suppose the chief motive of choice forgotten or neglected. Whenever I shall seek a wife, it shall be my first question, whether she be willing to be led by reason?'

'Thus it is, said Nekayah, that philsophers are deceived. There are a thousand familiar disputes which reason never can decide; questions that elude investigation, and make logick ridiculous; cases where something must be done, and where little can be said. Consider the state of mankind, and enquire how few can be supposed to act upon any occasions, whether small or great, with all the reasons of action present to their minds. Wretched would be the pair above all names of wretchedness, who should be doomed to adjust by reason every morning all the minute detail of a domestick day.

'Those who marry at an advanced age, will probably escape the encroachments of their children; but, in diminution of this advantage, they will be likely to leave them, ignorant and helpless, to a guardian's mercy: or, if that should not happen, they must at least go out of the world before they see those whom they love best either wise or great.

'From their children, if they have less to fear, they have less also to hope, and they lose, without equivalent, the joys of early love, and the convenience of uniting with manners pliant, and minds susceptible of new impressions, which might wear away their dissimilitudes by long cohabitation, as soft bodies, by continual attrition, conform their surfaces to each other.

'I believe it will be found that those who marry late are best pleased with their children, and those who marry early with their partners.'

'The union of these two affections, said Rasselas, would produce all that could be wished. Perhaps there is a time when marriage might unite them, a time neither too early for the father, nor too late for the husband.'

'Every hour, answered the princess, confirms my prejudice in favour of the position so often uttered by the mouth of Imlac, "That nature sets her gifts on the right hand and on the left." Those conditions, which flatter hope and attract desire, are so constituted, that, as we approach one, we recede from another. There are goods so opposed that we cannot seize both, but, by too much prudence, may pass between them at too great a distance to reach either. This is often the fate of long consideration; he does nothing who endeavours to do more than is allowed to humanity. Flatter not yourself with contrarieties of pleasure. Of the blessings set before you make your choice, and be content. No man can taste the fruits of autumn while he is delighting his scent with the flowers of the spring: no man can, at the same time, fill his cup from the source and from the mouth of the Nile.'

Chap. XLIV

The dangerous prevalence of imagination.

'Disorders of intellect, answered Imlac, happen much more often than superficial observers will easily believe.

Perhaps, if we speak with rigorous exactness, no human mind is in its right state. There is no man whose imagination does not sometimes predominate over his reason, who can regulate his attention wholly by his will, and whose ideas will come and go at his command. No man will be found in whose mind airy notions do not sometimes tyrannise, and force him to hope or fear beyond the limits of sober probability. All power of fancy over reason is a degree of insanity; but while this power is such as we can controul and repress, it is not visible to others, nor considered as any depravation of the mental faculties: it is not pronounced madness but when it comes ungovernable, and apparently influences speech or action.

'To indulge the power of fiction, and send imagination out upon the wing, is often the sport of those who delight too much in silent speculation. When we are alone we are not always busy; the labour of excogitation is too violent to last long; the ardour of enquiry will sometimes give way to idleness or satiety. He who has nothing external that can divert him, must find pleasure in his own thoughts, and must conceive himself what he is not; for who is pleased with what he is? He then expatiates in boundless futurity, and culls from all imaginable conditions that which for the present moment he should most desire, amuses his desires with impossible enjoyments, and confers upon his pride unattainable dominion. The mind dances from scene to scene, unites all pleasures in all combinations, and riots in delights which nature and fortune, with all their bounty, cannot bestow.

'In time some particular train of ideas fixes the attention, all other intellectual gratifications are rejected, the mind, in weariness or leisure, recurs constantly to the favourite conception, and feasts on the luscious falsehood whenever she is offended with the bitterness of truth. By degrees the reign of fancy is confirmed; she grows first imperious, and in time despotick. Then fictions begin to operate as realities, false opinions fasten upon the mind, and life passes in dreams of rapture or of anguish.

'This, Sir, is one of the dangers of solitude, which the hermit has confessed not always to promote goodness, and the astronomer's misery has proved to be not always propitious to wisdom.'

'I will no more, said the favourite, imagine myself the queen of Abissinia. I have often spent the hours, which the princess gave to my own disposal, in adjusting ceremonies and regulating the court; I have repressed the pride of the powerful, and granted the petitions of the poor; I have built new palaces in more happy situations, planted groves upon the tops of mountains, and have exulted in the beneficence of royalty, till, when the princess entered, I had almost forgotten to bow down before her.'

'And I, said the princess, will not allow myself any more to play the shepherdess in my waking dreams. I have often soothed my thoughts with the quiet and innocence of pastoral employments, till I have in my chamber heard the winds whistle, and the sheep bleat; sometimes freed the lamb entangled in the thicket, and sometimes with my crook encountered the wolf. I have a dress like that of the village maids, which I put on to help my imagination, and a pipe on which I play softly, and suppose myself followed by my flocks.'

'I will confess, said the prince, an indulgence of fantastick delight more dangerous than yours. I have frequently endeavoured to image the possibility of a perfect government, by which all wrong should be restrained, all vice reformed, and all the subjects preserved in tranquility and innocence. This thought produced innumerable schemes of reformation, and dictated many useful regulations and salutary edicts. This has been the sport and sometimes the labour of my solitude; and I start, when I think with how little anguish I once supposed the death of my father and my brothers.'

'Such, says Imlac, are the effects of visionary schemes: when we first form them we know them to be absurd, but familiarise them by degrees, and in time lose sight of their folly.'

Chap. XLIX

The conclusion, in which nothing is concluded.

It was now the time of the inundation of the Nile: a few

days after their visit to the catacombs, the river began to rise.

They were confined to their house. The whole region being under water gave them no invitation to any excursions, and, being well supplied with materials for talk, they diverted themselves with comparisons of the different forms of life which they had observed, and with various schemes of happiness which each of them had formed.

Pekuah was never so much charmed with any place as the convent of St. Anthony, where the Arab restored her to the princess, and wished only to fill it with pious maidens, and to be made prioress of the order: she was weary of expectation and disgust, and would gladly be fixed in some unvariable state.

The princess thought, that of all sublunary things, knowledge was the best: She desired first to learn all sciences, and then purposed to found a college of learned women, in which she would preside, that, by conversing with the old, and educating the young, she might divide her time between the acquisition and communication of wisdom, and raise up for the next age models of prudence, and patterns of piety.

The prince desired a little kingdom, in which he might administer justice in his own person, and see all the parts of government with his own eyes; but he could never fix the limits of his dominion, and was always adding to the number of his subjects.

Imlac and the astronomer were contented to be driven along the stream of life without directing their course to any particular port.

Of these wishes that they had formed they well knew that none could be obtained. They deliberated a while what was to be done, and resolved, when the inundation should cease, to return to Abissinia.

Literary Piracy

This paper [*The Idler*] was in such high estimation before it was collected into volumes, that it was seized on with avidity by various publishers of newspapers and magazines, to enrich their publications. Johnson, to put a stop to this unfair proceeding, wrote for the *Universal Chronicle* the following advertisement; in which there is, perhaps, more pomp of words than the occasion demanded:

'London, January 5, 1759. ADVERTISEMENT. The proprietors of the paper intitled *The Idler*, having found that those essays are inserted in the news-papers and magazines with so little regard to justice or decency, that the *Universal Chronicle*, in which they first appear, is not always mentioned, think it necessary to declare to the publishers of those collections, that however patiently they have hitherto endured these injuries, made yet more injurious by contempt, they have now determined to endure them no longer. They have already seen essays, for which a very large price is paid, transferred, with the most shameless rapacity, into the weekly or monthly compilations, and their right, at least for the present, alienated from them, before they could themselves be said to enjoy it. But they would not willingly be thought to want tenderness, even for men by whom no tenderness hath been shewn. The past is without remedy, and shall be without resentment. But those who have been thus busy with their sickles in the fields of their neighbours, are henceforward to take notice, that the time of impunity is at an end. Whoever shall, without our leave, lay the hand of rapine upon our papers, is to expect that we shall vindicate our due, by the means which justice prescribes, and which are warranted by the immemorial prescriptions of honourable trade. We shall lay hold, in our turn, on their copies, degrade them from the pomp of wide margin and diffuse typography, contract them into a narrow space, and sell them at an humble price; yet not with a view of growing rich by confiscations, for we think not much better of money got by punishment than by crimes. We shall, therefore, when our losses are repaid, give what profit shall remain to the *Magdalens*; for we know not who can be more properly taxed for the support of penitent prostitutes, than prostitutes in whom there yet appears neither penitence nor shame.'

Boswell, Life

The Evils of Discovery

In 1463, in the third year of the reign of John II. died
prince Henry, the first encourager of remote navigation,
by whose incitement, patronage and example, distant
nations have been made acquainted with each other,
unknown countries have been brought into general view,
and the power of Europe has been extended to the remotest parts of the world. What mankind has lost and
gained by the genius and designs of this prince, it would
be long to compare, and very difficult to estimate. Much
knowledge has been acquired, and much cruelty been
committed; the belief of religion has been very little propagated, and its laws have been outrageously and enor-
mously violated. The Europeans have scarcely visited
any coast, but to gratify avarice, and extend corruption;
to arrogate dominion without right, and practise cruelty
without incentive. Happy had it then been for the oppressed, if the designs of Henry had slept in his bosom,
and surely more happy for the oppressors. But there is
reason to hope that out of so much evil good may sometimes be produced; and that the light of the gospel will
at last illuminate the sands of Africa, and the deserts of
America, though its progress cannot but be slow, when
it is so much obstructed by the lives of christians.

Introduction to *The World Displayed*

1758–60

THE IDLER

1759

The Death of a Friend

The following Letter relates to an affliction perhaps not
necessary to be imparted to the publick; but I could not
persuade myself to suppress it, because I think I know
the sentiments to be sincere, and I feel no disposition to
provide for this day any other entertainment.

At tu quisquis eris, miseri qui cruda poetæ
Credideris fletu funera digna tuo,
Hæc postrema tibi sit flendi causa, fluatque
Lenis inoffenso vitaque morsque gradu.

Mr. Idler,

Notwithstanding the warnings of philosophers, and the daily examples of losses and misfortunes which life forces upon our observation, such is the absorption of our thoughts in the business of the present day, such the resignation of our reason to empty hopes of future felicity, or such our unwillingness to foresee what we dread, that every calamity comes suddenly upon us, and not only presses us as a burden, but crushes as a blow.

There are evils which happen out of the common course of nature, against which it is no reproach not to be provided. A flash of lightning intercepts the traveller in his way; the concussion of an earthquake heaps the ruins of cities upon their inhabitants. But other miseries time brings, though silently yet visibly, forward by its even lapse, which yet approach us unseen because we turn our eyes away, and seize us unresisted because we could not arm ourselves against them but by setting them before us.

That it is vain to shrink from what cannot be avoided, and to hide that from ourselves which must some time be found, is a truth which we all know, but which all neglect, and perhaps none more than the speculative reasoner, whose thoughts are always from home, whose eye wanders over life, whose fancy dances after meteors of happiness kindled by itself, and who examines every thing rather than his own state.

Nothing is more evident than that the decays of age must terminate in death; yet there is no man, says Tully, who does not believe that he may yet live another year; and there is none who does not, upon the same principle, hope another year for his parent or his friend: but the fallacy will be in time detected; the last year, the last day, must come. It has come, and is past. The life which made my own life pleasant is at an end, and the gates of death are shut upon my prospects.

The loss of a friend upon whom the heart was fixed, to whom every wish and endeavour tended, is a state of dreary desolation, in which the mind looks abroad impatient of itself, and finds nothing but emptiness and horrour. The blameless life, the artless tenderness, the pious simplicity, the modest resignation, the patient sickness, and the quiet death, are remembered only to add value to the loss, to aggravate regret for what cannot be amended, to deepen sorrow for what cannot be recalled.

These are the calamities by which Providence gradually disengages us from the love of life. Other evils fortitude may repel, or hope may mitigate; but irreparable privation leaves nothing to exercise resolution or flatter expectation. The dead cannot return, and nothing is left us here but languishment and grief.

Yet such is the course of nature, that whoever lives long must outlive those whom he loves and honours. Such is the condition of our present existence, that life must one time lose its associations, and every inhabitant of the earth must walk downward to the grave alone and unregarded, without any partner of his joy or grief, without any interested witness of his misfortunes or success.

Misfortune, indeed, he may yet feel; for where is the bottom of the misery of man? But what is success to him that has none to enjoy it? Happiness is not found in self-contemplation; it is perceived only when it is reflected from another.

We know little of the state of departed souls, because such knowledge is not necessary to a good life. Reason deserts us at the brink of the grave, and can give no farther intelligence. Revelation is not wholly silent. *There is joy in the angels of Heaven over one sinner that repenteth*; and surely this joy is not incommunicable to souls disentangled from the body, and made like angels.

Let hope therefore dictate, what revelation does not confute, that the union of souls may still remain; and that we who are struggling with sin, sorrow, and infirmities, may have our part in the attention and kindness of those who have finished their course, and are now receiving their reward.

These are the great occasions which force the mind to take refuge in religion: when we have no help in ourselves, what can remain but that we look up to a higher and a greater Power? and to what hope may we not raise our eyes and hearts, when we consider that the greatest POWER is the BEST?

Surely there is no man who, thus afflicted, does not seek succour in the *gospel*, which has brought *life and immortality to light*. The precepts of Epicurus, who teaches us to endure what the laws of the universe make necessary, may silence, but not content us. The dictates of Zeno, who commands us to look with indifference on external things, may dispose us to conceal our sorrow, but cannot assuage it. Real alleviation of the loss of friends, and rational tranquillity in the prospect of our own dissolution, can be received only from the promises of Him in whose hands are life and death, and from the assurance of another and better state, in which all tears will be wiped from the eyes, and the whole soul shall be filled with joy. Philosophy may infuse stubbornness, but Religion only can give patience.

Idler, No. 41

Molly Quick

Mr. Idler,

I am encouraged, by the notice you have taken of Betty Broom, to represent the miseries which I suffer from a species of tyranny which, I believe, is not very uncommon, though perhaps it may have escaped the observation of those who converse little with fine ladies, or see them only in their publick characters.

To this method of venting my vexation I am the more inclined, because if I do not complain to you, I must burst in silence; for my mistress has teased me and teased me till I can hold no longer, and yet I must not tell her of her tricks. The girls that live in common services can quarrel, and give warning, and find other places; but we that live with great ladies, if we once offend them, have nothing left but to return into the country.

I am waiting-maid to a lady who keeps the best

company, and is seen at every place of fashionable resort. I am envied by all the maids in the square, for few countesses leave off so many clothes as my mistress, and nobody shares with me: so that I supply two families in the country with finery for the assizes and horse-races, besides what I wear myself. The steward and housekeeper have joined against me to procure my removal, that they may advance a relation of their own; but their designs are found out by my lady, who says I need not fear them, for she will never have dowdies about her.

You would think Mr. *Idler*, like others, that I am very happy, and may well be contented with my lot. But I will tell you. My lady has an odd humour. She never orders any thing in direct words, for she loves a sharp girl that can take a hint.

I would not have you suspect that she has any thing to hint which she is ashamed to speak at length; for none can have greater purity of sentiment, or rectitude of intention. She has nothing to hide, yet nothing will she tell. She always gives her directions oblique and allusively, by the mention of something relative or consequential, without any other purpose than to exercise my acuteness and her own.

It is impossible to give a notion of this style otherwise than by examples. One night, when she had sat writing letters till it was time to be dressed, *Molly*, said she, *the Ladies are all to be at Court to-night in white aprons*. When she means that I should send to order the chair, she says, *I think the streets are clean, I may venture to walk*. When she would have something put into its place, she bids me *lay it on the floor*. If she would have me snuff the candles, she asks *whether I think her eyes are like a cat's?* If she thinks her chocolate delayed, she talks of *the benefit of abstinence*. If any needlework is forgotten, she supposes *that I have heard of the lady who died by pricking her finger*.

She always imagines that I can recall every thing past from a single word. If she wants her head from the milliner, she only says, *Molly, you know Mrs. Tape*. If she would have the mantua-maker sent for, she remarks *that Mr. Taffety, the mercer, was here last week*. She ordered, a fortnight ago, that the first time she was abroad all day I should chuse her a new set of coffee-cups at the china-shop: of this she reminded me yesterday, as she was going down stairs, by saying, *You can't find your way now to Pall-mall.*

All this would never vex me, if, by increasing my trouble, she spared her own; but, dear Mr. *Idler*, is it not as easy to say *coffee-cups*, as *Pall-mall?* and to tell me in plain words what I am to do, and when it is to be done, as to torment her own head with the labour of finding hints, and mine with that of understanding them?

When first I came to this lady, I had nothing like the learning that I have now; for she has many books, and I have much time to read; so that of late I seldom have missed her meaning: but when she first took me I was an ignorant girl; and she, who, as is very common, con-founded want of knowledge with want of understanding, began once to despair of bringing me to any thing, be-cause, when I came into her chamber at the call of her bell, she asked me, *Whether we lived in Zembla?* and I did not guess the meaning of her inquiry, but modestly answered, that *I could not tell.* She had happened to ring once when I did not hear her, and meant to put me in mind of that country where sounds are said to be con-gealed by the frost.

Another time, as I was dressing her head, she began to talk on a sudden of *Medusa*, and *snakes*, and *men turned into stone, and maids that, if they were not watched, would let their mistresses be Gorgons.* I looked round me half frightened and quite bewildered; till at last, finding that her litera-ture was thrown away upon me, she bid me, with great vehemence, reach the curling-irons.

It is not without some indignation, Mr. *Idler*, that I discover, in these artifices of vexation, something worse than foppery or caprice; a mean delight in superiority, which knows itself in no danger of reproof or opposition; a cruel pleasure in seeing the perplexity of a mind obliged to find what is studiously concealed, and a mean indulgence of petty malevolence, in the sharp censure of involuntary, and very often of inevitable, failings. When, beyond her expectation, I hit upon her meaning, I can perceive a sudden cloud of disappointment spread over her face; and have sometimes been afraid, lest I should lose her favour by understanding her when she means to puzzle me.

This day, however, she has conquered my sagacity. When she went out of her dressing-room, she said nothing, but, *Molly, you know*, and hastened to her chariot. What I am to know is yet a secret; but if I do not know, before she comes back, what I yet have no means of discovering, she will make my dulness a pretence for a fortnight's ill humour, treat me as a creature devoid of the faculties necessary to the common duties of life, and perhaps give the next gown to the housekeeper.

I am, Sir,
Your humble Servant,
Molly Quick.
Idler, No. 46

Dick Minim

Criticism is a study by which men grow important and formidable at a very small expense. The power of invention has been conferred by nature upon few, and the labour of learning those sciences which may by mere labour be obtained is too great to be willingly endured; but every man can exert such judgment as he has upon the works of others; and he whom nature has made weak, and idleness keeps ignorant, may yet support his vanity by the name of a Critick.

I hope it will give comfort to great numbers who are passing through the world in obscurity, when I inform them how easily distinction may be obtained. All the other powers of literature are coy and haughty, they must be long courted, and at last are not always gained; but Criticism is a goddess easy of access and forward of advance, who will meet the slow, and encourage the timorous; the want of meaning she supplies with words, and the want of spirit she recompenses with malignity.

This profession has one recommendation peculiar to

itself, that it gives vent to malignity without real mischief. No genius was ever blasted by the breath of criticks. The poison which, if confined, would have burst the heart, fumes away in empty hisses, and malice is set at ease with very little danger to merit. The Critick is the only man whose triumph is without another's pain, and whose greatness does not rise upon another's ruin.

To a study at once so easy and so reputable, so malicious and so harmless, it cannot be necessary to invite my readers by a long or laboured exhortation; it is sufficient, since all would be Criticks if they could, to show by one eminent example that all can be Criticks if they will.

Dick Minim, after the common course of puerile studies, in which he was no great proficient, was put an apprentice to a brewer, with whom he had lived two years, when his uncle died in the city, and left him a large fortune in the stocks. Dick had for six months before used the company of the lower players, of whom he had learned to scorn a trade, and, being now at liberty to follow his genius, he resolved to be a man of wit and humour. That he might be properly initiated in his new character, he frequented the coffee-houses near the theatres, where he listened very diligently, day after day, to those who talked of language and sentiments, and unities and catastrophes, till, by slow degrees, he began to think that he understood something of the stage, and hoped in time to talk himself.

But he did not trust so much to natural sagacity as wholly to neglect the help of books. When the theatres were shut, he retired to Richmond with a few select writers, whose opinions he impressed upon his memory by unwearied diligence; and, when he returned with other wits to the town, was able to tell, in very proper phrases, that the chief business of art is to copy nature; that a perfect writer is not to be expected, because genius decays as judgment increases; that the great art is the art of blotting; and that, according to the rule of Horace, every piece should be kept nine years.

Of the great authors he now began to display the

characters, laying down as an universal position, that all had beauties and defects. His opinion was, that Shakespear, committing himself wholly to the impulse of nature, wanted that correctness which learning would have given him; and that Jonson, trusting to learning, did not sufficiently cast his eye on nature. He blamed the stanza of Spenser, and could not bear the hexameters of Sidney. Denham and Waller he held the first reformers of English numbers; and thought that if Waller could have obtained the strength of Denham, or Denham the sweetness of Waller, there had been nothing wanting to complete a poet. He often expressed his commiseration of Dryden's poverty, and his indignation at the age which suffered him to write for bread; he repeated with rapture the first lines of *All for Love*, but wondered at the corruption of taste which could bear any thing so unnatural as rhyming tragedies. In Otway he found uncommon powers of moving the passions, but was disgusted by his general negligence, and blamed him for making a conspirator his hero; and never concluded his disquisition, without remarking how happily the sound of the clock is made to alarm the audience. Southern would have been his favourite, but that he mixes comick with tragick scenes, intercepts the natural course of the passions, and fills the mind with a wild confusion of mirth and melancholy. The versification of Rowe he thought too melodious for the stage, and too little varied in different passions. He made it the great fault of Congreve, that all his persons were wits, and that he always wrote with more art than nature. He considered Cato rather as a poem than a play and allowed Addison to be the complete master of allegory and grave humour, but paid no great deference to him as a critick. He thought the chief merit of Prior was in his easy tales and lighter poems, though he allowed that his *Solomon* had many noble sentiments elegantly expressed. In Swift he discovered an inimitable vein of irony, and an easiness which all would hope and few would attain. Pope he was inclined to degrade from a poet to a versifier, and thought his numbers rather luscious than sweet. He often lamented the neglect of

Phædra and Hippolitus, and wished to see the stage under better regulations.

These assertions passed commonly uncontradicted; and if now and then an opponent started up, he was quickly repressed by the suffrages of the company, and Minim went away from every dispute with elation of heart and increase of confidence.

He now grew conscious of his abilities, and began to talk of the present state of dramatick poetry; wondered what was become of the comick genius which supplied our ancestors with wit and pleasantry, and why no writer could be found that durst now venture beyond a farce. He saw no reason for thinking that the vein of humour was exhausted, since we live in a country where liberty suffers every character to spread itself to its utmost bulk, and which therefore produces more originals than all the rest of the world together. Of tragedy he concluded business to be the soul, and yet often hinted that love predominates too much upon the modern stage.

He was now an acknowledged critick, and had his own seat in a coffee-house, and headed a party in the pit. Minim has more vanity than ill-nature, and seldom desires to do much mischief; he will perhaps murmur a little in the ear of him that sits next him, but endeavours to influence the audience to favour, by clapping when an actor exclaims, *Ye gods!* or laments the misery of his country.

By degrees he was admitted to rehearsals; and many of his friends are of opinion, that our present poets are indebted to him for their happiest thoughts; by his contrivance the bell was rung twice in *Barbarossa,* and by his persuasion the author of *Cleone* concluded his play without a couplet; for what can be more absurd, said Minim, than that part of a play should be rhymed, and part written in blank verse? And by what acquisition of faculties is the speaker, who never could find rhymes before, enabled to rhyme at the conclusion of an act?

He is the great investigator of hidden beauties, and is particularly delighted when he finds *the sound an echo to the sense.* He has read all our poets with particular

attention to this delicacy of versification, and wonders at
the supineness with which their works have been hitherto
perused, so that no man has found the sound of a drum
in this distich:

> When pulpit, drum ecclesiastick,
> Was beat with fist instead of a stick;

and that the wonderful lines upon honour and a bubble
have hitherto passed without notice:

> Honour is like the glassy bubble,
> Which cost philosophers such trouble;
> Where, one part crack'd, the whole doth fly,
> And wits are crack'd to find out why.

In these verses, says Minim, we have two striking ac-
commodations of the sound to the sense. It is impossible
to utter the two lines emphatically without an act like
that which they describe; *bubble* and *trouble* causing a
momentary inflation of the cheeks by the retention of the
breath, which is afterwards forcibly emitted, as in the
practice of *blowing bubbles*. But the greatest excellence is
in the third line, which is *crack'd* in the middle to express
a crack, and then shivers into monosyllables. Yet has this
diamond lain neglected with common stones, and among
the innumerable admirers of *Hudibras*, the observation of
this superlative passage has been reserved for the sagacity
of Minim.

.   .   .   .

Mr. Minim had now advanced himself to the zenith of
critical reputation; when he was in the pit, every eye in
the boxes was fixed upon him; when he entered his coffee-
house, he was surrounded by circles of candidates, who
passed their noviciate of literature under his tuition: his
opinion was asked by all who had no opinion of their own,
and yet loved to debate and decide; and no composition
was supposed to pass in safety to posterity, till it had been
secured by Minim's approbation.

Minim professes great admiration of the wisdom and
munificence by which the academies of the continent
were raised; and often wishes for some standard of taste,

for some tribunal, to which merit may appeal from caprice, prejudice, and malignity. He has formed a plan for an academy of criticism, where every work of imagination may be read before it is printed, and which shall authoritatively direct the theatres what pieces to receive or reject, to exclude or to revive.

Such an institution would, in Dick's opinion, spread the fame of English literature over Europe, and make London the metropolis of elegance and politeness, the place to which the learned and ingenious of all countries would repair for instruction and improvement, and where nothing would any longer be applauded or endured that was not conformed to the nicest rules, and finished with the highest elegance.

Till some happy conjunction of the planets shall dispose our princes or ministers to make themselves immortal by such an academy, Minim contents himself to preside four nights in a week in a critical society selected by himself, where he is heard without contradiction, and whence his judgment is disseminated through the great vulgar and the small.

When he is placed in the chair of criticism, he declares loudly for the noble simplicity of our ancestors, in opposition to the petty refinements, and ornamental luxuriance. Sometimes he is sunk in despair, and perceives false delicacy daily gaining ground, and sometimes brightens his countenance with a gleam of hope, and predicts the revival of the true sublime. He then fulminates his loudest censures against the monkish barbarity of rhyme; wonders how beings that pretend to reason can be pleased with one line always ending like another; tells how unjustly and unnaturally sense is sacrificed to sound; how often the best thoughts are mangled by the necessity of confining or extending them to the dimensions of a couplet; and rejoices that genius has, in our days, shaken off the shackles which had encumbered it so long. Yet he allows that rhyme may sometimes be born, if the lines be often broken, and the pauses judiciously diversified.

From blank verse he makes an easy transition to Milton, whom he produces as an example of the slow advance of lasting reputation. Milton is the only writer in whose books Minim can read for ever without weariness. What cause it is that exempts this pleasure from satiety he has long and diligently inquired, and believes it to consist in the perpetual variation of the numbers, by which the ear is gratified and the attention awakened. The lines that are commonly thought rugged and unmusical, he conceives to have been written to temper the melodious luxury of the rest, or to express things by a proper cadence: for he scarcely finds a verse that has not this favourite beauty; he declares that he could shiver in a hot-house when he reads that

> the ground
> Burns frore, and cold performs th' effect of fire;

and that, when Milton bewails his blindness, the verse,

> So thick a drop serene has quench'd these orbs,

has, he knows not how, something that strikes him with an obscure sensation like that which he fancies would be felt from the sound of darkness.

Minim is not so confident of his rules of judgment as not very eagerly to catch new light from the name of the author. He is commonly so prudent as to spare those whom he cannot resist, unless, as will sometimes happen, he finds the publick combined against them. But a fresh pretender to fame he is strongly inclined to censure, till his own honour requires that he commend him. Till he knows the success of a composition, he intrenches himself in general terms; there are some new thoughts and beautiful passages, but there is likewise much which he would have advised the author to expunge. He has several favourite epithets, of which he has never settled the meaning, but which are very commodiously applied to books which he has not read, or cannot understand. One is *manly*, another is *dry*, another *stiff*, and another *flimsy*; sometimes he discovers delicacy of style, and sometimes meets with *strange expressions*.

He is never so great, or so happy, as when a youth of promising parts is brought to receive his directions for the prosecution of his studies. He then puts on a very serious air; he advises the pupil to read none but the best authors, and, when he finds one congenial to his own mind, to study his beauties, but avoid his faults, and, when he sits down to write, to consider how his favourite author would think at the present time on the present occasion. He exhorts him to catch those moments when he finds his thoughts expanded and his genius exalted, but to take care lest imagination hurry him beyond the bounds of nature. He holds diligence the mother of success; yet enjoins him, with great earnestness, not to read more than he can digest, and not to confuse his mind by pursuing studies of contrary tendencies. He tells him, that every man has his genius, and that Cicero could never be a poet. The boy retires illuminated, resolves to follow his genius, and to think how Milton would have thought: and Minim feasts upon his own beneficence till another day brings another pupil.

Idler, Nos. 60, 61

1760

Horrour of the Last

Respicere ad longæ jussit spatia ultima vitæ. Juv.

Much of the pain and pleasure of mankind arises from the conjectures which every one makes of the thoughts of others; we all enjoy praise which we do not hear, and resent contempt which we do not see. The *Idler* may therefore be forgiven, if he suffers his imagination to represent to him what his readers will say or think, when they are informed that they have now his last paper in their hands.

Value is more frequently raised by scarcity than by use. That which lay neglected when it was common, rises in estimation as its quantity becomes less. We seldom learn the true want of what we have, till it is discovered that we can have no more.

This essay will, perhaps, be read with care even by those who have not yet attended to any other; and he that finds this late attention recompensed, will not forbear to wish that he had bestowed it sooner.

Though the *Idler* and his readers have contracted no close friendship, they are perhaps both unwilling to part. There are few things not purely evil, of which we can say, without some emotion of uneasiness, *this is the last.* Those who never could agree together, shed tears when mutual discontent has determined them to final separation; of a place which has been frequently visited, though without pleasure, the last look is taken with heaviness of heart; and the *Idler*, with all his chillness of tranquillity, is not wholly unaffected by the thought that his last essay is now before him.

This secret horrour of the last is inseparable from a thinking being, whose life is limited, and to whom death is dreadful. We always make a secret comparison between a part and the whole; the termination of any period of life reminds us that life itself has likewise its termination; when we have done any thing for the last time, we involuntarily reflect that a part of the days allotted us is past, and that as more is past there is less remaining.

It is very happily and kindly provided, that in every life there are certain pauses and interruptions, which force consideration upon the careless, and seriousness upon the light; points of time where one course of action ends, and another begins; and by vicissitudes of fortune, or alteration of employment, by change of place or loss of friendship, we are forced to say of something, *this is the last.*

An even and unvaried tenour of life always hides from our apprehension the approach of its end. Succession is not perceived but by variation; he that lives to-day as he lived yesterday, and expects that as the present day is such will be the morrow, easily conceives time as running in a circle and returning to itself. The uncertainty of our duration is impressed commonly by dissimilitude of condition; it is only by finding life changeable that we are reminded of its shortness.

This conviction, however forcible at every new impression, is every moment fading from the mind; and partly

by the inevitable incursion of new images, and partly by
voluntary exclusion of unwelcome thoughts, we are again
exposed to the universal fallacy; and we must do another
thing for the last time, before we consider that the time
is nigh when we shall do no more.

As the last *Idler* is published in that solemn week which
the Christian world has always set apart for the examination of the conscience, the review of life, the extinction of
earthly desires, and the renovation of holy purposes; I
hope that my readers are already disposed to view every
incident with seriousness, and improve it by meditation;
and that, when they see this series of trifles brought to a
conclusion, they will consider that, by outliving the *Idler*,
they have passed weeks, months, and years, which are
no longer in their power; that an end must in time be put
to every thing great as to every thing little; that to life
must come its last hour, and to this system of being its
last day, the hour at which probation ceases, and repentance will be vain; the day in which every work of the
hand, and imagination of the heart, shall be brought to
judgment, and an everlasting futurity shall be determined
by the past.

Idler, No. 103

1760
Charity to Prisoners

It is far from certain, that a single Englishman will suffer
by the charity to the French. New scenes of misery make
new impressions; and much of the charity which produced these donations, may be supposed to have been
generated by a species of calamity never known among
us before. Some imagine that the laws have provided all
necessary relief in common cases, and remit the poor to
the care of the publick; some have been deceived by
fictitious misery, and are afraid of encouraging imposture; many have observed want to be the effect of vice,
and consider casual almsgivers as patrons of idleness. But
all these difficulties vanish in the present case: we know

that for the Prisoners of War there is no legal provision; we see their distress, and are certain of its cause; we know that they are poor and naked, and poor and naked without a crime.

But it is not necessary to make any concessions. The opponents of this charity must allow it to be good, and will not easily prove it not to be the best. That charity is best, of which the consequences are most extensive: the relief of enemies has a tendency to unite mankind in fraternal affection; to soften the acrimony of adverse nations, and dispose them to peace and amity: in the mean time, it alleviates captivity, and takes away something from the miseries of war. The rage of war, however mitigated, will always fill the world with calamity and horrour: let it not then be unnecessarily extended; let animosity and hostility cease together; and no man be longer deemed an enemy, than while his sword is drawn against us.

The effects of these contributions may, perhaps, reach still further. Truth is best supported by virtue: we may hope from those who feel or who see our charity, that they shall no longer detest as heresy that religion, which makes its professors the followers of Him, who has commanded us to 'do good to them that hate us.'

Introduction to *Proceedings of the Committee for Clothing French Prisoners*

1761

Easter Resolutions

Easter Eve, 1761.
Since the Communion of last Easter I have led a life so dissipated and useless, and my terrours and perplexities have so much encreased, that I am under great depression and discouragement, yet I purpose to present myself before God to-morrow with humble hope that he will not break the bruised reed,

Come unto me all ye that travail.

I have resolved, I hope not presumptuously, till I am

afraid to resolve again. Yet hoping in God I steadfastly purpose to lead a new life. O God, enable me, for Jesus Christ's sake.

My purpose is

To avoid Idleness.

To regulate my sleep as to length and choice of hours.

To set down every day what shall be done the day following.

To keep a Journal.

To worship God more diligently.

To go to Church every Sunday.

To study the Scriptures.

To read a certain portion every week.

Almighty and most merciful Father look down upon my misery with pity, strengthen me that I may overcome all sinful habits, grant that I may with effectual faith commemorate the death of thy Son Jesus Christ, so that all corrupt desires may be extinguished, and all vain thoughts may be dispelled. Enlighten me with true knowledge, animate me with reasonable hope, comfort me with a just sense of thy love, and assist me to the performance of all holy purposes, that after the sins, errours, and miseries of this world, I may obtain everlasting happiness for Jesus Christ's sake. To whom, &c. Amen.

I hope to attend on God in his ordinances to-morrow. Trust in God O my soul. O God, let me trust in Thee.

Prayers and Meditations 1785

1762

To a Lady

Madam

I hope you will believe that my delay in answering Your letter could proceed only from my unwillingness to destroy any hope that You had form'd. Hope is itself a species of happiness, & perhaps the chief happiness which this World affords, but like all other pleasures immoderately enjoyed, the excesses of hope must be expiated by pain, & expectations improperly indulged must end in disappointment. If it be asked, what is the improper expectation which it is dangerous to indulge, experience will quickly answer, that it is such expectation, dictated not by reason but by desire; expectation raised not by the common occurrences of life but by the wants of the Expectant; an Expectation that requires the common course of things to be changed, and the general rules of Action to be broken.

When you made Your request to me, You should have considered, Madam, what You were asking. You ask me to solicit a great Man to whom I never spoke, for a young Person whom I had never seen, upon a supposition which I had no means of knowing to be true. There is no reason why amongst all the great, I should chuse to supplicate the Archbishop, nor why among all the possible objects of his bounty, the Archbishop should chuse your Son. I know, Madam, how unwillingly conviction is admitted, when interest opposes it; but surely, Madam, You must allow that there is no reason why that should be done by me which every other man may do with equal reason, and which indeed no man can do properly without some very particular Relation both to the Archbishop & to You. If I could help You in this exigence by any proper means, it would give me pleasure, but this proposal is so very remote from all usual methods, that I cannot comply with it, but at the risque of such answer & suspicions, as I believe you do not wish me to undergo.

I have seen your Son this morning, he seems a pretty Youth, and will perhaps find some better friend than I can procure him, but though he should at last miss the University he may still be wise, useful, & happy.

　　　　　I am Madam, Your most humble Servant,
June 8, 1762.　　　　　　　　　　　　Sam: Johnson

To the Earl of Bute

My Lord
　　When the bills were yesterday delivered to me by Mr. Wedderburne, I was informed by him of the future favours which his Majesty has, by your Lordship's recommendation, been induced to intend for me.

Bounty always receives part of its value from the manner in which it is bestowed; your Lordship's kindness includes every circumstance that can gratify delicacy, or enforce obligation. You have conferred your favours on a man who has neither alliance nor interest, who has not merited them by services, nor courted them by officiousness; you have spared him the shame of solicitation, and the anxiety of suspense.

What has been thus elegantly given, will, I hope, not be reproachfully enjoyed; I shall endeavour to give your Lordship the only recompense which generosity desires, —the gratification of finding that your benefits are not improperly bestowed. I am, my Lord,

Your Lordship's most obliged, most obedient, and most humble Servant,

July 20, 1762.   Sam: Johnson

Fidei Defensor

To the KING.

Sir,

Having by long labour, and diligent enquiry, endeavoured to illustrate and establish the chronology of the Bible, I hope to be pardoned the ambition of inscribing my work to your Majesty.

An age of war is not often an age of learning: the tumult and anxiety of military preparations seldom leave attention vacant to the silent progress of study, and the placid conquests of investigation; yet, surely, a vindication of the inspired writers can never be unseasonably offered to the DEFENDER OF THE FAITH, nor can it ever be improper to promote that Religion, without which all other blessings are snares of destruction, without which armies cannot make us safe, nor victories make us happy.

I am far from imagining that my testimony can add any thing to the honours of your Majesty, to the splendour of a reign crowded with triumphs, to the beauty of a life dignified by virtue. I can only wish, that your reign may long continue such as it has begun, and that the effulgence of your example may spread its light through distant ages, till it shall be the highest praise of any future mon-arch, that he exhibits some resemblance of GEORGE THE THIRD.

I am, Sir,
Your Majesty's, &c.
JOHN KENNEDY
Dedication of Kennedy's *Astronomical Chronology*

1763

Kit Smart

I have preserved the following short minute of what passed this day:—

'Madness frequently discovers itself merely by un-necessary deviation from the usual modes of the world. My poor friend Smart shewed the disturbance of his mind, by falling upon his knees, and saying his prayers in the street, or in any other unusual place. Now although, rationally speaking, it is greater madness not to pray at all, than to pray as Smart did, I am afraid there are so many who do not pray, that their understanding is not called in question.'

Concerning this unfortunate poet, Christopher Smart, who was confined in a mad-house, he had, at another time, the following conversation with Dr. Burney:— BURNEY. 'How does poor Smart do, Sir; is he likely to recover?' JOHNSON. 'It seems as if his mind had ceased to struggle with the disease; for he grows fat upon it.' BURNEY. 'Perhaps, Sir, that may be from want of exercise.' JOHNSON. 'No, Sir; he has partly as much exercise as he used to have, for he digs in the garden. Indeed, before his confinement, he used for exercise to walk to the ale-house; but he was *carried* back again. I did not think he ought to be shut up. His infirmities were not noxious to society. He insisted on people praying with him; and I'd as lief pray with Kit Smart as any one else. Another charge was, that he did not love clean linen; and I have no passion for it.'—Johnson continued, 'Mankind have a great aversion to intellectual labour; but even supposing knowledge to be easily attainable, more people would be content to be ignorant than would take even a little trouble to acquire it.

'The morality of an action depends on the motive from which we act. If I fling half a crown to a beggar with intention to break his head, and he picks it up and buys victuals with it, the physical effect is good; but, with respect to me, the action is very wrong. So, religious exercises, if not performed with an intention to please GOD, avail us nothing. As our Saviour says of those who perform them from other motives, "Verily they have their reward."

'The Christian religion has very strong evidences. It, indeed, appears in some degree strange to reason; but in History we have undoubted facts, against which, reasoning *à priori*, we have more arguments than we have for them; but then, testimony has great weight, and casts the balance. I would recommend to every man whose faith is yet unsettled, Grotius,—Dr. Pearson,[1]—and Dr. Clarke.'

Boswell, *Life*

Armchair Critics

I mentioned Mallet's tragedy of *Elvira*, which had been acted the preceding winter at Drury-lane, and that the Honourable Andrew Erskine, Mr. Dempster, and myself, had joined in writing a pamphlet, entitled, *Critical Strictures*, against it. That the mildness of Dempster's disposition had, however, relented; and he had candidly said, 'We have hardly a right to abuse this tragedy: for bad as it is, how vain should either of us be to write one not near so good.' JOHNSON. 'Why no, Sir; this is not just reasoning. You *may* abuse a tragedy, though you cannot write one. You may scold a carpenter who has made you a bad table, though you cannot make a table. It is not your trade to make tables.'

Boswell, *Life*

[1 An error for Pearce.]

Noble Prospects

Mr. Ogilvie was unlucky enough to choose for the topick of his conversation the praises of his native country. He began with saying, that there was very rich land round Edinburgh. Goldsmith, who had studied physick there, contradicted this, very untruly, with a sneering laugh. Disconcerted a little by this, Mr. Ogilvie then took new ground, where, I suppose, he thought himself perfectly safe; for he observed, that Scotland had a great many noble wild prospects. JOHNSON. 'I believe, Sir, you have a great many. Norway, too, has noble wild prospects; and Lapland is remarkable for prodigious noble wild prospects. But, Sir, let me tell you, the noblest prospect which a Scotchman ever sees, is the high road that leads him to England!' This unexpected and pointed sally produced a roar of applause. After all, however, those, who admire the rude grandeur of Nature, cannot deny it to Caledonia.

Boswell, *Life*

In Praise of Rhyme

He enlarged very convincingly upon the excellence of rhyme over blank verse in English poetry. I mentioned to him that Dr. Adam Smith, in his lectures upon composition, when I studied under him in the College of Glasgow, had maintained the same opinion strenuously, and I repeated some of his arguments. JOHNSON. 'Sir, I was once in company with Smith, and we did not take to each other; but had I known that he loved rhyme as much as you tell me he does, I should have HUGGED him.'

Boswell, *Life*

Excess of Stupidity

He laughed heartily, when I mentioned to him a saying of his concerning Mr. Thomas Sheridan, which Foote took a wicked pleasure to circulate. 'Why, Sir, Sherry is dull, naturally dull; but it must have taken him a great deal of pains to become what we now see him. Such an excess of stupidity, Sir, is not in Nature.' 'So (said he,) I allowed him all his own merit.'

He now added, 'Sheridan cannot bear me. I bring his declamation to a point. I ask him a plain question, "What do you mean to teach?" Besides, Sir, what influence can Mr. Sheridan have upon the language of this great country, by his narrow exertions? Sir, it is burning a farthing candle at Dover, to shew light at Calais.'

Boswell, *Life*

To George Strahan

Dear George

To give pain ought always to be painful, and I am sorry that I have been the occasion of any uneasiness to you, to whom I hope never to do any thing but for your benefit or your pleasure. Your uneasiness was without any reason on your part, as you had written with sufficient frequency to me, and I had only neglected to answer then, because as nothing new had been proposed to your study no new direction or incitement could be offered you. But if it had happened that you had omitted what you did not omit, and that I had for an hour, or a week, or a much longer time thought myself put out of your mind by something to which presence gave that prevalence, which presence will sometimes give, even where there is the most prudence and experience, you are not to imagine that my friendship is light enough to be blown away by the first cross blast, or that my regard or kindness hangs by so slender a hair, as to be broken off by the unfelt weight of a petty offence. I love you, and hope to love you long. You have hitherto done nothing to diminish my goodwill, and though you had done much more than you have supposed imputed to you my goodwill would not have been diminished.

I write thus largely on this suspicion which you have suffered to enter your mind, because in youth we are apt to be too rigorous in our expectations, and to suppose that the duties of life are to be performed with unfailing exactness and regularity, but in our progress through life we are forced to abate much of our demands, and to take friends such as we can find them, not as we would make them.

These concessions every wise man is more ready to make to others as he knows that he shall often want them for himself; and when he remembers how often he fails in the observance or cultivation of his best friends, is willing to suppose that his friends may in their turn neglect him without any intention to offend him.

When therefore it shall happen, as happen it will, that you or I have disappointed the expectation of the other, you are not to suppose that you have lost me or that I intended to lose you; nothing will remain but to repair the fault, and to go on as if it never had been committed,

I am Sir Your affectionate servant
Thursday July 14, 1763.   Sam: Johnson

To James Boswell at Utrecht

Dear Sir

You are not to think yourself forgotten, or criminally neglected, that you have had yet no letter from me. I love to see my friends, to hear from them, to talk to them, and to talk of them; but it is not without a considerable effort of resolution that I prevail upon myself to write. I would not, however, gratify my own indolence by the omission of any important duty, or any office of real kindness.

To tell you that I am or am not well, that I have or have not been in the country, that I drank your health in the room in which we sat last together, and that your acquaintance continue to speak of you with their former kindness, topicks with which those letters are commonly filled which are written only for the sake of writing, I seldom shall think worth communicating; but if I can have it in my power to calm any harassing disquiet, to excite any virtuous desire, to rectify any important opinion, or fortify any generous resolution, you need not doubt but I shall at least wish to prefer the pleasure of gratifying a friend much less esteemed than yourself, before the gloomy calm of idle vacancy. Whether I shall easily arrive at an exact punctuality of correspondence,

I cannot tell. I shall, at present, expect that you will receive this in return for two which I have had from you. The first, indeed, gave me an account so hopeless of the state of your mind, that it hardly admitted or deserved an answer; by the second I was much better pleased; and the pleasure will still be increased by such a narrative of the progress of your studies, as may evince the continuance of an equal and rational application of your mind to some useful enquiry.

You will, perhaps, wish to ask, what study I would recommend. I shall not speak of theology, because it ought not to be considered as a question whether you shall endeavour to know the will of God.

I shall, therefore, consider only such studies as we are at liberty to pursue or to neglect; and of these I know not how you will make a better choice, than by studying the civil law, as your father advises, and the ancient languages, as you had determined for yourself; at least resolve, while you remain in any settled residence, to spend a certain number of hours every day amongst your books. The dissipation of thought, of which you complain, is nothing more than the vacillation of a mind suspended between different motives, and changing its direction as any motive gains or loses strength. If you can but kindle in your mind any strong desire, if you can but keep predominant any wish for some particular excellence or attainment, the gusts of imagination will break away, without any effect upon your conduct, and commonly without any traces left upon the memory.

There lurks, perhaps, in every human heart a desire of distinction, which inclines every man first to hope, and then to believe, that Nature has given him something peculiar to himself. This vanity makes one mind nurse aversions, and another actuate desires, till they rise by art much above their original state of power; and as affectation, in time, improves to habit, they at last tyrannise over him who at first encouraged them only for show. Every desire is a viper in the bosom, who, while he was chill, was harmless; but when warmth gave him strength, exerted it in poison. You know a gentleman, who, when first he set his foot in the gay world, as he prepared himself to whirl in the vortex of pleasure, imagined a total indifference and universal negligence to be the most agreeable concomitants of youth, and the strongest indication of an airy temper and a quick apprehension. Vacant to every object, and sensible of every impulse, he thought that all appearance of diligence would deduct something from the reputation of genius; and hoped that he should appear to attain, amidst all the ease of carelessness and all the tumult of diversion, that knowledge and those accomplishments which mortals of the common fabrick obtain only by mute abstraction and solitary drudgery. He tried this scheme of life awhile, was made weary of it by his sense and his virtue, he then wished to return to his studies; and finding long habits of idleness and pleasure harder to be cured than he expected, still willing to retain his claim to some extraordinary prerogatives, resolved the common consequences of irregularity into an unalterable decree of destiny, and concluded that Nature had originally formed him incapable of rational employment.

Let all such fancies, illusive and destructive, be banished henceforward from your thoughts for ever. Resolve, and keep your resolution; choose, and pursue your choice. If you spend this day in study, you will find yourself still more able to study to-morrow; not that you are to expect that you shall at once obtain a complete victory. Depravity is not very easily overcome. Resolution will sometimes relax, and diligence will sometimes be interrupted; but let no accidental surprize or deviation, whether short or long, dispose you to despondency. Consider these failings as incident to all mankind. Begin again where you left off, and endeavour to avoid the seducements that prevailed over you before.

This, my dear Boswell, is advice which, perhaps, has been often given you, and given you without effect. But this advice, if you will not take from others, you must take from your own reflections, if you purpose to do the duties of the station to which the bounty of Providence has called you.

Let me have a long letter from you as soon as you can. I hope you continue your journal, and enrich it with many observations upon the country in which you reside. It will be a favour if you can get me any books in the Frisick language, and can enquire how the poor are maintained in the Seven Provinces.

I am, dear Sir, Your most affectionate servant,
London, Dec. 8, 1763.   Sam: Johnson

Character of Collins

Having formerly written his character, while perhaps it was yet more distinctly impressed upon my memory, I shall insert it here.

'Mr. Collins was a man of extensive literature, and of vigorous faculties. He was acquainted not only with the learned tongues, but with the Italian, French, and Spanish languages. He had employed his mind chiefly upon works of fiction and subjects of fancy, and by indulging some peculiar habits of thought was eminently delighted with those flights of imagination which pass the bounds of nature, and to which the mind is reconciled only by a passive acquiescence in popular traditions. He loved fairies, genii, giants, and monsters; he delighted to rove through the meanders of inchantment, to gaze on the magnificence of golden palaces, to repose by the water-falls of Elysian gardens.

'This was, however, the character rather of his inclination than his genius; the grandeur of wildness and the novelty of extravagance were always desired by him, but were not always attained. Yet as diligence is never wholly lost, if his efforts sometimes caused harshness and obscurity, they likewise produced in happier moments sublimity and splendour. This idea which he had formed of excellence led him to oriental fictions and allegorical imagery, and perhaps, while he was intent upon description, he did not sufficiently cultivate sentiment. His poems are the productions of a mind not deficient in fire, nor unfurnished with knowledge either of books or life, but

somewhat obstructed in its progress by deviation in quest
of mistaken beauties.

'His morals were pure, and his opinions pious; in a
long continuance of poverty and long habits of dissipation it cannot be expected that any character should be
exactly uniform. There is a degree of want by which the
freedom of agency is almost destroyed; and long association with fortuitous companions will at last relax the
strictness of truth, and abate the fervour of sincerity.
That this man, wise and virtuous as he was, passed always
unentangled through the snares of life, it would be prejudice and temerity to affirm; but it may be said that at
least he preserved the source of action unpolluted, that
his principles were never shaken, that his distinctions of
right and wrong were never confounded, and that his
faults had nothing of malignity or design, but proceeded
from some unexpected pressure, or casual temptation.

'The latter part of his life cannot be remembered but
with pity and sadness. He languished some years under
that depression of mind which enchains the faculties
without destroying them, and leaves reason the knowledge of right without the power of pursuing it. These
clouds which he perceived gathering on his intellects he
endeavoured to disperse by travel, and passed into
France; but found himself constrained to yield to his
malady, and returned. He was for some time confined
in a house of lunaticks, and afterwards retired to the care
of his sister in Chichester, where death in 1756 came to
his relief.

'After his return from France the writer of this character
paid him a visit at Islington, where he was waiting for his
sister, whom he had directed to meet him: there was then
nothing of disorder discernible in his mind by any but
himself, but he had withdrawn from study, and travelled
with no other book than an English Testament, such as
children carry to the school; when his friend took it into
his hand, out of curiosity to see what companion a Man
of Letters had chosen, "I have but one book," said
Collins, "but that is the best."'

Such was the fate of Collins, with whom I once delighted to converse, and whom I yet remember with tenderness.

Life of Collins, 1763, reprinted 1781

1764
Strange Oblivion

April 21, 1764, –3–m.

My indolence, since my last reception of the Sacrament, has sunk into grosser sluggishness, and my dissipation spread into wilder negligence. My thoughts have been clouded with sensuality, and, except that from the beginning of this year I have in some measure forborn excess of Strong Drink my appetites have predominated over my reason. A kind of strange oblivion has overspread me, so that I know not what has become of the last year, and perceive that incidents and intelligence pass over me without leaving any impression.

This is not the life to which Heaven is promised. I purpose to approach the altar again to morrow. Grant, O Lord, that I may receive the Sacrament with such resolutions of a better life as may by thy grace be effectual, for the sake of Jesus Christ. Amen.

Prayers and Meditations, 1785

1765
Goldsmith's The Traveller

How small of all that human hearts endure,
That part which laws or kings can cause or cure.
Still to ourselves in every place consign'd,
Our own felicity we make or find:
With secret course, which no loud storms annoy,
Glides the smooth current of domestic joy.
The lifted ax, the agonizing wheel,
Luke's iron crown, and Damien's bed of steel,
To men remote from power but rarely known,
Leave reason, faith, and conscience, all our own.

[The lines in italic are Goldsmith's own.]

To Charles Burney

Sir

I am sorry that your kindness to me has brought upon you so much trouble, though you have taken care to abate that sorrow, by the pleasure which I receive from your approbation. I defend my criticism in the same manner with you. We must confess the faults of our favourite,[1] to gain credit to our praise of his excellencies. He that claims either for himself or for another the honours of perfection, will surely injure the reputation which he designs to assist.

Be pleased to make my compliments to your family. I am, Sir, Your most obliged and most humble Servant, Oct. 16 1765　　　　　　　　　Sam: Johnson

1745–65
SHAKESPEARE EDITED

1745
Hanmer's Shakespeare

The rest of this edition I have not read, but, from the little that I have seen, think it not dangerous to declare that, in my opinion, its pomp recommends it more than its accuracy. There is no distinction made between the ancient reading, and the innovations of the editor; there is no reason given for any of the alterations which are made; the emendations of former critics are adopted without any acknowledgment, and few of the difficulties are removed which have hitherto embarrassed the readers of Shakespeare.

I would not, however, be thought to insult the editor, nor to censure him with too much petulance, for having failed in little things, of whom I have been told, that he excels in greater. But I may without indecency, observe, that no man should attempt to teach others what he has never learned himself; and that those who, like Themisto-

[1 Shakespeare.]

cles, have studied the arts of policy, and *can teach a small state how to grow great*, should, like him, disdain to labour in trifles, and consider petty accomplishments as below their ambition.

Observations on Macbeth, 1745

Shakespeare and Dryden

——Now o'er one half the world
Nature seems dead.

That is, *over our hemisphere all action and motion seem to have ceased.* This image, which is perhaps the most striking that poetry can produce, has been adopted by Dryden in his *Conquest of Mexico*.

All things are hush'd as nature's self lay dead,
The mountains seem to nod their drowsy head;
The little birds in dreams their songs repeat,
And sleeping flow'rs beneath the night-dews sweat.
Even lust and envy sleep!

These lines, though so well known, I have transcribed, that the contrast between them and this passage of Shakespeare may be more accurately observed.

Night is described by two great poets, but one describes a night of quiet, the other of perturbation. In the night of Dryden, all the disturbers of the world are laid asleep; in that of Shakespeare, nothing but sorcery, lust, and murder is awake. He that reads Dryden, finds himself lulled with serenity, and disposed to solitude and contemplation. He that peruses Shakespeare, looks round alarmed, and starts to find himself alone. One is the night of a lover, the other that of a murderer.

Observations on Macbeth, 1745

Aroint thee, witch,———

In one of the folio editions the reading is *anoint thee*, in a sense very consistent with the common accounts of witches, who are related to perform many supernatural acts by the means of unguents, and particularly to fly through the air to the place where they meet at their hellish festivals. In this sense *anoint thee, witch*, will mean, *away, witch, to your infernal assembly.* This reading I was inclined to favour, because I had met with the word *aroint* in no other place; till looking into Herne's Collections, I found it in a very old drawing, that he has published, in which St. Patrick is represented visiting hell, and putting the devils into great confusion by his presence, of whom one that is driving the damned before him with a prong, has a label issuing out from his mouth with these words **out out aroingt**, of which the last is evidently the same with *aroint*, and used in the same sense as in this passage.

Observations on Macbeth, 1745

1756
The Proposals

When the works of Shakespeare are, after so many editions, again offered to the Publick, it will doubtless be inquired, why Shakespeare stands in more need of critical assistance than any other of the English writers, and what are the deficiencies of the late attempts, which another editor may hope to supply?

The business of him that republishes an ancient book, is, to correct what is corrupt, and to explain what is obscure. To have a text corrupt in many places, and in many doubtful, is, among the authors that have written since the use of types, almost peculiar to Shakespeare. Most writers, by publishing their own works, prevent all various readings, and preclude all conjectural criticism. Books indeed are sometimes published after the death of him who produced them; but they are better secured from corruption than these unfortunate compositions. They subsist in a single copy, written or revised by the author; and the faults of the printed volume can be only faults of one descent.

But of the works of Shakespeare the condition has been far different: he sold them, not to be printed, but to be played. They were immediately copied for the actors, and multiplied by transcript after transcript, vitiated by the blunders of the penman, or changed by the affectation of the player; perhaps enlarged to introduce a jest, or mutilated to shorten the representation; and printed at last without the concurrence of the author, without the consent of the proprietor, from compilations made by chance or by stealth out of the separate parts written for the theatre: and thus thrust into the world surreptitiously and hastily, they suffered another depravation from the ignorance and negligence of the printers, as every man who knows the state of the press in that age will readily conceive.

It is not easy for invention to bring together so many causes concurring to vitiate the text. No other author ever gave up his works to fortune and time with so little care: no books could be left in hands so likely to injure them, as plays frequently acted, yet continued in manuscript: no other transcribers were likely to be so little qualified for their task as those who copied for the stage, at a time when the lower ranks of the people were universally illiterate: no other editions were made from fragments so minutely broken, and so fortuitously reunited; and in no other age was the art of printing in such unskilful hands.

With the causes of corruption that make the revisal of Shakespeare's dramatick pieces necessary, may be enumerated the causes of obscurity, which may be partly imputed to his age, and partly to himself.

When a writer outlives his contemporaries, and remains almost the only unforgotten name of a distant time, he is necessarily obscure. Every age has its modes of speech, and its cast of thought; which, though easily explained when there are many books to be compared with each other, become sometimes unintelligible and always difficult, when there are no parallel passages that may conduce to their illustration. Shakespeare is the first considerable author of sublime or familiar dialogue in our language. Of the books which he read, and from which he formed his style, some perhaps have perished, and the rest are neglected. His imitations are therefore unnoted, his allusions are undiscovered, and many beauties, both of pleasantry and greatness, are lost with the objects to which they were united, as the figures vanish when the canvass has decayed.

It is the great excellence of Shakespeare, that he drew his scenes from nature, and from life. He copied the manners of the world then passing before him, and has more allusions than other poets to the traditions and superstition of the vulgar; which must therefore be traced before he can be understood.

He wrote at a time when our poetical language was yet unformed, when the meaning of our phrases was yet in fluctuation, when words were adopted at pleasure from the neighbouring languages, and while the Saxon was still visibly mingled in our diction. The reader is therefore embarrassed at once with dead and with foreign languages, with obsoleteness and innovation. In that age, as in all others, fashion produced phraseology, which succeeding fashion swept away before its meaning was generally known, or sufficiently authorized: and in that age, above all others, experiments were made upon our language, which distorted its combinations, and disturbed its uniformity.

If Shakespeare has difficulties above other writers, it is to be imputed to the nature of his work, which required the use of the common colloquial language, and consequently admitted many phrases allusive, elliptical, and proverbial, such as we speak and hear every hour without observing them; and of which, being now familiar, we do not suspect that they can ever grow uncouth, or that, being now obvious, they can ever seem remote.

These are the principal causes of the obscurity of Shakespeare; to which might be added the fulness of idea, which might sometimes load his words with more sentiment than they could conveniently convey, and that rapidity of imagination which might hurry him to a second thought before he had fully explained the first. But my opinion is, that very few of his lines were difficult to his audience, and that he used such expressions as were then common, though the paucity of contemporary writers makes them now seem peculiar.

Authors are often praised for improvement, or blamed for innovation, with very little justice, by those who read few other books of the same age. Addison himself has been so unsuccessful in enumerating the words with which Milton has enriched our language, as perhaps not to have named one of which Milton was the author; and Bentley has yet more unhappily praised him as the introducer of those elisions into English poetry, which had been used from the first essays of versification among us, and which Milton was indeed the last that practised.

Another impediment, not the least vexatious to the commentator, is the exactness with which Shakespeare followed his authors. Instead of dilating his thoughts into generalities, and expressing incidents with poetical latitude, he often combines circumstances unnecessary to his main design, only because he happened to find them together. Such passages can be illustrated only by him who has read the same story in the very book which Shakespeare consulted.

He that undertakes an edition of Shakespeare, has all these difficulties to encounter, and all these obstructions to remove.

Proposals, 1756

1765

The Preface

The Praise of Shakespeare

That praises are without reason lavished on the dead, and that the honours due only to excellence are paid to antiquity, is a complaint likely to be always continued by those, who, being able to add nothing to truth, hope for eminence from the heresies of paradox; or those, who, being forced by disappointment upon consolatory expedients, are willing to hope from posterity what the present age refuses, and flatter themselves that the regard, which is yet denied by envy, will be at last bestowed by time.

Antiquity, like every other quality that attracts the notice of mankind, has undoubtedly votaries that reverence it, not from reason, but from prejudice. Some seem to admire indiscriminately whatever has been long preserved, without considering that time has sometimes cooperated with chance; all perhaps are more willing to honour past than present excellence; and the mind contemplates genius through the shades of age, as the eye surveys the sun through artificial opacity. The great contention of criticism is to find the faults of the moderns, and the beauties of the ancients. While an author is yet living we estimate his powers by his worst performance, and when he is dead, we rate them by his best.

To works, however, of which the excellence is not absolute and definite, but gradual and comparative; to works not raised upon principles demonstrative and scientifick, but appealing wholly to observation and experience, no other test can be applied than length of duration and continuance of esteem. What mankind have long possessed they have often examined and compared; and if they persist to value the possession, it is because frequent comparisons have confirmed opinion in its favour. As among the works of nature no man can properly call a river deep, or a mountain high, without the knowledge of many mountains, and many rivers; so, in the productions of genius, nothing can be styled excellent till it has been compared with other works of the same kind. Demonstration immediately displays its power, and has nothing to hope or fear from the flux of years; but works tentative and experimental must be estimated by their proportion to the general and collective ability of man, as it is discovered in a long succession of endeavours. Of the first building that was raised, it might be with certainty determined that it was round or square; but whether it was spacious or lofty must have been referred to time. The Pythagorean scale of numbers was at once discovered to be perfect; but the poems of Homer we yet know not to transcend the common limits of human intelligence, but by remarking, that nation after nation, and century after century, has been able to do little more than transpose his incidents, new-name his characters, and paraphrase his sentiments.

The reverence due to writings that have long subsisted arises therefore not from any credulous confidence in the superior wisdom of past ages, or gloomy persuasion of the degeneracy of mankind, but is the consequence of acknowledged and indubitable positions, that what has been longest known has been most considered, and what is most considered is best understood.

The poet, of whose works I have undertaken the revision, may now begin to assume the dignity of an ancient, and claim the privilege of established fame and prescriptive veneration. He has long outlived his century, the term commonly fixed as the test of literary merit. Whatever advantages he might once derive from personal allusions, local customs, or temporary opinions, have for many years been lost; and every topick of merriment, or motive of sorrow which the modes of artificial life afforded him, now only obscure the scenes which they once illuminated. The effects of favour and competition are at an end; the tradition of his friendships and his enmities has perished; his works support no opinion with arguments, nor supply any faction with invectives; they can neither indulge vanity, nor gratify malignity; but are read without any other reason than the desire of pleasure, and are therefore praised only as pleasure is obtained; yet, thus unassisted by interest or passion, they have past through variations of taste and changes of manners, and, as they devolved from one generation to another, have received new honours at every transmission.

But because human judgment, though it be gradually gaining upon certainty, never becomes infallible; and approbation, though long continued, may yet be only the approbation of prejudice or fashion; it is proper to inquire, by what peculiarities of excellence Shakespeare has gained and kept the favour of his countrymen.

Nothing can please many, and please long, but just representations of general nature. Particular manners can be known to few, and therefore few only can judge how nearly they are copied. The irregular combinations of fanciful invention may delight awhile, by that novelty of which the common satiety of life sends us all in quest; but the pleasures of sudden wonder are soon exhausted, and the mind can only repose on the stability of truth.

Shakespeare is, above all writers, at least above all modern writers, the poet of nature; the poet that holds up to his readers a faithful mirror of manners and of life. His characters are not modified by the customs of particular places, unpractised by the rest of the world; by the peculiarities of studies or professions, which can operate but upon small numbers; or by the accidents of transient fashions or temporary opinions: they are the genuine progeny of common humanity, such as the world will always supply, and observation will always find. His persons act and speak by the influence of those general passions and principles by which all minds are agitated, and the whole system of life is continued in motion. In the writings of other poets a character is too often an individual: in those of Shakespeare it is commonly a species.

It is from this wide extension of design that so much instruction is derived. It is this which fills the plays of Shakespeare with practical axioms and domestic wisdom. It was said of Euripides, that every verse was a precept; and it may be said of Shakespeare, that from his works may be collected a system of civil and œconomical prudence. Yet his real power is not shown in the splendour of particular passages, but by the progress of his fable, and the tenor of his dialogue: and he that tries to recommend him by select quotations, will succeed like the pedant in Hierocles, who, when he offered his house to sale, carried a brick in his pocket as a specimen.

It will not easily be imagined how much Shakespeare excels in accommodating his sentiments to real life, but by comparing him with other authors. It was observed of the ancient schools of declamation, that the more diligently they were frequented, the more was the student disqualified for the world, because he found nothing there which he should ever meet in any other place. The same remark may be applied to every stage but that of Shakespeare. The theatre, when it is under any other direction, is peopled by such characters as were never seen, conversing in a language which was never heard, upon topics which will never arise in the commerce of mankind. But the dialogue of this author is often so evidently determined by the incident which produces it, and is pursued with so much ease and simplicity, that it seems scarcely to claim the merit of fiction, but to have been gleaned by diligent selection out of common conversation, and common occurrences.

Upon every other stage the universal agent is love, by whose power all good and evil is distributed, and every action quickened or retarded. To bring a lover, a lady, and a rival into the fable; to entangle them in contradictory obligations, perplex them with oppositions of interest, and harrass them with violence of desires inconsistent with each other; to make them meet in rapture, and part in agony; to fill their mouths with hyperbolical joy and outrageous sorrow; to distress them as nothing human ever was distressed; to deliver them as nothing human ever was delivered; is the business of a modern dramatist. For this, probability is violated, life is misrepresented, and language is depraved. But love is only one of many passions; and as it has no great influence upon the sum of life, it has little operation in the dramas of a poet, who caught his ideas from the living world, and exhibited only what he saw before him. He knew that any other passion, as it was regular or exorbitant, was a cause of happiness or calamity.

Characters thus ample and general were not easily discriminated and preserved, yet perhaps no poet ever kept his personages more distinct from each other. I will not say with Pope, that every speech may be assigned to the proper speaker, because many speeches there are which have nothing characteristical; but, perhaps, though some may be equally adapted to every person, it will be difficult to find that any can be properly transferred from the present possessor to another claimant. The choice is right, when there is reason for choice.

Other dramatists can only gain attention by hyperbolical or aggravated characters, by fabulous and unexampled excellence or depravity, as the writers of barbarous romances invigorated the reader by a giant and a dwarf; and he that should form his expectations of human affairs from the play, or from the tale, would be equally deceived. Shakespeare has no heroes; his scenes are occupied only by men, who act and speak as the reader thinks that he should himself have spoken or acted on the same occasion; even where the agency is supernatural, the dialogue is level with life. Other writers disguise the most natural passions and most frequent incidents; so that he who contemplates them in the book will not know them in the world: Shakespeare approximates the remote, and familiarizes the wonderful; the event which he represents will not happen, but, if it were possible, its effects would probably be such as he has assigned; and it may be said, that he has not only shown human nature as it acts in real exigencies, but as it would be found in trials, to which it cannot be exposed.

This therefore is the praise of Shakespeare, that his drama is the mirror of life; that he who has mazed his imagination, in following the phantoms which other writers raise up before him, may here be cured of his delirious ecstacies, by reading human sentiments in human language, by scenes from which a hermit may estimate the transactions of the world, and a confessor predict the progress of the passions.

Preface to Shakespeare, 1765

Shakespeare's Faults

Shakespeare with his excellencies has likewise faults, and faults sufficient to obscure and overwhelm any other merit. I shall show them in the proportion in which they appear to me, without envious malignity or superstitious veneration. No question can be more innocently discussed than a dead poet's pretensions to renown; and little regard is due to that bigotry which sets candour higher than truth.

His first defect is that to which may be imputed most of the evil in books or in men. He sacrifices virtue to convenience, and is so much more careful to please than to instruct, that he seems to write without any moral purpose. From his writings indeed a system of social duty may be selected, for he that thinks reasonably must think morally; but his precepts and axioms drop casually from him; he makes no just distribution of good or evil, nor is always careful to show in the virtuous a disapprobation of the wicked; he carries his persons indifferently through right and wrong, and at the close dismisses them without further care, and leaves their examples to operate by chance. This fault the barbarity of his age cannot extenuate; for it is always a writer's duty to make the world better, and justice is a virtue independent on time or place.

The plots are often so loosely formed, that a very slight consideration may improve them, and so carelessly pursued, that he seems not always fully to comprehend his own design. He omits opportunities of instructing or delighting, which the train of his story seems to force upon him, and apparently rejects those exhibitions which would be more affecting, for the sake of those which are more easy.

It may be observed, that in many of his plays the latter part is evidently neglected. When he found himself near the end of his work, and in view of his reward, he shortened the labour to snatch the profit. He therefore remits his efforts where he should most vigorously exert them, and his catastrophe is improbably produced or imperfectly represented.

He had no regard to distinction of time or place, but gives to one age or nation, without scruple, the customs, institutions, and opinions of another, at the expense not only of likelihood, but of possibility. These faults Pope has endeavoured, with more zeal than judgment, to transfer to his imagined interpolators. We need not wonder to find Hector quoting Aristotle, when we see the loves of Theseus and Hippolyta combined with the gothick mythology of fairies. Shakespeare, indeed, was not the only violator of chronology, for in the same age Sidney, who wanted not the advantages of learning, has, in his *Arcadia*, confounded the pastoral with the feudal times, the days of innocence, quiet, and security, with those of turbulence, violence, and adventure.

In his comick scenes he is seldom very successful, when he engages his characters in reciprocations of smartness and contests of sarcasm; their jests are commonly gross, and their pleasantry licentious; neither his gentlemen nor his ladies have much delicacy, nor are sufficiently distinguished from his clowns by any appearance of refined manners. Whether he represented the real conversation of his time is not easy to determine: the reign of Elizabeth is commonly supposed to have been a time of stateliness, formality, and reserve; yet perhaps the relaxations of that severity were not very elegant. There must, however, have been always some modes of gayety preferable to others, and a writer ought to choose the best.

In tragedy his performance seems constantly to be worse, as his labour is more. The effusions of passion, which exigence forces out, are for the most part striking and energetick; but whenever he solicits his invention, or strains his faculties, the offspring of his throes is tumour, meanness, tediousness, and obscurity.

In narration he affects a disproportionate pomp of diction, and a wearisome train of circumlocution, and tells the incident imperfectly in many words, which might have been more plainly delivered in few. Narration in dramatick poetry is naturally tedious, as it is unanimated and inactive, and obstructs the progress of the action; it should therefore always be rapid, and enlivened by frequent interruption. Shakespeare found it an incumbrance, and instead of lightening it by brevity, endeavoured to recommend it by dignity and splendour.

His declamations or set speeches are commonly cold and weak, for his power was the power of nature; when he endeavoured, like other tragick writers, to catch opportunities of amplification, and instead of inquiring what the occasion demanded, to show how much his stores of knowledge could supply, he seldom escapes without the pity or resentment of his reader.

It is incident to him to be now and then entangled with an unwieldy sentiment, which he cannot well express, and will not reject; he struggles with it a while, and, if it continues stubborn, comprises it in words such as occur, and leaves it to be disentangled and evolved by those who have more leisure to bestow upon it.

Not that always where the language is intricate the thought is subtle, or the image always great where the line is bulky; the equality of words to things is very often neglected, and trivial sentiments and vulgar ideas disappoint the attention, to which they are recommended by sonorous epithets and swelling figures.

But the admirers of this great poet have most reason to complain when he approaches nearest to his highest excellence, and seems fully resolved to sink them in dejection, and mollify them with tender emotions by the fall of greatness, the danger of innocence, or the crosses of love. What he does best, he soon ceases to do. He is not soft and pathetick without some idle conceit, or contemptible equivocation. He no sooner begins to move, than he counteracts himself; and terrour and pity, as they are rising in the mind, are checked and blasted by sudden frigidity.

A quibble is to Shakespeare, what luminous vapours are to the traveller: he follows it at all adventures; it is sure to lead him out of his way, and sure to engulf him in the mire. It has some malignant power over his mind, and its fascinations are irresistible. Whatever be the dignity or profundity of his disquisition, whether he be enlarging knowledge or exalting affection, whether he be amusing attention with incidents, or enchaining it in suspense, let but a quibble spring up before him, and he leaves his work unfinished. A quibble is the golden apple for which he will always turn aside from his career, or stoop from his elevation. A quibble, poor and barren as it is, gave him such delight, that he was content to purchase it, by the sacrifice of reason, propriety, and truth.

A quibble was to him the fatal Cleopatra for which he
lost the world, and was content to lose it.

Preface to Shakespeare, 1765

Textual Criticism

The part of criticism in which the whole succession of
editors has laboured with the greatest diligence, which
has occasioned the most arrogant ostentation, and excited
the keenest acrimony, is the emendation of corrupted
passages, to which the publick attention having been first
drawn by the violence of the contention between Pope
and Theobald, has been continued by the persecution,
which, with a kind of conspiracy, has been since raised
against all the publishers of Shakespeare.

That many passages have passed in a state of depravation through all the editions, is indubitably certain; of
these the restoration is only to be attempted by collation
of copies, or sagacity of conjecture. The collator's province is safe and easy, the conjecturer's perilous and
difficult. Yet as the greater part of the plays are extant
only in one copy, the peril must not be avoided, nor the
difficulty refused.

Of the readings which this emulation of amendment has
hitherto produced, some from the labours of every publisher I have advanced into the text; those are to be considered as in my opinion sufficiently supported; some I
have rejected without mention, as evidently erroneous;
some I have left in the notes without censure or approbation, as resting in equipoise between objection and defence; and some, which seemed specious but not right,
I have inserted with a subsequent animadversion.

Having classed the observations of others, I was at last
to try what I could substitute for their mistakes, and how
I could supply their omissions. I collated such copies as I
could procure, and wished for more, but have not found
the collectors of these rarities very communicative. Of the
editions which chance or kindness put into my hands I
have given an enumeration, that I may not be blamed
for neglecting what I had not the power to do.

By examining the old copies, I soon found that the

later publishers, with all their boasts of diligence, suffered many passages to stand unauthorized, and contented themselves with Rowe's regulation of the text, even where they knew it to be arbitrary, and with a little consideration might have found it to be wrong. Some of these alterations are only the ejection of a word for one that appeared to him more elegant or more intelligible. These corruptions I have often silently rectified; for the history of our language, and the true force of our words, can only be preserved, by keeping the text of authors free from adulteration. Others, and those very frequent, smoothed the cadence, or regulated the measure: on these I have not exercised the same rigour; if only a word was transposed, or a particle inserted or omitted, I have sometimes suffered the line to stand; for the inconstancy of the copies is such, as that some liberties may be easily permitted. But this practice I have not suffered to proceed far, having restored the primitive diction wherever it could for any reason be preferred.

The emendations, which comparison of copies supplied, I have inserted in the text: sometimes, where the improvement was slight, without notice, and sometimes with an account of the reasons of the change.

Conjecture, though it be sometimes unavoidable, I have not wantonly nor licentiously indulged. It has been my settled principle, that the reading of the ancient books is probably true, and therefore is not to be disturbed for the sake of elegance, perspicuity, or mere improvement of the sense. For though much credit is not due to the fidelity, nor any to the judgment of the first publishers, yet they who had the copy before their eyes were more likely to read it right, than we who read it only by imagination. But it is evident that they have often made strange mistakes by ignorance or negligence, and that therefore something may be properly attempted by criticism, keeping the middle way between presumption and timidity.

Such criticism I have attempted to practise, and, where any passage appeared inextricably perplexed, have endeavoured to discover how it may be recalled to sense, with least violence. But my first labour is, always to turn the old text on every side, and try if there be any interstice, through which light can find its way; nor would Huetius himself condemn me, as refusing the trouble of research, for the ambition of alteration. In this modest industry I have not been unsuccessful. I have rescued many lines from the violations of temerity, and secured many scenes from the inroads of correction. I have adopted the Roman sentiment, that it is more honourable to save a citizen, than to kill an enemy, and have been more careful to protect than to attack.

* * * * * * *

Yet conjectural criticism has been of great use in the learned world; nor is it my intention to depreciate a study, that has exercised so many mighty minds, from the revival of learning to our own age, from the bishop of Aleria to English Bentley. The criticks on ancient authors have, in the exercise of their sagacity, many assistances, which the editor of Shakespeare is condemned to want. They are employed upon grammatical and settled languages, whose construction contributes so much to perspicuity, that Homer has fewer passages unintelligible than Chaucer. The words have not only a known regimen, but invariable quantities, which direct and confine the choice. There are commonly more manuscripts than one; and they do not often conspire in the same mistakes. Yet Scaliger could confess to Salmasius how little satisfaction his emendations gave him. *Illudunt nobis conjecturæ nostræ, quarum nos pudet, posteaquam in meliores codices incidimus.* And Lipsius could complain, that criticks were making faults by trying to remove them, *Ut olim vitiis, ita nunc remediis laboratur.* And, indeed, where mere conjecture is to be used, the emendations of Scaliger and Lipsius, notwithstanding their wonderful sagacity and erudition, are often vague and disputable, like mine or Theobald's.

Perhaps I may not be more censured for doing wrong, than for doing little; for raising in the publick, expectations which at last I have not answered. The expectation of ignorance is indefinite, and that of knowledge is often

tyrannical. It is hard to satisfy those who know not what
to demand, or those who demand by design what they
think impossible to be done. I have indeed disappointed
no opinion more than my own; yet I have endeavoured
to perform my task with no slight solicitude. Not a single
passage in the whole work has appeared to me corrupt,
which I have not attempted to restore; or obscure, which
I have not endeavoured to illustrate. In many I have
failed, like others; and from many, after all my efforts, I
have retreated, and confessed the repulse. I have not
passed over with affected superiority, what is equally
difficult to the reader and to myself, but, where I could
not instruct him, have owned my ignorance. I might
easily have accumulated a mass of seeming learning upon
easy scenes; but it ought not to be imputed to negligence,
that, where nothing was necessary, nothing has been done,
or that, where others have said enough, I have said no
more.

Preface to Shakespeare, 1765

Our Myriad-minded Shakespeare

Notes are often necessary, but they are necessary evils.
Let him, that is yet unacquainted with the powers of
Shakespeare, and who desires to feel the highest pleasure
that the drama can give, read every play, from the first
scene to the last, with utter negligence of all his commentators. When his fancy is once on the wing, let it not
stoop at correction or explanation. When his attention is
strongly engaged, let it disdain alike to turn aside to the
name of Theobald and of Pope. Let him read on through
brightness and obscurity, through integrity and corruption; let him preserve his comprehension of the dialogue
and his interest in the fable. And when the pleasures of
novelty have ceased, let him attempt exactness, and read
the commentators.

Particular passages are cleared by notes, but the general
effect of the work is weakened. The mind is refrigerated
by interruption; the thoughts are diverted from the principal subject; the reader is weary, he suspects not why;

and at last throws away the book which he has too diligently studied.

Parts are not to be examined till the whole has been surveyed; there is a kind of intellectual remoteness necessary for the comprehension of any great work in its full design and in its true proportions; a close approach shows the smaller niceties, but the beauty of the whole is discerned no longer.

It is not very grateful to consider how little the succession of editors has added to this author's power of pleasing. He was read, admired, studied, and imitated, while he was yet deformed with all the improprieties which ignorance and neglect could accumulate upon him; while the reading was yet not rectified, nor his allusions understood; yet then did Dryden pronounce, that Shakespeare was the 'man, who, of all modern and perhaps ancient poets, had the largest and most comprehensive soul. All the images of nature were still present to him, and he drew them not laboriously, but luckily: when he describes any thing, you more than see it, you feel it too. Those, who accuse him to have wanted learning, give him the greater commendation: he was naturally learned: he needed not the spectacles of books to read nature; he looked inwards, and found her there. I cannot say he is every where alike; were he so I should do him injury to compare him with the greatest of mankind. He is many times flat and insipid; his comick wit degenerating into clenches, his serious swelling into bombast. But he is always great when some great occasion is presented to him: no man can say, he ever had a fit subject for his wit, and did not then raise himself as high above the rest of poets,

Quantum lenta solent inter viburna cupressi.'[1]

It is to be lamented, that such a writer should want a commentary; that his language should become obsolete, or his sentiments obscure. But it is vain to carry wishes beyond the condition of human things; that which must happen to all, has happened to Shakespeare, by accident

[1 Virgil, *Ecl.* i. 25: 'as the cypresses tower above the bushes'.]

and time; and more than has been suffered by any other writer since the use of types, has been suffered by him through his own negligence of fame, or perhaps by that superiority of mind, which despised its own performances, when it compared them with its powers, and judged those works unworthy to be preserved, which the criticks of following ages were to contend for the fame of restoring and explaining.

Among these candidates of inferiour fame, I am now to stand the judgment of the Publick; and wish that I could confidently produce my commentary as equal to the encouragement which I have had the honour of receiving. Every work of this kind is by its nature deficient, and I should feel little solicitude about the sentence, were it to be pronounced only by the skilful and the learned.

Preface to Shakespeare, 1765

1 and *2 Henry IV*

None of Shakespeare's plays are more read than the *First and Second Parts of Henry the Fourth.* Perhaps no author has ever in two plays afforded so much delight. The great events are interesting, for the fate of kingdoms depends upon them; the slighter occurrences are diverting, and, except one or two, sufficiently probable; the incidents are multiplied with wonderful fertility of invention, and the characters diversified with the utmost nicety of discernment, and the profoundest skill in the nature of man.

The prince, who is the hero both of the comick and tragick part, is a young man of great abilities and violent passions, whose sentiments are right, though his actions are wrong; whose virtues are obscured by negligence, and whose understanding is dissipated by levity. In his idle hours he is rather loose than wicked; and when the occasion forces out his latent qualities, he is great without effort, and brave without tumult. The trifler is roused into a hero, and the hero again reposes in the trifler. This character is great, original, and just.

Percy is a rugged soldier, cholerick, and quarelsome, and has only the soldier's virtues, generosity and courage.

But Falstaff, unimitated, unimitable Falstaff, how shall I describe thee? Thou compound of sense and vice; of sense which may be admired, but not esteemed; of vice which may be despised, but hardly detested. Falstaff is a character loaded with faults, and with those faults which naturally produce contempt. He is a thief and a glutton, a coward and a boaster, always ready to cheat the weak, and prey upon the poor; to terrify the timorous, and insult the defenceless. At once obsequious and malignant, he satirises in their absence those with whom he lives by flattering. He is familiar with the prince only as an agent of vice, but of this familiarity he is so proud, as not only to be supercilious and haughty with common men, but to think his interest of importance to the duke of Lancaster. Yet the man thus corrupt, thus despicable, makes himself necessary to the prince that despises him, by the most pleasing of all qualities, perpetual gayety, by an unfailing power of exciting laughter, which is the more freely indulged, as his wit is not of the splendid or ambitious kind, but consists in easy escapes and sallies of levity, which make sport, but raise no envy. It must be observed, that he is stained with no enormous or sanguinary crimes, so that his licentiousness is not so offensive but that it may be born for his mirth.

Cymbeline

This play has many just sentiments, some natural dialogues, and some pleasing scenes, but they are obtained at the expense of much incongruity. To remark the folly of the fiction, the absurdity of the conduct, the confusion of the names, and manners of different times, and the impossibility of the events in any system of life, were to waste criticism upon unresisting imbecility, upon faults too evident for detection, and too gross for aggravation.

Othello

The beauties of this play impress themselves so strongly upon the attention of the reader, that they can draw no aid from critical illustration. The fiery openness of Othello, magnanimous, artless, and credulous, boundless in his confidence, ardent in his affection, inflexible in his resolution, and obdurate in his revenge; the cool malignity of Iago, silent in his resentment, subtle in his designs, and studious at once of his interest and his vengeance; the soft simplicity of Desdemona, confident of merit, and conscious of innocence, her artless perseverance in her suit, and her slowness to suspect that she can be suspected, are such proofs of Shakespeare's skill in human nature, as, I suppose, it is vain to seek in any modern writer. The gradual progress which Iago makes in the Moor's conviction, and the circumstances which he employs to inflame him, are so artfully natural, that, though it will perhaps not be said of him as he says of himself, that he is *a man not easily jealous*, yet we cannot but pity him, when at last we find him *perplexed in the extreme*.

Selected Notes

Two Gentlemen of Verona (II. iv. 137)

> *Love's a mighty lord:*
> *And hath so humbled me as, I confess,*
> *There is no woe to his correction.*

No misery that *can be compared to* the punishment inflicted by love. Herbert called for the prayers of the *Liturgy* a little before his death, saying, *None to them, none to them.*

Measure for Measure (III. i. 32)

> *Thou hast nor youth, nor age:*
> *But as it were an after dinner's sleep,*
> *Dreaming on both.*

This is exquisitely imagined. When we are young we busy ourselves in forming schemes for succeeding time, and miss the gratifications that are before us; when we are old we amuse the languour of age with the recollection of youthful pleasures or performances; so that our life, of which no part is filled with the business of the present

time, resembles our dreams after dinner, when the events
of the morning are mingled with the designs of the
evening.

All's Well that Ends Well (v. iii. 20)

Shakespeare is now hastening to the end of the play, finds
his matter sufficient to fill up his remaining scenes, and
therefore, as on other such occasions, contracts his dialogue and precipitates his action. Decency required that
Bertram's double crime of cruelty and disobedience, joined
likewise with some hypocrisy, should raise more resentment; and that though his mother might easily forgive
him, his king should more pertinaciously vindicate his
own authority and Helen's merit: of all this Shakespeare
could not be ignorant, but Shakespeare wanted to conclude his play.

2 Henry IV (v. v. 68)

Mr. Rowe observes, that many readers lament to see
Falstaff so hardly used by his old friend. But if it be considered that the fat knight has never uttered one sentiment of generosity, and with all his power of exciting
mirth, has nothing in him that can be esteemed, no great
pain will be suffered from the reflection that he is compelled to live honestly, and maintained by the king, with
a promise of advancement when he shall deserve it.

I think the poet more blameable for Poins, who is
always represented as joining some virtues with his vices,
and is therefore treated by the prince with apparent distinction, yet he does nothing in the time of action, and
though after the bustle is over he is again a favourite, at
last vanishes without notice. Shakespeare certainly lost
him by heedlessness, in the multiplicity of his characters,
the variety of his action, and his eagerness to end the
play.

Henry V (iv. i. 250)

There is something very striking and solemn in this
soliloquy, into which the king breaks immediately as

soon as he is left alone. Something like this, on less occasions, every breast has felt. Reflection and seriousness rush upon the mind upon the separation of a gay company, and especially after forced and unwilling merriment.

(v. ii. 125)

I know not why Shakespeare now gives the king nearly such a character as he made him formerly ridicule in Percy. This military grossness and unskilfulness in all the softer arts, does not suit very well with the gaieties of his youth, with the general knowledge ascribed to him at his accession, or with the contemptuous message sent him by the Dauphin, who represents him as fitter for the ball room than the field, and tells him that he is not *to revel into dutchies*, or win provinces *with a nimble galliard*. The truth is, that the poet's matter failed him in the fifth act, and he was glad to fill it up with whatever he could get; and not even Shakespeare can write well without a proper subject. It is a vain endeavour for the most skilful hand to cultivate barrenness, or to paint upon vacuity.

King Lear (v. iii. 168)

The injury done by Edmund to the simplicity of the action is abundantly recompensed by the addition of variety, by the art with which he is made to co-operate with the chief design, and the opportunity which he gives the poet of combining perfidy with perfidy, and connecting the wicked son with the wicked daughters, to impress this important moral, that villany is never at a stop, that crimes lead to crimes, and at last terminate in ruin.

But though this moral be incidentally enforced, Shakespeare has suffered the virtue of Cordelia to perish in a just cause, contrary to the natural ideas of justice, to the hope of the reader, and, what is yet more strange, to the faith of chronicles. Yet this conduct is justified by the Spectator, who blames Tate for giving Cordelia success and happiness in his alteration, and declares, that, in his opinion, *the tragedy has lost half its beauty*. Dennis has remarked, whether justly or not, that, to secure the favourable reception of *Cato, the town was poisoned with much false and abominable criticism*, and that endeavours had been used to discredit and decry poetical justice. A play in which the wicked prosper, and the virtuous miscarry, may doubtless be good, because it is a just representation of the common events of human life: but since all reasonable beings naturally love justice, I cannot easily be persuaded, that the observation of justice makes a play worse; or, that if other excellencies are equal, the audience will not always rise better pleased from the final triumph of persecuted virtue.

In the present case the publick has decided. Cordelia, from the time of Tate, has always retired with victory and felicity. And, if my sensations could add any thing to the general suffrage, I might relate, that I was many years ago so shocked by Cordelia's death, that I know not whether I ever endured to read again the last scenes of the play till I undertook to revise them as an editor.

1766
To William Drummond

Sir

I did not expect to hear that it could be, in an assembly convened for the propagation of Christian knowledge, a question whether any nation uninstructed in religion should receive instruction; or whether that instruction should be imparted to them by a translation of the holy books into their own language. If obedience to the will of God be necessary to happiness, and knowledge of his will be necessary to obedience, I know not how he that with-holds this knowledge, or delays it, can be said to love his neighbour as himself. He, that voluntarily continues ignorance, is guilty of all the crimes which ignorance produces; as to him, that should extinguish the tapers of a light-house, might justly be imputed the calamities of shipwrecks. Christianity is the highest perfection of humanity; and as no man is good but as he wishes the good of others, no man can be good in the highest degree, who wishes not to others the largest measures of the greatest good. To omit for a year, or for a day, the most efficacious method of advancing Christianity, in compliance with any purposes that terminate on this side of the grave, is a crime of which I know not that the world has yet had an example, except in the practice of the planters of America, a race of mortals whom, I suppose, no other man wishes to resemble.

The Papists have, indeed, denied to the laity the use of the bible; but this prohibition, in few places now very rigorously enforced, is defended by arguments, which have for their foundation the care of souls. To obscure, upon motives merely political, the light of revelation, is a practice reserved for the reformed; and, surely, the blackest midnight of popery is meridian sunshine to such a reformation.

I am not very willing that any language should be totally extinguished. The similitude and derivation of languages afford the most indubitable proof of the traduction of nations, and the genealogy of mankind. They add often physical certainty to historical evidence; and often supply the only evidence of ancient migrations, and of the revolutions of ages which left no written monuments behind them.

Every man's opinions, at least his desires, are a little influenced by his favourite studies. My zeal for languages may seem, perhaps, rather over-heated, even to those by whom I desire to be well esteemed. To those who have nothing in their thoughts but trade or policy, present power, or present money, I should not think it necessary to defend my opinions; but with men of letters I would not unwillingly compound, by wishing the continuance of every language, however narrow in its extent, or however incommodious for common purposes, till it is re-posited in some version of a known book, that it may be always hereafter examined and compared with other languages, and then permitting its disuse. For this purpose, the translation of the bible is most to be desired. It is not certain that the same method will not preserve the Highland language, for the purposes of learning, and abolish it from daily use. When the Highlanders read the Bible, they will naturally wish to have its obscurities cleared, and to know the history, collateral or appendant. Knowledge always desires increase: it is like fire, which must first be kindled by some external agent, but which will afterwards propagate itself. When they once desire to learn, they will naturally have recourse to the nearest language by which that desire can be gratified; and one will tell another that if he would attain knowledge, he must learn English.

This speculation may, perhaps, be thought more subtle than the grossness of real life will easily admit. Let it, however, be remembered, that the efficacy of ignorance has been long tried, and has not produced the consequence expected. Let knowledge, therefore, take its turn; and let the patrons of privation stand awhile aside, and admit the operation of positive principles.

You will be pleased, Sir, to assure the worthy man who is employed in the new translation, that he has my wishes for his success; and if here or at Oxford I can be of any use, that I shall think it more than honour to promote his undertaking.

I am sorry that I delayed so long to write.

I am, Sir, Your most humble servant, Sam. Johnson.

Johnson's-court, Fleet-street, Aug. 13, 1766.

Writing and Talking

Another evening Dr. Goldsmith and I called on him, with the hope of prevailing on him to sup with us at the Mitre. We found him indisposed, and resolved not to go abroad. 'Come then, (said Goldsmith,) we will not go to the Mitre to-night, since we cannot have the big man with us.' Johnson then called for a bottle of port, of which Goldsmith and I partook, while our friend, now a water-drinker, sat by us. GOLDSMITH. 'I think, Mr. Johnson, you don't go near the theatres now. You give yourself no more concern about a new play, than if you had never had any thing to do with the stage.' JOHNSON. 'Why, Sir, our tastes greatly alter. The lad does not care for the child's rattle, and the old man does not care for the young man's whore.' GOLDSMITH. 'Nay, Sir, but your Muse was not a whore.' JOHNSON. 'Sir, I do not think she was. But as we advance in the journey of life, we drop some of the things which have pleased us; whether it be that we are fatigued and don't choose to carry so many things any farther, or that we find other things which we like better.' BOSWELL. 'But, Sir, why don't you give us something in some other way?' GOLDSMITH. 'Ay, Sir, we have a claim upon you.' JOHNSON. 'No, Sir, I am not obliged to do any more. No man is obliged to do as much as he can do. A man is to have part of his life to himself. If a soldier has fought a good many campaigns, he is not to be blamed if he retires to ease and tranquillity. A physician, who has practised long in a great city, may be excused if he retires to a small town, and takes less practice. Now, Sir, the good I can do by my conversation bears the same pro- portion to the good I can do by my writings, that the practice of a physician, retired to a small town, does to his practice in a great city.' BOSWELL. 'But I wonder, Sir, you have not more pleasure in writing than in not writing.' JOHNSON. 'Sir, you *may* wonder.'

He talked of making verses, and observed, 'The great difficulty is to know when you have made good ones. When composing, I have generally had them in my mind, perhaps fifty at a time, walking up and down in my room; and then I have written them down, and often, from laziness, have written only half lines. I have written a hundred lines in a day. I remember I wrote a hundred lines of *The Vanity of Human Wishes* in a day. Doctor, (turning to Goldsmith,) I am not quite idle; I made one line t'other day; but I made no more.' GOLDSMITH. 'Let us hear it; we'll put a bad one to it.' JOHNSON. 'No, Sir, I have forgot it.'

Boswell, *Life*

1767

Epidemick Bravery

By those who have compared the military genius of the English with that of the French nation, it is remarked, that *the French officers will always lead, if the soldiers will follow*; and that *the English soldiers will always follow, if their officers will lead.*

In all pointed sentences, some degree of accuracy must be sacrificed to conciseness; and, in this comparison, our officers seem to lose what our soldiers gain. I know not any reason for supposing that the English officers are less willing than the French to lead; but it is, I think, universally allowed, that the English soldiers are more willing to follow. Our nation may boast, beyond any other people in the world, of a kind of epidemick bravery, diffused equally through all its ranks. We can show a peasantry of heroes, and fill our armies with clowns, whose courage may vie with that of their general.

There may be some pleasure in tracing the causes of this plebeian magnanimity. The qualities which commonly make an army formidable, are long habits of regularity, great exactness of discipline, and great confidence in the commander. Regularity may, in time, produce a kind of mechanical obedience to signals and commands, like that which the perverse Cartesians impute to animals; discipline may impress such an awe upon the mind, that any danger shall be less dreaded than the danger of punishment; and confidence in the wisdom or fortune of the general, may induce the soldiers to follow him blindly to the most dangerous enterprise.

What may be done by discipline and regularity, may be seen in the troops of the Russian empress and Prussian monarch. We find that they may be broken without confusion, and repulsed without flight.

But the English troops have none of these requisites in any eminent degree. Regularity is by no means part of their character: they are rarely exercised, and therefore show very little dexterity in their evolutions as bodies of men, or in the manual use of their weapons as individuals; they neither are thought by others nor by themselves, more active or exact than their enemies, and therefore derive none of their courage from such imaginary superiority.

The manner in which they are dispersed in quarters

over the country during times of peace, naturally produces laxity of discipline: they are very little in sight of
their officers; and, when they are not engaged in the
slight duty of the guard, are suffered to live every man his
own way.

.   .   .   .   .   .

Whence then is the courage of the English vulgar? It
proceeds, in my opinion, from that dissolution of dependence which obliges every man to regard his own
character. While every man is fed by his own hands, he
has no need of any servile arts; he may always have wages
for his labour; and is no less necessary to his employer,
than his employer is to him. While he looks for no protection from others, he is naturally roused to be his own
protector; and having nothing to abate his esteem of himself, he consequently aspires to the esteem of others. Thus
every man that crowds our streets is a man of honour,
disdainful of obligation, impatient of reproach, and desirous of extending his reputation among those of his own
rank; and as courage is in most frequent use, the fame
of courage is most eagerly pursued. From this neglect of
subordination I do not deny that some inconveniencies
may from time to time proceed: the power of the law does
not always sufficiently supply the want of reverence, or
maintain the proper distinction between different ranks:
but good and evil will grow up in this world together;
and they who complain, in peace, of the insolence of the
populace, must remember, that their insolence in peace
is bravery in war.

On the Bravery of the English Common Soldiers

Johnson and his King

In February, 1767, there happened one of the most remarkable incidents of Johnson's life, which gratified his
monarchical enthusiasm, and which he loved to relate
with all its circumstances, when requested by his friends.
This was his being honoured by a private conversation
with his Majesty, in the library at the Queen's house. He
had frequently visited those splendid rooms and noble

collection of books, which he used to say was more numerous and curious than he supposed any person could
have made in the time which the King had employed.
Mr. Barnard, the librarian, took care that he should have
every accommodation that could contribute to his ease
and convenience, while indulging his literary taste in
that place; so that he had here a very agreeable resource
at leisure hours.

His Majesty having been informed of his occasional
visits, was pleased to signify a desire that he should be
told when Dr. Johnson came next to the library. Accordingly, the next time that Johnson did come, as soon as he
was fairly engaged with a book, on which, while he sat by
the fire, he seemed quite intent, Mr. Barnard stole round
to the apartment where the King was, and, in obedience
to his Majesty's commands, mentioned that Dr. Johnson
was then in the library. His Majesty said he was at leisure,
and would go to him; upon which Mr. Barnard took one
of the candles that stood on the King's table, and lighted
his Majesty through a suite of rooms, till they came to a
private door into the library, of which his Majesty had
the key. Being entered, Mr. Barnard stepped forward
hastily to Dr. Johnson, who was still in a profound study,
and whispered him, 'Sir, here is the King.' Johnson
started up, and stood still. His Majesty approached him,
and at once was courteously easy.

His Majesty began by observing, that he understood
he came sometimes to the library; and then mentioning
his having heard that the Doctor had been lately at
Oxford, asked him if he was not fond of going thither.
To which Johnson answered, that he was indeed fond of
going to Oxford sometimes, but was likewise glad to
come back again. The King then asked him what they
were doing at Oxford. Johnson answered, he could not
much commend their diligence, but that in some respects
they were mended, for they had put their press under
better regulations, and were at that time printing Poly-
bius. He was then asked whether there were better
libraries at Oxford or Cambridge. He answered, he
believed the Bodleian was larger than any they had at

Cambridge; at the same time adding, 'I hope, whether we have more books or not than they have at Cambridge, we shall make as good use of them as they do.' Being asked whether All-Souls or Christ-Church library was the largest, he answered, 'All-Souls library is the largest we have, except the Bodleian.' 'Aye, (said the King,) that is the publick library.'

His Majesty enquired if he was then writing any thing. He answered, he was not, for he had pretty well told the world what he knew, and must now read to acquire more knowledge. The King, as it should seem with a view to urge him to rely on his own stores as an original writer, and to continue his labours, then said 'I do not think you borrow much from any body.' Johnson said, he thought he had already done his part as a writer. 'I should have thought so too, (said the King,) if you had not written so well.'—Johnson observed to me, upon this, that 'No man could have paid a handsomer compliment; and it was fit for a King to pay. It was decisive.' When asked by another friend, at Sir Joshua Reynolds's, whether he made any reply to this high compliment, he answered, 'No, Sir. When the King had said it, it was to be so. It was not for me to bandy civilities with my Sovereign.' Perhaps no man who had spent his whole life in courts could have shewn a more nice and dignified sense of true politeness, than Johnson did in this instance.

His Majesty having observed to him that he supposed he must have read a great deal; Johnson answered, that he thought more than he read; that he had read a great deal in the early part of his life, but having fallen into ill health, he had not been able to read much, compared with others: for instance, he said he had not read much, compared with Dr. Warburton. Upon which the King said, that he heard Dr. Warburton was a man of such general knowledge, that you could scarce talk with him on any subject on which he was not qualified to speak; and that his learning resembled Garrick's acting, in its universality. His Majesty then talked of the controversy between Warburton and Lowth, which he seemed to have read, and asked Johnson what he thought of it.

Johnson answered, 'Warburton has most general, most scholastick learning; Lowth is the more correct scholar. I do not know which of them calls names best.' The King was pleased to say he was of the same opinion; adding, 'You do not think, then, Dr. Johnson, that there was much argument in the case.' Johnson said, he did not think there was. 'Why truly, (said the King,) when once it comes to calling names, argument is pretty well at an end.'

His Majesty then asked him what he thought of Lord Lyttelton's *History*, which was then just published. Johnson said, he thought his style pretty good, but that he had blamed Henry the Second rather too much. 'Why, (said the King,) they seldom do these things by halves.' 'No, Sir, (answered Johnson,) not to Kings.' But fearing to be misunderstood, he proceeded to explain himself; and immediately subjoined, 'That for those who spoke worse of Kings than they deserved, he could find no excuse; but that he could more easily conceive how some might speak better of them than they deserved, without any ill intention; for, as Kings had much in their power to give, those who were favoured by them would frequently, from gratitude, exaggerate their praises; and as this proceeded from a good motive, it was certainly excusable, as far as errour could be excusable.'

The King then asked him what he thought of Dr. Hill. Johnson answered, that he was an ingenious man, but had no veracity; and immediately mentioned, as an instance of it, an assertion of that writer, that he had seen objects magnified to a much greater degree by using three or four microscopes at a time, than by using one. 'Now, (added Johnson,) every one acquainted with microscopes knows, that the more of them he looks through, the less the object will appear.' 'Why, (replied the King,) this is not only telling an untruth, but telling it clumsily; for, if that be the case, every one who can look through a microscope will be able to detect him.'

'I now, (said Johnson to his friends, when relating what had passed) began to consider that I was depreciating this man in the estimation of his Sovereign, and thought

it was time for me to say something that might be more
favourable.' He added, therefore, that Dr. Hill was, notwithstanding, a very curious observer; and if he would
have been contented to tell the world no more than he
knew, he might have been a very considerable man, and
needed not to have recourse to such mean expedients to
raise his reputation.

The King then talked of literary journals, mentioned
particularly the *Journal des Savans*, and asked Johnson if it
was well done. Johnson said, it was formerly very well
done, and gave some account of the persons who began it,
and carried it on for some years; enlarging, at the same
time, on the nature and use of such works. The King
asked him if it was well done now. Johnson answered, he
had no reason to think that it was. The King then asked
him if there were any other literary journals published in
this kingdom, except the *Monthly* and *Critical Reviews*; and
on being answered there were no other, his Majesty asked
which of them was the best: Johnson answered, that the
Monthly Review was done with most care, the *Critical* upon
the best principles; adding that the authours of the
Monthly Review were enemies to the Church. This the King
said he was sorry to hear.

The conversation next turned on the Philosophical
Transactions, when Johnson observed, that they had now
a better method of arranging their materials than formerly. 'Aye, (said the King,) they are obliged to Dr.
Johnson for that;' for his Majesty had heard and remembered the circumstance, which Johnson himself had
forgot.

His Majesty expressed a desire to have the literary biography of this country ably executed, and proposed to
Dr. Johnson to undertake it. Johnson signified his readiness to comply with his Majesty's wishes.

During the whole of this interview, Johnson talked to
his Majesty with profound respect, but still in his firm
manly manner, with a sonorous voice, and never in that
subdued tone which is commonly used at the levee and
in the drawing-room. After the King withdrew, Johnson shewed himself highly pleased with his Majesty's

conversation, and gracious behaviour. He said to Mr. Barnard, 'Sir, they may talk of the King as they will; but he is the finest gentleman I have ever seen.' And he afterwards observed to Mr. Langton, 'Sir, his manners are those of as fine a gentleman as we may suppose Lewis the Fourteenth or Charles the Second.'

At Sir Joshua Reynolds's, where a circle of Johnson's friends was collected round him to hear his account of this memorable conversation, Dr. Joseph Warton, in his frank and lively manner, was very active in pressing him to mention the particulars. 'Come now, Sir, this is an interesting matter; do favour us with it.' Johnson, with great good humour, complied.

He told them, 'I found his Majesty wished I should talk, and I made it my business to talk. I find it does a man good to be talked to by his Sovereign. In the first place, a man cannot be in a passion—.' Here some question interrupted him, which is to be regretted, as he certainly would have pointed out and illustrated many circumstances of advantage, from being in a situation, where the powers of the mind are at once excited to vigorous exertion, and tempered by reverential awe.

Boswell, *Life*

The Science of Princes

To the KING.

Sir,

It is the privilege of real greatness not to be afraid of diminution by condescending to the notice of little things: and I therefore can boldly solicit the patronage of your Majesty to the humble labours by which I have endeavoured to improve the instruments of science, and make the globes on which the earth and sky are delineated less defective in their construction, and less difficult in their use.

Geography is in a peculiar manner the science of Princes. When a private student revolves the terraqueous globe, he beholds a succession of countries in which he has no more interest than in the imaginary regions of Jupiter and Saturn. But your Majesty must contemplate the scientific picture with other sentiments, and consider, as oceans and continents are rolling before you, how large a part of mankind is now waiting on your determinations, and may receive benefits or suffer evils, as your influence is extended or withdrawn.

The provinces which your Majesty's arms have added to your dominions, make no inconsiderable part of the orb allotted to human beings. Your power is acknowledged by nations whose names we know not yet how to write, and whose boundaries we cannot yet describe. But your Majesty's lenity and beneficence give us reason to expect the time, when science shall be advanced by the diffusion of happiness: when the desarts of America shall become pervious and safe: when those who are now restrained by fear shall be attracted by reverence: and multitudes who now range the woods for prey, and live at the mercy of winds and seasons, shall by the paternal care of your Majesty enjoy the plenty of cultivated lands, the pleasures of society, the security of law, and the light of revelation.

I am, Sir,

Your Majesty's most humble, most obedient,

and most dutiful Subject and Servant,

GEORGE ADAMS

Dedication of Adams's *Treatise on the Globes,* 1766

1768

Legal Advocacy

I asked him whether, as a moralist, he did not think that the practice of the law, in some degree, hurt the nice feeling of honesty. JOHNSON. 'Why no, Sir, if you act properly. You are not to deceive your clients with false representations of your opinion: you are not to tell lies to a judge.' BOSWELL. 'But what do you think of supporting a cause which you know to be bad?' JOHNSON. 'Sir, you do not know it to be good or bad till the Judge determines it. I have said that you are to state facts fairly; so

that your thinking, or what you call knowing, a cause
to be bad, must be from reasoning, must be from your
supposing your arguments to be weak and inconclusive.
But, Sir, that is not enough. An argument which does not
convince yourself, may convince the Judge to whom you
urge it: and if it does convince him, why, then, Sir, you
are wrong, and he is right. It is his business to judge; and
you are not to be confident in your own opinion that a
cause is bad, but to say all you can for your client, and
then hear the Judge's opinion.' BOSWELL. 'But, Sir, does
not affecting a warmth when you have no warmth, and
appearing to be clearly of one opinion when you are in
reality of another opinion, does not such dissimulation
impair one's honesty? Is there not some danger that a
lawyer may put on the same mask in common life, in the
intercourse with his friends?' JOHNSON. 'Why no, Sir.
Everybody knows you are paid for affecting warmth for
your client; and it is, therefore, properly no dissimulation:
the moment you come from the bar you resume your
usual behaviour. Sir, a man will no more carry the artifice of the bar into the common intercourse of society,
than a man who is paid for tumbling upon his hands will
continue to tumble upon his hands when he should walk
on his feet.'

Boswell, *Life*

1769
Shakespeare and Congreve

After dinner our conversation first turned upon Pope.
Johnson said, his characters of men were admirably
drawn, those of women not so well. He repeated to us,
in his forcible melodious manner, the concluding lines of
the *Dunciad*. While he was talking loudly in praise of those
lines, one of the company ventured to say, 'Too fine for
such a poem:—a poem on what?' JOHNSON, (with a disdainful look,) 'Why, on *dunces*. It was worth while being
a dunce then. Ah, Sir, hadst *thou* lived in those days! It is
not worth while being a dunce now, when there are no

wits.' Bickerstaff observed, as a peculiar circumstance, that Pope's fame was higher when he was alive than it was then. Johnson said, his Pastorals were poor things, though the versification was fine. He told us, with high satisfaction, the anecdote of Pope's inquiring who was the authour of his *London*, and saying, he will be soon *déterré*. He observed, that in Dryden's poetry there were passages drawn from a profundity which Pope could never reach. He repeated some fine lines on love, by the former, (which I have now forgotten,) and gave great applause to the character of Zimri. Goldsmith said, that Pope's character of Addison shewed a deep knowledge of the human heart. Johnson said, that the description of the temple, in the *Mourning Bride*, was the finest poetical passage he had ever read; he recollected none in Shakspeare equal to it. 'But, (said Garrick, all alarmed for the 'God of his idolatry,') we know not the extent and variety of his powers. We are to suppose there are such passages in his works. Shakspeare must not suffer from the badness of our memories.' Johnson, diverted by this enthusiastick jealousy, went on with greater ardour: 'No, Sir; Congreve has *nature*;' (smiling on the tragick eagerness of Garrick;) but composing himself, he added, 'Sir, this is not comparing Congreve on the whole, with Shakspeare on the whole; but only maintaining that Congreve has one finer passage than any that can be found in Shakspeare. Sir, a man may have no more than ten guineas in the world, but he may have those ten guineas in one piece; and so may have a finer piece than a man who has ten thousand pounds: but then he has only one ten-guinea piece. What I mean is, that you can shew me no passage where there is simply a description of material objects, without any intermixture of moral notions, which produces such an effect.' Mr. Murphy mentioned Shakspeare's description of the night before the battle of Agincourt; but it was observed, it had *men* in it. Mr. Davies suggested the speech of Juliet, in which she figures herself awaking in the tomb of her ancestors. Some one mentioned the description of Dover Cliff. JOHNSON. 'No, Sir; it should be all precipice,—all vacuum. The crows impede your fall. The diminished appearance of the boats, and other circumstances, are all very good description; but do not impress the mind at once with the horrible idea of immense height. The impression is divided; you pass on by computation, from one stage of the tremendous space to another. Had the girl in *The Mourning Bride* said, she could not cast her shoe to the top of one of the pillars in the temple, it would not have aided the idea, but weakened it.'

Boswell, *Life*

Talking of Trade

Talking of trade, he observed, 'It is a mistaken notion that a vast deal of money is brought into a nation by trade. It is not so. Commodities come from commodities; but trade produces no capital accession of wealth. However, though there should be little profit in money, there is a considerable profit in pleasure, as it gives to one nation the productions of another; as we have wines and fruits, and many other foreign articles, brought to us.' BOSWELL. 'Yes, Sir, and there is a profit in pleasure, by its furnishing occupation to such numbers of mankind.' JOHNSON. 'Why, Sir, you cannot call that pleasure to which all are averse, and which none begin but with the hope of leaving off; a thing which men dislike before they have tried it, and when they have tried it.' BOSWELL. 'But, Sir, the mind must be employed, and we grow weary when idle.' JOHNSON. 'That is, Sir, because, others being busy, we want company; but if we were all idle, there would be no growing weary; we should all entertain one another. There is, indeed, this in trade:—it gives men an opportunity of improving their situation. If there were no trade, many who are poor would always remain poor. But no man loves labour for itself.' BOSWELL. 'Yes, Sir, I know a person who does. He is a very laborious Judge, and he loves the labour.' JOHNSON. 'Sir, that is because he loves respect and distinction. Could he have them without labour, he would like it less.' BOSWELL.

'He tells me he likes it for itself.'—'Why, Sir, he fancies so, because he is not accustomed to abstract.'

Boswell, *Life*

Babies

I know not how so whimsical a thought came into my mind, but I asked, 'If, Sir, you were shut up in a castle, and a newborn child with you, what would you do?' JOHNSON. 'Why, Sir, I should not much like my company.' BOWELL. 'But would you take the trouble of rearing it?' He seemed, as may well be supposed, unwilling to pursue the subject: but upon my persevering in my question, replied, 'Why yes, Sir, I would; but I must have all conveniencies. If I had no garden, I would make a shed on the roof, and take it there for fresh air. I should feed it, and wash it much, and with warm water to please it, not with cold water to give it pain.' BOSWELL, 'But, Sir, does not heat relax?' JOHNSON. 'Sir, you are not to imagine the water is to be very hot. I would not *coddle* the child. No, Sir, the hardy method of treating children does no good. I'll take you five children from London, who shall cuff five Highland children. Sir, a man bred in London will carry a burthen, or run, or wrestle, as well as a man brought up in the hardiest manner in the country.' BOSWELL. 'Good living, I suppose, makes the Londoners strong.' JOHNSON. 'Why, Sir, I don't know that it does. Our chairmen from Ireland, who are as strong men as any, have been brought up upon potatoes. Quantity makes up for quality.' BOSWELL. 'Would you teach this child that I have furnished you with, any thing?' JOHNSON. 'No, I should not be apt to teach it.' BOSWELL. 'Would not you have a pleasure in teaching it?' JOHNSON. 'No, Sir, I should *not* have a pleasure in teaching it.' BOSWELL. 'Have you not a pleasure in teaching men?—*There* I have you. You have the same pleasure in teaching men, that I should have in teaching children.' JOHNSON. 'Why, something about that.'

Boswell, *Life*

Purgatory

I proceeded: 'What do you think, Sir, of Purgatory, as believed by the Roman Catholicks?' JOHNSON. 'Why, Sir, it is a very harmless doctrine. They are of opinion that the generality of mankind are neither so obstinately wicked as to deserve everlasting punishment, nor so good as to merit being admitted into the society of blessed spirits; and therefore that God is graciously pleased to allow of a middle state, where they may be purified by certain degrees of suffering. You see, Sir, there is nothing unreasonable in this.' BOSWELL. 'But then, Sir, their masses for the dead?' JOHNSON. 'Why, Sir, if it be once established that there are souls in purgatory, it is as proper to pray for *them*, as for our brethren of mankind who are yet in this life.' BOSWELL. 'The idolatry of the Mass?' JOHNSON. 'Sir, there is no idolatry in the Mass. They believe GOD to be there, and they adore him.' BOSWELL. 'The worship of Saints?' JOHNSON. 'Sir, they do not worship saints; they invoke them; they only ask their prayers. I am talking all this time of the *doctrines* of the Church of Rome. I grant you that in *practice*, Purgatory is made a lucrative imposition, and that the people do become idolatrous as they recommend themselves to the tutelary protection of particular saints. I think their giving the sacrament only in one kind is criminal, because it is contrary to the express institution of CHRIST, and I wonder how the Council of Trent admitted it.' BOSWELL. 'Confession?' JOHNSON. 'Why, I don't know but that is a good thing. The scripture says, "Confess your faults one to another," and the priests confess as well as the laity. Then it must be considered that their absolution is only upon repentance, and often upon penance also. You think your sins may be forgiven without penance, upon repentance alone.'

Boswell, *Life*

To Louise Flint

Mademoiselle

Il faut avouer que la lettre que vous m'avez fait

l'honeur de m'ecrire, a ete longtems sans rêponse. Voici
mon Apologie. J'ai eté affligé d'une Maladie de Violence
pteu supportable, & d'un lenteur bien ennuiant. Tout
êat a ses droits particuliers. On compte parmi les droits
d'un Malade ce de manquer aux offices de respect, et
aux devoirs de reconoissance. Géné par ses douleurs il ne
scait veiller qu'a soimême. Il ne pense qu'a se soulager,
et a se retablir, peu attentif a tout autre soin, et peu sensible á la gloire d'etre traduit d'une main telle que vôtre.

Neanmoins Mademoiselle votre merite auroit exige
que je m'efforcasse a vous rendre graces de vos egards si
je l'aurois pu faire sans y meler des querelles. Mais comment m'empescher de me plaindre de ces appas par les-
quelles vous avez gagne sur l'Esprit de Mademoiselle
Reynolds jusqu'a ce qu'elle ne se souvient plus ni de sa
patrie ni de ses amis. C'est peu de nous louer, c'est peu de
repandre nos ouvrages par des traductions les plus belles,
pendant que vous nous privez du plaisir de voir Mademoiselle Reynolds & de l'êcouter.—Enfin Mademoiselle
il faut etre moins aimable, afin que nous vous aimions
plus.

Je suis Mademoiselle, Vôtre tres humble et Obeissant
Serviteur

a Londres Mars 31. 1769.   Sam: Johnson

To Mrs. Thrale

Madam

I set out on Thursday Morning, and found my Companion, to whom I was very much a Stranger, more
agreeable than I expected. We went cheerfully forward,
and passed the night at Coventry. We came in late and
went out early, and therefore I did not send for my Cousin
Tom, but I design to make him some amends for the
omission.

Next day we came early to Lucy who was, I believe,
glad to see us. She had saved her best gooseberries upon
the tree for me, and, as Steele says, *I was neither too proud
nor too wise* to gather them. I have rambled a very little
inter fontes et flumina nota, but am not yet well. They

have cut down the trees in George Lane. Evelyn in his book of forest trees tells us of wicked men that cut down trees and never prospered afterwards, yet nothing has deterred these audacious aldermen from violating the Hamadryads of George Lane. As an impartial traveller I must however tell that in Stow street where I left a draw-well, I have found a pump, but the lading well in this ill-fated George Lane lyes shamefully neglected.

I am going to day or to morrow to Ashbourne, but I am at a loss how I shall get back in time to London. Here are only chance Coaches, so that there is no certainty of a place. If I do not come, let it not hinder your journey. I can be but a few days behind you, and I will follow in the Brighthelmston Coach. But I hope to come.

I took care to tell Miss Porter, that I have got another Lucy. I hope she is well. Tell Mrs. Salusbury that I beg her to stay at Streatham, for little Lucy's sake.

I am Madam Your most obliged humble Servant
Lichfield August 14. 1769   Sam: Johnson

1770

A New Year's Prayer

Primâ mane, *Jan.* 1, 1770.

Almighty God by whose mercy I am permitted to behold the beginning of another year, succour with thy help and bless with thy favour, the creature whom Thou vouchsafest to preserve. Mitigate, if it shall seem best unto thee, the diseases of my body, and compose the disorders of my mind. Dispel my terrours; and grant that the time which thou shalt yet allow me, may not pass unprofitably away. Let not pleasure seduce me, Idleness lull me, or misery depress me. Let me perform to thy glory, and the good of my fellow creatures the work which thou shalt yet appoint me. And grant that as I draw nearer to my dissolution, I may, by the help of thy Holy Spirit feel my knowledge of Thee encreased, my hope exalted, and my Faith strengthened, that, when the hour which is coming shall

come, I may pass by a holy death to everlasting happiness, for the sake of Jesus Christ our Lord. Amen.

Prayers and Meditations, 1785

The Progress of a Petition

The progress of a petition is well known. An ejected place-
man goes down to his county or his borough, tells his friends
of his inability to serve them, and his constituents of the
corruption of the government. His friends readily understand that he who can get nothing, will have nothing to
give. They agree to proclaim a meeting; meat and drink
are plentifully provided; a crowd is easily brought together,
and those who think that they know the reason of their
meeting, undertake to tell those who know it not. Ale
and clamour unite their powers, the crowd, condensed
and heated, begins to ferment with the leven of sedition.
All see a thousand evils, though they cannot show them,
and grow impatient for a remedy, though they know not
what.

A speech is then made by the Cicero of the day; he says
much, and suppresses more, and credit is equally given
to what he tells, and what he conceals. The petition is
read and universally approved. Those who are sober
enough to write, add their names, and the rest would sign
it if they could.

Every man goes home and tells his neighbour of the
glories of the day; how he was consulted and what he
advised; how he was invited into the great room, where
his lordship called him by his name; how he was caressed
by Sir Francis, Sir Joseph, or Sir George; how he eat turtle
and venison, and drank unanimity to the three brothers.

The poor loiterer, whose shop had confined him, or
whose wife had locked him up, hears the tale of luxury
with envy, and at last inquires what was their petition.
Of the petition nothing is remembered by the narrator,
but that it spoke much of fears and apprehensions, and
something very alarming, and that he is sure it is against
the government; the other is convinced that it must be
right, and wishes he had been there, for he loves wine

and venison, and is resolved as long as he lives to be against the government.

The petition is then handed from town to town, and from house to house, and wherever it comes the inhabitants flock together, that they may see that which must be sent to the king. Names are easily collected. One man signs because he hates the papists; another because he has vowed destruction to the turnpikes; one because it will vex the parson; another because he owes his landlord nothing; one because he is rich; another because he is poor; one to show that he is not afraid, and another to show that he can write.

The False Alarm, 1770

1771
The Horrors of War

As war is the last of remedies, *cuncta prius tentanda*, all lawful expedients must be used to avoid it. As war is the extremity of evil, it is surely the duty of those whose station intrusts them with the care of nations, to avert it from their charge. There are diseases of animal nature which nothing but amputation can remove; so there may, by the depravation of human passions, be sometimes a gangrene in collective life for which fire and the sword are the necessary remedies; but in what can skill or caution be better shown than preventing such dreadful operations, while there is yet room for gentler methods?

It is wonderful with what coolness and indifference the greater part of mankind see war commenced. Those that hear of it at a distance or read of it in books, but have never presented its evils to their minds, consider it as little more than a splendid game, a proclamation, an army, a battle, and a triumph. Some indeed must perish in the most successful field, but they die upon the bed of honour, *resign their lives amidst the joys of conquest, and filled with England's glory, smile in death.*

The life of a modern soldier is ill represented by heroick fiction. War has means of destruction more formidable than the cannon and the sword. Of the thousands and ten thousands that perished in our late contests with France and Spain, a very small part ever felt the stroke of an enemy; the rest languished in tents and ships, amidst damps and putrefaction; pale, torpid, spiritless, and helpless; gasping and groaning unpitied, among men made obdurate by long continuance of hopeless misery; and were at last whelmed in pits, or heaved into the ocean, without notice and without remembrance. By incommodious encampments and unwholesome stations, where courage is useless, and enterprise impracticable, fleets are silently dispeopled, and armies sluggishly melted away.

Thus is a people gradually exhausted, for the most part, with little effect. The wars of civilized nations make very slow changes in the system of empire. The publick perceives scarcely any alteration but an increase of debt; and the few individuals who are benefited, are not supposed to have the clearest right to their advantages. If he that shared the danger enjoyed the profit, and after bleeding in the battle grew rich by the victory, he might show his gains without envy. But at the conclusion of a ten years war, how are we recompensed for the death of multitudes and the expense of millions, but by contemplating the sudden glories of paymasters and agents, contractors and commissaries, whose equipages shine like meteors, and whose palaces rise like exhalations?

These are the men who, without virtue, labour, or hazard, are growing rich as their country is impoverished; they rejoice when obstinacy or ambition adds another year to slaughter and devastation; and laugh from their desks at bravery and science, while they are adding figure to figure, and cipher to cipher, hoping for a new contract from a new armament, and computing the profits of a siege or tempest.

Falkland's Islands

To Mrs. Thrale

Dear Madam

Last Saturday I came to Ashbourn; the dangers or the pleasures of the journey I have at present no disposition to recount. Else might I paint the beauties of my native plain, might I tell of 'the smiles of Nature and the charms of art', else might I relate how I crossed the Staffordshire Canal one of the great efforts of human labour and human contrivance, which from the bridge on which I viewed it, passed away on either side, and loses itself in distant regions uniting waters that Nature had divided, and dividing lands which Nature had united. I might tell how these reflections fermented in my mind till the chaise stopped at Ashbourne, at Ashbourne in the Peak. Let not the barren name of the peak terrify you; I have never wanted Strawberries and cream. The great Bull has no disease but age. I hope in time to be like the great Bull; and hope you will be like him too a hundred years hence.

In the mean time, dearest Madam, you have many dangers to pass. I hope the danger of this year is now over, and you are safe in Bed with a pretty little Stranger in the cradle. I hope you do not think me indifferent about you, and therefore will take care to have me informed.

I am Madam Your most obedient and most humble servant

Ashbourn July 3. 1771   Sam: Johnson

Epitaph on Hogarth

The Hand of Art here torpid lies
    That wav'd th' essential form of Grace,
Here death has clos'd the curious eyes
    That saw the manners in the Face.

If Genius warm thee, Reader, stay,
    If Merit touch thee, shed a tear,
Be Vice and Dulness far away
    Great Hogarth's honour'd Dust is here.

1772

Γνῶθι σεαυτόν

(Post Lexicon Anglicanum auctum et emendatum.)

Lexicon ad finem longo luctamine tandem
Scaliger ut duxit, tenuis pertæsus opellæ,
Vile indignatus studium, nugasque molestas,
Ingemit exosus, scribendaque lexica mandat
Damnatis, pœnam pro pœnis omnibus unam.

    Ille quidem recte, sublimis, doctus, et acer,
Quem decuit majora sequi, majoribus aptum,
Qui veterum modo facta ducum, modo carmina vatum,
Gesserat et quicquid Virtus, Sapientia quicquid
Dixerat, imperiique vices, cœlique meatus,
Ingentemque animo seclorum volverat orbem.

    Fallimur exemplis; temere sibi turba scholarum
Ima tuas credit permitti, Scaliger, iras.
Quisque suum nôrit modulum; tibi, prime virorum,
Ut studiis sperem, aut ausim par esse querelis,
Non mihi sorte datum; lenti seu sanguinis obsint
Frigora, seu nimium longo jacuisse veterno,
Sive mihi mentem dederit Natura minorem.

    Te sterili functum cura, vocumque salebris
Tuto eluctatum spatiis Sapientia dia
Excipit æthereis, Ars omnis plaudit amica,
Linguarumque omni terra discordia concors
Multiplici reducem circumsonat ore magistrum.

    Me, pensi immunis cum jam mihi reddor, inertis
Desidiæ sors dura manet, graviorque labore
Tristis et atra quies, et tardæ tædia vitæ.
Nascuntur curis curæ, vexatque dolorum
Importuna cohors, vacuæ mala somnia mentis.
Nunc clamosa juvant nocturnæ gaudia mensæ,
Nunc loca sola placent; frustra te, Somne, recumbens
Alme voco, impatiens noctis metuensque diei.
Omnia percurro trepidus, circum omnia lustro,
Si qua usquam pateat melioris semita vitæ,
Nec quid agam invenio, meditatus grandia, cogor
Notior ipse mihi fieri, incultumque fateri

Pectus, et ingenium vano se robore jactans.
Ingenium, nisi materiem Doctrina ministret,
Cessat inops rerum, ut torpet, si marmoris absit
Copia, Phidiaci fœcunda potentia cœli.
Quicquid agam, quocunque ferar, conatibus obstat
Res angusta domi, et macræ penuria mentis.

　　Non Rationis opes Animus, nunc parta recensens,
Conspicit aggestas, et se miratur in illis,
Nec sibi de gaza præsens quód postulet usus
Summus adesse jubet celsa dominator ab arce;
Non operum serie, seriem dum computat ævi,
Præteritis fruitur, lætos aut sumit honores
Ipse sui judex, actæ bene munera vitæ;
Sed sua regna videns, loca nocte silentia late
Horret, ubi vanæ species, umbræque fugaces,
Et rerum volitant raræ per inane figuræ.

　　Quid faciam? tenebrisne pigram damnare senectam
Restat? an accingar studiis gravioribus audax?
Aut, hoc si nimium est, tandem nova lexica poscam?

　　　　　　　　　　　　　　　12. Dec. 1772.

Translation by Arthur Murphy

KNOW YOURSELF

(AFTER REVISING AND ENLARGING THE
ENGLISH LEXICON, OR DICTIONARY.)

　　When Scaliger, whole years of labour past,
Beheld his Lexicon complete at last,
And weary of his task, with wond'ring eyes,
Saw from words pil'd on words a fabric rise,
He curs'd the industry, inertly strong,
In creeping toil that could persist so long,
And if, enrag'd he cried, Heav'n meant to shed
Its keenest vengeance on the guilty head,
The drudgery of words the damn'd would know,
Doom'd to write Lexicons in endless woe.
　　Yes, you had cause, great Genius, to repent;
'You lost good days, that might be better spent;'

You well might grudge the hours of ling'ring pain,
And view your learned labours with disdain.
To you were given the large expanded mind,
The flame of genius, and the taste refin'd.
'Twas yours on eagle wings aloft to soar,
And amidst rolling worlds the Great First Cause explore;
To fix the æras of recorded time,
And live in ev'ry age and ev'ry clime;
Record the Chiefs, who propt their Country's cause;
Who founded Empires, and establish'd Laws;
To learn whate'er the Sage with virtue fraught,
Whate'er the Muse of moral wisdom taught.
These were your quarry; these to you were known,
And the world's ample volume was your own.

Yet warn'd by me, ye pigmy Wits, beware,
Nor with immortal Scaliger compare.
For me, though his example strike my view,
Oh! not for me his footsteps to pursue.
Whether first Nature, unpropitious, cold,
This clay compounded in a ruder mould;
Or the slow current, loit'ring at my heart,
No gleam of wit or fancy can impart;
Whate'er the cause, from me no numbers flow,
No visions warm me, and no raptures glow.
A mind like Scaliger's, superior still,
No grief could conquer, no misfortune chill.
Though for the maze of words his native skies
He seem'd to quit, 'twas but again to rise;
To mount once more to the bright source of day,
And view the wonders of th' æthereal way.
The love of Fame his gen'rous bosom fir'd;
Each Science hail'd him, and each Muse inspir'd.
For him the Sons of Learning trimm'd the bays,
And Nations grew harmonious in his praise.

My task perform'd, and all my labours o'er,
For me what lot has Fortune now in store?
The listless will succeeds, that worst disease,
The rack of indolence, the sluggish ease.

Care grows on care, and o'er my aching brain
Black Melancholy pours her morbid train.
No kind relief, no lenitive at hand,
I seek at midnight clubs the social Band;
But midnight clubs, where wit with noise conspires,
Where Comus revels, and where wine inspires,
Delight no more: I seek my lonely bed,
And call on Sleep to sooth my languid head.
But Sleep from these sad lids flies far away;
I mourn all night, and dread the coming day.
Exhausted, tir'd, I throw my eyes around,
To find some vacant spot on classic ground;
And soon, vain hope! I form a grand design;
Languor succeeds, and all my powers decline.
If Science open not her richest vein,
Without materials all our toil is vain.
A form to rugged stone when Phidias gives,
Beneath his touch a new creation lives.
Remove his marble, and his genius dies;
With Nature then no breathing statue vies.

Whate'er I plan, I feel my pow'rs confin'd
By Fortune's frown and penury of mind.
I boast no knowledge glean'd with toil and strife,
That bright reward of a well-acted life.
I view myself, while Reason's feeble light
Shoots a pale glimmer through the gloom of night,
While passions, error, phantoms of the brain,
And vain opinions, fill the dark domain;
A dreary void, where fears with grief combin'd
Waste all within, and desolate the mind.

What then remains? Must I in slow decline
To mute inglorious ease old age resign?
Or, bold Ambition kindling in my breast,
Attempt some arduous task? Or, were it best
Brooding o'er Lexicons to pass the day,
And in that labour drudge my life away?

Methodists at Oxford

I talked of the recent expulsion of six students from the
University of Oxford, who were methodists and would
not desist from publickly praying and exhorting. JOHN-
SON. 'Sir, that expulsion was extremely just and proper.
What have they to do at an University who are not
willing to be taught, but will presume to teach? Where is
religion to be learnt but at an University? Sir, they were
examined, and found to be mighty ignorant fellows.'
BOSWELL. 'But, was it not hard, Sir, to expel them, for I
am told they were good beings?' JOHNSON. 'I believe they
might be good beings; but they were not fit to be in the
University of Oxford. A cow is a very good animal in the
field; but we turn her out of a garden.' Lord Elibank used
to repeat this as an illustration uncommonly happy.

Boswell, *Life*

A Flea and a Lion

A learned gentleman who in the course of conversation
wished to inform us of this simple fact, that the Counsel
upon the circuit at Shrewsbury were much bitten by
fleas, took, I suppose, seven or eight minutes in relating
it circumstantially. He in a plenitude of phrase told us,
that large bales of woollen cloth were lodged in the town-
hall;—that by reason of this, fleas nestled there in prodigious numbers; that the lodgings of the counsel were
near to the town-hall;—and that those little animals
moved from place to place with wonderful agility. Johnson sat in great impatience till the gentleman had finished
his tedious narrative, and then burst out (playfully however,) 'It is a pity, Sir, that you have not seen a lion;
for a flea has taken you such a time, that a lion must have
served you a twelvemonth.'

Boswell, *Life*

To Hester ('Queeney') Thrale

Dear Sweeting   Ashbourn, Nov. 2, 1772
    Your pretty letter was too short. If Lucy is not good,

you must try to mend her by good advice, and good example, for all the little girls will try to be like you. I am glad to hear of the improvement and prosperity of my hen. Miss Porter has buried her fine black cat. So things come and go. Generations, as Homer says, are but like leaves; and you now see the faded leaves falling about you.

You are sorry to come to town, and I am sorry for dear Granmamma that will be left in the country, be sure that you make my compliments to her.

I am, Dear Miss, Your most obedient servant
Sam: Johnson

1773
Goldsmith's Powers

Goldsmith being mentioned; JOHNSON. 'It is amazing how little Goldsmith knows. He seldom comes where he is not more ignorant than any one else.' SIR JOSHUA REYNOLDS. 'Yet there is no man whose company is more liked.' JOHNSON. 'To be sure, Sir. When people find a man of the most distinguished abilities as a writer, their inferiour while he is with them, it must be highly gratifying to them. What Goldsmith comically says of himself is very true,—he always gets the better when he argues alone; meaning, that he is master of a subject in his study, and can write well upon it; but when he comes into company, grows confused, and unable to talk. Take him as a poet, his *Traveller* is a very fine performance; ay, and so is his *Deserted Village*, were it not sometimes too much the echo of his *Traveller*. Whether, indeed, we take him as a poet,—as a comick writer,—or as an historian, he stands in the first class.' BOSWELL. 'An historian! My dear Sir, you surely will not rank his compilation of the Roman History with the works of other historians of this age?' JOHNSON. 'Why, who are before him?' BOSWELL. 'Hume,—Robertson, —Lord Lyttelton.' JOHNSON (his antipathy to the Scotch beginning to rise). 'I have not read Hume; but, doubtless, Goldsmith's *History* is better than the *verbiage* of Robertson, or the foppery of Dalrymple.' BOSWELL. 'Will you not admit the superiority of Robertson, in whose *History* we find such penetration—such painting?' JOHNSON. 'Sir, you must consider how that penetration and that painting are employed. It is not history, it is imagination. He who describes what he never saw, draws from fancy. Robertson paints minds as Sir Joshua paints faces in a history-piece: he imagines an heroic countenance. You must look upon Robertson's work as romance, and try it by that standard. History it is not. Besides, Sir, it is the great excellence of a writer to put into his book as much as his book will hold. Goldsmith has done this in his *History*. Now Robertson might have put twice as much into his book. Robertson is like a man who has packed gold in wool: the wool takes up more room than the gold. No, Sir; I always thought Robertson would be crushed by his own weight,—would be buried under his own ornaments. Goldsmith tells you shortly all you want to know: Robertson detains you a great deal too long. No man will read Robertson's cumbrous detail a second time; but Goldsmith's plain narrative will please again and again. I would say to Robertson what an old tutor of a college said to one of his pupils: "Read over your compositions, and where ever you meet with a passage which you think is particularly fine, strike it out." Goldsmith's abridgement is better than that of Lucius Florus or Eutropius; and I will venture to say, that if you compare him with Vertot, in the same places of the Roman History, you will find that he excels Vertot. Sir, he has the art of compiling, and of saying every thing he has to say in a pleasing manner. He is now writing a Natural History and will make it as entertaining as a Persian Tale.'

Boswell, Life

To William Samuel Johnson

Sir

Of all those whom the various accidents of life have brought within my notice there is scarce any man whose acquaintance I have more desired to cultivate than yours. I cannot indeed charge you with neglecting me, yet our mutual inclination could never gratify itself with opportunities,—the current of the day always bore us away from one another. And now the Atlantick is between us.

Whether you carried away an impression of me as pleasing as that which you left me of yourself, I know not; if you did you have not forgotten me, and will be glad that I do not forget you. Merely to be remembred is indeed a barren pleasure, but it is one of the pleasures which is more sensibly felt, as human Nature is more exalted.

To make you wish that I should have you in my mind, I would be glad to tell you something which you do not know, but all publick affairs are printed; and as you and I had no common friends I can tell you no private history.

The Government I think grows stronger, but I am afraid the next general Election will be a time of uncommon turbulence, violence, and outrage.

Of Literature no great product has appeared or is expected; the attention of the people has for some years been otherwise employed.

I was told two days ago of a design which must excite some curiosity. Two ships are preparing here, which are under the command of Captain Constantine Phipps to explore the Northern Ocean, not to seek the Northeast or the Northwest passage, but to sail directly North, as near the pole as they can go. They hope to find an open Ocean, but I suspect it is one mass of perpetual congelation. I do not much wish well to discoveries, for I am always afraid they will end in conquest and robbery.

I have been out of order this winter but am grown better. Can I ever hope to see you again, or must I be always content to tell you that in another hemisphere
I am Sir Your most humble Servant

Sam: Johnson

Johnson's Court, Fleetstreet London.
March. 4. 1773

To Mrs. Thrale from Scotland

Dear Madam   Bamff, Aug. 25. 1773

It has so happened that though I am perpetually thinking on you, I could seldom find opportunity to write. I have in fourteen days sent only one Letter. You must consider the fatigues of travel, and the difficulties encountered in a strange Country.

August 18. I passed with Boswel the Firth of Forth, and began our Journey. In the passage We observed an Island which I persuaded my companions to survey. We found it a Rock somewhat troublesome to climb, about a mile long and half a mile broad; in the middle were the ruins of an old fort, which had on one of the stones Maria Re. 1564. It had been only a blockhouse one story high. I measured two apartments of which the walls were entire and found them 27 feet long and 23 broad. The Rock had some grass and many thistles, both cows and sheep were grazing. There was a spring of water. The name is Inchkeith. Look on your Maps.

This visit took about an hour. We pleased ourselves with being in a country all our own, and then went back to the boat, and landed at Kinghorn, a mean town, and travelling through Kirkaldie, a very long town meanly built, and Cowpar, which I could not see because it was night, we came late to St. Andrews, the most ancient of the Scotch universities, and once the See of the Primate of Scotland. The inn was full, but Lodgings were provided for us at the house of the professor of Rhetorick, a Man of elegant manners who showed us in the morning the poor remains of a stately Cathedral, demolished in Knox's reformation, and now only to be imaged by tracing its foundation and contemplating the little ruins that are left. Here was once a religious house. Two of the vaults or cellars of the Subprior are yet entire. In one of them lives an old Woman who claims an hereditary residence in it, boasting that her husband was the sixth tenant of this gloomy mansion in a lineal descent, and claiming by her marriage with this Lord of the cavern, an alliance with the Bruces. Mr. Boswel staid a while to interrogate her, because he understood her language. She told him, that she and her Cat lived together; that she had two sons somewhere, who might perhaps be dead; that when there were quality in the town, notice was taken of her; and that now she was neglected, but did not trouble them. Her habitation contained all that she had, her turf for fire was laid in one place, and her balls of coaldust in another, but her bed seemed to be clean. Boswel asked her if she never heard any noises, but she could tell him of nothing supernatural, though she sometimes wandered in the night among the graves and ruins, only she had some notice by dreams of the death of her relations.

We then viewed the remains of a Castle on the margin of the sea, in which the Archbishops resided, and in which Cardinal Beatoun was killed.

The Professors, who happened to be resident in the vacation, made a publick dinner, and treated us very kindly and respectfully. They shewed us their Colleges in one of which there is a library, that for luminousness and elegance may vie at least with the new edifice at Streatham. But Learning seems not to prosper among them, one of their Colleges has been lately alienated, and one of their churches lately deserted. An experiment was made of planting a shrubbery in the church, but it did not thrive.

Why the place should thus fall to decay I know not, for Education, such as is here to be had, is sufficiently cheap. Their term or as they call it their session lasts seven months in the year which the students of the highest rank and greatest expence may pass here for twenty pounds in which are included, Board, Lodging, Books, and the continual instruction of three Professors.

20 We left St Andrews well satisfied with our reception, and crossing the Firth of Tay, came to Dundee, a dirty despicable town. We past afterwards through Aberbrothick, famous once for an Abbey of which there are only a few fragments left, but those fragments testify that the fabrick was once of great extent, and stupendous magnificence; two of the towers are yet standing though shattered, into one of them Boswel climbed, but found

the stairs broken. The way into the other we did not see, and had not time to search, I believed it might be ascended but the top, I think, is open.

We lay at Montrose, a neat place, with a spacious area for the market, and an elegant townhouse.

21 We travelled towards Aberdeen, another University, and in the way dined at Lord Monbodo's, the Scotch Judge who has lately written a strange book about the origin of Language, in which he traces Monkeys up to Men, and says that in some countries the human species have tails like other beasts. He enquired for these long-tailed Men of Banks, and was not well pleased, that they had not been found in all his peregrination. He talked nothing of this to me, and I hope, we parted friends, for we agreed pretty well, only we differed in adjusting the claims of merit between a Shopkeeper of London, and a Savage of the American wildernesses. Our opinions were, I think, maintained on both sides without full conviction; Monbodo declared boldly for the Savage, and I perhaps for that reason sided with the Citizen.

We came late to Aberdeen, where I found my dear Mistress's Letter, and learned that all our little people were happily recovered of the Measles. Every part of your letter was pleasing. I am glad that the presents are made, and that Mr. Perkins is sent to Ireland, and sent with full powers both by my Master and you. I do not well understand the question of the tithes, if you can follow Mr Robson's advice without open War upon your unkle, it will be best to do it; but it would be wrong to raise new quarrels for a small matter.

There are two cities of the name of Aberdeen. The old town built about a mile inland, once the see of a Bishop, which contains the King's College, and the remains of the Cathedral, and the new town which stands for the sake of trade, upon a firth or arm of the sea, so that ships rest against the Key.

The two cities have their separate Magistrates, and the two Colleges are in effect two Universities which confer degrees independently on each other.

New Aberdeen is a large town, built almost wholly of

that Granite which is used for the new pavement in London, which, hard as it is, they square with very little difficulty. Here I first saw the women in plaids. The plaid makes at once a hood and cloak without cutting or sewing, merely by the manner of drawing the opposite sides over the Shoulders. The Maids at the Inns run over the house barefoot, and children, not dressed in rags, go without shoes or stockings. Shoes are indeed not yet in universal use they came late into this country. One of the Professors told us, as we were mentioning a fort built by Cromwel, that the Country owed much of its present industry to Cromwel's soldiers. They taught us said he, to raise cabbage, and make shoes. How they lived without shoes may yet be seen, but in the passage through villages, it seems to him that surveys their gardens, that when they had not cabbage they had nothing.

Education is here of the same price as at St. Andrews only the session is but from the first of November to the first of April. The academical buildings, seem rather to advance than decline. They shewed their libraries which were not very splendid, but some manuscripts were so exquisitely penned, that I wished my dear Mistress to have seen them.

I had an unexpected pleasure by finding an old acquaintance, now professor of physick in the King's College. We were on both sides glad of the interview, having not seen nor perhaps thought on one another for many years. But we had no emulation, nor had either of us risen to the other's envy, and our old kindness was easily renewed. I hope We shall never try the effect of so long an absence, and that I shall always be

Madam Your most humble servant
Sam: Johnson

To Mrs. Thrale

Dearest Madam

I am so vexed at the necessity of sending yesterday so short a Letter that I purpose to get a long letter before-hand by writing something every day, which I may the more easily do, as a cold makes me now too deaf to take the usual pleasure in conversation. Lady Macleod is very kind to me, and the place at which we now are, is equal in strength of situation, in the wildness of the adjacent country, and in the plenty and elegance of the domestick entertainment, to a Castle in Gothick romances. The sea with a little Island is before us, cascades play within view. Close to the house is the formidable skeleton of an old Castle probably Danish; and the whole mass of building stands upon a protuberance of rock, inaccessible till of late but by a pair of stairs on the sea side, and secure in ancient times against any Enemy that was likely to invade the kingdom of Skie. Macleod has offered me an Island, if it were not too far off I should hardly refuse it; my Island would be pleasanter than Brighthelmston, if you and Master could come to it, but I cannot think it pleasant to live quite alone. Oblitusque meorum, obliviscendus et illis. That I should be elated by the dominion of an Island to forgetfulness of my friends at Streatham, and I hope never to deserve that they should be willing to forget me.

It has happened that I have been often recognized in my journey where I did not expect it. At Aberdeen I found one of my acquaintance Professor of Physick. Turning aside to dine with a country Gentleman, I was owned at a table by one who had seen me at a Philosophical Lecture. At Macdonald's I was claimed by a Naturalist, who wanders about the Islands to pick up curiosities, and I had once in London attracted the notice of Lady Macleod. I will now go on with my Account.

The Highland Girl made tea, and looked and talked not inelegantly. Her Father was by no means an ignorant or a weak man. There were books in the cottage, among which were some volumes of Prideaux's Connexion. This man's conversation we were glad of while we staid. He had been *out* as they call it, in forty five, and still retained his old opinions. He was going to America, because his rent was raised beyond what he thought himself able to pay.

At night our beds were made, but we had some difficulty in persuading ourselves to lye down in them, though we had put on our own sheets. At last we ventured, and I slept very soundly, in the vale called Glenmorison amidst the rocks and mountains. Next morning our Landlord liked us so well, that he walked some miles with us for our company through a country so wild and barren that the proprietor does not with all his pressure upon his tenants raise more than four hundred a year from near an hundred square miles, or sixty thousand acres. He let us know that he had forty head of black cattle, an hundred Goats, and an hundred sheep upon a farm which he remembred let at five pounds a year, but for which he now paid twenty. He told us some stories of their march into England. At last he left us, and we went forward, winding among mountains sometimes green and sometimes naked, commonly so steep as not easily to be climbed by the greatest vigour and activity. Our way was often crossed by little rivulets, and we were entertained with small streams trickling from the rocks, which after heavy rains must be tremendous torrents.

About noon, we came to a small glen, so they call a valley, which compared with other places appeared rich and fertile. Here our Guides desired us to stop that the horses might graze, for the journey was very laborious, and no more grass would be found. We made no difficulty of compliance, and I sat down to take notes on a green bank, with a small stream running at my feet, in the midst of savage solitude, with Mountains before me, and on either hand covered with heath. I looked round me, and wondered that I was not more affected, but the mind is not at all times equally ready to be put in motion. If my Mistress, and Master, and Queeny had been there we should have produced some reflections among us either poetical or philosophical, for though *Solitude* be *the nurse of woe*, conversation is often the parent of remarks and discoveries.

In about an hour we remounted, and persued our journey. The lake by which we had travelled from some time ended in a river, which we passed by a bridge and came to another Glen with a collection of huts, called Auknashealds, the huts were generally built of clods of earth held together by the intertexture of vegetable fibres, of which earth there are great levels in Scotland which they call mosses. Moss in Scotland, is Bog in Ireland, and Moss trooper is Bog trotter. There was however one hut built of loose stones piled up with great thickness into a strong though not solid wall. From this house we obtained some great pails of milk, and having brought bread with us, were very liberally regaled. The Inhabitants, a very coarse tribe, ignorant of any language but Earse, gathered so fast about us, that if we had not had Highlanders with us, they might have caused more alarm than pleasure. They are called the clan of Macrae.

We have been told that nothing gratified the Highlanders so much as snuff and tobacco, and had accordingly stored ourselves with both at fort Augustus. Boswel opened his treasure and gave them each a piece of tobacco roll. We had more bread than we could eat for the present, and were more liberal than provident. Boswel cut it in slices and gave each of them an opportunity of tasting wheaten bread for the first time. I then got some halfpence for a shilling and made up the deficiencies of Boswels distribution, who had given some money among the children. We then directed that the mistress of the stone house should be asked what we must pay her, she who perhaps had never sold any thing but cattle before, knew not, I believe, well what to ask, and referred herself to us. We obliged her to make some demand, and our Highlanders settled the account with her at a shilling. One of the men advised her, with the cunning that clowns never can be without, to ask more but she said that a shilling was enough. We gave her half a crown and she offered part of it again. The Macraes were so well pleased with our behaviour, that they declared it the best day they had seen since the time of the old Laird of MacLeod, who I suppose, like us, stopped in their valley, as he was travelling to Skie.

We were mentioning this view of the Highlander's life at Macdonald's, and mentioning the Macraes with some degree of pity, when a Highland Lady informed us, that we might spare our tenderness, for she doubted not, but the Woman who supplied us with milk, was Mistress of thirteen or fourteen milch cows.

I cannot forbear to interrupt my Narrative. Boswel, with some of his troublesome kindness, has informed this family, and reminded me that the eighteenth of September is my birthday. The return of my Birthday, if I remember it, fills me with thoughts which it seems to be the general care of humanity to escape. I can now look back upon threescore and four years, in which little has been done, and little has been enjoyed, a life diversified by misery, spent part in the sluggishness of penury, and part under the violence of pain, in gloomy discontent, or importunate distress. But perhaps I am better than I should have been, if I had been less afflicted. With this I will try to be content.

In proportion as there is less pleasure in retrospective considerations the mind is more disposed to wander forward into futurity, but at sixty four what promises, however liberal of imaginary good, can Futurity venture to make. Yet something will be always promised, and some promises will always be credited. I am hoping, and I am praying that I may live better in the time to come, whether long or short, than I have yet lived, and in the solace of that hope endeavour to repose. Dear Queeney's day is next, I hope, she at sixty four will have less to regret.

I will now complain no more, but tell my Mistress of my travels.

After we left the Macraes, we travelled on through a country like that which we passed in the morning, the highlands are very uniform, for there is little variety in universal barrenness. The rocks however are not all naked, some have grass on their sides, and Birches and Alders on their tops, and in the vallies are often broad and clear streams which have little depth, and commonly run very quick. The channels are made by the violence of wintry floods, the quickness of the stream is in proportion to the declivity of the descent, and the breadth of the channel makes the water shallow in a dry season.

There are Red Deer and Roebucks in the mountains,

but we found only Goats in the road, and had very little entertainment as we travelled either for the eye or ear. There are, I fancy, no singing birds in the Highlands.

Towards Night we came to a very formidable Hill called Rattiken, which we climbed with more difficulty than we had yet experienced, and at last came to Glanelg a place on the Seaside opposite to Skie. We were by this time weary and disgusted, nor was our humour much mended, by an inn, which, though it was built with lime and slate, the highlander's description of a house which he thinks magnificent, had neither wine, bread, eggs, nor any thing that we could eat or drink. When we were taken up stairs, a dirty fellow bounced out of the bed in which one of us was to lie. Boswel blustered, but nothing could be got. At last a Gentleman in the Neighbourhood who heard of our arrival sent us rum and white sugar. Boswel was now provided for in part, and the Landlord prepared some mutton chops, which we could not eat, and killed two Hens, of which Boswel made his servant broil a limb, with what effect I know not. We had a lemon, and a piece of bread, which supplied me with my supper.

When the repast was ended, we began to deliberate upon bed. Mrs Boswel had warned us that we should *catch something*, and had given us Sheets for our security; for Sir Alexander and Lady Macdonald, she said, came back from Skie, so scratching themselves—. I thought sheets a slender defence, against the confederacy with which we were threatned, and by this time our highlanders had found a place where they could get some hay; I ordered hay to be laid thick upon the bed, and slept upon it in my great coat. Boswell laid sheets upon his hay, and reposed in Linen like a Gentleman. The horses were turned out to grass, with a man to watch them. The hill Ratiken, and the inn at Glanelg, are the only things of which we or travellers yet more delicate, could find any pretensions to complain.

Sept. 2. I rose rustling from the hay, and went to tea, which I forget whether we found or brought. We saw the Isle of Skie before us darkening the horizon with its rocky coast. A boat was procured, and we launched into one of the Straits of the Atlantick Ocean. We had a passage of about twelve miles to the point where Sir Alexander resided, having come from his Seat in the midland part, to a small house on the shore, as we believe, that he might with less reproach entertain us meanly. If he aspired to meanness his retrograde ambition was completely gratified, but he did not succeed equally in escaping reproach. He had no cook, nor, I suppose, much provision, nor had the Lady the common decencies of her tea table. We picked up our Sugar with our fingers. Boswel was very angry, and reproached him with his improper parsimony. I did not much reflect upon the conduct of a man with whom I was not likely to converse as long at any other time.

You will now expect that I should give you some account of the Isle of Skie, of which though I have been twelve days upon it, I have little to say. It is an Island perhaps fifty miles long, so much indented by inlets of the Sea, that there is no part of it removed from the water more than six miles. No part that I have seen is plain you are always climbing or descending, and every step is upon rock or mire. A walk upon plowed ground in England is a dance upon carpets, compared to the toilsome drudgery, of wandering in Skie. There is neither town nor village in the Island, nor have I seen any house but Macleod's, that is not much below your habitation at Brighthelmston. In the mountains there are Stags and Roebucks, but no hares and few rabbits, nor have I seen any thing that interested me, as Zoologist, except an Otter, bigger than I thought an otter could have been.

You are perhaps imagining that I am withdrawn from the gay and the busy world into regions of peace and pastoral felicity, and am enjoying the reliques of the golden age; that I am surveying Nature's magnificence from a mountain, or remarking her minuter beauties on the flowery bank of a winding rivulet, that I am invigorating myself in the sunshine, or delighting my imagination with being hidden from the invasion of human evils and human passions, in the darkness of a

Thicket, that I am busy in gathering shells and pebbles on the Shore, or contemplative on a rock, from which I look upon the water and consider how many waves are rolling between me and Streatham.

The use of travelling is to regulate imagination by reality, and instead of thinking how things may be, to see them as they are. Here are mountains which I should once have climbed, but to climb steeps is now very laborious, and to descend them dangerous, and I am now content with knowing that by a scrambling up a rock, I shall only see other rocks, and a wider circuit of barren desolation. Of streams we have here a sufficient number, but they murmur not upon pebbles but upon rocks; of flowers, if Chloris herself were here, I could present her only with the bloom of Heath. Of Lawns and Thickets, he must read, that would know them, for here is little sun and no shade. On the sea I look from my window, but am not much tempted to the shore for since I came to this Island, almost every Breath of air has been a storm, and what is worse, a storm with all its severity, but without its magnificence, for the sea is here so broken into channels, that there is not a sufficient volume of water either for lofty surges, or loud roar.

On Sept. 6. We left Macdonald, to visit Raarsa, the Island which I have already mentioned. We were to cross part of Skie on horseback, a mode of travelling very uncomfortable, for the road is so narrow, where any road can be found that only one can go, and so craggy that the attention can never be remitted, it allows therefore neither the gayety of conversation nor the laxity of solitude, nor has it in itself the amusement of much variety, as it affords only all the possible transpositions of Bog, Rock, and Rivulet. Twelve Miles, by computation, make a reasonable journey for a day.

At night we came to a tenants house of the first rank of tenants where we were entertained better than the Landlord's. There were books, both English and Latin. Company gathered about us, and we heard some talk of the Second sight and some talk of the events of forty five, a year which will not soon be forgotten among the

Islanders. The next day we were confined by a storm, the company, I think, encreased and our entertainment was not only hospitable but elegant. At night, a Minister's sister in very fine Brocade, sung Earse songs. I wished to know the meaning, but the Highlanders are not much used to scholastick questions, and no translation could be obtained.

Next day, Sept. 8. The weather allowed us to depart, a good boat was provided us, and we went to Raarsa, under the conduct of Mr Malcolm Macleod, a Gentleman who conducted Prince Charles through the mountains in his distresses. The prince, he says, was more active than himself, they were at least one night, without any shelter.

The wind blew enough to give the boat a kind of dancing agitation, and in about three or four hours we arrived at Raarsa, where we were met by the Laird and his friends upon the Shore. Raarsa, for such is his title, is Master of two Islands, upon the smaller of which, called Rona, he has only flocks and herds. Rona gives title to his eldest Son. The money which he raises by rent from all his dominions which contain at least fifty thousand acres, is not believed to exceed two hundred and fifty pounds, but as he keeps a large farm in his own hands, he sells every year great numbers of cattle which he adds to his revenue, and his table is furnished from the Farm and from the sea with little expence, except for those things this country does not produce, and of those he is very liberal. The Wine circulates vigorously, and the tea and Chocolate and Coffee, however they are got are always at hand.

I am Madam Your most obedient servant

Skie. Sep. 21. 1773　　　　　　　　　　Sam: Johnson

We are this morning trying to get out of Skie.

1773-5
JOHNSON AND BOSWELL
IN SCOTLAND

1773
Insula Sancti Kennethi

Parva quidem regio, sed relligione priorum
    Nota, Caledonias panditur inter aquas;
Voce ubi Cennnethus populos domuisse feroces
    Dicitur, et vanos dedocuisse deos.
Huc ego delatus placido per cœrula cursu
    Scire locum volui quid daret ille novi.
Illic Leniades humili regnabat in aula,
    Leniades magnis nobilitatus avis:
Una duas habuit casa cum genitore puellas,
    Quas Amor undarum fingeret esse deas:
Non tamen inculti gelidis latuere sub antris,
    Accola Danubii qualia sævus habet;
Mollia non deerant vacuæ solatia vitæ,
    Sive libros poscant otia, sive lyram.
Luxerat illa dies, legis gens docta supernæ
    Spes hominum ac curas cum procul esse jubet.
Ponti inter strepitus sacri non munera cultus
    Cessarunt; pietas hic quoque cura fuit:
Quid quod sacrifici versavit femina libros,
    Legitimas faciunt pectora pura preces.
Quo vagor ulterius? quod ubique requiritur hic est;
    Hic secura quies, hic et honestus amor.

Beattie and Hume

Of Dr. Beattie, Mr. Johnson said, 'Sir, he has written
like a man conscious of the truth, and feeling his own
strength. Treating your adversary with respect, is giving
him an advantage to which he is not entitled. The greatest
part of men cannot judge of reasoning, and are impressed
by character; so that, if you allow your adversary a re-
spectable character, they will think, that though you

differ from him, you may be in the wrong. Sir, treating your adversary with respect, is striking soft in a battle. And as to Hume,—a man who has so much conceit as to tell all mankind that they have been bubbled for ages, and he is the wise man who sees better than they,—a man who has so little scrupulosity as to venture to oppose those principles which have been thought necessary to human happiness,—is he to be surprised if another man comes and laughs at him? If he is the great man he thinks himself, all this cannot hurt him: it is like throwing peas against a rock.' He added *something much too rough,* both as to Mr. Hume's head and heart, which I suppress.

Boswell, Tour to the Hebrides

Genius and Application

We talked of Mr. Burke.—Dr. Johnson said, he had great variety of knowledge, store of imagery, copiousness of language.—ROBERTSON. 'He has wit too.'—JOHNSON, 'No, sir; he never succeeds there. 'Tis low; 'tis conceit. I used to say, Burke never once made a good joke. What I most envy Burke for, is, his being constantly the same. He is never what we call hum-drum; never unwilling to begin to talk, nor in haste to leave off.'—BOSWELL. 'Yet he can listen.'—JOHNSON. 'No; I cannot say he is good at that. So desirous is he to talk, that, if one is speaking at this end of the table, he'll speak to somebody at the other end. Burke, sir, is such a man, that if you met him for the first time in a street where you were stopped by a drove of oxen, and you and he stepped aside to take shelter but for five minutes, he'd talk to you in such a manner, that, when you parted, you would say, this is an extraordinary man. Now, you may be long enough with me, without finding any thing extraordinary.' He said, he believed Burke was intended for the law; but either had not money enough to follow it, or had not diligence enough. He said, he could not understand how a man could apply to one thing, and not to another. ROBERTSON said, one man had more judgment, another more imagination.—JOHNSON. 'No, sir; it is only, one man has more mind than another.

He may direct it differently; he may, by accident, see the success of one kind of study, and take a desire to excel in it. I am persuaded that, had Sir Isaac Newton applied to poetry, he would have made a very fine epick poem. I could as easily apply to law as to tragick poetry.'—BOSWELL. 'Yet, sir, you did apply to tragick poetry, not to law.'—JOHNSON. 'Because, sir, I had not money to study law. Sir, the man who has vigour, may walk to the east, just as well as to the west, if he happens to turn his head that way.'—BOSWELL. 'But, sir, 'tis like walking up and down a hill; one man will naturally do the one better than the other. A hare will run up a hill best, from her forelegs being short; a dog down.'—JOHNSON. 'Nay, sir; that is from mechanical powers. If you make mind mechanical, you may argue in that manner. One mind is a vice, and holds fast; there's a good memory. Another is a file; and he is a disputant, a controversialist. Another is a razor; and he is sarcastical.'

Boswell, *Tour to the Hebrides*

Patronage

Dr. Watson observed, that Glasgow University had fewer home-students, since trade increased, as learning was rather incompatible with it.—JOHNSON. 'Why, sir, as trade is now carried on by subordinate hands, men in trade have as much leisure as others; and now learning itself is a trade. A man goes to a bookseller, and gets what he can. We have done with patronage. In the infancy of learning, we find some great man praised for it. This diffused it among others. When it becomes general, an author leaves the great, and applies to the multitude.'—BOSWELL. 'It is a shame that authors are not now better patronized.'—JOHNSON. 'No, sir. If learning cannot support a man, if he must sit with his hands across till somebody feeds him, it is as to him a bad thing, and it is better as it is. With patronage, what flattery! what falsehood! While a man is in equilibrio, he throws truth among the multitude, and lets them take it as they please: in patronage, he must say what pleases his patron, and it is

an equal chance whether that be truth or falsehood.'—
WATSON. 'But is not the case now, that, instead of flattering one person, we flatter the age?'—JOHNSON. 'No, sir.
The world always lets a man tell what he thinks, his own
way. I wonder however, that so many people have written,
who might have let it alone. That people should endeavour to excel in conversation, I do not wonder; because
in conversation praise is instantly reverberated.'

Boswell, Tour to the Hebrides

Monasticism

As we walked in the cloisters, there was a solemn echo,
while he talked loudly of a proper retirement from the
world. Mr. Nairne said, he had an inclination to retire.
I called Dr. Johnson's attention to this, that I might hear
his opinion if it was right.—JOHNSON. 'Yes, when he has
done his duty to society. In general, as every man is
obliged not only to "love GOD, but his neighbour as himself," he must bear his part in active life; yet there are
exceptions. Those who are exceedingly scrupulous, (which
I do not approve, for I am no friend to scruples,) and
find their scrupulosity invincible, so that they are quite
in the dark, and know not what they shall do,—or those
who cannot resist temptations, and find they make themselves worse by being in the world, without making it
better, may retire. I never read of a hermit, but in imagination I kiss his feet; never of a monastery, but I could
fall on my knees, and kiss the pavement. But I think
putting young people there, who know nothing of life,
nothing of retirement, is dangerous and wicked. It is a
saying as old as Hesiod,

Ἔργα νεῶν, βουλαίτε μέσων, εὐχαίτε γερόντων.

That is a very noble line: not that young men should not
pray, or old men not give counsel, but that every season
of life has its proper duties. I have thought of retiring,
and have talked of it to a friend; but I find my vocation
is rather to active life.'

Boswell, Tour to the Hebrides

A Sailor's Life

I yesterday expressed my wonder that John Hay, one of our guides, who had been pressed aboard a man of war, did not choose to continue in it longer than nine months, after which time he got off.—JOHNSON. 'Why, sir, no man will be a sailor, who has contrivance enough to get himself into a jail; for, being in a ship is being in a jail, with the chance of being drowned.'

Boswell, *Tour to the Hebrides*

His negro servant, Francis Barber, having left him, and been some time at sea, not pressed as has been supposed, but with his own consent, it appears from a letter to John Wilkes, Esq., from Dr. Smollet, that his master kindly interested himself in procuring his release from a state of life of which Johnson always expressed the utmost abhorrence. He said, 'No man will be a sailor who has contrivance enough to get himself into a jail; for being in a ship is being in a jail, with the chance of being drowned.' And at another time, 'A man in a jail has more room, better food, and commonly better company.'

Boswell, *Life*, s.a. 1759

Johnson's Seraglio

After the ladies were gone from table, we talked of the Highlanders not having sheets; and this led us to consider the advantage of wearing linen.—JOHNSON. 'All animal substances are less cleanly than vegetables. Wool, of which flannel is made, is an animal substance; flannel therefore is not so cleanly as linen. I remember I used to think tar dirty; but when I knew it to be only a preparation of the juice of the pine, I thought so no longer. It is not disagreeable to have the gum that oozes from a plumb-tree upon your fingers, because it is vegetable; but if you have any candle-grease, any tallow upon your fingers, you are uneasy till you rub it off.—I have often thought, that, if I kept a seraglio, the ladies should all wear linen gowns,—or cotton;—I mean stuffs made of

vegetable substances. I would have no silk; you cannot
tell when it is clean: It will be very nasty before it is
perceived to be so. Linen detects its own dirtiness.'

Boswell, Tour to the Hebrides

Unpliability

'Beauclerk and I, and Langton, and Lady Sydney Beauclerk, mother to our friend, were one day driving in a
coach by Cuper's Gardens, which were then unoccupied.
I, in sport, proposed that Beauclerk and Langton, and
myself should take them; and we amused ourselves with
scheming how we should all do our parts. Lady Sydney
grew angry, and said, "an old man should not put such
things in young people's heads." She had no notion of
a joke, sir; had come late into life, and had a mighty
unpliable understanding.'

Boswell, Tour to the Hebrides

Seeing the World

Mrs. M'Sweyn, who officiated as our landlady here, had
never been on the main land. On hearing this, Dr. Johnson said to me, before her, 'That is rather being behind-
hand with life. I would at least go and see Glenelg.'
—Boswell. 'You yourself, sir, have never seen, till now,
any thing but your native island.'—Johnson. 'But, sir,
by seeing London, I have seen as much of life as the
world can shew.'—Boswell. 'You have not seen Pekin.'
—Johnson. 'What is Pekin? Ten thousand Londoners
would *drive* all the people of Pekin: they would drive
them like deer.'

Boswell, Tour to the Hebrides

Homo Caudatus

Young Col told us he could run down a grey-hound; 'for,
(said he,) the dog runs himself out of breath, by going
too quick, and then I get up with him.' I accounted for
his advantage over the dog, by remarking that Col had

the faculty of reason, and knew how to moderate his pace, which the dog had not sense enough to do. Dr. Johnson said, 'He is a noble animal. He is as complete an islander as the mind can figure. He is a farmer, a sailor, a hunter, a fisher: he will run you down a dog: if any man has a *tail*, it is Col. He is hospitable; and he has an intrepidity of talk, whether he understands the subject or not. I regret that he is not more intellectual.'

Boswell, *Tour to the Hebrides*

1775

St. Andrews

At an hour somewhat late we came to St. Andrews, a city once archiepiscopal; where that university still subsists in which philosophy was formerly taught by Buchanan, whose name has as fair a claim to immortality as can be conferred by modern latinity, and perhaps a fairer than the instability of vernacular languages admits.

We found, that by the interposition of some invisible friend, lodgings had been provided for us at the house of one of the professors, whose easy civility quickly made us forget that we were strangers; and in the whole time of our stay we were gratified by every mode of kindness, and entertained with all the elegance of lettered hospitality.

In the morning we rose to perambulate a city, which only history shews to have once flourished, and surveyed the ruins of ancient magnificence, of which even the ruins cannot long be visible, unless some care be taken to preserve them; and where is the pleasure of preserving such mournful memorials? They have been till very lately so much neglected, that every man carried away the stones who fancied that he wanted them.

The cathedral, of which the foundations may be still traced, and a small part of the wall is standing, appears to have been a spacious and majestick building, not unsuitable to the primacy of the kingdom. Of the architecture, the poor remains can hardly exhibit, even to an artist, a sufficient specimen. It was demolished, as is well known, in the tumult and violence of Knox's reformation.

Not far from the cathedral, on the margin of the water, stands a fragment of the castle, in which the archbishop anciently resided. It was never very large, and was built with more attention to security than pleasure. Cardinal Beatoun is said to have had workmen employed in improving its fortifications at the time when he was murdered by the ruffians of reformation, in the manner of which Knox has given what he himself calls a merry narrative.

The change of religion in Scotland, eager and vehement as it was, raised an epidemical enthusiasm, compounded of sullen scrupulousness and warlike ferocity, which, in a people whom idleness resigned to their own thoughts, and who, conversing only with each other, suffered no dilution of their zeal from the gradual influx of new opinions, was long transmitted in its full strength from the old to the young, but by trade and intercourse with England, is now visibly abating, and giving way too fast to that laxity of practice and indifference of opinion, in which men, not sufficiently instructed to find the middle point, too easily shelter themselves from rigour and constraint.

The city of St. Andrews, when it had lost its archiepiscopal preeminence, gradually decayed: One of its streets is now lost; and in those that remain, there is the silence and solitude of inactive indigence and gloomy depopulation.

The university, within a few years, consisted of three colleges, but is now reduced to two; the college of St. Leonard being lately dissolved by the sale of its buildings and the appropriation of its revenues to the professors of the two others. The chapel of the alienated college is yet standing, a fabrick not inelegant of external structure; but I was always, by some civil excuse, hindred from entering it. A recent attempt, as I was since told, has been made to convert it into a kind of green-house, by planting its area with shrubs. This new method of gardening is unsuccessful; the plants do not hitherto prosper. To what use it will next be put I have no pleasure in conjecturing. It is something that its present state is at least not ostentatiously displayed. Where there is yet shame, there may in time be virtue.

The dissolution of St. Leonard's college was doubtless necessary; but of that necessity there is reason to complain. It is surely not without just reproach, that a nation, of which the commerce is hourly extending, and the wealth encreasing, denies any participation of its prosperity to its literary societies; and while its merchants or its nobles are raising palaces, suffers its universities to moulder into dust.

Of the two colleges yet standing, one is by the institution of its founder appropriated to Divinity. It is said to be capable of containing fifty students; but more than one must occupy a chamber. The library, which is of late erection, is not very spacious, but elegant and luminous.

The doctor, by whom it was shewn, hoped to irritate or subdue my English vanity by telling me, that we had no such repository of books in England.

Saint Andrews seems to be a place eminently adapted to study and education, being situated in a populous, yet a cheap country, and exposing the minds and manners of young men neither to the levity and dissoluteness of a capital city, nor to the gross luxury of a town of commerce, places naturally unpropitious to learning; in one the desire of knowledge easily gives way to the love of pleasure, and in the other, is in danger of yielding to the love of money.

The students however are represented as at this time not exceeding a hundred. Perhaps it may be some obstruction to their increase that there is no episcopal chapel in the place. I saw no reason for imputing their paucity to the present professors; nor can the expence of an academical education be very reasonably objected. A student of the highest class may keep his annual session, or as the English call it, his term, which lasts seven months, for about fifteen pounds, and one of lower rank for less than ten; in which board, lodging, and instruction are all included.

The chief magistrate resident in the university, answering to our vice-chancellor, and to the *rector magnificus* on the continent, had commonly the title of Lord Rector; but being addressed only as *Mr. Rector* in an inauguratory speech by the present chancellor, he has fallen from his former dignity of style. Lordship was very liberally annexed by our ancestors to any station or character of dignity: They said, the *Lord General*, and *Lord Ambassador*; so we still say, *my Lord*, to the judge upon the circuit, and yet retain in our Liturgy *the Lords of the Council*.

In walking among the ruins of religious buildings, we came to two vaults over which had formerly stood the house of the sub-prior. One of the vaults was inhabited by an old woman, who claimed the right of abode there, as the widow of a man whose ancestors had possessed the same gloomy mansion for no less than four generations. The right, however it began, was considered as established by legal prescription, and the old woman lives undisturbed. She thinks however that she has a claim to something more than sufferance; for as her husband's name was Bruce, she is allied to royalty, and told Mr. Boswell that when there were persons of quality in the place, she was distinguished by some notice; that indeed she is now neglected, but she spins a thread, has the company of her cat, and is troublesome to nobody.

Having now seen whatever this ancient city offered to our curiosity, we left it with good wishes, having reason to be highly pleased with the attention that was paid us. But whoever surveys the world must see many things that give him pain. The kindness of the professors did not contribute to abate the uneasy remembrance of a university declining, a college alienated, and a church profaned and hastening to the ground.

St. Andrews indeed has formerly suffered more atrocious ravages and more extensive destruction, but recent evils affect with greater force. We were reconciled to the sight of archiepiscopal ruins. The distance of a calamity from the present time seems to preclude the mind from contact or sympathy. Events long past are barely known; they are not considered. We read with as little emotion the violence of Knox and his followers, as the irruptions of Alaric and the Goths. Had the university been destroyed two centuries ago, we should not have regretted it; but to see it pining in decay and struggling for life, fills the mind with mournful images and ineffectual wishes.

A Journey to the Western Islands

The Glazier's Art

The art of joining squares of glass with lead is little used in Scotland, and in some places is totally forgotten. The frames of their windows are all of wood. They are more frugal of their glass than the English, and will often, in houses not otherwise mean, compose a square of two pieces, not joining like cracked glass, but with one edge laid perhaps half an inch over the other. Their windows do not move upon hinges, but are pushed up and drawn down in grooves, yet they are seldom accommodated with weights and pullies. He that would have his window open must hold it with his hand, unless what may be sometimes found among good contrivers, there be a nail which he may stick into a hole, to keep it from falling.

What cannot be done without some uncommon trouble or particular expedient, will not often be done at all. The incommodiousness of the Scotch windows keeps them very closely shut. The necessity of ventilating human habitations has not yet been found by our northern neighbours; and even in houses well built and elegantly furnished, a stranger may be sometimes forgiven, if he allows himself to wish for fresher air.

These diminutive observations seem to take away something from the dignity of writing, and therefore are never communicated but with hesitation, and a little fear of abasement and contempt. But it must be remembered, that life consists not of a series of illustrious actions, or elegant enjoyments; the greater part of our time passes in compliance with necessities, in the performance of daily duties, in the removal of small inconveniencies, in the procurement of petty pleasures; and we are well or ill at ease, as the main stream of life glides on smoothly, or is ruffled by small obstacles and frequent interruption. The true state of every nation is the state of common life.

The manners of a people are not to be found in the schools of learning, or the palaces of greatness, where the national character is obscured or obliterated by travel or instruction, by philosophy or vanity; nor is public happiness to be estimated by the assemblies of the gay, or the banquets of the rich. The great mass of nations is neither rich nor gay: they whose aggregate constitutes the people, are found in the streets, and the villages, in the shops and farms; and from them collectively considered, must the measure of general prosperity be taken. As they approach to delicacy a nation is refined, as their conveniencies are multiplied, a nation, at least a commercial nation, must be denominated wealthy.

A Journey to the Western Islands

Travelling Light

We were now to bid farewel to the luxury of travelling, and to enter a country upon which perhaps no wheel has ever rolled. We could indeed have used our post-chaise one day longer, along the military road to Fort *Augustus*, but we could have hired no horses beyond Inverness, and we were not so sparing of ourselves, as to lead them, merely that we might have one day longer the indulgence of a carriage.

At Inverness therefore we procured three horses for ourselves and a servant, and one more for our baggage, which was no very heavy load. We found in the course of our journey the convenience of having disencumbered ourselves, by laying aside whatever we could spare; for it is not to be imagined without experience, how in climbing crags, and treading bogs, and winding through narrow and obstructed passages, a little bulk will hinder, and a little weight will burthen; or how often a man that has pleased himself at home with his own resolution, will, in the hour of darkness and fatigue, be content to leave behind him every thing but himself.

A Journey to the Western Islands

The Falls of Foyers

Towards evening we crossed, by a bridge, the river which makes the celebrated fall of Fiers. The country at the bridge strikes the imagination with all the gloom and grandeur of Siberian solitude. The way makes a flexure, and the mountains, covered with trees, rise at once on the left hand and in the front. We desired our guides to shew us the fall, and dismounting, clambered over very rugged crags, till I began to wish that our curiosity might have been gratified with less trouble and danger. We came at last to a place where we could overlook the river, and saw a channel torn, as it seems, through black piles of stone, by which the stream is obstructed and broken, till it comes to a very steep descent, of such dreadful depth, that we were naturally inclined to turn aside our eyes.

But we visited the place at an unseasonable time, and found it divested of its dignity and terror. Nature never gives every thing at once. A long continuance of dry weather, which made the rest of the way easy and delightful, deprived us of the pleasure expected from the fall of Fiers. The river having now no water but what the springs supply, showed us only a swift current, clear and shallow, fretting over the asperities of the rocky bottom, and we were left to exercise our thoughts, by endeavouring to conceive the effect of a thousand streams poured from the mountains into one channel, struggling for expansion in a narrow passage, exasperated by rocks rising in their way, and at last discharging all their violence of waters by a sudden fall through the horrid chasm.

A Journey to the Western Islands

Contemplation

As the day advanced towards noon, we entered a narrow valley not very flowery, but sufficiently verdant. Our guides told us, that the horses could not travel all day without rest or meat, and intreated us to stop here, because no grass would be found in any other place. The request was reasonable and the argument cogent. We therefore willingly dismounted and diverted ourselves as the place gave us opportunity.

I sat down on a bank, such as a writer of Romance might have delighted to feign. I had indeed no trees to whisper over my head, but a clear rivulet streamed at my feet. The day was calm, the air soft, and all was rudeness, silence, and solitude. Before me, and on either side, were high hills, which by hindering the eye from ranging, forced the mind to find entertainment for itself. Whether I spent the hour well I know not; for here I first conceived the thought of this narration.

We were in this place at ease and by choice, and had no evils to suffer or to fear; yet the imaginations excited by the view of an unknown and untravelled wilderness are not such as arise in the artificial solitude of parks and gardens, a flattering notion of self-sufficiency, a placid indulgence of voluntary delusions, a secure expansion of the fancy, or a cool concentration of the mental powers. The phantoms which haunt a desert are want, and misery, and danger; the evils of dereliction rush upon the thoughts; man is made unwillingly acquainted with his own weakness, and meditation shows him only how little he can sustain, and how little he can perform. There were no traces of inhabitants, except perhaps a rude pile of clods called a summer hut, in which a herdsman had rested in the favourable seasons. Whoever had been in the place where I then sat, unprovided with provisions and ignorant of the country, might, at least before the roads were made, have wandered among the rocks, till he had perished with hardship, before he could have found either food or shelter. Yet what are these hillocks to the ridges of Taurus, or these spots of wildness to the desarts of America?

A Journey to the Western Islands

Glenelg

We left *Auknasheals* and the *Macraes* in the afternoon, and in the evening came to *Ratiken*, a high hill on which a road is cut, but so steep and narrow, that it is very difficult. There is now a design of making another way round the bottom. Upon one of the precipices, my horse, weary with the steepness of the rise, staggered a little, and I called in haste to the Highlander to hold him. This was the only moment of my journey, in which I thought myself endangered.

Having surmounted the hill at last, we were told that at *Glenelg*, on the sea-side, we should come to a house of lime and slate and glass. This image of magnificence raised our expectation. At last we came to our inn weary and peevish, and began to inquire for meat and beds.

Of the provisions the negative catalogue was very copious. Here was no meat, no milk, no bread, no eggs, no wine. We did not express much satisfaction. Here however we were to stay. Whisky we might have, and I believe at last they caught a fowl and killed it. We had some bread, and with that we prepared ourselves to be contented, when we had a very eminent proof of Highland hospitality. Along some miles of the way, in the evening, a gentleman's servant had kept us company on foot with very little notice on our part. He left us near *Glenelg*, and we thought on him no more till he came to us again, in about two hours, with a present from his master of rum and sugar. The man had mentioned his company, and the gentleman, whose name, I think, is *Gordon*, well knowing the penury of the place, had this attention to two men, whose names perhaps he had not heard, by whom his kindness was not likely to be ever repaid, and who could be recommended to him only by their necessities.

We were now to examine our lodging. Out of one of the beds, on which we were to repose, started up, at our entrance, a man black as a Cyclops from the forge. Other circumstances of no elegant recital concurred to disgust us. We had been frighted by a lady at Edinburgh, with discouraging representations of Highland lodgings. Sleep, however, was necessary. Our Highlanders had at last found some hay, with which the inn could not supply them. I directed them to bring a bundle into the room, and slept upon it in my riding coat. Mr. Boswell being more delicate, laid himself sheets with hay over and under him, and lay in linen like a gentleman.

A Journey to the Western Islands

Island Hospitality

It is not only in *Raasay* that the chapel is unroofed and useless; through the few islands which we visited, we neither saw nor heard of any house of prayer, except in *Sky*, that was not in ruins. The malignant influence of *Calvinism* has blasted ceremony and decency together; and if the remembrance of papal superstition is obliterated, the monuments of papal piety are likewise effaced.

It has been, for many years, popular to talk of the lazy devotion of the Romish clergy; over the sleepy laziness of men that erected churches, we may indulge our superiority with a new triumph, by comparing it with the fervid activity of those who suffer them to fall.

Of the destruction of churches, the decay of religion must in time be the consequence; for while the publick acts of the ministry are now performed in houses, a very small number can be present; and as the greater part of the Islanders make no use of books, all must necessarily live in total ignorance who want the opportunity of vocal instruction.

From these remains of ancient sanctity, which are every where to be found, it has been conjectured, that, for the last two centuries, the inhabitants of the Islands have decreased in number. This argument, which supposes that the churches have been suffered to fall, only because they were no longer necessary, would have some force, if the houses of worship still remaining were sufficient for the people. But since they have now no churches at all, these venerable fragments do not prove the people of former times to have been more numerous, but to have been more devout. If the inhabitants were doubled with their present principles, it appears not that any provision for publick worship would be made. Where the religion of a country enforces consecrated buildings, the number of those buildings may be supposed to afford some indication, however uncertain, of the populousness of the place; but where by a change of manners a nation is contented to live without them, their decay implies no diminution of inhabitants.

Some of these dilapidations are said to be found in islands now uninhabited; but I doubt whether we can thence infer that they were ever peopled. The religion of the middle age, is well known to have placed too much hope in lonely austerities. Voluntary solitude was the great act of propitiation, by which crimes were effaced, and conscience was appeased; it is therefore not unlikely, that oratories were often built in places where retirement was sure to have no disturbance.

Raasay has little that can detain a traveller, except the Laird and his family; but their power wants no auxiliaries. Such a seat of hospitality, amidst the winds and waters, fills the imagination with a delightful contrariety of images. Without is the rough ocean and the rocky land, the beating billows and the howling storm: within is plenty and elegance, beauty and gaiety, the song and the dance. In *Raasay*, if I could have found an Ulysses, I had fancied a *Phæacia*.

A Journey to the Western Islands

National Honour

To disarm part of the Highlands, could give no reasonable occasion of complaint. Every government must be allowed the power of taking away the weapon that is lifted against it. But the loyal clans murmured, with some appearance of justice, that after having defended the King, they were forbidden for the future to defend themselves; and that the sword should be forfeited, which had been legally employed. Their case is undoubtedly hard, but in political regulations, good cannot be complete, it can only be predominant.

Whether by disarming a people thus broken into several tribes, and thus remote from the seat of power, more good than evil has been produced, may deserve inquiry. The supreme power in every community has the

right of debarring every individual, and every subordinate society from self-defence, only because the supreme
power is able to defend them; and therefore where the
governor cannot act, he must trust the subject to act for
himself. These Islands might be wasted with fire and
sword before their sovereign would know their distress.
A gang of robbers, such as has been lately found con-
federating themselves in the Highlands, might lay a
wide region under contribution. The crew of a petty
privateer might land on the largest and most wealthy
of the Islands, and riot without control in cruelty and
waste. It was observed by one of the Chiefs of Sky, that
fifty armed men might, without resistance, ravage the
country. Laws that place the subjects in such a state,
contravene the first principles of the compact of authority:
they exact obedience, and yield no protection.

It affords a generous and manly pleasure to conceive
a little nation gathering its fruits and tending its herds
with fearless confidence, though it lies open on every side
to invasion, where, in contempt of walls and trenches,
every man sleeps securely with his sword beside him;
where all on the first approach of hostility come together
at the call to battle, as at a summons to a festal show; and
committing their cattle to the care of those whom age or
nature has disabled, engage the enemy with that competition for hazard and for glory, which operate in men that
fight under the eye of those, whose dislike or kindness
they have always considered as the greatest evil or the
greatest good.

This was, in the beginning of the present century, the
state of the Highlands. Every man was a soldier, who
partook of national confidence, and interested himself
in national honour. To lose this spirit, is to lose what no
small advantage will compensate.

A Journey to the Western Islands

Emigration

Some method to stop this epidemick desire of wandering, which spreads its contagion from valley to valley,

deserves to be sought with great diligence. In more fruitful countries, the removal of one only makes room for the succession of another: but in the *Hebrides*, the loss of an inhabitant leaves a lasting vacuity; for nobody born in any other parts of the world will choose this country for his residence, and an Island once depopulated will remain a desert, as long as the present facility of travel gives every one, who is discontented and unsettled, the choice of his abode.

Let it be inquired, whether the first intention of those who are fluttering on the wing, and collecting a flock that they may take their flight, be to attain good, or to avoid evil. If they are dissatisfied with that part of the globe, which their birth has allotted them, and resolve not to live without the pleasures of happier climates; if they long for bright suns, and calm skies, and flowery fields, and fragrant gardens, I know not by what eloquence they can be persuaded, or by what offers they can be hired to stay.

But if they are driven from their native country by positive evils, and disgusted by ill-treatment, real or imaginary, it were fit to remove their grievances, and quiet their resentment; since, if they have been hitherto undutiful subjects, they will not much mend their principles by American conversation.

To allure them into the army, it was thought proper to indulge them in the continuance of their national dress. If this concession could have any effect, it might easily be made. That dissimilitude of appearance, which was supposed to keep them distinct from the rest of the nation, might disincline them from coalescing with the *Pensylvanians*, or people of *Connecticut*. If the restitution of their arms will reconcile them to their country, let them have again those weapons, which will not be more mischievous at home than in the Colonies. That they may not fly from the increase of rent, I know not whether the general good does not require that the landlords be, for a time, restrained in their demands, and kept quiet by pensions proportionate to their loss.

To hinder insurrection, by driving away the people,

and to govern peaceably, by having no subjects, is an expedient that argues no great profundity of politicks. To soften the obdurate, to convince the mistaken, to mollify the resentful, are worthy of a statesman; but it affords a legislator little self-applause to consider, that where there was formerly an insurrection, there is now a wilderness.

.   .   .   .

The great business of insular policy is now to keep the people in their own country. As the world has been let in upon them, they have heard of happier climates, and less arbitrary government; and if they are disgusted, have emissaries among them ready to offer them land and houses, as a reward for deserting their chief and clan. Many have departed both from the main of *Scotland*, and from the Islands; and all that go may be considered as subjects lost to the *British* crown; for a nation scattered in the boundless regions of *America* resembles rays diverging from a focus. All the rays remain, but the heat is gone. Their power consisted in their concentration: when they are dispersed, they have no effect.

It may be thought that they are happier by the change; but they are not happy as a nation, for they are a nation no longer. As they contribute not to the prosperity of any community, they must want that security, that dignity, that happiness, whatever it be, which a prosperous community throws back upon individuals.

The inhabitants of *Col* have not yet learned to be weary of their heath and rocks, but attend their agriculture and their dairies, without listening to American seducements.

There are some however who think that this emigration has raised terrour disproportionate to its real evil; and that it is only a new mode of doing what was always done. The Highlands, they say, never maintained their natural inhabitants; but the people, when they found themselves too numerous, instead of extending cultivation, provided for themselves by a more compendious method, and sought better fortune in other countries. They did not indeed go away in collective bodies; but

withdrew invisibly, a few at a time; but the whole
number of fugitives was not less, and the difference
between other times and this, is only the same as between
evaporation and effusion.

This is plausible, but I am afraid it is not true. Those
who went before, if they were not sensibly missed, as the
argument supposes, must have gone either in less number,
or in a manner less detrimental, than at present; because
formerly there was no complaint. Those who then left the
country were generally the idle dependants on overburdened families, or men who had no property; and
therefore carried away only themselves. In the present
eagerness of emigration, families, and almost communities, go away together. Those who were considered as
prosperous and wealthy sell their stock and carry away
the money. Once none went away but the useless and
poor; in some parts there is now reason to fear, that none
will stay but those who are too poor to remove themselves,
and too useless to be removed at the cost of others.

A Journey to the Western Islands

The Second Sight

I do not find it to be true, as it is reported, that to the
Second Sight nothing is presented but phantoms of evil.
Good seems to have the same proportion in those visionary
scenes, as it obtains in real life: almost all remarkable
events have evil for their basis; and are either miseries
incurred, or miseries escaped. Our sense is so much
stronger of what we suffer, than of what we enjoy, that
the ideas of pain predominate in almost every mind.
What is recollection but a revival of vexations, or history
but a record of wars, treasons, and calamities? Death,
which is considered as the greatest evil, happens to all.
The greatest good, be it what it will, is the lot but of
a part.

That they should often see death is to be expected;
because death is an event frequent and important. But
they see likewise more pleasing incidents. A gentleman
told me, that when he had once gone far from his own

Island, one of his labouring servants predicted his return, and described the livery of his attendant, which he
had never worn at home; and which had been, without
any previous design, occasionally given him.

Our desire of information was keen, and our inquiry
frequent. Mr. Boswell's frankness and gaiety made every
body communicative; and we heard many tales of these
airy shows, with more or less evidence and distinctness.

It is the common talk of the Lowland *Scots*, that the
notion of the *Second Sight* is wearing away with other
superstitions; and that its reality is no longer supposed,
but by the grossest people. How far its prevalence ever
extended, or what ground it has lost, I know not. The
Islanders of all degrees, whether of rank or understanding,
universally admit it, except the Ministers, who universally deny it, and are suspected to deny it, in consequence
of a system, against conviction. One of them honestly told
me, that he came to *Sky* with a resolution not to believe it.

Strong reasons for incredulity will readily occur. This
faculty of seeing things out of sight is local, and commonly
useless. It is a breach of the common order of things, without any visible reason or perceptible benefit. It is ascribed
only to a people very little enlightened; and among them,
for the most part, to the mean and the ignorant.

To the confidence of these objections it may be replied,
that by presuming to determine what is fit, and what is
beneficial, they presuppose more knowledge of the universal system than man has attained; and therefore
depend upon principles too complicated and extensive
for our comprehension; and that there can be no security
in the consequence, when the premises are not understood, that the *Second Sight* is only wonderful because it is
rare, for, considered in itself, it involves no more difficulty
than dreams, or perhaps than the regular exercise of the
cogitative faculty; that a general opinion of communicative impulses, or visionary representations, has prevailed
in all ages and all nations; that particular instances have
been given, with such evidence, as neither *Bacon* nor
Bayle[1] has been able to resist; that sudden impressions,

[1 Johnson probably wrote *Boyle*.]

which the event has verified, have been felt by more
than own or publish them; that the *Second Sight* of the
Hebrides implies only the local frequency of a power,
which is nowhere totally unknown; and that where we
are unable to decide by antecedent reason, we must be
content to yield to the force of testimony.

.   .   .   .

To collect sufficient testimonies for the satisfaction of the
publick, or of ourselves, would have required more time
than we could bestow. There is, against it, the seeming
analogy of things confusedly seen, and little understood;
and for it, the indistinct cry of national persuasion, which
may be perhaps resolved at last into prejudice and tradition. I never could advance my curiosity to conviction;
but came away at last only willing to believe.

A Journey to the Western Islands

Ossian

I suppose my opinion of the poems of Ossian is already
discovered. I believe they never existed in any other form
than that which we have seen. The editor, or author,
never could shew the original; nor can it be shewn by any
other; to revenge reasonable incredulity, by refusing
evidence, is a degree of insolence, with which the world
is not yet acquainted; and stubborn audacity is the last
refuge of guilt. It would be easy to shew it if he had it;
but whence could it be had? It is too long to be remembered, and the language formerly had nothing written.
He has doubtless inserted names that circulate in popular
stories, and may have translated some wandering ballads,
if any can be found; and the names, and some of the
images being recollected, make an inaccurate auditor
imagine, by the help of Caledonian bigotry, that he has
formerly heard the whole.

I asked a very learned Minister in Sky, who had used
all arts to make me believe the genuineness of the book,
whether at last he believed it himself? but he would not
answer. He wished me to be deceived, for the honour of

his country; but would not directly and formally deceive me. Yet has this man's testimony been publickly produced, as of one that held Fingal to be the work of Ossian.

It is said, that some men of integrity profess to have heard parts of it, but they all heard them when they were boys; and it was never said that any of them could recite six lines. They remember names, and perhaps some proverbial sentiments; and, having no distinct ideas, coin a resemblance without an original. The persuasion of the Scots, however, is far from universal; and in a question so capable of proof, why should doubt be suffered to continue? The editor has been heard to say, that part of the poem was received by him, in the Saxon character. He has then found, by some peculiar fortune, an unwritten language, written in a character which the natives probably never beheld.

I have yet supposed no imposture but in the publisher, yet I am far from certainty, that some translations have not been lately made, that may now be obtruded as parts of the original work. Credulity on one part is a strong temptation to deceit on the other, especially to deceit of which no personal injury is the consequence, and which flatters the author with his own ingenuity. The Scots have something to plead for their easy reception of an improbable fiction: they are seduced by their fondness for their supposed ancestors. A Scotchman must be a very sturdy moralist, who does not love *Scotland* better than truth: he will always love it better than inquiry; and if falsehood flatters his vanity, will not be very diligent to detect it. Neither ought the *English* to be much influenced by *Scotch* authority; for of the past and present state of the whole *Earse* nation, the Lowlanders are at least as ignorant as ourselves. To be ignorant is painful; but it is dangerous to quiet our uneasiness by the delusive opiate of hasty persuasion.

But this is the age in which those who could not read, have been supposed to write; in which the giants of antiquated romance have been exhibited as realities. If we know little of the ancient Highlanders, let us not fill the vacuity with *Ossian*. If we have not searched the

Magellanick regions, let us however forbear to people them with *Patagons*.

A Journey to the Western Islands

Planting

It is natural, in traversing this gloom of desolation, to inquire, whether something may not be done to give nature a more cheerful face, and whether those hills and moors that afford heath cannot with a little care and labour bear something better? The first thought that occurs is to cover them with trees, for that in many of these naked regions trees will grow, is evident, because stumps and roots are yet remaining; and the speculatist hastily proceeds to censure that negligence and laziness that has omitted for so long a time so easy an improvement.

To drop seeds into the ground, and attend their growth, requires little labour and no skill. He who remembers that all the woods, by which the wants of man have been supplied from the Deluge till now, were self-sown, will not easily be persuaded to think all the art and preparation necessary, which the Georgick writers prescribe to planters. Trees certainly have covered the earth with very little culture. They wave their tops among the rocks of *Norway*, and might thrive as well in the Highlands and *Hebrides*.

But there is a frightful interval between the seed and timber. He that calculates the growth of trees, has the unwelcome remembrance of the shortness of life driven hard upon him. He knows that he is doing what will never benefit himself; and when he rejoices to see the stem rise, is disposed to repine that another shall cut it down.

Plantation is naturally the employment of a mind unburdened with care, and vacant to futurity, saturated with present good, and at leisure to derive gratification from the prospect of posterity. He that pines with hunger, is in little care how others shall be fed. The poor man is seldom studious to make his grandson rich. It may be soon discovered, why in a place, which hardly supplies the cravings of necessity, there has been little attention to the delights of fancy, and why distant convenience is unregarded, where the thoughts are turned with incessant solicitude upon every possibility of immediate advantage.

Neither is it quite so easy to raise large woods, as may be conceived. Trees intended to produce timber must be sown where they are to grow; and ground sown with trees must be kept useless for a long time, inclosed at an expence from which many will be discouraged by the remoteness of the profit, and watched with that attention, which, in places where it is most needed, will neither be given nor bought. That it cannot be plowed is evident; and if cattle be suffered to graze upon it, they will devour the plants as fast as they rise. Even in coarser countries, where herds and flocks are not fed, not only the deer and the wild goats will browse upon them, but the hare and rabbit will nibble them. It is therefore reasonable to believe, what I do not remember any naturalist to have remarked, that there was a time when the world was very thinly inhabited by beasts, as well as men, and that the woods had leisure to rise high before animals had bred numbers sufficient to intercept them.

A Journey to the Western Islands

Iona

The evening was now approaching, and we were yet at a considerable distance from the end of our expedition. We could therefore stop no more to make remarks in the way, but set forward with some degree of eagerness. The day soon failed us, and the moon presented a very solemn and pleasing scene. The sky was clear, so that the eye commanded a wide circle: the sea was neither still nor turbulent: the wind neither silent nor loud. We were never far from one coast or another, on which, if the weather had become violent, we could have found shelter, and therefore contemplated at ease the region through which we glided in the tranquillity of the night, and saw now a rock and now an island grow gradually conspicuous and gradually obscure. I committed the fault which I have just been censuring, in neglecting, as we passed, to note the series of this placid navigation.

We were very near an Island, called *Nun's Island*, perhaps from an ancient convent. Here is said to have been dug the stone that was used in the buildings of *Icolmkill*. Whether it is now inhabited we could not stay to inquire.

At last we came to *Icolmkill*, but found no convenience for landing. Our boat could not be forced very near the dry ground, and our Highlanders carried us over the water.

We were now treading that illustrious Island, which was once the luminary of the *Caledonian* regions, whence savage clans and roving barbarians derived the benefits of knowledge, and the blessings of religion. To abstract the mind from all local emotion would be impossible, if it were endeavoured, and would be foolish, if it were possible. Whatever withdraws us from the power of our senses; whatever makes the past, the distant, or the future predominate over the present, advances us in the dignity of thinking beings. Far from me and from my friends, be such frigid philosophy as may conduct us indifferent and unmoved over any ground which has been dignified by wisdom, bravery, or virtue. That man is little to be envied, whose patriotism would not gain force upon the plain of *Marathon*, or whose piety would not grow warmer among the ruins of *Iona*!

A Journey to the Western Islands

Nature's Music

On the next day we began our journey southwards. The weather was tempestuous. For half the day the ground was rough, and our horses were still small. Had they required much restraint, we might have been reduced to difficulties; for I think we had amongst us but one bridle. We fed the poor animals liberally, and they performed their journey well. In the latter part of the day, we came to a firm and smooth road, made by the soldiers, on which we travelled with great security, busied with

contemplating the scene about us. The night came on
while we had yet a great part of the way to go, though
not so dark, but that we could discern the cataracts which
poured down the hills, on one side, and fell into one
general channel that ran with great violence on the other.
The wind was loud, the rain was heavy, and the whistling
of the blast, the fall of the shower, the rush of the
cataracts, and the roar of the torrent, made a nobler
chorus of the rough musick of nature than it had ever
been my chance to hear before. The streams, which ran
cross the way from the hills to the main current, were so
frequent, that after a while I began to count them; and,
in ten miles, reckoned fifty-five, probably missing some,
and having let some pass before they forced themselves
upon my notice. At last we came to *Inverary*, where we
found an inn, not only commodious, but magnificent.

A Journey to the Western Islands

Scottish Learning

To describe a city so much frequented as *Glasgow*, is
unnecessary. The prosperity of its commerce appears by
the greatness of many private houses, and a general appearance of wealth. It is the only episcopal city whose
cathedral was left standing in the rage of Reformation.
It is now divided into many separate places of worship,
which, taken all together, compose a great pile, that had
been some centuries in building, but was never finished;
for the change of religion intercepted its progress, before
the cross isle was added, which seems essential to a
Gothick cathedral.

The college has not had a sufficient share of the increasing magnificence of the place. The session was begun;
for it commences on the tenth of *October*, and continues to
the tenth of *June*, but the students appeared not numerous,
being, I suppose, not yet returned from their several
homes. The division of the academical year into one
session, and one recess, seems to me better accommodated
to the present state of life, than that variegation of time
by terms and vacations derived from distant centuries,

in which it was probably convenient, and still continued in the *English* universities. So many solid months as the *Scotch* scheme of education joins together, allow and encourage a plan for each part of the year; but with us, he that has settled himself to study in the college is soon tempted into the country, and he that has adjusted his life in the country, is summoned back to his college.

Yet when I have allowed to the universities of *Scotland* a more rational distribution of time, I have given them, so far as my inquiries have informed me, all that they can claim. The students, for the most part, go thither boys, and depart before they are men; they carry with them little fundamental knowledge, and therefore the superstructure cannot be lofty. The grammar schools are not generally well supplied; for the character of a schoolmaster being there less honourable than in *England*, is seldom accepted by men who are capable to adorn it, and where the school has been deficient, the college can effect little.

Men bred in the universities of *Scotland* cannot be expected to be often decorated with the splendours of ornamental erudition, but they obtain a mediocrity of knowledge, between learning and ignorance, not inadequate to the purposes of common life, which is, I believe, very widely diffused among them, and which countenanced in general by a national combination so invidious, that their friends cannot defend it, and actuated in particulars by a spirit of enterprise, so vigorous, that their enemies are constrained to praise it, enables them to find, or to make their way to employment, riches, and distinction.

A Journey to the Western Islands

1774
Epitaph on Goldsmith

Τὸν τάφον εἰσοράας τὸν Ὀλιβαρίοιο, κονίην
Ἄφροσι μὴ σεμνήν, Ξεῖνε, πόδεσσι πάτει·
Οἷσι μέμηλε φύσις, μέτρων χάρις, ἔργα παλαιῶν,
Κλαίετε ποιητήν, ἱστορικόν, φυσικόν.

To William Strahan on Literary Property

Sir

I will tell you in a few words, what is, in my opinion, the most desirable state of Copyright or literary Property.

The Authour has a natural and peculiar right to the profits of his own work.

But as every Man who claims the protection of Society must purchase it by resigning some part of his natural right, the authour must recede from so much of his claim, as shall be deemed injurious or inconvenient to Society.

It is inconvenient to Society that an useful book should become perpetual and exclusive property.

The Judgement of the Lords was therefore legally and politically right.

But the Authours enjoyment of his natural right might without any inconvenience be protracted beyond the term settled by the statute. And it is, I think, to be desired

1 That an Authour should retain during his life the sole right of printing and selling his work.

This is agreeable to moral right, and not inconvenient to the publick, for who will be so diligent as the authour to improve the book, or who can know so well how to improve it?

2 That the authour be allowed, as by the present act, to alienate his right only for fourteen years.

A shorter time would not procure a sufficient price, and a longer would cut off all hope of future profit, and consequently all solicitude for correction or addition.

3 That when after fourteen years the copy shall revert to the authour, he be allowed to alienate it again only for seven years at a time.

After fourteen years the value of the work will be known, and it will be no longer bought at hazard. Seven years of possession will therefore have an assignable price. It is proper that the authour be always incited to polish and improve his work, by that prospect of accruing interest which those shorter periods of alienation will afford him.

4 That after the Authours death his work should con-

tinue an exclusive property capable of bequest and inheritance, and of conveyance by gift or sale for thirty
years.

By these regulations a book may continue the property
of the authour or of those who claim from him about
fifty years, a term sufficient to reward the writer without
any loss to the publick. In fifty years far the greater
number of books are forgotten and annihilated, and it is
for the advantage of learning that those which fifty years
have not destroyed should become bona communia, to be
used by every scholar as he shall think best.

In fifty years almost every book begins to require notes
either to explain forgotten allusions and obsolete words;
or to subjoin those discoveries which have been made by
the gradual advancement of knowledge; or to correct
those mistakes which time may have discovered.

Such Notes cannot be written to any useful purpose
without the text, and the text will frequently be refused
while it is any man's property.

I am Sir Your humble servant,
Sam: Johnson

March 7. 1774

To Warren Hastings

Sir

Though I have had but little personal knowledge of
you, I have had enough to make me wish for more and
though it be now a long time since I was honoured by
your visit, I had too much pleasure from it to forget it. By
those whom we delight to remember we are unwilling to
be forgotten, and therefore I cannot omit this opportunity of reviving myself in your memory, by a letter
which you will receive from the hands of my friend Mr
Chambers, a man whose purity of manners and vigour of
mind are sufficient to make every thing welcome that he
brings.

That this is my only reason for writing will be too
apparent by the uselessness of my letter to any other
purpose. I have no questions to ask, not that I want
curiosity after either the ancient or present state of regions

in which have been seen all the power and splendour of wide-extended empire; and which as by some grant of natural superiority supply the rest of the world with almost all that pride desires and luxury enjoys; but my knowledge of them is too scanty to furnish me with proper topicks of enquiry. I can only wish for information, and hope that a Mind comprehensive like yours will find leisure amidst the cares of your important station to enquire into many subjects of which the European world either thinks not at all, or thinks with deficient intelligence and uncertain conjecture. I shall hope that he who once intended to encrease the learning of his country by the introduction of the Persian language, will examine nicely the Traditions and Histories of the East, that he will survey the remains of its ancient Edifices, and trace the vestiges of its ruined cities; and that at his return we shall know the arts and opinions of a Race of Men from whom very little has been hitherto derived.

You, Sir, have no need of being told by me how much may be added by your attention and patronage to experimental knowledge and natural history. There are arts of manufacture practised in the countries in which you preside which are yet very imperfectly known here either to artificers or philosophers. Of the natural productions animate and inanimate we yet have so little intelligence that our books are filled, I fear, with conjectures about things which an Indian Peasant knows by his senses.

Many of those things my first Wish is to see; my second to know by such accounts as a Man like You will be able to give.

As I have not skill to ask proper questions, I have likewise no such access to great men, as can enable me to send you any political information. Of the agitations of an unsettled government, and the struggles of a feeble ministry, care is doubtless taken, to give you more exact accounts than I can obtain. If you are inclined to interest yourself much in publick transactions, it is no misfortune to you, to be so distant from them.

That literature is not totally forsaking us, and that your

favourite language is not neglected will appear from the book[1] which I should have pleased myself more with sending if I could have procured it bound: but time was wanting. I beg however, Sir, that you will accept it, from a man very desirous of your regard, and that if you think me able to gratify you by any thing more important, you will employ me.

I am now going to take leave, perhaps a very long leave of my dear Mr Chambers. That he is going to live where you govern may justly alleviate the regret of parting, and the hope of seeing both him and You again, which I am not willing to mingle with doubt, must at present content as it can,

                    Sir, Your most humble servant,
March 30, 1774.   Sam: Johnson.

1775

To James Macpherson[2]

Mr James Macpherson—I received your foolish and impudent note. Whatever insult is offered me I will do my best to repel, and what I cannot do for myself the law will do for me. I will not desist from detecting what I think a cheat, from any fear of the menaces of a Ruffian.

You want me to retract. What shall I retract? I thought your book an imposture from the beginning, I think it upon yet surer reasons an imposture still. For this opinion I give the publick my reasons which I here dare you to refute.

But however I may despise you, I reverence truth and if you can prove the genuineness of the work I will confess it. Your rage I defy, your abilities since your Homer are not so formidable, and what I have heard of your morals disposes me to pay regard not to what you shall say, but to what you can prove.

You may print this if you will.
Jan. 20. 1775   Sam: Johnson

[1 Jones's *Persian Grammar*.]
[2 The 'translator' of Ossian.]

To the Vice-Chancellor of Oxford

Viro Reverendo Thomae Fothergill, S.T.P. Universitatis
Oxoniensis Vice-Cancellario.

S.P.D.

Sam. Johnson.

Multis non est opus, ut testimonium quo, te praeside,
Oxonienses nomen meum posteris commendârunt, quali
animo acceperim compertum faciam. Nemo sibi placens
non laetatur; nemo sibi non placet, qui vobis, literarum
arbitris, placere potuit. Hoc tamen habet incommodi
tantum beneficium, quod mihi nunquam posthàc sine
vestrae famae detrimento vel labi liceat vel cessare; sem-
perque sit timendum, ne quod mihi tam eximiae laudi
est, vobis aliquando fiat opprobrio. Vale.

7. Id. Apr. 1775.

To Mrs. Thrale

Dear Madam

I hope it is very true that Ralph mends, and wish you
were gone to see that you might come back again.

Queeney revenges her long tasks upon Mr Baretti's
hen, who must sit on Duck eggs a week longer than on her
own. I hope she takes great care of my Hen, and the
Guinea hen and her pretty little brood.

I was afraid Mawbey would succeed, and have little
hope from the scrutiny. Did you ever know a scrutiny
change the account?

Miss Adey does not run after me, but I do not want
her, here are other Ladies.

Invenies alium, si te hic fastidit Alexis.

Miss Turton grows old; and Miss Vyse has been ill,
but I believe, she came to me as soon as she got out. And
I can always go to Stowhill. So never grieve about me.
Only flatulencies are come again.

Do you read Boswell's Journals? He moralised, and
found my faults, and laid them up to reproach me. Boswel's narrative is very natural, and therefore very enter-

taining, he never made any scruple of showing it to me.
He is a very fine fellow. He has established Rasa's Chief-
tainship in the Edinburgh papers, and quieted all commotion in the Hebridean world. These little things are
great to little Man.

Small letters will undoubtedly gain room for more
words, but words are useless if they cannot be read. The
lines need not all be kept distinct, and some words I shall
wish to leave out, though very few. It must be revised
before it is engraved.[1] I always told you that Mr Thrale
was a man take him for all in all, you ne'er will look upon
his like, but you never mind him nor me, till time forces
conviction into your steely bosom. You will perhaps find
all right about the house and the windows.

Pray always suppose that I send my respects to Master,
and Mr. Baretti, and Queeney, and Harry, and Susey,
and Sophy.

Poor Lucy mends very slowly, but she is very good
humoured, while I do just as she would have me.

Lady Smith has got a new postchaise, which is not
nothing to talk on at Lichfield. Little things here serve
for conversation. Mrs Aston's Parrot pecked my leg, and
I heard of it some time after at Mrs Cobb's.

       —We deal in nicer things
    Than routing armies, and dethroning kings.

a week ago Mrs Cobb gave me sweetmeats to breakfast,
and I heard of it last night at Stowhill.

If you are for small talk.

       —Come on, and do the best you can
    I fear not you, nor yet a better man.

I could tell you about Lucy's two cats, and Brill her
brother's old dog, who is gone deaf, but the day would
fail me. Suadentque cadentia sidera somnum. So said
Aeneas but I have not yet had my diner. I have begun
early for what would become of the nation if a Letter of
this importance should miss the post? Pray write to

Dear Madam Your most obedient and most humble
Servant

Lichfield. June 19. 1775   Sam: Johnson

    [1 Johnson's inscription for Mrs. Thrale's mother's tomb.]

To Mrs. Thrale

Dear Madam

I wonder how it could happen. I forgot that the post went out yester night, and so omitted to write. I therefore send this by the bypost, and hope it will come that I may not lose my regular letter.

This was to have been my last letter from this place but Lucy says I must not go this week. Fits of tenderness with Mrs Lucy are not common, but she seems now to have a little paroxysm, and I was not willing to counteract it. When I am to go I shall take care to inform you.

The Lady at Stowhill says, how comes Lucy to be such a sovereign; all the town besides could not have kept you.

America now fills every mouth, and some heads; and a little of it shall come into my letter. I do not much like the news. Our troops have indeed the superiority, five and twenty hundred have driven five thousand from their intrenchment but the Americans fought skilfully; had coolness enough in the battle to carry off their men; and seem to have retreated orderly for they were not persued. They want nothing but confidence in their leaders and familiarity with danger. Our business is to persue their main army, and disperse it by a decisive battle and then waste the country till they sue for peace. If we make war by parties and detachments, dislodge them from one place, and exclude them from another, we shall by a local, gradual, and ineffectual war, teach them our own knowledge, harden their obstinacy, and strengthen their confidence, and at last come to fight on equal terms of skill and bravery, without equal numbers.

Mrs Williams wrote me word that you had honoured her with a visit, and *behaved lovely*.

Mr Thrale left off digging his pool, I suppose for want of water. The first thing to be done is by digging in three or four places to try how near the springs will rise to the surface; for though we cannot hope to be always full, we must be sure never to be dry.

Poor Sir Lynch! I am sorry for him. It is sad to give a family of children no pleasure but by dying. It was said

of Otho. Hoc tantum fecit nobile quod periit. It may be
changed to Sir Lynch, hoc tantum fecit utile.

If I could do Mr Carter any good at Oxford, I could
easily stop there, for through it, if I go by Birmingham I
am likely to pass; but the place is now a sullen solitude.
Whatever can be done, I am ready to do; but our operations must for the present be at London.

I am, Madam, Your most humble servant,
August 1. 1775 Sam: Johnson

Good Friday

Apr. 14, GOOD FRIDAY.
Boswel came in before I was up. We breakfasted, I only
drank tea without milk or bread. We went to Church,
saw Dr. Wetherel in the pew, and by his desire took him
home with us. He did not go very soon, and Boswel staid.
Dilly and Millar called. Boswel and I went to Church,
but came very late. We then took tea, by Boswel's desire,
and I eat one bun, I think, that I might not seem to fast
ostentatiously. Boswel sat with me till night; we had
some serious talk. When he went I gave Francis some
directions for preparation to communicate. Thus has
passed hitherto this awful day. 10°30′ p.m.

When I look back upon resolutions of improvement and
amendments, which have year after year been made and
broken, either by negligence, forgetfulness, vicious idleness, casual interruption, or morbid infirmity, when I
find that so much of my life has stolen unprofitably away,
and that I can descry by retrospection scarcely a few
single days properly and vigorously employed, why do I
yet try to resolve again? I try because Reformation is
necessary and despair is criminal. I try in humble hope of
the help of God.

As my life has from my earliest years been wasted in
a morning bed my purpose is from Easter day to rise
early, not later than eight. 11°15′ p.m. D.j.

Prayers and Meditations, 1785

Principles of Taxation

Of every empire all the subordinate communities are liable to taxation, because they all share the benefits of government, and therefore ought all to furnish their proportion of the expense.

This the Americans have never openly denied. That it is their duty to pay the costs of their own safety they seem to admit; nor do they refuse their contribution to the exigencies, whatever they may be, of the British empire; but they make this participation of the publick burden a duty of very uncertain extent, and imperfect obligation, a duty temporary, occasional, and elective, of which they reserve to themselves the right of settling the degree, the time, and the duration, of judging when it may be required, and when it has been performed.

They allow to the supreme power nothing more than the liberty of notifying to them its demands or its necessities. Of this notification they profess to think for themselves, how far it shall influence their counsels, and of the necessities alleged, how far they shall endeavour to relieve them. They assume the exclusive power of settling not only the mode, but the quantity of this payment. They are ready to cooperate with all the other dominions of the king; but they will cooperate by no means which they do not like, and at no greater charge than they are willing to bear.

This claim, wild as it may seem, this claim, which supposes dominion without authority, and subjects without subordination, has found among the libertines of policy many clamorous and hardy vindicators. The laws of nature, the rights of humanity, the faith of charters, the danger of liberty, the encroachments of usurpation, have been thundered in our ears, sometimes by interested faction, and sometimes by honest stupidity.

It is said by Fontenelle, that if twenty philosophers shall resolutely deny that the presence of the sun makes the day, he will not despair but whole nations may adopt the opinion. So many political dogmatists have denied to the Mother-country the power of taxing the

Colonies, and have enforced their denial with so much violence of outcry, that their sect is already very numerous, and the publick voice suspends its decision.

Taxation No Tyranny

The Limits of Freedom

There are some, and those not inconsiderable for number, nor contemptible for knowledge, who except the power of taxation from the general dominion of parliament, and hold, that whatever degrees of obedience may be exacted, or whatever authority may be exercised in other acts of government, there is still reverence to be paid to money, and that legislation passes its limits when it violates the purse.

Of this exception, which by a head not fully impregnated with politicks is not easily comprehended, it is alleged as an unanswerable reason, that the Colonies send no representatives to the House of Commons.

It is, say the American advocates, the natural distinction of a freeman, and the legal privilege of an Englishman, that he is able to call his possessions his own, that he can sit secure in the enjoyment of inheritance or acquisition, that his house is fortified by the law, and that nothing can be taken from him but by his own consent. This consent is given for every man by his representative in parliament. The Americans unrepresented cannot consent to English taxations, as a corporation, and they will not consent as individuals.

Of this argument, it has been observed by more than one, that its force extends equally to all other laws, for a freeman is not to be exposed to punishment, or be called to any onerous service but by his own consent. The Congress has extracted a position from the fanciful Montesquieu, that, *in a free state every man being a free agent ought to be concerned in his own government.* Whatever is true of taxation is true of every other law, that he who is bound by it, without his consent, is not free, for he is not concerned in his own government.

He that denies the English parliament the right of taxation, denies it likewise the right of making any other laws civil or criminal, yet this power over the Colonies was never yet disputed by themselves. They have always admitted statutes for the punishment of offences, and for the redress or prevention of inconveniencies, and the reception of any law draws after it, by a chain which cannot be broken, the unwelcome necessity of submitting to taxation.

That a freeman is governed by himself, or by laws to which he has consented, is a position of mighty sound: but every man that utters it, with whatever confidence, and every man that hears it, with whatever acquiescence, if consent be supposed to imply the power of refusal, feels it to be false. We virtually and implicitly allow the institutions of any government of which we enjoy the benefit, and solicit the protection. In wide-extended dominions, though power has been diffused with the most even hand, yet a very small part of the people are either primarily or secondarily consulted in legislation. The business of the Publick must be done by delegation. The choice of delegates is made by a select number, and those who are not electors stand idle and helpless spectators of the commonweal, *wholly unconcerned in the government of themselves.*

Of the electors the hap is but little better. They are often far from unanimity in their choice, and where the numbers approach to equality, almost half must be governed not only without, but against their choice.

Taxation No Tyranny

A Particularity

Next morning I won a small bet from Lady Diana Beauclerk, by asking him as to one of his particularities, which her Ladyship laid I durst not do. It seems he had been frequently observed at the Club to put into his pocket the Seville oranges, after he had squeezed the juice of them into the drink which he made for himself. Beauclerk and Garrick talked of it to me, and seemed to think that he had a strange unwillingness to be discovered. We could not divine what he did with them; and this was the bold question to be put. I saw on his table the spoils of the preceding night, some fresh peels nicely scraped and cut into pieces. 'O, Sir, (said I,) I now partly see what you do with the squeezed oranges which you put into your pocket at the Club.' JOHNSON. 'I have a great love for them.' BOSWELL. 'And pray, Sir, what do you do with them? You scrape them, it seems, very neatly, and what next?' JOHNSON. 'Let them dry, Sir.' BOSWELL. 'And what next?' JOHNSON. 'Nay, Sir, you shall know their fate no further.' BOSWELL. 'Then the world must be left in the dark. It must be said (assuming a mock solemnity,) he scraped them, and let them dry, but what he did with them next, he never could be prevailed upon to tell.' JOHNSON. 'Nay, Sir, you should say it more emphatically:— he could not be prevailed upon, even by his dearest friends, to tell.'

Boswell, Life

Gentility

Dr. Johnson, as usual, spoke contemptuously of Colley Cibber. 'It is wonderful that a man, who for forty years had lived with the great and the witty, should have acquired so ill the talents of conversation: and he had but half to furnish; for one half of what he said was oaths.' He, however, allowed considerable merit to some of his comedies, and said there was no reason to believe that the *Careless Husband* was not written by himself. Davies said, he was the first dramatick writer who introduced genteel ladies upon the stage. Johnson refuted this observation by instancing several such characters in comedies before his time. DAVIES. (trying to defend himself from a charge of ignorance,) 'I mean genteel moral characters.' 'I think (said Hicky,) gentility and morality are inseparable.' BOSWELL. 'By no means, Sir. The genteelest characters are often the most immoral. Does not Lord Chesterfield give precepts for uniting wickedness and the graces? A man, indeed, is not genteel when he gets drunk; but most vices may be committed very genteelly: a man may debauch his friend's wife genteelly: he may cheat at cards genteelly.' HICKY. 'I do not think *that* is genteel.'

BOSWELL. 'Sir, it may not be like a gentleman, but it may be genteel.' JOHNSON. 'You are meaning two different things. One means exteriour grace; the other honour. It is certain that a man may be very immoral with exteriour grace. Lovelace, in *Clarissa*, is a very genteel and a very wicked character. Tom Hervey, who died t'other day, though a vicious man, was one of the genteelest men that ever lived.' Tom Davies instanced Charles the Second. JOHNSON. (taking fire at any attack upon that Prince, for whom he had an extraordinary partiality,) 'Charles the Second was licentious in his practice; but he always had a reverence for what was good. Charles the Second knew his people, and rewarded merit. The Church was at no time better filled than in his reign. He was the best King we have had from his time till the reign of his present Majesty, except James the Second, who was a very good King, but unhappily believed that it was necessary for the salvation of his subjects that they should be Roman Catholicks. *He* had the merit of endeavouring to do what he thought was for the salvation of the souls of his subjects, till he lost a great Empire. *We*, who thought that we should *not* be saved if we were Roman Catholicks, had the merit of maintaining our religion, at the expence of submitting ourselves to the government of King William, (for it could not be done otherwise,)—to the government of one of the most worthless scoundrels that ever existed. No; Charles the Second was not such a man as ——,[1] (naming another King). He did not destroy his father's will. He took money, indeed, from France: but he did not betray those over whom he ruled: he did not let the French fleet pass ours. George the First knew nothing, and desired to know nothing; did nothing, and desired to do nothing: and the only good thing that is told of him is, that he wished to restore the crown to its hereditary successor.' He roared with prodigious violence against George the Second. When he ceased, Moody interjected, in an Irish tone, and with a comick look, 'Ah! poor George the Second.'

Boswell, *Life*

[1 George II.]

Johnson in Paris

Dear Sir   Paris, Oct. 22, 1775.
We are still here, commonly very busy in looking
about us. We have been to day at Versailles. You have
seen it, and I shall not describe it. We came yesterday
from Fontainbleau, where the Court is now. We went
to see the King and Queen at dinner, and the Queen was
so impressed by Miss, that she sent one of the gentlemen
to enquire who she was. I find all true that you have ever
told me of Paris. Mr. Thrale is very liberal, and keeps us
two coaches, and a very fine table; but I think our
cookery very bad. Mrs. Thrale got into a convent of
English nuns, and I talked with her through the grate,
and I am very kindly used by the English Benedictine
friars. But upon the whole I cannot make much acquaintance here, and though the churches, palaces, and some
private houses are very magnificent, there is no very
great pleasure after having seen many, in seeing more;
at least the pleasure, whatever it be, must some time have
an end, and we are beginning to think when we shall
come home. Mr. Thrale calculates that as we left Streatham on the fifteenth of September, we shall see it again
about the fifteenth of November.

I think I had not been on this side of the sea five days
before I found a sensible improvement in my health. I
ran a race in the rain this day, and beat Baretti. Baretti
is a fine fellow, and speaks French, I think, quite as well
as English.

Make my compliments to Mrs. Williams, and give my
love to Francis, and tell my friends that I am not lost.
I am, dear Sir, Your affectionate humble, &c.

Sam. Johnson.

1776
Vexing Thoughts

I enjoyed the luxury of our approach to London, that
metropolis which we both loved so much, for the high

and varied intellectual pleasure which it furnishes. I experienced immediate happiness while whirled along with such a companion, and said to him, 'Sir, you observed one day at General Oglethorpe's, that a man is never happy for the present, but when he is drunk. Will you not add,—or when driving rapidly in a post-chaise?' JOHNSON. 'No, Sir, you are driving rapidly *from* something, or *to* something.'

Talking of melancholy, he said, 'Some men, and very thinking men too, have not those vexing thoughts. Sir Joshua Reynolds is the same all the year round. Beauclerk, except when ill and in pain, is the same. But I believe most men have them in the degree in which they are capable of having them. If I were in the country, and were distressed by that malady, I would force myself to take a book; and every time I did it I should find it the easier. Melancholy, indeed, should be diverted by every means but drinking.'

Boswell, Life

Defending Truth

Mr. Murray praised the ancient philosophers for the candour and good humour with which those of different sects disputed with each other. JOHNSON. 'Sir, they disputed with good humour, because they were not in earnest as to religion. Had the ancients been serious in their belief, we should not have had their Gods exhibited in the manner we find them represented in the Poets. The people would not have suffered it. They disputed with good humour upon their fanciful theories, because they were not interested in the truth of them: when a man has nothing to lose, he may be in good humour with his opponent. Accordingly you see in Lucian, the Epicurean, who argues only negatively, keeps his temper; the Stoick, who has something positive to preserve, grows angry. Being angry with one who controverts an opinion which you value, is a necessary consequence of the uneasiness which you feel. Every man who attacks my belief, diminishes in some degree my confidence in it, and therefore makes me uneasy; and I am angry with him who makes me uneasy. Those only who believed in revelation have been angry at having their faith called in question; because they only had something upon which they could rest as matter of fact.' MURRAY. 'It seems to me that we are not angry at a man for controverting an opinion which we believe and value; we rather pity him.' JOHNSON. 'Why, Sir; to be sure when you wish a man to have that belief which you think is of infinite advantage, you wish well to him; but your primary consideration is your own quiet. If a madman were to come into this room with a stick in his hand, no doubt we should pity the state of his mind; but our primary consideration would be to take care of ourselves. We should knock him down first, and pity him afterwards. No, Sir; every man will dispute with great good humour upon a subject in which he is not interested. I will dispute very calmly upon the probability of another man's son being hanged; but if a man zealously enforces the probability that my own son will be hanged, I shall certainly not be in a very good humour with him.' I added this illustration, 'If a man endeavours to convince me that my wife, whom I love very much, and in whom I place great confidence, is a disagreeable woman, and is even unfaithful to me, I shall be very angry, for he is putting me in fear of being unhappy.' MURRAY. 'But, Sir, truth will always bear an examination.' JOHNSON. 'Yes, Sir, but it is painful to be forced to defend it. Consider, Sir, how should you like, though conscious of your innocence, to be tried before a jury for a capital crime, once a week.'

Boswell, *Life*

What is Poetry?

I related a dispute between Goldsmith and Mr. Robert Dodsley, one day when they and I were dining at Tom Davies's, in 1762. Goldsmith asserted, that there was no poetry produced in this age. Dodsley appealed to his own *Collection*, and maintained, that though you could not find a palace like Dryden's *Ode on St. Cecilia's Day*, you had villages composed of very pretty houses; and he mentioned particularly *The Spleen*. JOHNSON. 'I think Dodsley gave up the question. He and Goldsmith said the same thing; only he said it in a softer manner than Goldsmith did; for he acknowledged that there was no poetry, nothing that towered above the common mark. You may find wit and humour in verse, and yet no poetry. *Hudibras* has a profusion of these; yet it is not to be reckoned a poem. *The Spleen*, in Dodsley's *Collection*, on which you say he chiefly rested, is not poetry.' BOSWELL. 'Does not Gray's poetry, Sir, tower above the common mark?' JOHNSON. 'Yes, Sir; but we must attend to the difference between what men in general cannot do if they would, and what every man may do if he would. Sixteen-string Jack towered above the common mark.' BOSWELL. 'Then, Sir, what is poetry?' JOHNSON. 'Why, Sir, it is much easier to say what it is not. We all *know* what light is; but it is not easy to *tell* what it is.'

Boswell, *Life*

The Graces

No man was a more attentive and nice observer of behaviour in those in whose company he happened to be, than Johnson; or, however strange it may seem to many, had a higher estimation of its refinements. Lord Eliot informs me, that one day when Johnson and he were at dinner at a gentleman's house in London, upon Lord Chesterfield's Letters being mentioned, Johnson surprized the company by this sentence: 'Every man of any education would rather be called a rascal, than accused of deficiency in *the graces*.' Mr. Gibbon, who was present, turned to a lady who knew Johnson well, and lived much with him, and in his quaint manner, tapping his box, addressed her thus: 'Don't you think, Madam, (looking towards Johnson,) that among *all* your acquaintance, you could find *one* exception?' The lady smiled, and seemed to acquiesce.

Boswell, *Life*

Censure from the Pulpit

During my stay in London this spring, I solicited his attention to another law case, in which I was engaged. In the course of a contested election for the Borough of Dumfermline, which I attended as one of my friend Colonel (afterwards Sir Archibald) Campbell's counsel; one of his political agents, who was charged with having been unfaithful to his employer, and having deserted to the opposite party for a pecuniary reward—attacked very rudely in a news-paper the Reverend Mr. James Thomson, one of the ministers of that place, on account of a supposed allusion to him in one of his sermons. Upon this the minister, on a subsequent Sunday, arraigned him by name from the pulpit with some severity; and the agent, after the sermon was over, rose up and asked the minister aloud, 'What bribe he had received for telling so many lies from the chair of verity.' I was present at this very extraordinary scene. The person arraigned, and his father and brother, who had also had a share both of the reproof from the pulpit, and in the retaliation, brought an action against Mr. Thomson, in the Court of Session, for defamation and damages, and I was one of the counsel for the reverend defendant. The *Liberty of the Pulpit* was our great ground of defence; but we argued also on the provocation of the previous attack, and on the instant retaliation. The Court of Session, however—the fifteen Judges, who are at the same time the Jury, decided against the minister, contrary to my humble opinion; and several of them expressed themselves with indignation against him. He was an aged gentleman, formerly a military chaplain, and a man of high spirit and honour. Johnson was satisfied that the judgement was wrong, and dictated to me the following argument in confutation of it:—

'Of the censure pronounced from the pulpit, our determination must be formed, as in other cases, by a consideration of the action itself, and the particular circumstances with which it is invested.

'The right of censure and rebuke seems necessarily

appendant to the pastoral office. He, to whom the care of a congregation is entrusted, is considered as the shepherd of a flock, as the teacher of a school, as the father of a family. As a shepherd tending not his own sheep but those of his master, he is answerable for those that stray, and that lose themselves by straying. But no man can be answerable for losses which he has not power to prevent, or for vagrancy which he has not authority to restrain.

'As a teacher giving instruction for wages, and liable to reproach, if those whom he undertakes to inform make no proficiency, he must have the power of enforcing attendance, of awakening negligence, and repressing contradiction.

'As a father, he possesses the paternal authority of admonition, rebuke, and punishment. He cannot, without reducing his office to an empty name, be hindered from the exercise of any practice necessary to stimulate the idle, to reform the vicious, to check the petulant, and correct the stubborn.

'If we enquire into the practice of the primitive Church, we shall, I believe, find the ministers of the word exercising the whole authority of this complicated character. We shall find them not only encouraging the good by exhortation, but terrifying the wicked by reproof and denunciation. In the earliest ages of the Church, while religion was yet pure from secular advantages, the punishment of sinners was publick censure, and open penance; penalties inflicted merely by ecclesiastical authority, at a time while the Church had yet no help from the civil power; while the hand of the magistrate lifted only the rod of persecution; and when governours were ready to afford a refuge to all those who fled from clerical authority.

'That the Church, therefore, had once a power of publick censure is evident, because that power was frequently exercised. That it borrowed not its power from the civil authority, is likewise certain, because civil authority was at that time its enemy.

'The hour came at length, when after three hundred years of struggle and distress, Truth took possession of imperial power, and the civil laws lent their aid to the ecclesiastical constitutions. The magistrate from that time co-operated with the priest, and clerical sentences were made efficacious by secular force. But the State, when it came to the assistance of the Church, had no intention to diminish its authority. Those rebukes and those censures which were lawful before, were lawful still. But they had hitherto operated only upon voluntary submission. The refractory and contemptuous were at first in no danger of temporal severities, except what they might suffer from the reproaches of conscience, or the detestation of their fellow Christians. When religion obtained the support of law, if admonitions and censures had no effect, they were seconded by the magistrates with coercion and punishment.

'It therefore appears from ecclesiastical history, that the right of inflicting shame by publick censure, has been always considered as inherent in the Church; and that this right was not conferred by the civil power; for it was exercised when the civil power operated against it. By the civil power it was never taken away; for the Christian magistrate interposed his office, not to rescue sinners from censure, but to supply more powerful means of reformation; to add pain where shame was insufficient; and when men were proclaimed unworthy of the society of the faithful, to restrain them by imprisonment, from spreading abroad the contagion of wickedness.

'It is not improbable that from this acknowledged power of publick censure, grew in time the practice of auricular confession. Those who dreaded the blast of publick reprehension, were willing to submit themselves to the priest, by a private accusation of themselves; and to obtain a reconciliation with the Church by a kind of clandestine absolution and invisible penance; conditions with which the priest would in times of ignorance and corruption, easily comply, as they increased his influence, by adding the knowledge of secret sins to that of notorious offences, and enlarged his authority, by making him the sole arbiter of the terms of reconcilement.

'From this bondage the Reformation set us free. The

minister has no longer power to press into the retire-
ments of conscience, to torture us by interrogatories, or
put himself in possession of our secrets and our lives. But
though we have thus controlled his usurpations, his just
and original power remains unimpaired. He may still
see, though he may not pry: he may yet hear, though he
may not question. And that knowledge which his eyes and
ears force upon him it is still his duty to use, for the benefit
of his flock. A father who lives near a wicked neighbour,
may forbid a son to frequent his company. A minister
who has in his congregation a man of open and scanda-
lous wickedness, may warn his parishioners to shun his
conversation. To warn them is not only lawful, but not to
warn them would be criminal. He may warn them one
by one in friendly converse, or by a parochial visitation.
But if he may warn each man singly, what shall forbid
him to warn them altogether? Of that which is to be
made known to all, how is there any difference whether
it be communicated to each singly, or to all together?
What is known to all, must necessarily be publick.
Whether it shall be publick at once, or publick by degrees, is the only question. And of a sudden and solemn
publication the impression is deeper, and the warning
more effectual.

'It may easily be urged, if a minister be thus left at
liberty to delate sinners from the pulpit, and to publish
at will the crimes of a parishioner, he may often blast the
innocent, and distress the timorous. He may be suspicious, and condemn without evidence; he may be rash,
and judge without examination; he may be severe, and
treat slight offences with too much harshness; he may be
malignant and partial, and gratify his private interest or
resentment under the shelter of his pastoral character.

'Of all this there is possibility, and of all this there is
danger. But if possibility of evil be to exclude good, no good
can be done. If nothing is to be attempted in which there
is danger, we must all sink into hopeless inactivity. The
evils that may be feared from this practice arise not from
any defect in the institution, but from the infirmities of
human nature. Power, in whatever hands it is placed,

will be sometimes improperly exerted; yet courts of law must judge, though they will sometimes judge amiss. A father must instruct his children, though he himself may often want instruction. A minister must censure sinners, though his censure may be sometimes erroneous by want of judgement, and sometimes unjust by want of honesty.

'If we examine the circumstances of the present case, we shall find the sentence neither erroneous nor unjust; we shall find no breach of private confidence, no intrusion into secret transactions. The fact was notorious and indubitable; so easy to be proved, that no proof was desired. The act was base and treacherous, the perpetration insolent and open, and the example naturally mischievous. The minister however, being retired and recluse, had not yet heard what was publickly known throughout the parish; and on occasion of a publick election, warned his people, according to his duty, against the crimes which publick elections frequently produce. His warning was felt by one of his parishioners, as pointed particularly at himself. But instead of producing, as might be wished, private compunction and immediate reformation, it kindled only rage and resentment. He charged his minister, in a publick paper, with scandal, defamation, and falsehood. The minister, thus reproached, had his own character to vindicate, upon which his pastoral authority must necessarily depend. To be charged with a defamatory lie is an injury which no man patiently endures in common life. To be charged with polluting the pastoral office with scandal and falsehood, was a violation of character still more atrocious, as it affected not only his personal but his clerical veracity. His indignation naturally rose in proportion to his honesty, and with all the fortitude of injured honesty, he dared this calumniator in the church, and at once exonerated himself from censure, and rescued his flock from deception and from danger. The man whom he accuses pretends not to be innocent; or at least only pretends; for he declines a trial. The crime of which he is accused has frequent opportunities and strong temptations. It has already spread far, with much depravation of private morals, and much injury to publick happiness. To warn the people, therefore, against it was not wanton and officious, but necessary and pastoral.

'What then is the fault with which this worthy minister is charged? He has usurped no dominion over conscience. He has exerted no authority in support of doubtful and controverted opinions. He has not dragged into light a bashful and corrigible sinner. His censure was directed against a breach of morality, against an act which no man justifies. The man who appropriated this censure to himself, is evidently and notoriously guilty. His consciousness of his own wickedness incited him to attack his faithful reprover with open insolence and printed accusations. Such an attack made defence necessary; and we hope it will be at last decided that the means of defence were just and lawful.'

Boswell, Life

Foote and Garrick

Foote being mentioned, Johnson said, 'He is not a good mimick.' One of the company added, 'A merry Andrew, a buffoon.' JOHNSON. 'But he has wit too, and is not deficient in ideas, or in fertility and variety of imagery, and not empty of reading; he has knowledge enough to fill up his part. One species of wit he has in an eminent degree, that of escape. You drive him into a corner with both hands; but he's gone, Sir, when you think you have got him—like an animal that jumps over your head. Then he has a great range for wit; he never lets truth stand between him and a jest, and he is sometimes mighty coarse. Garrick is under many restraints from which Foote is free.' WILKES. 'Garrick's wit is more like Lord Chesterfield's.' JOHNSON. 'The first time I was in company with Foote was at Fitzherbert's. Having no good opinion of the fellow, I was resolved not to be pleased; and it is very difficult to please a man against his will. I went on eating my dinner pretty sullenly, affecting not to mind him. But the dog was so very comical, that I was obliged to lay down my knife and fork, throw myself back upon my chair, and fairly laugh it out. No, Sir, he was irresistible. He upon one occasion experienced, in an extraordinary degree, the efficacy of his powers of entertaining. Amongst the many and various modes which he tried of getting money, he became a partner with a small-beer brewer, and he was to have a share of the profits for procuring customers amongst his numerous acquaintance. Fitzherbert was one who took his small-beer; but it was so bad that the servants resolved not to drink it. They were at some loss how to notify their resolution, being afraid of offending their master, who they knew liked Foote much as a companion. At last they fixed upon a little black boy, who was rather a favourite, to be their deputy, and deliver their remonstrance; and having invested him with the whole authority of the kitchen, he was to inform Mr. Fitzherbert, in all their names, upon a certain day, that they would drink Foote's small-beer no longer. On that day Foote happened to dine at Fitzherbert's, and this boy served at table; he was so delighted with Foote's stories, and merriment, and grimace, that when he went down stairs, he told them, "This is the finest man I have ever seen. I will not deliver your message. I will drink his small-beer."'

Somebody observed that Garrick could not have done this. WILKES. 'Garrick would have made the small-beer still smaller. He is now leaving the stage; but he will play *Scrub* all his life.' I knew that Johnson would let nobody attack Garrick but himself, as Garrick once said to me, and I had heard him praise his liberality; so to bring out his commendation of his celebrated pupil, I said, loudly, 'I have heard Garrick is liberal.' JOHNSON. 'Yes, Sir, I know that Garrick has given away more money than any man in England that I am acquainted with, and that not from ostentatious views. Garrick was very poor when he began life; so when he came to have money, he probably was very unskilful in giving away, and saved when he should not. But Garrick began to be liberal as soon as he could; and I am of opinion, the reputation of avarice which he has had, has been very lucky for him, and prevented his having many enemies. You despise a man for avarice, but do not hate him. Garrick might have been much better attacked for living with more splendour than is suitable to a player: if they had had the wit to have assaulted him in that quarter, they might have galled him more. But they have kept clamouring about his avarice, which has rescued him from much obloquy and envy.'

Boswell, *Life*

To Mrs. Thrale

Dear Madam

This letter will not, I hope, reach you many days before me, in a distress which can be so little relieved, nothing remains for a friend but to come and partake it.

Poor dear sweet little Boy. When I read the letter this day to Mrs Aston, she said 'such a death is the next to Translation'. Yet, however I may convince myself of this, the tears are in my eyes, and yet I could not love him as you loved him, nor reckon on him for a future comfort, as you and his Father reckoned upon him.

He is gone, and we are going. We could not have enjoyed him long, and shall not long be separated from him. He has probably escaped many such pangs as you are now feeling.

Nothing remains but that with humble confidence We resign ourselves to almighty Goodness, and fall down without irreverent murmurs before the Sovereign Distributer of good and evil, with hope that though sorrow endureth for a night, yet joy may come in the Morning.

I have known you, Madam, too long to think that you want any arguments for submission to the supreme will, nor can my consolation have any effect but that of showing that I wish to comfort you. What can be done you must do for yourself. Remember first that your Child is happy, and then, that he is safe not only from the ills of this world, but from those more formidable dangers which extend their mischief to eternity. You have brought into the world a rational Being, have seen him happy during the little life that has been granted him, and can have no doubt but that his Happiness is now permanent and immutable.

When you have obtained by Prayer such tranquillity as nature will admit, force your attention, as you can, upon your accustomed duties, and accustomed entertainments. You can do no more for our dear Boy, but you must not therefore think less on those whom your attention may make fitter for the place to which he is gone.

I am Dearest, dearest Madam Your most affectionate humble servant,

Lichfield. March 25. 1776   Sam: Johnson

1777

Fitzherbert of Derbyshire

Johnson gave us this evening, in his happy discriminative manner, a portrait of the late Mr. Fitzherbert, of Derbyshire. 'There was (said he,) no sparkle, no brilliancy in Fitzherbert; but I never knew a man who was so generally acceptable. He made every body quite easy, overpowered nobody by the superiority of his talents, made no man think worse of himself by being his rival, seemed always to listen, did not oblige you to hear much from him, and did not oppose what you said. Every body liked him; but he had no friend, as I understand the word, nobody with whom he exchanged intimate thoughts. People were willing to think well of every thing about him. A gentleman was making an affected rant, as many people do, of great feelings about "his dear son," who was at school near London; how anxious he was lest he might be ill, and what he would give to see him. "Can't you (said Fitzherbert,) take a post-chaise and go to him." This, to be sure, *finished* the affected man, but there was not much in it. However, this was circulated as wit for a whole winter, and I believe part of a summer too; a proof that he was no very witty man. He was an instance of the truth of the observation, that a man will please

more upon the whole by negative qualities than by positive; by never offending, than by giving a great deal of
delight. In the first place, men hate more steadily than
they love; and if I have said something to hurt a man
once, I shall not get the better of this, by saying many
things to please him.'

Boswell, *Life*

Johnson's Parodists

I mentioned to him that Dr. Hugh Blair, in his lectures
on Rhetorick and Belles Lettres, which I heard him deliver at Edinburgh, had animadverted on the Johnsonian
style as too pompous; and attempted to imitate it, by
giving a sentence of Addison in *The Spectator*. No. 411, in
the manner of Johnson. When treating of the utility of
the pleasures of imagination in preserving us from vice, it
is observed of those 'who know not how to be idle and
innocent,' that 'their very first step out of business is into
vice or folly;' which Dr. Blair supposed would have been
expressed in *The Rambler* thus: 'Their very first step out
of the regions of business is into the perturbation of vice,
or the vacuity of folly.' JOHNSON. 'Sir, these are not the
words I should have used. No, Sir; the imitators of my
style have not hit it. Miss Aikin has done it the best; for
she has imitated the sentiment as well as the diction.'

Boswell, *Life*

Anonymous Authorship

Johnson disapproved of Dr. Dodd's leaving the world
persuaded that *The Convict's Address to his unhappy Brethren*
was of his own writing. 'But, Sir, (said I,) you contributed
to the deception; for when Mr. Seward expressed a
doubt to you that it was not Dodd's own, because it had
a great deal more force of mind in it than any thing known
to be his, you answered,—"Why should you think so?
Depend upon it, Sir, when a man knows he is to be
hanged in a fortnight, it concentrates his mind wonder-
fully." ' JOHNSON. 'Sir, as Dodd got it from me to pass as

his own, while that could do him any good, there was an *implied promise* that I should not own it. To own it, therefore, would have been telling a lie, with the addition of breach of promise, which was worse than simply telling a lie to make it be believed it was Dodd's. Besides, Sir, I did not *directly* tell a lie: I left the matter uncertain. Perhaps I thought that Seward would not believe it the less to be mine for what I said; but I would not put it in his power to say I had owned it.'

.   .   .   .

Talking of the wonderful concealment of the authour of the celebrated letters signed *Junius*; he said, 'I should have believed Burke to be Junius, because I know no man but Burke who is capable of writing these letters; but Burke spontaneously denied it to me. The case would have been different had I asked him if he was the authour; a man so questioned, as to an anonymous publication, may think he has a right to deny it.'

Boswell, *Life*

To William Vyse

Sir,

I doubt not but you will readily forgive me for taking the liberty of requesting your assistance in recommending an old friend to his Grace the Archbishop, as Governour of the Charter-house.

His name is De Groot; he was born at Gloucester; I have known him many years. He has all the common claims to charity, being old, poor, and infirm, in a great degree. He has likewise another claim, to which no scholar can refuse attention; he is by several descents the nephew of Hugo Grotius; of him, from whom perhaps every man of learning has learned something. Let it not be said that in any lettered country a nephew of Grotius asked a charity and was refused.

I am, reverend Sir, Your most humble servant,

July 19, 1777.   Sam. Johnson

To Mrs. Thrale from Ashbourne

Dear Madam

I think I have already told you that Bos is gone. The day before he went we met the Duke and Dutchess of Argyle in the street, and went to speak to them while they changed horses, and in the afternoon Mrs. Langton and Juliet stopped in their way to London, and sent for me, I went to them and sent for Boswel whom Mrs Langton had never seen.

And so, here is this post without a letter. I am old, I am old, says Sir John Falstaff. 'Take heed, my dear, youth flies apace.' You will be wanting a letter sometime. I wish I were with you, but I cannot come yet.—

> Glacies et frigora Rheni
> Me sine sola vides. Ah! ne te frigora lædant
> Ah tibi ne glacies teneras secet aspera plantas! Ecl. x.

I wish you well; Burney and all, and shall be glad to know your adventures. Do not however think wholly to escape me, you will, I hope, see me at Brighthelmston. Dare you answer me as Brutus answered his evil genius? I know not when I shall write again now you are going to the world's end. Extra anni solisque vias, where the post will be a long time in reaching you. I shall notwithstanding all distance continue to think on you, and to please myself with the hope of being once again

Madam, Your most humble servant,

Sept. 27. 1777 Ashbourne   Sam: Johnson.

Good King George

To the KING.

Sir

I presume to lay before your Majesty the last labours of a learned bishop, who died in the toils and duties of his calling. He is now beyond the reach of all earthly honours and rewards; and only the hope of inciting others to imitate him, makes it now fit to be remembered, that he enjoyed in his life the favour of your Majesty.

The tumultuary life of Princes seldom permits them to
survey the wide extent of national interest, without losing
sight of private merit: to exhibit qualities which may be
imitated by the highest and the humblest of mankind:
and to be at once amiable and great.

Such characters, if now and then they appear in history, are contemplated with admiration. May it be the
ambition of all your subjects to make haste with their
tribute of reverence: and as posterity may learn from
your Majesty how kings should live, may they learn, likewise from your people how they should be honoured.

I am,

May it please your Majesty,

with the most profound respect,

Your Majesty's

most dutiful and devoted

Subject and Servant.

Dedication of Zachary Pearce's *Commentary on the Four
Evangelists and the Acts of the Apostles*

1778

Soldiers and Sailors

We talked of war. JOHNSON. 'Every man thinks meanly of
himself for not having been a soldier, or not having been
at sea.' BOSWELL. 'Lord Mansfield does not.' JOHNSON.
'Sir, if Lord Mansfield were in a company of General
Officers and Admirals who have been in service, he
would shrink; he'd wish to creep under the table.'
BOSWELL. 'No; he'd think he could *try* them all.' JOHN-
SON. 'Yes, if he could catch them: but they'd try him
much sooner. No, Sir; were Socrates and Charles the
Twelfth of Sweden both present in any company, and
Socrates to say, "Follow me, and hear a lecture on
philosophy;" and Charles, laying his hand on his sword,
to say, "Follow me, and dethrone the Czar;" a man
would be ashamed to follow Socrates. Sir, the impression
is universal; yet it is strange. As to the sailor, when you

nothing by which the pride of other authors might be gratified or favour gained, no exchange of praise nor solicitation of support. His great works were performed under discountenance and in blindness, but difficulties vanished at his touch; he was born for whatever is arduous; and his work is not the greatest of heroick poems, only because it is not the first.

Life of Milton

Butler: Wit and Wisdom

The great source of pleasure is variety. Uniformity must tire at last, though it be uniformity of excellence. We love to expect; and, when expectation is disappointed or gratified, we want to be again expecting. For this impatience of the present, whoever would please must make provision. The skilful writer *irritat, mulcet*;[1] makes a due distribution of the still and animated parts. It is for want of this artful intertexture and those necessary changes that the whole of a book may be tedious, though all the parts are praised.

If inexhaustible wit could give perpetual pleasure no eye would ever leave half-read the work of Butler; for what poet has ever brought so many remote images so happily together? It is scarcely possible to peruse a page without finding some association of images that was never found before. By the first paragraph the reader is amused, by the next he is delighted, and by a few more strained to astonishment; but astonishment is a toilsome pleasure; he is soon weary of wondering, and longs to be diverted.

'Omnia vult [vis] belle, Matho, dicere: dic aliquando
    Et bene, dic neutrum, dic aliquando male.'

Imagination is useless without knowledge: nature gives in vain the power of combination, unless study and observation supply materials to be combined. Butler's treasures of knowledge appear proportioned to his expence; whatever topick employs his mind he shews himself qualified to expand and illustrate it with all the accessories that books can furnish: he is found not only to have

[1 'Now stimulates, now soothes'. Horace.]

look down from the quarter deck to the space below, you
see the utmost extremity of human misery; such croud-
ing, such filth, such stench!' BOSWELL. 'Yet sailors are
happy.' JOHNSON. 'They are happy as brutes are happy,
with a piece of fresh meat,—with the grossest sensuality.
But, Sir, the profession of soldiers and sailors has the
dignity of danger. Mankind reverence those who have
got over fear, which is so general a weakness.' SCOTT. 'But
is not courage mechanical, and to be acquired?' JOHN-
SON. 'Why yes, Sir, in a collective sense. Soldiers consider themselves only as parts of a great machine.'
SCOTT. 'We find people fond of being sailors.' JOHNSON.
'I cannot account for that, any more than I can account
for other strange perversions of imagination.'

Boswell, Life

Canting

On Sunday, April 12, I found him at home before dinner;
Dr. Dodd's poem entitled *Thoughts in Prison* was lying
upon his table. This appearing to me an extraordinary
effort by a man who was in Newgate for a capital crime,
I was desirous to hear Johnson's opinion of it: to my
surprize, he told me he had not read a line of it. I took up
the book and read a passage to him. JOHNSON. 'Pretty
well, if you are previously disposed to like them.' I read
another passage, with which he was better pleased. He
then took the book into his own hands, and having looked
at the prayer at the end of it, he said, 'What *evidence* is
there that this was composed the night before he suffered?
I do not believe it.' He then read aloud where he prays
for the King, &c. and observed, 'Sir, do you think that
a man the night before he is to be hanged cares for the
succession of a royal family?—Though, he *may* have
composed this prayer, then. A man who has been canting
all his life, may cant to the last.—And yet a man who
has been refused a pardon after so much petitioning,
would hardly be praying thus fervently for the King.'

Boswell, Life

To Hester ('Queeney') Thrale

My dearest Love,   London, 24 Oct. 1778

I was in hopes that your letter about the camp would have been longer, and that you would have considered yourself as surveying in a camp perhaps the most important scene of human existence, the real scene of heroick life. If you are struck with the inconveniences of the military in a camp where there is no danger, where all the materials of pleasure are supplied, and where there is little but jollity and festivity, reflect what a camp must be surrounded by enemies in a wasted or a hostile country, where provisions can scarcely be had, and what can be had must be snatched in haste by men who when they put the bread into their mouths, are uncertain whether they shall swallow it.

Sir Robert Cotton, whose degradation seems to touch you, is not the greatest man that has inhabited a tent. He is not considered out of Cheshire, nor perhaps in it, as standing on even ground with Alexander and Darius; Cæsar and Pompey; Tamerlane and Bajazet; Charles, Peter, and Augustus. These and many more like these, have lived in a camp like Sir Robert Cotton.

In a camp you see what is the lowest and most portable accommodation with which Life can be contented; what shelter it is that can be most expeditiously erected and removed. There is in a camp what human wit sharpened by the greatest exigencies has been able to contrive, and it gives ladies the particular pleasure of seeing evils which they are not to share.

I am, Sweeting, Your most humble servant
                                        Sam: Johnson

The Manners of the Great

As he was a zealous friend of subordination, he was at all times watchful to repress the vulgar cant against the manners of the great; 'High people, Sir, (said he,) are the best; take a hundred ladies of quality, you'll find them better wives, better mothers, more willing to sacrifice their own pleasure to their children than a hundred other women. Tradeswomen (I mean the wives of tradesmen) in the city, who are worth from ten to fifteen thousand pounds, are the worst creatures upon the earth, grossly ignorant, and thinking viciousness fashionable. Farmers, I think, are often worthless fellows. Few lords will cheat; and, if they do, they'll be ashamed of it: farmers cheat and are not ashamed of it: they have all the sensual vices too of the nobility, with cheating into the bargain. There is as much fornication and adultery among farmers as amongst noblemen.' BOSWELL. 'The notion of the world, Sir, however is, that the morals of women of quality are worse than those in lower stations.' JOHNSON. 'Yes, Sir, the licentiousness of one woman of quality makes more noise than that of a number of women in lower stations; then, Sir, you are to consider the malignity of women in the city against women of quality, which will make them believe any thing of them, such as that they call their coachmen to bed. No, Sir, so far as I have observed, the higher in rank, the richer ladies are, they are the better instructed and the more virtuous.'

Boswell, Life

1779–81
THE LIVES OF THE POETS

1779
Cowley

Wit, like all other things subject by their nature to the choice of man, has its changes and fashions, and at different times takes different forms. About the beginning of the seventeenth century appeared a race of writers that may be termed the metaphysical poets, of whom in a criticism on the works of Cowley it is not improper to give some account.

The metaphysical poets were men of learning, and to shew their learning was their whole endeavour; but, un-

luckily resolving to shew it in rhyme, instead of writing
poetry they only wrote verses, and very often such verses
as stood the trial of the finger better than of the ear; for
the modulation was so imperfect that they were only found
to be verses by counting the syllables.

If the father of criticism has rightly denominated
poetry τέχνη μιμητική, *an imitative* art, these writers will
without great wrong lose their right to the name of
poets, for they cannot be said to have imitated any thing:
they neither copied nature nor life; neither painted the
forms of matter nor represented the operations of intellect.

Those however who deny them to be poets allow them
to be wits. Dryden confesses of himself and his contemporaries that they fall below Donne in wit, but maintains
that they surpass him in poetry.

If Wit be well described by Pope as being 'that which
has been often thought, but was never before so well expressed,' they certainly never attained nor ever sought it,
for they endeavoured to be singular in their thoughts, and
were careless of their diction. But Pope's account of wit
is undoubtedly erroneous; he depresses it below its
natural dignity, and reduces it from strength of thought
to happiness of language.

If by a more noble and more adequate conception that
be considered as Wit which is at once natural and new,
that which though not obvious is, upon its first production, acknowledged to be just; if it be that, which he that
never found it, wonders how he missed; to wit of this
kind the metaphysical poets have seldom risen. Their
thoughts are often new, but seldom natural; they are
not obvious, but neither are they just; and the reader,
far from wondering that he missed them, wonders more
frequently by what perverseness of industry they were
ever found.

But Wit, abstracted from its effects upon the hearer,
may be more rigorously and philosophically considered as
a kind of *discordia concors*; a combination of dissimilar
images, or discovery of occult resemblances in things
apparently unlike. Of wit, thus defined, they have more
than enough. The most heterogeneous ideas are yoked by

violence together; nature and art are ransacked for illustrations, comparisons, and allusions; their learning instructs, and their subtilty surprises; but the reader commonly thinks his improvement dearly bought, and, though he sometimes admires, is seldom pleased.

From this account of their compositions it will be readily inferred that they were not successful in representing or moving the affections. As they were wholly employed on something unexpected and surprising they had no regard to that uniformity of sentiment, which enables us to conceive and to excite the pains and the pleasure of other minds: they never enquired what on any occasion they should have said or done, but wrote rather as beholders than partakers of human nature; as beings looking upon good and evil, impassive and at leisure; as Epicurean deities making remarks on the actions of men and the vicissitudes of life, without interest and without emotion. Their courtship was void of fondness and their lamentation of sorrow. Their wish was only to say what they hoped had been never said before.

Nor was the sublime more within their reach than the pathetick; for they never attempted that comprehension and expanse of thought which at once fills the whole mind, and of which the first effect is sudden astonishment, and the second rational admiration. Sublimity is produced by aggregation, and littleness by dispersion. Great thoughts are always general, and consist in positions not limited by exceptions, and in descriptions not descending to minuteness. It is with great propriety that subtlety, which in its original import means exility of particles, is taken in its metaphorical meaning for nicety of distinction. Those writers who lay on the watch for novelty could have little hope of greatness; for great things cannot have escaped former observation. Their attempts were always analytick: they broke every image into fragments, and could no more represent by their slender conceits and laboured particularities the prospects of nature or the scenes of life, than he who dissects a sun-beam with a prism can exhibit the wide effulgence of a summer noon.

What they wanted however of the sublime they endeavoured to supply by hyperbole; their amplification had no limits: they left not only reason but fancy behind them, and produced combinations of confused magnificence that not only could not be credited, but could not be imagined.

Yet great labour directed by great abilities is never wholly lost: if they frequently threw away their wit upon false conceits, they likewise sometimes struck out unexpected truth: if their conceits were far-fetched, they were often worth the carriage. To write on their plan it was at least necessary to read and think. No man could be born a metaphysical poet, nor assume the dignity of a writer by descriptions copied from descriptions, by imitations borrowed from imitations, by traditional imagery and hereditary similes, by readiness of rhyme and volubility of syllables.

In perusing the works of this race of authors the mind is exercised either by recollection or inquiry; either something already learned is to be retrieved, or something new is to be examined. If their greatness seldom elevates their acuteness often surprises; if the imagination is not always gratified, at least the powers of reflection and comparison are employed; and in the mass of materials, which ingenious absurdity has thrown together, genuine wit and useful knowledge may be sometimes found, buried perhaps in grossness of expression, but useful to those who know their value, and such as, when they are expanded to perspicuity and polished to elegance, may give lustre to works which have more propriety though less copiousness of sentiment.

Life of Cowley

Denham

Cooper's Hill if it be maliciously inspected will not be found without its faults. The digressions are too long, the morality too frequent, and the sentiments sometimes such as will not bear a rigorous enquiry.

The four verses, which, since Dryden has commended

them, almost every writer for a century past has imitated,
are generally known:

> 'O could I flow like thee, and make thy stream
> My great example, as it is my theme!
> Though deep, yet clear; though gentle, yet not dull;
> Strong without rage, without o'erflowing full.'

The lines are in themselves not perfect, for most of the
words thus artfully opposed are to be understood simply
on one side of the comparison, and metaphorically on the
other; and if there be any language which does not express
intellectual operations by material images, into that
language they cannot be translated. But so much meaning is comprised in so few words; the particulars of resemblance are so perspicaciously collected, and every
mode of excellence separated from its adjacent fault by
so nice a line of limitation; the different parts of the sentence are so accurately adjusted; and the flow of the last
couplet is so smooth and sweet—that the passage however
celebrated has not been praised above its merit. It has
beauty peculiar to itself, and must be numbered among
those felicities which cannot be produced at will by wit
and labour, but must arise unexpectedly in some hour
propitious to poetry.

Life of Denham

Milton: The Schoolmaster

He now hired a lodging at the house of one Russel, a
taylor in St. Bride's Churchyard, and undertook the
education of John and Edward Philips, his sister's sons.
Finding his rooms too little he took a house and garden
in Aldersgate street, which was not then so much out of
the world as it is now, and chose his dwelling at the upper
end of a passage that he might avoid the noise of the
street. Here he received more boys, to be boarded and
instructed.

Let not our veneration for Milton forbid us to look
with some degree of merriment on great promises and
small performance, on the man who hastens home be-

cause his countrymen are contending for their liberty, and, when he reaches the scene of action, vapours away his patriotism in a private boarding-school. This is the period of his life from which all his biographers seem inclined to shrink. They are unwilling that Milton should be degraded to a schoolmaster; but, since it cannot be denied that he taught boys, one finds out that he taught for nothing, and another that his motive was only zeal for the propagation of learning and virtue; and all tell what they do not know to be true, only to excuse an act which no wise man will consider as in itself disgraceful. His father was alive, his allowance was not ample, and he supplied its deficiencies by an honest and useful employment.

It is told that in the art of education he performed wonders, and a formidable list is given of the authors, Greek and Latin, that were read in Aldersgate-street by youth between ten and fifteen or sixteen years of age. Those who tell or receive these stories should consider that nobody can be taught faster than he can learn. The speed of the horseman must be limited by the power of his horse. Every man that has ever undertaken to instruct others can tell what slow advances he has been able to make, and how much patience it requires to recall vagrant inattention, to stimulate sluggish indifference, and to rectify absurd misapprehension.

The purpose of Milton, as it seems, was to teach something more solid than the common literature of schools, by reading those authors that treat of physical subjects; such as the Georgick, and astronomical treatises of the ancients. This was a scheme of improvement which seems to have busied many literary projectors of that age. Cowley, who had more means than Milton of knowing what was wanting to the embellishments of life, formed the same plan of education in his imaginary College.

But the truth is that the knowledge of external nature, and the sciences which that knowledge requires or includes, are not the great or the frequent business of the human mind. Whether we provide for action or conversation, whether we wish to be useful or pleasing, the first

requisite is the religious and moral knowledge of right
and wrong; the next is an acquaintance with the history
of mankind, and with those examples which may be said
to embody truth and prove by events the reasonableness
of opinions. Prudence and Justice are virtues and excellences of all times and of all places; we are perpetually
moralists, but we are geometricians only by chance. Our
intercourse with intellectual nature is necessary; our
speculations upon matter are voluntary and at leisure.
Physiological learning is of such rare emergence that one
man may know another half his life without being able to
estimate his skill in hydrostaticks or astronomy, but his
moral and prudential character immediately appears.

Those authors, therefore, are to be read at schools that
supply most axioms of prudence, most principles of moral
truth, and most materials for conversation; and these purposes are best served by poets, orators, and historians.

Let me not be censured for this digression as pedantick
or paradoxical, for if I have Milton against me I have
Socrates on my side. It was his labour to turn philosophy
from the study of nature to speculations upon life, but the
innovators whom I oppose are turning off attention from
life to nature. They seem to think that we are placed
here to watch the growth of plants, or the motions of the
stars. Socrates was rather of opinion that what we had
to learn was, how to do good and avoid evil.

Ὅττι τοι ἐν μεγάροισι κακόν τ᾽ ἀγαθόν τε τέτυκται.

Of institutions we may judge by their effects. From this
wonder-working academy I do not know that there ever
proceeded any man very eminent for knowledge; its only
genuine product, I believe, is a small *History of Poetry*,
written in Latin by his nephew Philips, of which perhaps
none of my readers has ever heard.

Life of Milton

Lycidas, L'Allegro, Il Penseroso

One of the poems on which much praise has been
bestowed is *Lycidas*; of which the diction is harsh, the
rhymes uncertain, and the numbers unpleasing. What

beauty there is we must therefore seek in the sentiments and images. It is not to be considered as the effusion of real passion; for passion runs not after remote allusions and obscure opinions. Passion plucks no berries from the myrtle and ivy, nor calls upon Arethuse and Mincius, nor tells of 'rough satyrs and fauns with cloven heel.' Where there is leisure for fiction there is little grief.

In this poem there is no nature, for there is no truth; there is no art, for there is nothing new. Its form is that of a pastoral, easy, vulgar, and therefore disgusting: whatever images it can supply are long ago exhausted; and its inherent improbability always forces dissatisfaction on the mind. When Cowley tells of Hervey that they studied together, it is easy to suppose how much he must miss the companion of his labours and the partner of his discoveries; but what image of tenderness can be excited by these lines!

'We drove a field, and both together heard
What time the grey fly winds her sultry horn,
Battening our flocks with the fresh dews of night.'

We know that they never drove a field, and that they had no flocks to batten; and though it be allowed that the representation may be allegorical, the true meaning is so uncertain and remote that it is never sought because it cannot be known when it is found.

Among the flocks and copses and flowers appear the heathen deities, Jove and Phœbus, Neptune and Æolus, with a long train of mythological imagery, such as a College easily supplies. Nothing can less display knowledge or less exercise invention than to tell how a shepherd has lost his companion and must now feed his flocks alone, without any judge of his skill in piping; and how one god asks another god what is become of Lycidas, and how neither god can tell. He who thus grieves will excite no sympathy; he who thus praises will confer no honour.

This poem has yet a grosser fault. With these trifling fictions are mingled the most awful and sacred truths, such as ought never to be polluted with such irreverent combinations. The shepherd likewise is now a feeder of sheep, and afterwards an ecclesiastical pastor, a super-intendent of a Christian flock. Such equivocations are always unskilful; but here they are indecent, and at least approach to impiety, of which, however, I believe the writer not to have been conscious.

Such is the power of reputation justly acquired that its blaze drives away the eye from nice examination. Surely no man could have fancied that he read *Lycidas* with pleasure had he not known its author.

Of the two pieces, *L'Allegro* and *Il Penseroso*, I believe opinion is uniform; every man that reads them, reads them with pleasure. The author's design is not, what Theobald has remarked, merely to shew how objects derived their colours from the mind, by representing the operation of the same things upon the gay and the melancholy temper, or upon the same man as he is differently disposed; but rather how, among the successive variety of appearances, every disposition of mind takes hold on those by which it may be gratified.

Life of Milton

Paradise Lost: *Milton's Powers*

He had considered creation in its whole extent, and his descriptions are therefore learned. He had accustomed his imagination to unrestrained indulgence, and his con-ceptions therefore were extensive. The characteristick quality of his poem is sublimity. He sometimes descends to the elegant, but his element is the great. He can occa-sionally invest himself with grace; but his natural port is gigantick loftiness. He can please when pleasure is required; but it is his peculiar power to astonish.

He seems to have been well acquainted with his own genius, and to know what it was that Nature had bes-towed upon him more bountifully than upon others; the power of displaying the vast, illuminating the splendid, enforcing the awful, darkening the gloomy, and aggravat-ing the dreadful: he therefore chose a subject on which too much could not be said, on which he might tire his fancy without the censure of extravagance.

The appearances of nature and the occurrences of life did not satiate his appetite of greatness. To paint things as they are requires a minute attention, and employs the memory rather than the fancy. Milton's delight was to sport in the wide regions of possibility; reality was a scene too narrow for his mind. He sent his faculties out upon discovery, into worlds where only imagination can travel, and delighted to form new modes of existence, and furnish sentiment and action to superior beings, to trace the counsels of hell, or accompany the choirs of heaven.

Life of Milton

Paradise Lost: *Its Weaknesses*

But original deficience cannot be supplied. The want of human interest is always felt. *Paradise Lost* is one of the books which the reader admires and lays down, and forgets to take up again. None ever wished it longer than it is. Its perusal is a duty rather than a pleasure. We read Milton for instruction, retire harassed and overburdened, and look elsewhere for recreation; we desert our master, and seek for companions.

Life of Milton

The Highest Praise

The highest praise of genius is original invention. Milton cannot be said to have contrived the structure of an epick poem, and therefore owes reverence to that vigour and amplitude of mind to which all generations must be indebted for the art of poetical narration, for the texture of the fable, the variation of incidents, the interposition of dialogue, and all the stratagems that surprise and enchain attention. But of all the borrowers from Homer Milton is perhaps the least indebted. He was naturally a thinker for himself, confident of his own abilities and disdainful of help or hindrance; he did not refuse admission to the thoughts or images of his predecessors, but he did not seek them. From his contemporaries he neither courted nor received support; there is in his writings

travelled the beaten road, but the bye-paths of literature; not only to have taken general surveys, but to have examined particulars with minute inspection.

If the French boast the learning of Rabelais, we need not be afraid of confronting them with Butler.

But the most valuable parts of his performance are those which retired study and native wit cannot supply. He that merely makes a book from books may be useful, but can scarcely be great. Butler had not suffered life to glide beside him unseen or unobserved. He had watched with great diligence the operations of human nature and traced the effects of opinion, humour, interest, and passion. From such remarks proceeded that great number of sententious distichs which have passed into conversation, and are added as proverbial axioms to the general stock of practical knowledge.

Life of Butler

Roscommon: An Academy of Letters

He now busied his mind with literary projects, and formed the plan of a society for refining our language, and fixing its standard; 'in imitation,' says Fenton, 'of those learned and polite societies with which he had been acquainted abroad.' In this design his friend Dryden is said to have assisted him.

The same design, it is well known, was revived by Dr. Swift in the ministry of Oxford; but it has never since been publickly mentioned, though at that time great expectations were formed, by some, of its establishment and its effects. Such a society might perhaps without much difficulty be collected; but that it would produce what is expected from it may be doubted.

The Italian academy seems to have obtained its end. The language was refined, and so fixed that it has changed but little. The French academy thought that they refined their language, and doubtless thought rightly: but the event has not shewn that they fixed it; for the French of the present time is very different from that of the last century.

In this country an academy could be expected to do but little. If an academician's place were profitable it would be given by interest; if attendance were gratuitous it would be rarely paid, and no man would endure the least disgust. Unanimity is impossible, and debate would separate the assembly.

But suppose the philological decree made and promulgated, what would be its authority? In absolute governments there is sometimes a general reverence paid to all that has the sanction of power and the countenance of greatness. How little this is the state of our country needs not to be told. We live in an age in which it is a kind of publick sport to refuse all respect that cannot be enforced. The edicts of an English academy would probably be read by many, only that they might be sure to disobey them.

That our language is in perpetual danger of corruption cannot be denied; but what prevention can be found? The present manners of the nation would deride authority, and therefore nothing is left but that every writer should criticise himself.

Life of Roscommon

Waller: Poetical Devotion

It has been the frequent lamentation of good men that verse has been too little applied to the purposes of worship, and many attempts have been made to animate devotion by pious poetry; that they have very seldom attained their end is sufficiently known, and it may not be improper to enquire why they have miscarried.

Let no pious ear be offended if I advance, in opposition to many authorities, that poetical devotion cannot often please. The doctrines of religion may indeed be defended in a didactick poem, and he who has the happy power of arguing in verse will not lose it because his subject is sacred. A poet may describe the beauty and the grandeur of Nature, the flowers of the Spring, and the harvests of Autumn, the vicissitudes of the Tide, and the revolutions of the Sky, and praise the Maker for his works in lines which no reader shall lay aside. The subject of the disputation is not piety, but the motives to piety; that of the description is not God, but the works of God.

Contemplative piety, or the intercourse between God and the human soul, cannot be poetical. Man admitted to implore the mercy of his Creator and plead the merits of his Redeemer is already in a higher state than poetry can confer.

The essence of poetry is invention; such invention as, by producing something unexpected, surprises and delights. The topicks of devotion are few, and being few are universally known; but, few as they are, they can be made no more; they can receive no grace from novelty of sentiment, and very little from novelty of expression.

Poetry pleases by exhibiting an idea more grateful to the mind than things themselves afford. This effect proceeds from the display of those parts of nature which attract, and the concealment of those which repel, the imagination: but religion must be shewn as it is; suppression and addition equally corrupt it, and such as it is, it is known already.

From poetry the reader justly expects, and from good poetry always obtains, the enlargement of his comprehension and elevation of his fancy; but this is rarely to be hoped by Christians from metrical devotion. Whatever is great, desirable, or tremendous, is comprised in the name of the Supreme Being. Omnipotence cannot be exalted; Infinity cannot be amplified; Perfection cannot be improved.

The employments of pious meditation are Faith, Thanksgiving, Repentance, and Supplication. Faith, invariably uniform, cannot be invested by fancy with decorations. Thanksgiving, the most joyful of all holy effusions, yet addressed to a Being without passions, is confined to a few modes, and is to be felt rather than expressed. Repentance, trembling in the presence of the judge, is not at leisure for cadences and epithets. Supplication of man to man may diffuse itself through many topicks of persuasion, but supplication to God can only cry for mercy.

Of sentiments purely religious, it will be found that the most simple expression is the most sublime. Poetry loses its lustre and its power, because it is applied to the decoration of something more excellent than itself. All that pious verse can do is to help the memory and delight the ear, and for these purposes it may be very useful; but it supplies nothing to the mind. The ideas of Christian Theology are too simple for eloquence, too sacred for fiction, and too majestick for ornament; to recommend them by tropes and figures is to magnify by a concave mirror the sidereal hemisphere.

Life of Waller

Dryden: his Conversion

Soon after the accession of king James, when the design of reconciling the nation to the church of Rome became apparent, and the religion of the court gave the only efficacious title to its favours, Dryden declared himself a convert to popery. This at any other time might have passed with little censure. Sir Kenelm Digby embraced popery; the two Rainolds reciprocally converted one another; and Chillingworth himself was a while so entangled in the wilds of controversy as to retire for quiet to an infallible church. If men of argument and study can find such difficulties or such motives, as may either unite them to the church of Rome or detain them in uncertainty, there can be no wonder that a man, who perhaps never enquired why he was a protestant, should by an artful and experienced disputant be made a papist, overborne by the sudden violence of new and unexpected arguments, or deceived by a representation which shews only the doubts on one part and only the evidence on the other.

That conversion will always be suspected that apparently concurs with interest. He that never finds his error till it hinders his progress towards wealth or honour will not be thought to love Truth only for herself. Yet it may easily happen that information may come at a commodious time; and as truth and interest are not by

any fatal necessity at variance, that one may by accident
introduce the other. When opinions are struggling into
popularity the arguments by which they are opposed or
defended become more known; and he that changes his
profession would perhaps have changed it before, with
the like opportunities of instruction. This was then the
state of popery; every artifice was used to shew it in its
fairest form: and it must be owned to be a religion of
external appearance sufficiently attractive.

It is natural to hope that a comprehensive is likewise an
elevated soul, and that whoever is wise is also honest. I
am willing to believe that Dryden, having employed his
mind, active as it was, upon different studies, and filled
it, capacious as it was, with other materials, came unprovided to the controversy, and wanted rather skill to
discover the right than virtue to maintain it. But en-
quiries into the heart are not for man; we must now leave
him to his Judge.

Life of Dryden

Dryden: Dramatic Immorality

Congreve represents him as ready to advise and instruct; but there is reason to believe that his communication was rather useful than entertaining. He declares of
himself that he was saturnine, and not one of those whose
spritely sayings diverted company; and one of his cen-
surers makes him say,

'Nor wine nor love could ever see me gay;
To writing bred, I knew not what to say.'

There are men whose powers operate only at leisure
and in retirement, and whose intellectual vigour deserts
them in conversation; whom merriment confuses, and
objection disconcerts; whose bashfulness restrains their
exertion, and suffers them not to speak till the time of
speaking is past; or whose attention to their own character
makes them unwilling to utter at hazard what has not
been considered, and cannot be recalled.

Of Dryden's sluggishness in conversation it is vain to

search or to guess the cause. He certainly wanted neither
sentiments nor language; his intellectual treasures were
great, though they were locked up from his own use.
'His thoughts,' when he wrote, 'flowed in upon him so
fast, that his only care was which to chuse, and which
to reject.' Such rapidity of composition naturally promises a flow of talk, yet we must be content to believe
what an enemy says of him, when he likewise says it of
himself. But whatever was his character as a companion,
it appears that he lived in familiarity with the highest
persons of his time. It is related by Carte of the duke of
Ormond that he used often to pass a night with Dryden,
and those with whom Dryden consorted: who they were
Carte has not told; but certainly the convivial table at
which Ormond sat was not surrounded with a plebeian
society. He was indeed reproached with boasting of his
familiarity with the great; and Horace will support him
in the opinion that to please superiors is not the lowest
kind of merit.

The merit of pleasing must, however, be estimated by
the means. Favour is not always gained by good actions
or laudable qualities. Caresses and preferments are often
bestowed on the auxiliaries of vice, the procurers of
pleasure, or the flatterers of vanity. Dryden has never
been charged with any personal agency unworthy of a
good character: he abetted vice and vanity only with his
pen. One of his enemies has accused him of lewdness in
his conversation; but if accusation without proof be
credited, who shall be innocent?

His works afford too many examples of dissolute licentiousness and abject adulation; but they were probably,
like his merriment, artificial and constrained—the effects
of study and meditation, and his trade rather than his
pleasure.

Of the mind that can trade in corruption, and can
deliberately pollute itself with ideal wickedness for the
sake of spreading the contagion in society, I wish not to
conceal or excuse the depravity.—Such degradation of
the dignity of genius, such abuse of superlative abilities,
cannot be contemplated but with grief and indignation.

What consolation can be had Dryden has afforded, by living to repent, and to testify his repentance.

Of dramatick immorality he did not want examples among his predecessors, or companions among his contemporaries; but in the meanness and servility of hyperbolical adulation I know not whether, since the days in which the Roman emperors were deified, he has been ever equalled, except by Afra Behn in an address to Eleanor Gwyn. When once he has undertaken the task of praise he no longer retains shame in himself, nor supposes it in his patron. As many odoriferous bodies are observed to diffuse perfumes from year to year without sensible diminution of bulk or weight, he appears never to have impoverished his mint of flattery by his expences, however lavish. He had all forms of excellence, intellectual and moral, combined in his mind, with endless variation; and when he had scattered on the hero of the day the golden shower of wit and virtue, he had ready for him, whom he wished to court on the morrow, new wit and virtue with another stamp. Of this kind of meanness he never seems to decline the practice, or lament the necessity: he considers the great as entitled to encomiastick homage, and brings praise rather as a tribute than a gift, more delighted with the fertility of his invention than mortified by the prostitution of his judgement. It is indeed not certain that on these occasions his judgement much rebelled against his interest. There are minds which easily sink into submission, that look on grandeur with undistinguishing reverence, and discover no defect where there is elevation of rank and affluence of riches.

Life of Dryden

Dryden: Criticism

Criticism, either didactick or defensive, occupies almost all his prose, except those pages which he has devoted to his patrons; but none of his prefaces were ever thought tedious. They have not the formality of a settled style, in which the first half of the sentence betrays the other. The clauses are never balanced, nor the periods modelled; every word seems to drop by chance, though it falls into its proper place. Nothing is cold or languid; the whole is airy, animated, and vigorous: what is little is gay; what is great is splendid. He may be thought to mention himself too frequently; but while he forces himself upon our esteem, we cannot refuse him to stand high in his own. Every thing is excused by the play of images and the spriteliness of expression. Though all is easy, nothing is feeble; though all seems careless, there is nothing harsh; and though since his earlier works more than a century has passed they have nothing yet uncouth or obsolete.

He who writes much will not easily escape a manner, such a recurrence of particular modes as may be easily noted. Dryden is always 'another and the same'; he does not exhibit a second time the same elegances in the same form, nor appears to have any art other than that of expressing with clearness what he thinks with vigour. His style could not easily be imitated, either seriously or ludicrously; for, being always equable and always varied, it has no prominent or discriminative characters. The beauty who is totally free from disproportion of parts and features cannot be ridiculed by an overcharged resemblance.

From his prose however Dryden derives only his accidental and secondary praise; the veneration with which his name is pronounced by every cultivator of English literature is paid to him as he refined the language, improved the sentiments, and tuned the numbers of English Poetry.

After about half a century of forced thoughts and rugged metre some advances towards nature and harmony had been already made by Waller and Denham; they had shewn that long discourses in rhyme grew more pleasing when they were broken into couplets, and that verse consisted not only in the number but the arrangement of syllables.

But though they did much, who can deny that they left much to do? Their works were not many, nor were their minds of very ample comprehension. More examples of more modes of composition were necessary for the establishment of regularity, and the introduction of propriety in word and thought.

Every language of a learned nation necessarily divides itself into diction scholastick and popular, grave and familiar, elegant and gross; and from a nice distinction of these different parts arises a great part of the beauty of style. But if we except a few minds, the favourites of nature, to whom their own original rectitude was in the place of rules, this delicacy of selection was little known to our authors: our speech lay before them in a heap of confusion, and every man took for every purpose what chance might offer him.

There was therefore before the time of Dryden no poetical diction: no system of words at once refined from the grossness of domestick use and free from the harshness of terms appropriated to particular arts. Words too familiar or too remote defeat the purpose of a poet. From those sounds which we hear on small or on coarse occasions, we do not easily receive strong impressions or delightful images; and words to which we are nearly strangers, whenever they occur, draw that attention on themselves which they should transmit to things.

Those happy combinations of words which distinguish poetry from prose had been rarely attempted; we had few elegances or flowers of speech: the roses had not yet been plucked from the bramble or different colours had not been joined to enliven one another.

It may be doubted whether Waller and Denham could have over-borne the prejudices which had long prevailed, and which even then were sheltered by the protection of Cowley. The new versification, as it was called, may be considered as owing its establishment to Dryden; from whose time it is apparent that English poetry has had no tendency to relapse to its former savageness.

Life of Dryden

Dryden's Virgil

Not long afterwards he undertook perhaps the most arduous work of its kind, a translation of Virgil, for which

he had shewn how well he was qualified by his version of
the *Pollio,* and two episodes, one of Nisus and Euryalus,
the other of Mezentius and Lausus.

In the comparison of Homer and Virgil the discriminative excellence of Homer is elevation and comprehension
of thought, and that of Virgil is grace and splendor of
diction. The beauties of Homer are therefore difficult to
be lost, and those of Virgil difficult to be retained. The
massy trunk of sentiment is safe by its solidity, but the
blossoms of elocution easily drop away. The author,
having the choice of his own images, selects those which
he can best adorn; the translator must at all hazards
follow his original, and express thoughts which perhaps
he would not have chosen. When to this primary difficulty is added the inconvenience of a language so much
inferior in harmony to the Latin, it cannot be expected
that they who read the *Georgick* and the *Eneid* should be
much delighted with any version.

All these obstacles Dryden saw, and all these he determined to encounter. The expectation of his work was
undoubtedly great; the nation considered its honour as
interested in the event. One gave him the different editions
of his author, and another helped him in the subordinate
parts. The arguments of the several books were given
him by Addison.

The hopes of the publick were not disappointed.
He produced, says Pope, 'the most noble and spirited
translation that I know in any language.' It certainly
excelled whatever had appeared in English, and appears
to have satisfied his friends, and, for the most part, to
have silenced his enemies. Milbourne, indeed, a clergyman, attacked it; but his outrages seem to be the ebullitions of a mind agitated by stronger resentment than
bad poetry can excite, and previously resolved not to be
pleased.

Life of Dryden

Dryden: his Violence of Wit

Next to argument, his delight was in wild and daring
sallies of sentiment, in the irregular and excentrick

violence of wit. He delighted to tread upon the brink of
meaning, where light and darkness begin to mingle; to
approach the precipice of absurdity, and hover over the
abyss of unideal vacancy. This inclination sometimes
produced nonsense, which he knew, as

> 'Move swiftly, sun, and fly a lover's pace,
> Leave weeks and months behind thee in thy race.'

> 'Amariel flies . . .
> To guard thee from the demons of the air;
> My flaming sword above them to display,
> All keen, and ground upon the edge of day.'

And sometimes it issued in absurdities, of which perhaps
he was not conscious:

> 'Then we upon our orb's last verge shall go,
> And see the ocean leaning on the sky;
> From thence our rolling neighbours we shall know,
> And on the lunar world securely pry.'

These lines have no meaning; but may we not say, in
imitation of Cowley on another book

> ''Tis so like *sense* 'twill serve the turn as well'?
> *Life of Dryden*

Edmund Smith: Character of
Gilbert Walmsley

Of Gilbert Walmsley, thus presented to my mind, let me
indulge myself in the remembrance. I knew him very
early; he was one of the first friends that literature procured me, and I hope that at least my gratitude made me
worthy of his notice.

He was of an advanced age, and I was only not a boy;
yet he never received my notions with contempt. He was
a Whig, with all the virulence and malevolence of his
party; yet difference of opinion did not keep us apart.
I honoured him, and he endured me.

He had mingled with the gay world without exemption from its vices or its follies, but had never neglected
the cultivation of his mind; his belief of Revelation was

unshaken; his learning preserved his principles: he grew
first regular, and then pious.

His studies had been so various that I am not able to
name a man of equal knowledge. His acquaintance with
books was great; and what he did not immediately know
he could at least tell where to find. Such was his amplitude of learning and such his copiousness of communication that it may be doubted whether a day now passes in
which I have not some advantage from his friendship.

At this man's table I enjoyed many chearful and instructive hours, with companions such as are not often
found: with one who has lengthened and one who has
gladdened life; with Dr. James, whose skill in physick
will be long remembered; and with David Garrick, whom
I hoped to have gratified with this character of our common friend: but what are the hopes of man! I am disappointed by that stroke of death, which has eclipsed the
gaiety of nations and impoverished the publick stock of
harmless pleasure.

Life of Smith

Charles Montagu, Earl of Halifax: The Ethics of Dedication

He was, as Pope says, 'fed with dedications'; for Tickell
affirms that no dedicator was unrewarded. To charge all
unmerited praise with the guilt of flattery, and to suppose
that the encomiast always knows and feels the falsehood
of his assertions, is surely to discover great ignorance of
human nature and human life. In determinations de-
pending not on rules, but on experience and comparison,
judgement is always in some degree subject to affection.
Very near to admiration is the wish to admire.

Every man willingly gives value to the praise which he
receives, and considers the sentence passed in his favour
as the sentence of discernment. We admire in a friend
that understanding that selected us for confidence; we
admire more in a patron that judgement which, instead
of scattering bounty indiscriminately, directed it to us;
and, if the patron be an author, those performances

which gratitude forbids us to blame, affection will easily dispose us to exalt.

To these prejudices, hardly culpable, interest adds a power always operating, though not always, because not willingly, perceived. The modesty of praise wears gradually away; and perhaps the pride of patronage may be in time so increased that modest praise will no longer please.

Life of Halifax

1781

Rowe's Lucan

The version of Lucan is one of the greatest productions of English poetry; for there is perhaps none that so completely exhibits the genius and spirit of the original. Lucan is distinguished by a kind of dictatorial or philosophic dignity, rather, as Quintilian observes, declamatory than poetical; full of ambitious morality and pointed sentences, comprised in vigorous and animated lines. This character Rowe has very diligently and successfully preserved. His versification, which is such as his contemporaries practised without any attempt at innovation or improvement, seldom wants either melody or force. His author's sense is sometimes a little diluted by additional infusions, and sometimes weakened by too much expansion. But such faults are to be expected in all translations, from the constraint of measures and dissimilitude of languages. The *Pharsalia* of Rowe deserves more notice than it obtains, and as it is more read will be more esteemed.

Life of Rowe

Addison: Tatler *and* Spectator

To *The Tatler* in about two months succeeded *The Spectator*, a series of essays of the same kind, but written with less levity, upon a more regular plan, and published daily. Such an undertaking shewed the writers not to distrust their own copiousness of materials or facility of composition, and their performance justified their confidence. They found, however, in their progress many auxiliaries. To attempt a single paper was no terrifying labour: many pieces were offered, and many were received.

Addison had enough of the zeal of party, but Steele had at that time almost nothing else. *The Spectator* in one of the first papers shewed the political tenets of its authors; but a resolution was soon taken of courting general approbation by general topicks, and subjects on which faction had produced no diversity of sentiments; such as literature, morality, and familiar life. To this practice they adhered with very few deviations. The ardour of Steele once broke out in praise of Marlborough; and when Dr. Fleetwood prefixed to some sermons a preface overflowing with whiggish opinions, that it might be read by the Queen, it was reprinted in *The Spectator*.

To teach the minuter decencies and inferior duties, to regulate the practice of daily conversation, to correct those depravities which are rather ridiculous than criminal, and remove those grievances which, if they produce no lasting calamities, impress hourly vexation, was first attempted by Casa in his book of *Manners*, and Castiglione in his *Courtier*, two books yet celebrated in Italy for purity and elegance, and which, if they are now less read, are neglected only because they have effected that reformation which their authors intended, and their precepts now are no longer wanted. Their usefulness to the age in which they were written is sufficiently attested by the translations which almost all the nations of Europe were in haste to obtain.

This species of instruction was continued and perhaps advanced by the French; among whom La Bruyère's *Manners of the Age*, though, as Boileau remarked, it is written without connection, certainly deserves great praise for liveliness of description and justness of observation.

Before *The Tatler* and *Spectator*, if the writers for the theatre are excepted, England had no masters of common life. No writers had yet undertaken to reform either the savageness of neglect or the impertinence of civility; to shew when to speak, or to be silent; how to refuse, or how to comply. We had many books to teach us our more important duties, and to settle opinions in philosophy or politicks; but an *Arbiter elegantiarum*, a judge of propriety, was yet wanting, who should survey the track of daily conversation and free it from thorns and prickles, which teaze the passer, though they do not wound him.

For this purpose nothing is so proper as the frequent publication of short papers, which we read not as study but amusement. If the subject be slight, the treatise likewise is short. The busy may find time, and the idle may find patience.

This mode of conveying cheap and easy knowledge began among us in the Civil War, when it was much the interest of either party to raise and fix the prejudices of the people. At that time appeared *Mercurius Aulicus*, *Mercurius Rusticus*, and *Mercurius Civicus*. It is said that when any title grew popular it was stolen by the antagonist, who by this stratagem conveyed his notions to those who would not have received him had he not worn the appearance of a friend. The tumult of those unhappy days left scarcely any man leisure to treasure up occasional compositions; and so much were they neglected that a complete collection is nowhere to be found.

These *Mercuries* were succeeded by L'Estrange's *Observator*, and that by Lesley's *Rehearsal*, and perhaps by others; but hitherto nothing had been conveyed to the people in this commodious manner but controversy relating to the Church or State: of which they taught many to talk, whom they could not teach to judge.

It has been suggested that the Royal Society was instituted soon after the Restoration to divert the attention of the people from publick discontent. *The Tatler* and *Spectator* had the same tendency; they were published at a time when two parties, loud, restless, and violent, each with plausible declarations, and each perhaps without any distinct termination of its views, were agitating the nation: to minds heated with political contest they supplied cooler and more inoffensive reflections; and it is

said by Addison, in a subsequent work, that they had a
perceptible influence upon the conversation of that time,
and taught the frolick and the gay to unite merriment
with decency—an effect which they can never wholly
lose, while they continue to be among the first books by
which both sexes are initiated in the elegances of knowledge.

Life of Addison

Addison: His Character

Of his habits, or external manners, nothing is so often
mentioned as that timorous or sullen taciturnity, which
his friends called modesty by too mild a name. Steele
mentions with great tenderness 'that remarkable bashfulness, which is a cloak that hides and muffles merit';
and tells us that 'his abilities were covered only by
modesty, which doubles the beauties which are seen,
and gives credit and esteem to all that are concealed.'
Chesterfield affirms that 'Addison was the most timorous
and awkward man that he ever saw.' And Addison,
speaking of his own deficience in conversation, used to
say of himself, that, with respect to intellectual wealth,
'he could draw bills for a thousand pounds, though he
had not a guinea in his pocket.'

That he wanted current coin for ready payment, and
by that want was often obstructed and distressed; that
he was oppressed by an improper and ungraceful timidity, every testimony concurs to prove: but Chesterfield's representation is doubtless hyperbolical. That man
cannot be supposed very unexpert in the arts of conversation and practice of life, who, without fortune or alliance,
by his usefulness and dexterity became secretary of state,
and who died at forty-seven, after having not only stood
long in the highest rank of wit and literature, but filled
one of the most important offices of state.

The time in which he lived had reason to lament his
obstinacy of silence, 'for he was,' says Steele, 'above all
men in that talent called humour, and enjoyed it in such
perfection that I have often reflected, after a night spent

with him apart from all the world, that I had had the
pleasure of conversing with an intimate acquaintance of
Terence and Catullus, who had all their wit and nature,
heightened with humour more exquisite and delightful
than any other man ever possessed.' This is the fondness
of a friend; let us hear what is told us by a rival. 'Addison's conversation,' says Pope, 'had something in it more
charming than I have found in any other man. But this
was only when familiar: before strangers, or perhaps a
single stranger, he preserved his dignity by a stiff silence.'

This modesty was by no means inconsistent with a very
high opinion of his own merit. He demanded to be the
first name in modern wit; and, with Steele to echo him,
used to depreciate Dryden, whom Pope and Congreve
defended against them. There is no reason to doubt that
he suffered too much pain from the prevalence of Pope's
poetical reputation; nor is it without strong reason suspected that by some disingenuous acts he endeavoured to
obstruct it: Pope was not the only man whom he insidiously
injured, though the only man of whom he could be
afraid.

His own powers were such as might have satisfied him
with conscious excellence. Of very extensive learning he
has indeed given no proofs. He seems to have had small
acquaintance with the sciences, and to have read little
except Latin and French; but of the Latin poets his
Dialogues on Medals shew that he had perused the works
with great diligence and skill. The abundance of his
own mind left him little need of adventitious sentiments:
his wit always could suggest what the occasion demanded.
He had read with critical eyes the important volume of
human life, and knew the heart of man from the depths
of stratagem to the surface of affection.

Life of Addison

Addison: Virtue and Religion

If any judgement be made from his books of his moral
character nothing will be found but purity and excellence. Knowledge of mankind indeed, less extensive than

that of Addison, will shew that to write and to live are
very different. Many who praise virtue, do no more than
praise it. Yet it is reasonable to believe that Addison's
professions and practice were at no great variance, since,
amidst that storm of faction in which most of his life
was passed, though his station made him conspicuous
and his activity made him formidable, the character
given him by his friends was never contradicted by his
enemies: of those with whom interest or opinion united
him he had not only the esteem, but the kindness; and
of others, whom the violence of opposition drove against
him, though he might lose the love, he retained the
reverence.

It is justly observed by Tickell that he employed wit on
the side of virtue and religion. He not only made the
proper use of wit himself, but taught it to others; and
from his time it has been generally subservient to the
cause of reason and of truth. He has dissipated the prejudice that had long connected gaiety with vice, and
easiness of manners with laxity of principles. He has restored virtue to its dignity, and taught innocence not to
be ashamed. This is an elevation of literary character,
'above all Greek, above all Roman fame.' No greater
felicity can genius attain than that of having purified
intellectual pleasure, separated mirth from indecency,
and wit from licentiousness; of having taught a succession of writers to bring elegance and gaiety to the aid of
goodness; and, if I may use expressions yet more awful,
of having 'turned many to righteousness.'

Life of Addison

1779

Addison: The Campaign

No passage in *The Campaign* has been more often mentioned than the simile of the Angel, which is said in *The
Tatler* to be 'one of the noblest thoughts that ever entered
into the heart of man,' and is therefore worthy of attentive consideration. Let it be first enquired whether it be

a simile. A poetical simile is the discovery of likeness
between two actions in their general nature dissimilar,
or of causes terminating by different operations in some
resemblance of effect. But the mention of another like
consequence from a like cause, or of a like performance
by a like agency, is not a simile, but an exemplification.
It is not a simile to say that the Thames waters fields as
the Po waters fields; or that as Hecla vomits flames in
Iceland, so Ætna vomits flames in Sicily. When Horace
says of Pindar, that he pours his violence and rapidity
of verse, as a river swoln with rain rushes from the
mountain; or of himself, that his genius wanders in
quest of poetical decorations, as the bee wanders to
collect honey; he, in either case, produces a simile: the
mind is impressed with the resemblance of things generally
unlike, as unlike as intellect and body. But if Pindar had
been described as writing with the copiousness and grandeur of Homer, or Horace had told that he reviewed and
finished his own poetry with the same care as Isocrates
polished his orations, instead of similitude he would have
exhibited almost identity: he would have given the same
portraits with different names. In the poem now examined,
when the English are represented as gaining a fortified
pass by repetition of attack and perseverance of resolution, their obstinacy of courage and vigour of onset is well
illustrated by the sea that breaks with incessant battery
the dikes of Holland. This is a simile: but when Addison,
having celebrated the beauty of Marlborough's person,
tells us that 'Achilles thus was formed with every grace,'
here is no simile, but a mere exemplification. A simile
may be compared to lines converging at a point and is
more excellent as the lines approach from greater distance: an exemplification may be considered as two
parallel lines which run on together without approxima-
tion, never far separated, and never joined.

Marlborough is so like the angel in the poem that the
action of both is almost the same, and performed by both
in the same manner. Marlborough 'teaches the battle to
rage'; the angel 'directs the storm': Marlborough is
'unmoved in peaceful thought'; the angel is 'calm and

serene': Marlborough stands 'unmoved amidst the shock
of hosts'; the angel rides 'calm in the whirlwind.' The
lines on Marlborough are just and noble; but the simile
gives almost the same images a second time.

Life of Addison

1781
Addison: His Style

As a describer of life and manners he must be allowed to
stand perhaps the first of the first rank. His humour,
which, as Steele observes, is peculiar to himself, is so
happily diffused as to give the grace of novelty to domestick scenes and daily occurrences. He never 'outsteps the
modesty of nature,' nor raises merriment or wonder by
the violation of truth. His figures neither divert by distor-
tion, nor amaze by aggravation. He copies life with so
much fidelity that he can be hardly said to invent; yet
his exhibitions have an air so much original that it is
difficult to suppose them not merely the product of
imagination.

As a teacher of wisdom he may be confidently followed.
His religion has nothing in it enthusiastick or superstitious: he appears neither weakly credulous nor wantonly sceptical; his morality is neither dangerously lax,
nor impracticably rigid. All the enchantment of fancy
and all the cogency of argument are employed to recommend to the reader his real interest, the care of pleasing
the Author of his being. Truth is shewn sometimes as
the phantom of a vision, sometimes appears half-veiled
in an allegory, sometimes attracts regard in the robes of
fancy, and sometimes steps forth in the confidence of
reason. She wears a thousand dresses, and in all is pleasing.

'Mille habet ornatus, mille decenter habet.'

His prose is the model of the middle style; on grave
subjects not formal, on light occasions not groveling;
pure without scrupulosity, and exact without apparent
elaboration; always equable, and always easy, without
glowing words or pointed sentences. Addison never de-

viates from his track to snatch a grace; he seeks no ambitious ornaments, and tries no hazardous innovations. His
page is always luminous, but never blazes in unexpected
splendour.

It was apparently his principal endeavour to avoid all
harshness and severity of diction; he is therefore sometimes verbose in his transitions and connections, and
sometimes descends too much to the language of conversation: yet if his language had been less idiomatical it
might have lost somewhat of its genuine Anglicism. What
he attempted, he performed; he is never feeble, and he
did not wish to be energetick; he is never rapid, and he
never stagnates. His sentences have neither studied amplitude, nor affected brevity; his periods, though not
diligently rounded, are voluble and easy. Whoever wishes
to attain an English style, familiar but not coarse, and
elegant but not ostentatious, must give his days and nights
to the volumes of Addison.

Life of Addison

Prior

Solomon is the work to which he entrusted the protection
of his name, and which he expected succeeding ages to
regard with veneration. His affection was natural; it had
undoubtedly been written with great labour, and who is
willing to think that he has been labouring in vain? He
had infused into it much knowledge and much thought;
had often polished it to elegance, often dignified it with
splendour, and sometimes heightened it to sublimity: he
perceived in it many excellences, and did not discover
that it wanted that without which all others are of small
avail, the power of engaging attention and alluring
curiosity.

Tediousness is the most fatal of all faults; negligences
or errors are single and local, but tediousness pervades
the whole; other faults are censured and forgotten, but
the power of tediousness propagates itself. He that is
weary the first hour is more weary the second; as bodies
forced into motion, contrary to their tendency, pass more

and more slowly through every successive interval of space.

Unhappily this pernicious failure is that which an author is least able to discover. We are seldom tiresome to ourselves; and the act of composition fills and delights the mind with change of language and succession of images: every couplet when produced is new, and novelty is the great source of pleasure. Perhaps no man ever thought a line superfluous when he first wrote it, or contracted his work till his ebullitions of invention had subsided. And even if he should controul his desire of immediate renown, and keep his work *nine years*[1] unpublished, he will be still the author, and still in danger of deceiving himself; and if he consults his friends, he will probably find men who have more kindness than judgement, or more fear to offend than desire to instruct.

Life of Prior

Congreve

Congreve has merit of the highest kind: he is an original writer, who borrowed neither the models of his plot nor the manner of his dialogue. Of his plays I cannot speak distinctly, for since I inspected them many years have passed; but what remains upon my memory is that his characters are commonly fictitious and artificial, with very little of nature, and not much of life. He formed a peculiar idea of comick excellence, which he supposed to consist in gay remarks and unexpected answers; but that which he endeavoured, he seldom failed of performing. His scenes exhibit not much of humour, imagery, or passion; his personages are a kind of intellectual gladiators; every sentence is to ward or strike; the contest of smartness is never intermitted; his wit is a meteor playing to and fro with alternate coruscations. His comedies have therefore, in some degree, the operation of tragedies: they surprise rather than divert, and raise admiration oftener than merriment. But they are the works of a mind replete with images, and quick in combination.

Life of Congreve

[1 The Horatian maxim, *nonum prematur in annum.*]

Gay

Of this performance, when it was printed, the reception was different according to the different opinion of its readers. Swift commended it for the excellence of its morality, as a piece 'that placed all kinds of vice in the strongest and most odious light'; but others, and among them Dr. Herring, afterwards archbishop of Canterbury, censured it as giving encouragement not only to vice but to crimes, by making a highwayman the hero, and dismissing him at last unpunished. It has been even said, that after the exhibition of *The Beggar's Opera* the gangs of robbers were evidently multiplied.

Both these decisions are surely exaggerated. The play, like many others, was plainly written only to divert, without any moral purpose, and is therefore not likely to do good; nor can it be conceived, without more speculation than life requires or admits, to be productive of much evil. Highwaymen and housebreakers seldom frequent the play-house or mingle in any elegant diversion; nor is it possible for any one to imagine that he may rob with safety because he sees Macheath reprieved upon the stage.

Life of Gay

Tickell

He was now intimately united to Mr. Addison, who, when he went into Ireland as secretary to the lord Sunderland, took him thither, and employed him in publick business; and when (1717) afterwards he rose to be secretary of state made him under-secretary. Their friendship seems to have continued without abatement; for when Addison died he left him the charge of publishing his works, with a solemn recommendation to the patronage of Craggs.

To these works he prefixed an elegy on the author, which could owe none of its beauties to the assistance which might be suspected to have strengthened or embellished his earlier compositions; but neither he nor Addison ever produced nobler lines than are contained in the third and fourth paragraphs, nor is a more sublime or more elegant funeral poem to be found in the whole compass of English literature.

Life of Tickell

Swift

Beauty and the power of pleasing, the greatest external advantages that woman can desire or possess, were fatal to the unfortunate Stella. The man whom she had the misfortune to love was, as Delany observes, fond of singularity, and desirous to make a mode of happiness for himself, different from the general course of things and order of Providence. From the time of her arrival in Ireland he seems resolved to keep her in his power, and therefore hindered a match sufficiently advantageous by accumulating unreasonable demands and prescribing conditions that could not be performed. While she was at her own disposal he did not consider his possession as secure; resentment, ambition, or caprice might separate them; he was therefore resolved to make 'assurance double sure,' and to appropriate her by a private marriage, to which he had annexed the expectation of all the pleasures of perfect friendship, without the uneasiness of conjugal restraint. But with this state poor Stella was not satisfied; she never was treated as a wife, and to the world she had the appearance of a mistress. She lived sullenly on, in hope that in time he would own and receive her; but the time did not come till the change of his manners and depravation of his mind made her tell him, when he offered to acknowledge her, that 'it was too late.' She then gave up herself to sorrowful resentment, and died under the tyranny of him by whom she was in the highest degree loved and honoured.

Life of Swift

Pope

Friendship

Of his social qualities, if an estimate be made from his Letters, an opinion too favourable cannot easily be formed; they exhibit a perpetual and unclouded effulgence of general benevolence and particular fondness. There is nothing but liberality, gratitude, constancy, and tenderness. It has been so long said as to be commonly believed that the true characters of men may be found in their letters, and that he who writes to his friend lays his heart open before him. But the truth is that such were simple friendships of the *Golden Age*, and are now the friendships only of children. Very few can boast of hearts which they dare lay open to themselves, and of which, by whatever accident exposed, they do not shun a distinct and continued view; and certainly what we hide from ourselves we do not shew to our friends. There is, indeed, no transaction which offers stronger temptations to fallacy and sophistication than epistolary intercourse. In the eagerness of conversation the first emotions of the mind often burst out before they are considered; in the tumult of business interest and passion have their genuine effect; but a friendly letter is a calm and deliberate performance in the cool of leisure, in the stillness of solitude, and surely no man sits down to depreciate by design his own character.

Friendship has no tendency to secure veracity, for by whom can a man so much wish to be thought better than he is as by him whose kindness he desires to gain or keep? Even in writing to the world there is less constraint: the author is not confronted with his reader, and takes his chance of approbation among the different dispositions of mankind; but a letter is addressed to a single mind of which the prejudices and partialities are known, and must therefore please, if not by favouring them, by forbearing to oppose them.

To charge those favourable representations, which men give of their own minds, with the guilt of hypocritical falsehood, would shew more severity than knowledge. The writer commonly believes himself. Almost every man's thoughts, while they are general, are right; and most hearts are pure while temptation is away. It is easy to awaken generous sentiments in privacy; to despise death when there is no danger; to glow with benevolence when there is nothing to be given. While such ideas are formed they are felt, and self-love does not suspect the gleam of virtue to be the meteor of fancy.

Life of Pope

Dryden and Pope

Of genius, that power which constitutes a poet; that quality without which judgement is cold and knowledge is inert; that energy which collects, combines, amplifies, and animates—the superiority must, with some hesitation, be allowed to Dryden. It is not to be inferred that of this poetical vigour Pope had only a little, because Dryden had more, for every other writer since Milton must give place to Pope; and even of Dryden it must be said that if he has brighter paragraphs, he has not better poems. Dryden's performances were always hasty, either excited by some external occasion, or extorted by domestick necessity; he composed without consideration, and published without correction. What his mind could supply at call, or gather in one excursion, was all that he sought, and all that he gave. The dilatory caution of Pope enabled him to condense his sentiments, to multiply his images, and to accumulate all that study might produce, or chance might supply. If the flights of Dryden therefore are higher, Pope continues longer on the wing. If of Dryden's fire the blaze is brighter, of Pope's the heat is more regular and constant. Dryden often surpasses expectation, and Pope never falls below it. Dryden is read with frequent astonishment, and Pope with perpetual delight.

This parallel will, I hope, when it is well considered, be found just; and if the reader should suspect me, as I suspect myself, of some partial fondness for the memory of Dryden, let him not too hastily condemn me; for meditation and enquiry may, perhaps, shew him the reasonableness of my determination.

Life of Pope

Pope's Homer

The train of my disquisition has now conducted me to
that poetical wonder, the translation of the *Iliad*; a performance which no age or nation can pretend to equal.
To the Greeks translation was almost unknown; it was
totally unknown to the inhabitants of Greece. They had
no recourse to the Barbarians for poetical beauties, but
sought for every thing in Homer, where, indeed, there is
but little which they might not find.

The Italians have been very diligent translators; but
I can hear of no version, unless perhaps Anguillara's
Ovid may be excepted, which is read with eagerness. The
Iliad of Salvini every reader may discover to be puncti-
liously exact; but it seems to be the work of a linguist skilfully pedantick, and his countrymen, the proper judges of
its power to please, reject it with disgust.

Their predecessors the Romans have left some speci-
mens of translation behind them, and that employment
must have had some credit in which Tully and Germa-
nicus engaged; but unless we suppose, what is perhaps
true, that the plays of Terence were versions of Menander,
nothing translated seems ever to have risen to high
reputation. The French, in the meridian hour of their
learning, were very laudably industrious to enrich their
own language with the wisdom of the ancients; but found
themselves reduced, by whatever necessity, to turn the
Greek and Roman poetry into prose. Whoever could read
an author could translate him. From such rivals little
can be feared.

The chief help of Pope in this arduous undertaking was
drawn from the versions of Dryden. Virgil had borrowed
much of his imagery from Homer, and part of the debt
was now paid by his translator. Pope searched the pages
of Dryden for happy combinations of heroick diction,
but it will not be denied that he added much to what he
found. He cultivated our language with so much diligence and art that he has left in his *Homer* a treasure of
poetical elegances to posterity. His version may be said
to have tuned the English tongue, for since its appearance

no writer, however deficient in other powers, has wanted melody. Such a series of lines so elaborately corrected and so sweetly modulated took possession of the publick ear; the vulgar was enamoured of the poem, and the learned wondered at the translation.

But in the most general applause discordant voices will always be heard. It has been objected by some, who wish to be numbered among the sons of learning, that Pope's version of Homer is not Homerical; that it exhibits no resemblance of the original and characteristick manner of the Father of Poetry, as it wants his awful simplicity, his artless grandeur, his unaffected majesty. This cannot be totally denied, but it must be remembered that 'necessitas quod cogit defendit,' that may be lawfully done which cannot be forborne. Time and place will always enforce regard. In estimating this translation consideration must be had of the nature of our language, the form of our metre, and, above all, of the change which two thousand years have made in the modes of life and the habits of thought. Virgil wrote in a language of the same general fabrick with that of Homer, in verses of the same measure, and in an age nearer to Homer's time by eighteen hundred years; yet he found even then the state of the world so much altered, and the demand for elegance so much increased, that mere nature would be endured no longer; and perhaps, in the multitude of borrowed passages, very few can be shewn which he has not embellished.

There is a time when nations emerging from barbarity, and falling into regular subordination, gain leisure to grow wise, and feel the shame of ignorance and the craving pain of unsatisfied curiosity. To this hunger of the mind plain sense is grateful; that which fills the void removes uneasiness, and to be free from pain for a while is pleasure; but repletion generates fastidiousness, a saturated intellect soon becomes luxurious, and knowledge finds no willing reception till it is recommended by artificial diction. Thus it will be found in the progress of learning that in all nations the first writers are simple, and that every age improves in elegance. One refinement always makes way for another, and what was expedient to Virgil was necessary to Pope.

I suppose many readers of the English *Iliad*, when they have been touched with some unexpected beauty of the lighter kind, have tried to enjoy it in the original, where, alas! it was not to be found. Homer doubtless owes to his translator many Ovidian graces not exactly suitable to his character; but to have added can be no great crime if nothing be taken away. Elegance is surely to be desired if it be not gained at the expence of dignity. A hero would wish to be loved as well as to be reverenced.

To a thousand cavils one answer is sufficient; the purpose of a writer is to be read, and the criticism which would destroy the power of pleasing must be blown aside. Pope wrote for his own age and his own nation: he knew that it was necessary to colour the images and point the sentiments of his author; he therefore made him graceful, but lost him some of his sublimity.

Life of Pope

The Dunciad

Of *The Dunciad* the hint is confessedly taken from Dryden's *Mac Flecknoe*, but the plan is so enlarged and diversified as justly to claim the praise of an original, and affords perhaps the best specimen that has yet appeared of personal satire ludicrously pompous.

That the design was moral, whatever the author might tell either his readers or himself, I am not convinced. The first motive was the desire of revenging the contempt with which Theobald had treated his *Shakespeare*, and regaining the honour which he had lost, by crushing his opponent. Theobald was not of bulk enough to fill a poem, and therefore it was necessary to find other enemies with other names, at whose expence he might divert the publick.

In this design there was petulance and malignity enough; but I cannot think it very criminal. An author places himself uncalled before the tribunal of criticism, and solicits fame at the hazard of disgrace. Dulness or deformity are not culpable in themselves, but may be very justly reproached when they pretend to the honour of wit or the influence of beauty. If bad writers were to pass without reprehension what should restrain them? 'impune diem consumpserit ingens Telephus'; and upon bad writers only will censure have much effect. The satire which brought Theobald and Moore into contempt, dropped impotent from Bentley, like the javelin of Priam.

All truth is valuable, and satirical criticism may be considered as useful when it rectifies error and improves judgement: he that refines the publick taste is a publick benefactor.

The beauties of this poem are well known; its chief fault is the grossness of its images. Pope and Swift had an unnatural delight in ideas physically impure, such as every other tongue utters with unwillingness, and of which every ear shrinks from the mention.

But even this fault, offensive as it is, may be forgiven for the excellence of other passages; such as the formation and dissolution of Moore, the account of the Traveller, the misfortune of the Florist, and the crowded thoughts and stately numbers which dignify the concluding paragraph.

Life of Pope

The Essay on Man

The *Essay on Man* was a work of great labour and long consideration, but certainly not the happiest of Pope's performances. The subject is perhaps not very proper for poetry, and the poet was not sufficiently master of his subject, metaphysical morality was to him a new study, he was proud of his acquisitions, and, supposing himself master of great secrets, was in haste to teach what he had not learned. Thus he tells us, in the first Epistle, that from the nature of the Supreme Being may be deduced an order of beings such as mankind, because Infinite Excellence can do only what is best. He finds out that these beings must be 'somewhere,' and that 'all the question is whether man be in a wrong place.' Surely if, according to the poet's Leibnitian reasoning, we may infer that man ought to be only because he is, we may allow that his place is the right place, because he has it. Supreme Wisdom is not less infallible in disposing than in creating. But what is meant by 'somewhere' and 'place' and 'wrong place' it had been vain to ask Pope, who probably had never asked himself.

Having exalted himself into the chair of wisdom he tells us much that every man knows, and much that he does not know himself; that we see but little, and that the order of the universe is beyond our comprehension, an opinion not very uncommon; and that there is a chain of subordinate beings 'from infinite to nothing,' of which himself and his readers are equally ignorant. But he gives us one comfort which, without his help, he supposes unattainable, in the position 'that though we are fools, yet God is wise.'

This *Essay* affords an egregious instance of the predominance of genius, the dazzling splendour of imagery, and the seductive powers of eloquence. Never were penury of knowledge and vulgarity of sentiment so happily disguised. The reader feels his mind full, though he learns nothing; and when he meets it in its new array no longer knows the talk of his mother and his nurse. When these wonder-working sounds sink into sense and the doctrine of the *Essay*, disrobed of its ornaments, is left to the powers of its naked excellence, what shall we discover? That we are, in comparison with our Creator, very weak and ignorant; that we do not uphold the chain of existence; and that we could not make one another with more skill than we are made. We may learn yet more: that the arts of human life were copied from the instinctive operations of other animals; that if the world be made for man, it may be said that man was made for geese. To these profound principles of natural knowledge are added some moral instructions equally new: that self-interest well understood will produce social concord; that men are mutual gainers by mutual benefits; that evil is sometimes balanced by good; that human advantages are unstable and fallacious, of uncertain duration and doubtful effect; that our true honour is not to have a great part, but to act it well; that virtue only is our own; and that happiness is always in our power.

Surely a man of no very comprehensive search may venture to say that he has heard all this before, but it was never till now recommended by such a blaze of embellishment or such sweetness of melody. The vigorous contraction of some thoughts, the luxuriant amplification of others, the incidental illustrations, and sometimes the dignity, sometimes the softness of the verses, enchain philosophy, suspend criticism, and oppress judgement by overpowering pleasure.

Life of Pope

Pope: his Versification

Poetical expression includes sound as well as meaning. 'Musick,' says Dryden, 'is inarticulate poetry'; among the excellences of Pope, therefore, must be mentioned the melody of his metre. By perusing the works of Dryden he discovered the most perfect fabrick of English verse, and habituated himself to that only which he found the best; in consequence of which restraint his poetry has been censured as too uniformly musical, and as glutting the ear with unvaried sweetness. I suspect this objection to be the cant of those who judge by principles rather than perception; and who would even themselves have less pleasure in his works if he had tried to relieve attention by studied discords, or affected to break his lines and vary his pauses.

But though he was thus careful of his versification he did not oppress his powers with superfluous rigour. He seems to have thought with Boileau that the practice of writing might be refined till the difficulty should overbalance the advantage. The construction of his language is not always strictly grammatical; with those rhymes which prescription had conjoined he contented himself, without regard to Swift's remonstrances, though there was no striking consonance; nor was he very careful to vary his terminations or to refuse admission at a small distance to the same rhymes.

Life of Pope

Was Pope a Poet?

After all this it is surely superfluous to answer the question that has once been asked, Whether Pope was a poet? otherwise than by asking in return, If Pope be not a poet, where is poetry to be found? To circumscribe poetry by a definition will only shew the narrowness of the definer, though a definition which shall exclude Pope will not easily be made. Let us look round upon the present time, and back upon the past; let us enquire to whom the voice of mankind has decreed the wreath of poetry; let their productions be examined and their claims stated, and the pretensions of Pope will be no more disputed. Had he given the world only his version the name of poet must have been allowed him; if the writer of the *Iliad* were to class his successors he would assign a very high place to his translator, without requiring any other evidence of genius.

Life of Pope

Thomson

As a writer he is entitled to one praise of the highest kind: his mode of thinking and of expressing his thoughts is original. His blank verse is no more the blank verse of Milton or of any other poet than the rhymes of Prior are the rhymes of Cowley. His numbers, his pauses, his diction, are of his own growth, without transcription, without imitation. He thinks in a peculiar train, and he thinks always as a man of genius; he looks round on Nature and on Life with the eye which Nature bestows only on a poet, the eye that distinguishes in every thing presented to its view whatever there is on which imagination can delight to be detained, and with a mind that at once comprehends the vast, and attends to the minute. The reader of *The Seasons* wonders that he never saw before what Thomson shews him, and that he never yet has felt what Thomson impresses.

His is one of the works in which blank verse seems properly used; Thomson's wide expansion of general views, and his enumeration of circumstantial varieties, would have been obstructed and embarrassed by the frequent intersections of the sense, which are the necessary effects of rhyme.

His descriptions of extended scenes and general effects bring before us the whole magnificence of Nature, whether pleasing or dreadful. The gaiety of *Spring*, the splendour of *Summer*, the tranquillity of *Autumn*, and the horror of *Winter*, take in their turns possession of the mind. The poet leads us through the appearances of things as they are successively varied by the vicissitudes of the year, and imparts to us so much of his own enthusiasm that our thoughts expand with his imagery and kindle with his sentiments. Nor is the naturalist without his part in the entertainment; for he is assisted to recollect and to combine, to arrange his discoveries, and to amplify the sphere of his contemplation.

Life of Thomson

Watts

By his natural temper he was quick of resentment, but by his established and habitual practice he was gentle, modest, and inoffensive. His tenderness appeared in his attention to children and to the poor. To the poor, while he lived in the family of his friend, he allowed the third part of his annual revenue, though the whole was not a hundred a year; and for children he condescended to lay aside the scholar, the philosopher, and the wit, to write little poems of devotion and systems of instruction, adapted to their wants and capacities, from the dawn of reason through its gradations of advance in the morning of life. Every man acquainted with the common principles of human action will look with veneration on the writer who is at one time combating Locke, and at another making a catechism for children in their fourth year. A voluntary descent from the dignity of science is perhaps the hardest lesson that humility can teach.

Life of Watts

Ambrose Philips: Pastorals

The work which had procured him the first notice from the publick was his six *Pastorals*, which, flattering the imagination with Arcadian scenes, probably found many readers, and might have long passed as a pleasing amusement had they not been unhappily too much commended.

The rustick Poems of Theocritus were so highly valued by the Greeks and Romans that they attracted the imitation of Virgil, whose *Eclogues* seem to have been considered as precluding all attempts of the same kind; for no shepherds were taught to sing by any succeeding poet till Nemesian and Calphurnius ventured their feeble efforts in the lower age of Latin literature.

At the revival of learning in Italy it was soon discovered that a dialogue of imaginary swains might be composed with little difficulty, because the conversation of shepherds excludes profound or refined sentiment; and, for images and descriptions, Satyrs and Fauns, and Naiads and Dryads, were always within call, and woods and meadows, and hills and rivers, supplied variety of matter, which, having a natural power to sooth the mind, did not quickly cloy it.

Petrarch entertained the learned men of his age with the novelty of modern Pastorals in Latin. Being not ignorant of Greek, and finding nothing in the word *Eclogue* of rural meaning, he supposed it to be corrupted by the copiers, and therefore called his own productions *Æglogues*, by which he meant to express the talk of goatherds, though it will mean only the talk of goats. This new name was adopted by subsequent writers, and amongst others by our Spenser.

More than a century afterwards (1498) Mantuan published his *Bucolicks* with such success that they were soon dignified by Badius with a comment, and, as Scaliger complained, received into schools and taught as classical; his complaint was vain, and the practice, however injudicious, spread far and continued long. Mantuan was read, at least in some of the inferior schools of this kingdom, to the beginning of the present century. The speakers of Mantuan carried their disquisitions beyond the country, to censure the corruptions of the Church; and from him Spenser learned to employ his swains on topicks of controversy.

The Italians soon transferred Pastoral Poetry into their own language: Sannazaro wrote *Arcadia* in prose and verse; Tasso and Guarini wrote *Favole Boscareccie*, or Sylvan Dramas; and all nations of Europe filled volumes with Thyrsis and Damon, and Thestylis and Phyllis.

Life of Ambrose Philips

Ambrose Philips: his Pindar

In his translations from Pindar he found the art of reaching all the obscurity of the Theban bard, however he may fall below his sublimity: he will be allowed, if he has less fire, to have more smoke.

Life of Ambrose Philips

Shenstone

Now was excited his delight in rural pleasures, and his ambition of rural elegance; he began from this time to point his prospects, to diversify his surface, to entangle his walks, and to wind his waters, which he did with such judgement and such fancy as made his little domain the envy of the great and the admiration of the skilful: a place to be visited by travellers, and copied by designers. Whether to plant a walk in undulating curves, and to place a bench at every turn where there is an object to catch the view; to make water run where it will be heard, and to stagnate where it will be seen; to leave intervals where the eye will be pleased, and to thicken the plantation where there is something to be hidden, demands any great powers of mind, I will not enquire: perhaps a sullen and surly speculator may think such performances rather the sport than the business of human reason. But it must be at least confessed that to embellish the form of nature is an innocent amusement, and some praise must be allowed by the most supercilious observer to him who does best what such multitudes are contending to do well.

This praise was the praise of Shenstone; but, like all other modes of felicity, it was not enjoyed without its abatements. Lyttelton was his neighbour and his rival, whose empire, spacious and opulent, looked with disdain on the *petty State* that *appeared behind it*. For a while the inhabitants of Hagley affected to tell their acquaintance of the little fellow that was trying to make himself admired; but when by degrees the Leasowes forced themselves into notice, they took care to defeat the curiosity which they could not suppress, by conducting their visitants perversely to inconvenient points of view, and introducing them at the wrong end of a walk to detect a deception; injuries of which Shenstone would heavily complain. Where there is emulation there will be vanity, and where there is vanity there will be folly.

Life of Shenstone

Young's Love of Fame

The Universal Passion is indeed a very great performance. It is said to be a series of Epigrams; but if it be it is what the author intended: his endeavour was at the production of striking distichs and pointed sentences; and his distichs have the weight of solid sentiment, and his points the sharpness of resistless truth. His characters are often selected with discernment and drawn with nicety; his illustrations are often happy and his reflections often just. His species of satire is between those of Horace and of Juvenal: he has the gaiety of Horace without his laxity of numbers, and the morality of Juvenal with greater variation of images. He plays, indeed, only on the surface of life; he never penetrates the recesses of the mind, and therefore the whole power of his poetry is exhausted by a single perusal: his conceits please only when they surprise.

Life of Young

Young's Night Thoughts

In his *Night Thoughts* he has exhibited a very wide display of original poetry, variegated with deep reflections and striking allusions, a wilderness of thought in which the fertility of fancy scatters flowers of every hue and of every odour. This is one of the few poems in which blank verse could not be changed for rhyme but with disadvantage. The wild diffusion of the sentiments and the digressive sallies of imagination would have been compressed and restrained by confinement to rhyme. The excellence of this work is not exactness, but copiousness; particular lines are not to be regarded: the power is in the whole, and in the whole there is a magnificence like that ascribed to Chinese Plantation, the magnificence of vast extent and endless diversity.

Life of Young

Akenside

Akenside is to be considered as a didactick and lyrick poet. His great work is *The Pleasures of Imagination*, a performance which, published as it was at the age of twenty-three, raised expectations that were not afterwards very amply satisfied. It has undoubtedly a just claim to very particular notice as an example of great felicity of genius and uncommon amplitude of acquisitions, of a young mind stored with images, and much exercised in combining and comparing them.

With the philosophical or religious tenets of the author I have nothing to do; my business is with his poetry. The subject is well chosen, as it includes all images that can strike or please, and thus comprises every species of poetical delight. The only difficulty is in the choice of examples and illustrations, and it is not easy in such exuberance of matter to find the middle point between penury and satiety. The parts seem artificially disposed, with sufficient coherence, so as that they cannot change their places without injury to the general design.

His images are displayed with such luxuriance of

expression that they are hidden, like Butler's Moon, by a 'Veil of Light'; they are forms fantastically lost under superfluity of dress. 'Pars minima est ipsa puella sui.' The words are multiplied till the sense is hardly perceived; attention deserts the mind and settles in the ear. The reader wanders through the gay diffusion, sometimes amazed and sometimes delighted; but after many turnings in the flowery labyrinth comes out as he went in. He remarked little, and laid hold on nothing.

To his versification justice requires that praise should not be denied. In the general fabrication of his lines he is perhaps superior to any other writer of blank verse; his flow is smooth and his pauses are musical, but the concatenation of his verses is commonly too long continued, and the full close does not recur with sufficient frequency. The sense is carried on through a long intertexture of complicated clauses, and as nothing is distinguished, nothing is remembered.

The exemption which blank verse affords from the necessity of closing the sense with the couplet, betrays luxuriant and active minds into such self-indulgence that they pile image upon image, ornament upon ornament, and are not easily persuaded to close the sense at all. Blank verse will therefore, I fear, be too often found in description exuberant, in argument loquacious, and in narration tiresome.

Life of Akenside

Gray's Odes *and* Elegy

These odes are marked by glittering accumulations of ungraceful ornaments: they strike, rather than please; the images are magnified by affectation; the language is laboured into harshness. The mind of the writer seems to work with unnatural violence. 'Double, double, toil and trouble.' He has a kind of strutting dignity, and is tall by walking on tiptoe. His art and his struggle are too visible, and there is too little appearance of ease and nature.

To say that he has no beauties would be unjust: a man like him, of great learning and great industry, could not but produce something valuable. When he pleases least, it can only be said that a good design was ill directed.

His translations of Northern and Welsh Poetry deserve praise: the imagery is preserved, perhaps often improved; but the language is unlike the language of other poets.

In the character of his *Elegy* I rejoice to concur with the common reader; for by the common sense of readers uncorrupted with literary prejudices, after all the refinements of subtilty and the dogmatism of learning, must be finally decided all claim to poetical honours. The *Church-yard* abounds with images which find a mirrour in every mind, and with sentiments to which every bosom returns an echo. The four stanzas beginning 'Yet even these bones' are to me original: I have never seen the notions in any other place; yet he that reads them here persuades himself that he has always felt them. Had Gray written often thus it had been vain to blame, and useless to praise him.

Life of Gray

Lyttelton

His last literary production was his *History of Henry the Second*, elaborated by the searches and deliberations of twenty years, and published with such anxiety as only vanity can dictate.

The story of this publication is remarkable. The whole work was printed twice over, a great part of it three times, and many sheets four or five times. The booksellers paid for the first impression; but the charges and repeated operations of the press were at the expence of the author, whose ambitious accuracy is known to have cost him at least a thousand pounds. He began to print in 1755. Three volumes appeared in 1764, a second edition of them in 1767, a third edition in 1768, and the conclusion in 1771.

Andrew Reid, a man not without considerable abilities, and not unacquainted with letters or with life, undertook to persuade Lyttelton, as he had persuaded himself, that he was master of the secret of punctuation; and, as fear begets credulity, he was employed, I know not at what price, to point the pages of *Henry the Second*. The book was at last pointed and printed, and sent into the world. Lyttelton took money for his copy, of which, when he had paid the Pointer, he probably gave the rest away; for he was very liberal to the indigent.

When time brought the *History* to a third edition, Reid was either dead or discarded; and the superintendence of typography and punctuation was committed to a man originally a combmaker, but then known by the style of Doctor. Something uncommon was probably expected, and something uncommon was at last done; for to the Doctor's edition is appended, what the world had hardly seen before, a list of errors in nineteen pages.

Life of Lyttelton

1779
Ireland and the Irish

He, I know not why, shewed upon all occasions an aversion to go to Ireland, where I proposed to him that we should make a tour. JOHNSON. 'It is the last place where I should wish to travel.' BOSWELL. 'Should you not like to see Dublin, Sir?' JOHNSON. 'No, Sir! Dublin is only a worse capital.' BOSWELL. 'Is not the Giant's-Causeway worth seeing?' JOHNSON. 'Worth seeing? yes; but not worth going to see.'

Yet he had a kindness for the Irish nation, and thus generously expressed himself to a gentleman from that country, on the subject of an UNION which artful Politicians have often had in view—'Do not make an union with us, Sir. We should unite with you, only to rob you. We should have robbed the Scotch, if they had had any thing of which we could have robbed them.'

Boswell, Life

To Mrs. Garrick

Dr Johnson sends most respectful condolence to Mrs Garrick, and wishes that any endeavour of his could enable her support a loss which the world cannot repair.

1780

Long-expected One and Twenty

Long-expected one and twenty
Ling'ring year at last is flown,
Pomp and Pleasure, Pride and Plenty
Great Sir John, are all your own.

Loosen'd from the Minor's tether,
Free to mortgage or to sell,
Wild as wind, and light as feather
Bid the slaves of thrift farewell.

Call the Bettys, Kates, and Jennys
Ev'ry name that laughs at Care,
Lavish of your Grandsire's guineas,
Show the Spirit of an heir.

All that prey on vice and folly
Joy to see their quarry fly,
Here the Gamester light and jolly
There the Lender grave and sly.

Wealth, Sir John, was made to wander,
Let it wander as it will;
See the Jocky, see the Pander,
Bid them come, and take their fill.

When the bonny Blade carouses,
Pockets full, and Spirits high,
What are acres? What are houses?
Only dirt, or wet or dry.

If the Guardian or the Mother
Tell the woes of wilful waste,
Scorn their counsel and their pother,
You can hang or drown at last.

To Thomas Lawrence

Dear Sir,
    At a time when all your friends ought to shew their
kindness, and with a character which ought to make all

that know you, your friends, you may wonder that you have yet heard nothing of me.

I have been hindred by a vexatious and incessant cough, for which within these ten days, I have bled once, fasted four or five times, taken physick five times and opiates I think six. This day it seems to remit.

The loss, dear Sir, which you have lately suffered, I felt many years ago; and know therefore how much has been taken from you, and how little help can be had from consolation. He that outlives a wife whom he has long loved, sees himself disjoined from the only mind that had the same hopes, and fears, and interest; from the only companion with whom he has shared much good or evil, and with whom he could set his mind at liberty to retrace the past, or anticipate the future. The continuity of being is lacerated. The settled course of sentiment and action is stopped, and life stands suspended and motionless till it is driven by external causes into a new channel. But the time of suspense is dreadful.

Our first recourse in this distresful solitude, is perhaps for want of habitual piety, to a gloomy acquiescence in necessity. Of two mortal Beings one must lose the other. But surely there is a higher and a better comfort to be drawn from the consideration of that Providence which watches over all; and belief that the living and the dead are equally in the hands of God, who will re-unite those whom he has separated, or who sees that it is best not to re-unite them.

I am Dear Sir Your most affectionate and Most humble Servant,

Jan. 20. 1780. Sam: Johnson.

To Mrs. Thrale at Bath

Dear Madam

Of the petticoat Government I had never heard. Of the Shakespeare I was once told by Miss Laurence, and that is all that I know of it. I have not seen nor heard of any body that has seen the wonders. You may be sure I should tell you any thing that would gratify your curiosity, and furnish you for your present expences of intellectual entertainment. But of this dramatick discovery I know nothing.

I cannot see but my Master may with stuborn regularity totally recover. But surely though the invasion has been repelled from life, the waste it has made will require some time and much attention to repair it. You must not grow weary of watching him, and he must not grow impatient of being watched.

Pray, of what wonders do you tell me? You make verses, and they are read in publick, and I know nothing about them. This very crime, I think, broke the link of amity between Richardson and Miss Mulso, after a tenderness and confidence of many years. However you must do a great deal more before I leave you for Lucan or Montague, or any other charmer, if any other charmer would have me.

I am sorry that you have seen Mrs. Walmesley.[1] She and her husband exhibited two very different appearances of human Nature.—But busy, busy, still art thou.—He prevailed on himself to treat her with great tenderness, and to show how little sense will serve for common life, she has passed through the world with less imprudence than any of her Family.

Sir Philip's bill has been rejected by the Lords. There was, I think, nothing to be objected to it, but the time at which it was proposed, and the intention with which it was projected. It was fair in itself, but tended to weaken government, when it is too weak already.

Scrase is doubtless pleased with the payment of your debts. My Master, if I understand him right, talked of putting the other eight thousand pounds into the Bank, till it could be commodiously received. I wish it were done. I love that money should be in the Bank, and I love that debt should be discharged.

. . . has no business about you, but to be taught. Poor Biron's tenderness is very affecting. Comfort her all you can. I sincerely wish her well. Declining life is a very awful scene.

[¹ Johnson dropped a negative?]

Please to tell Mr. Thrale, that I think I grow rather less, and that I was last week almost dizzy with vacuity. I repeat my challenge to alternate diet, and doubt not but both of us by adhering to it may live more at ease, and a much longer time.

Though I am going to dine with Lady Craven,
I am Madam Your most humble servant
London. 18 April. 1780   Sam: Johnson.

1781
To Warren Hastings

Sir

Amidst the importance and multiplicity of affairs in which your great Office engages you I take the liberty of recalling your attention for a moment to literature, and will not prolong the interruption by an apology which your character makes needless.

Mr. Hoole, a Gentleman long known and long esteemed in the India house, after having translated Tasso, has undertaken Ariosto. How well he is qualified for his undertaking he has already shown. He is desirous Sir, of your favour in promoting his proposals, and flatters me by supposing that my testimony may advance his interest.

It is a new thing for a Clerk of the India house to translate Poets. It is new for a Governour of Bengal to patronise Learning. That he may find his ingenuity rewarded, and that Learning may flourish under your protection is the wish of, Sir,

Jan. 29. 1781   Your most humble servant,
Sam: Johnson

Henry Thrale's Death

Dearest Madam

Of your injunctions to pray for You and write to You I hope to leave neither unobserved, and I hope to find You willing in a short time to alleviate your trouble by some other exercise of the mind. I am not without my part of the calamity. No death since that of my Wife has ever oppressed me like this. But let us remember that we are in the hands of him who knows when to give, and when to take away, who will look upon us with mercy through all our variations of existence, and who invites us to call on him in the day of trouble. Call upon him in this great revolution of life, and call with confidence. You will then find comfort for the past, and support for the future. He that has given You happiness in marriage to a degree of which without personal knowledge, I should have thought the description fabulous, can give You another mode of happiness as a Mother, and at last the happiness of losing all temporal cares in the thoughts of an eternity in heaven.

I do not exhort You to reason yourself into tranquillity, we must first pray, and then labour, first implore the Blessing of God and then employ those means which he puts into our hands. Cultivated ground has few weeds, a mind occupied by lawful business, has little room for useless regret.

We read the will to day, but I will not fill my first letter with any other account than that with all my zeal for your advantage I am satisfied, and that the other executors, more used to consider property than I, commended it for wisdom and equity. Yet why should I not tell You that You have five hundred pounds for your immediate expences, and two thousand pounds a year with both the houses and all the goods?

Let us pray for one another, that the time whether long or short that shall yet be granted us, may be well spent, and that when this life which at the longest is very short, shall come to an end, a better may begin which shall never end.

I am, Dearest Madam, Your most humble Servant
London Apr. 5. 1781   Sam: Johnson

1782

Robert Levet's Death

Condemn'd to hope's delusive mine,
   As on we toil from day to day,
By sudden blasts, or slow decline,
   Our social comforts drop away.

Well tried through many a varying year,
   See Levet to the grave descend;
Officious, innocent, sincere,
   Of ev'ry friendless name the friend.

Yet still he fills affection's eye,
   Obscurely wise, and coarsely kind;
Nor, letter'd arrogance, deny
   Thy praise to merit unrefin'd.

When fainting nature call'd for aid,
   And hov'ring death prepar'd the blow,
His vig'rous remedy display'd
   The power of art without the show.

In misery's darkest caverns known,
   His useful care was ever nigh,
Where hopeless anguish pour'd his groan,
   And lonely want retir'd to die.

No summons mock'd by chill delay,
   No petty gain disdain'd by pride,
The modest wants of ev'ry day
   The toil of ev'ry day supplied.

His virtues walk'd their narrow round,
   Nor made a pause, nor left a void;
And sure th' Eternal Master found
   The single talent well employ'd.

The busy day, the peaceful night,
   Unfelt, uncounted, glided by;
His frame was firm, his powers were bright,
   Tho' now his eightieth year was nigh.

> Then with no throbbing fiery pain,
>   No cold gradations of decay,
> Death broke at once the vital chain,
>   And free'd his soul the nearest way.

To James Boswell: Evils of Poverty

Dear Sir

The earnestness and tenderness of your letter is such, that I cannot think myself shewing it more respect than it claims by sitting down to answer it the day on which I received it.

This year has afflicted me with a very irksome and severe disorder. My respiration has been much impeded, and much blood has been taken away. I am now harrassed by a catarrhous cough, from which my purpose is to seek relief by change of air; and I am, therefore, preparing to go to Oxford.

Whether I did right in dissuading you from coming to London this spring, I will not determine. You have not lost much by missing my company; I have scarcely been well for a single week. I might have received comfort from your kindness; but you would have seen me afflicted, and, perhaps, found me peevish. Whatever might have been your pleasure or mine, I know not how I could have honestly advised you to come hither with borrowed money. Do not accustom yourself to consider debt only as an inconvenience; you will find it a calamity. Poverty takes away so many means of doing good, and produces so much inability to resist evil, both natural and moral, that it is by all virtuous means to be avoided. Consider a man whose fortune is very narrow; whatever be his rank by birth, or whatever his reputation by intellectual excellence, what good can he do? or what evil can he prevent? That he cannot help the needy is evident, he has nothing to spare. But, perhaps, his advice or admonition may be useful. His poverty will destroy his influence: many more can find that he is poor, than that he is wise; and few will reverence the understanding that is of so little advantage to its owner. I say nothing of the personal

wretchedness of a debtor, which, however, has passed
into a proverb. Of riches, it is not necessary to write the
praise. Let it, however, be remembered, that he who
has money to spare, has it always in his power to benefit
others; and of such power a good man must always be
desirous.

I am pleased with your account of Easter. We shall
meet, I hope, in autumn, both well and both chearful;
and part each the better for the other's company.

Make my compliments to Mrs. Boswell, and to the
young charmers. I am, &c.

London, June 3, 1782.   Sam. Johnson.

1783

Crabbe's Village

Soon after this time I had an opportunity of seeing, by
means of one of his friends, a proof that his talents, as well
as his obliging service to authours, were ready as ever.
He had revised *The Village*, an admirable poem, by the
Reverend Mr. Crabbe. Its sentiments as to the false
notions of rustick happiness and rustick virtue were quite
congenial with his own; and he had taken the trouble not
only to suggest slight corrections and variations, but to
furnish some lines, when he thought he could give the
writer's meaning better than in the words of the manuscript.

I shall give an instance, marking the original by
Roman, and Johnson's substitution in Italick characters:

'In fairer scenes, where peaceful pleasures spring,
Tityrus, the pride of Mantuan swains, might sing:
But charmed by him, or smitten with his views,
Shall modern poets court the Mantuan muse?
From Truth and Nature shall we widely stray,
Where Fancy leads, or Virgil led the way?'
'*On Mincio's banks, in Cæsar's bounteous reign,*
If Tityrus found the golden age again,

Must sleepy bards the flattering dream prolong,
Mechanick echoes of the Mantuan song?
From Truth and Nature shall we widely stray,
Where Virgil, not where Fancy, leads the way?'

Here we find Johnson's poetical and critical powers un-
diminished. I must, however, observe, that the aids he
gave to this poem, as to *The Traveller* and *Deserted Village*
of Goldsmith, were so small as by no means to impair
the distinguished merit of the authour.

Boswell, *Life*

Cant

I have no minute of any interview with Johnson till
Thursday, May 15, when I find what follows:—BOSWELL.
'I wish much to be in Parliament, Sir.' JOHNSON. 'Why,
Sir, unless you come resolved to support any administration, you would be the worse for being in Parliament,
because you would be obliged to live more expensively.'
BOSWELL. 'Perhaps, Sir, I should be the less happy for
being in Parliament, I never would sell my vote, and I
should be vexed if things went wrong.' JOHNSON. 'That's
cant, Sir. It would not vex you more in the house, than
in the gallery: publick affairs vex no man.' BOSWELL.
'Have not they vexed yourself a little, Sir? Have not you
been vexed by all the turbulence of this reign, and by
that absurd vote of the House of Commons, "That the
influence of the Crown has increased, is increasing, and
ought to be diminished"?' JOHNSON. 'Sir, I have never
slept an hour less, nor eat an ounce less meat. I would
have knocked the factious dogs on the head, to be sure;
but I was not *vexed*.' BOSWELL. 'I declare, Sir, upon my
honour, I did imagine I was vexed, and took a pride in
it; but it *was*, perhaps, cant; for I own I neither ate less,
nor slept less.' JOHNSON. 'My dear friend, clear your
mind of cant. You may *talk* as other people do: you may
say to a man, "Sir, I am your most humble servant." You
are *not* his most humble servant. You may say, "These
are bad times; it is a melancholy thing to be reserved to
such times." You don't mind the times. You tell a man,

"I am sorry you had such bad weather the last day of your journey, and were so much wet." You don't care six-pence whether he is wet or dry. You may *talk* in this manner; it is a mode of talking in Society: but don't *think* foolishly.'

Boswell, Life

To Mrs. Thrale at Bath: a Paralytic Stroke

Dear Madam

I am sitting down in no chearful solitude to write a narrative which would once have affected you with tenderness and sorrow, but which you will perhaps pass over now with the careless glance of frigid indifference. For this diminution of regard however, I know not whether I ought to blame You, who may have reasons which I cannot know, and I do not blame myself who have for a great part of human life done You what good I could, and have never done you evil.

I had been disordered in the usual way, and had been relieved by the usual methods, by opium and catharticks, but had rather lessened my dose of opium.

On Monday the 16. I sat for my picture, and walked a considerable way with little inconvenience. In the afternoon and evening I felt myself light and easy, and began to plan schemes of life. Thus I went to bed, and in a short time waked and sat up as has been long my custom, when I felt a confusion and indistinctness in my head which lasted, I suppose about half a minute; I was alarmed and prayed God, that however he might afflict my body he would spare my understanding. This prayer, that I might try the integrity of my faculties I made in Latin verse. The lines were not very good, but I knew them not to be very good, I made them easily, and concluded myself to be unimpaired in my faculties.

Soon after I perceived that I had suffered a paralytick stroke, and that my Speech was taken from me. I had no pain, and so little dejection in this dreadful state that I wondered at my own apathy, and considered that perhaps death itself when it should come, would excite less horrour than seems now to attend it.

In order to rouse the vocal organs I took two drams. Wine has been celebrated for the production of eloquence; I put myself into violent motion, and, I think, repeated it. But all was vain; I then went to bed, and, strange as it may seem, I think, slept. When I saw light, it was time to contrive what I should do. Though God stopped my speech he left me my hand, I enjoyed a mercy which was not granted to my Dear Friend Laurence, who now perhaps overlooks me as I am writing and rejoices that I have what he wanted. My first note was necessarily to my servant, who came in talking, and could not immediately comprehend why he should read what I put into his hands.

I then wrote a card to Mr Allen, that I might have a discreet friend at hand to act as occasion should require. In penning this note I had some difficulty, my hand, I knew not how nor why, made wrong letters. I then wrote to Dr Taylor to come to me, and bring Dr Heberden, and I sent to Dr Brocklesby, who is my neighbour. My Physicians are very friendly and very disinterested, and give me great hopes, but you may imagine my situation. I have so far recovered my vocal powers, as to repeat the Lord's Prayer with no very imperfect articulation. My memory, I hope, yet remains as it was. But such an attack produces solicitude for the safety of every Faculty.

How this will be received by You I know not, I hope You will sympathise with me, but perhaps

> My Mistress gracious, mild, and good,
> Cries, Is he dumb? 'tis time he shou'd.

But can this be possible, I hope it cannot. I hope that what, when I could speak, I spoke of You, and to You, will be in a sober and serious hour remembred by You, and surely it cannot be remembred but with some degree of kindness. I have loved you with virtuous affection, I have honoured You with sincere Esteem. Let not all our endearment be forgotten, but let me have in this great distress your pity and your prayers. You see I yet turn to

You with my complaints as a settled and unalienable friend, do not, do not drive me from You, for I have not deserved either neglect or hatred.

To the Girls, who do not write often, for Susy has written only once, and Miss Thrale owes me a letter, I earnestly recommend as their Guardian and Friend, that They remember their Creator in the days of their Youth.

I suppose you may wish to know how my disease is treated by the physitians. They put a blister upon my back, and two from my ear to my throat, one on a side. The blister on the back has done little, and those on the throat have not risen. I bullied, and bounced, (it sticks to our last sand) and compelled the apothecary to make his salve according to the Edinburgh dispensatory, that it might adhere better. I have two on now of my own prescription. They likewise give me salt of hartshorn, which I take with no great confidence, but am satisfied that what can be done is done for me.

O God, give me comfort and confidence in Thee, forgive my sins, and if it be thy good pleasure, relieve my diseases for Jesus Christs sake, Amen.

I am almost ashamed of this querulous letter, but now it is written, let it go.

I am, Madam Your most humble servant
Bolt Court Fleet street June 19. 1783   Sam: Johnson.

To Hester ('Queeney') Thrale

Dear Madam,   London, 24 July 1783

It is long since I wrote to you, and indeed it is long since I wrote to anybody. Rochester was out of the way, and I sent no letters from that place that could be omitted. The heat was sufficient besides to produce laziness. The thermometer was, as I am told, within four degrees of the greatest heat in Jamaica.

Your account of your time gives me pleasure. Never lose the habit of reading, nor ever suffer yourself to acquiesce in total vacuity. Encourage in yourself an implacable impatience of doing nothing. He that cannot be idle, and will not be wicked, must be useful and

valuable, he must be always improving himself or benefit-
ing others. If you cannot at any particular time reconcile
yourself to any thing important, be busy upon trifles. Of
trifles the mind grows tired, and turns for its own satisfaction to something better; but if it learns to sooth itself
with the opiate of musing idleness, if it can once be content with inactivity, all the time to come is in danger of
being lost. And, I believe that life has been so dozed
away by many whom Nature had originally qualified not
only to be esteemed but admired.

If ever therefore you catch yourself contentedly and
placidly doing nothing, *sors de l'enchantement*, break away
from the snare, find your book or your needle, or snatch
the broom from the maid.

To Susannah Arabella Thral

Dear Miss

Here is a whole week, and nothing heard from your
house. Baretti said what a wicked house it would be, and
a wicked house it is. Of you however I have no complaint
to make for I owe you a letter. Still I live here by my own
self, and have had of late very bad nights, but then
I have had a pig to dinner which Mr. Perkins gave me.
Thus life is checquered.

I cannot tell you much news because I see nobody that
you know. Do you read the Tatlers? They are part of the
books which every body should read, because they are
the Sources of conversation, therefore make them part of
your library. Bickerstaff in the Tatler gives as a specimen
of familiar letters, an account of his Cat. I could tell you
as good things of Lily the white kitling, who is now at full
growth, and very well behaved, but I do not see why we
should descend below human Beings, and of one human
Being I can tell something that you will like to hear.

A Friend, whose name I will tell when your Mamma
has tried to guess it, sent to My Physician to enquire
whether this long train of ilness had brought me into any
difficulties for want of money, with an invitation to send

to him for what occasion required. I shall write this night
to thank him, having no need to borrow.

I have seen Mr. Seward since his return only once, he
gave no florid account of my Mistress's health. Tell her
that I hearken every day after a letter from her, and do
not be long before you write yourself to,

My dear, Your most humble servant
Novr 18. 1783   Sam: Johnson.

1784
To Jane Langton

My dearest Miss Jenny

I am sorry that your pretty Letter has been so long
without being answered; but when I am not pretty well,
I do not always write plain enough for young Ladies.

I am glad, my Dear, to see that you write so well, and
hope that you mind your pen, your book, and your needle,
for they are all necessary. Your books will give you knowledge, and make you respected, and your needle will
find you useful employment when you do not care to
read. When you are a little older, I hope you will be very
diligent in learning arithmetick; and above all, that
through your whole life, you will carefully say your
prayers, and read your Bible.

I am, my Dear Your most humble servant,
Bolt court, Fleetstreet. May 10. 1784.   Sam: Johnson.

To Hester ('Queeney') Thrale

My Dearest,   London, July 1, 1784
I read your letter with anguish and astonishment, such
as I never felt before. I had fondly flattered myself that
time had produced better thoughts. I can only give you
this consolation that, in my opinion, you have hitherto
done rightly. You have not left your Mother, but your
Mother has left you.

You must now be to your sisters what your Mother
ought to have been, and if I can give you any help, I hope
never to desert you. I will write to the other Guardians.

I send my kindest respects to your sisters, and exhort them to attend to your counsels, and recommend you all to the care of Him who is the Father of the fatherless.

I am, Dear Madam, Your most humble servant
Sam: Johnson

To Mrs. Piozzi at Bath: Anger and Forgiveness

Madam

If I interpret your letter right, you are ignominiously married, if it is yet undone, let us once talk together. If you have abandoned your children and your religion, God forgive your wickedness; if you have forfeited your Fame, and your country, may your folly do no further mischief.

If the last act is yet to do, I, who have loved you, esteemed you, reverenced you, and served you, I who long thought you the first of human kind, entreat that before your fate is irrevocable, I may once more see you. I was, I once was,

Madam, most truly yours.

July 2. 1784   Sam: Johnson.

I will come down if you permit it.

Dear Madam

What you have done, however I may lament it, I have no pretence to resent, as it has not been injurious to me. I therefore breathe out one sigh more of tenderness perhaps useless, but at least sincere.

I wish that God may grant you every blessing, that you may be happy in this world for its short continuance, and eternally happy in a better state. and whatever I can contribute to your happiness, I am very ready to repay for that kindness which soothed twenty years of a life radically wretched.

Do not think slightly of the advice which I now presume to offer. Prevail upon Mr. Piozzi to settle in England. You may live here with more dignity than in Italy, and with more security. Your rank will be higher, and your fortune more under your own eye. I desire not to detail all my reasons; but every argument of prudence and interest is for England, and only some phantoms of imagination seduce you to Italy.

I am afraid, however, that my counsel is vain, yet I have eased my heart by giving it.

When Queen Mary took the resolution of sheltering herself in England, the Archbishop of St. Andrew's attempting to dissuade her, attended on her journey and when they came to the irremeable stream that separated the two kingdoms, walked by her side into the water, in the middle of which he seized her bridle, and with earnestness proportioned to her danger and his own affection, pressed her to return. The Queen went forward.——If the parallel reaches thus far; may it go no further. The tears stand in my eyes.

I am going into Derbyshire, and hope to be followed by your good wishes, for I am with great affection

Your most humble servant,

London July 8. 1784   Sam: Johnson

Any letters that come for me hither, will be sent me.

Tom's Great Work

Dr. Newton, the Bishop of Bristol, having been mentioned, Johnson, recollecting the manner in which he had been censured by that Prelate, thus retaliated:—'Tom knew he should be dead before what he has said of me would appear. He durst not have printed it while he was alive.' DR. ADAMS. 'I believe his *Dissertations on the Prophecies* is his great work.' JOHNSON. 'Why, Sir, it is Tom's great work; but how far it is great, or how much of it is Tom's, are other questions. I fancy a considerable part of it was borrowed.' DR. ADAMS. 'He was a very successful man.' JOHNSON. 'I don't think so, Sir. He did not get very high. He was late in getting what he did get; and he did not get it by the best means. I believe he was a gross flatterer.'

Boswell, *Life*

To Lord Thurlow

My Lord

After a long and attentive observation of Mankind, the generosity of your Lordship's offer, excites in me no less wonder than gratitude. Bounty, so liberally bestowed if my condition made it necessary, I should gladly receive, for to such a Mind who would not be proud to own his obligations? But it has pleased God to restore me such a measure of health, that if I should now appropriate so much of a fortune destined to do good I should not escape from myself the charge of advancing a false claim. My journey to the Continent though I once thought it necessary was never much encouraged by my Physicians, and I was very desirous that your Lordship be told of it by Sir Joshua Reynolds as an event very uncertain; for if I grew much better, I should not be willing, if much worse, I should not be able, to migrate.

Your Lordship was Solicited without my knowledge, but when I was told that you were pleased to honour me with your patronage, I did not expect to hear of a refusal. Yet as I had little time to form hopes, and have not rioted in imaginary opulence, this cold reception has been scarce a disappointment; and from your Lordship's kindness I have received a benefit which only Men like You can bestow, I shall live *mihi charior* with a higher opinion of my own merit.

To Richard Brocklesby from Lichfield

Dear Sir

The day on which I received your letter I sent for castor oil, having just a stoppage in the rectum, but being afraid in such an exigency to trust too much to a medicine of which I had no experience, I took near an ounce of the oil at night and followed it with another purge in the morning, and all passed without inconvenience.

My dropsy keeps down, my breath is much obstructed, and I do not get strength, nor in any great degree lose it.

However I do not advance, and am afraid of winter. Give me what help and what hope You can.

The fate of the balloon I do not much lament to make new balloons is to repeat the jest again. We now know a method of mounting into the air, and I think, are not likely to know more. The vehicles can serve no use, till we can guide them, and they can gratify no curiosity till we mount with them to greater heights than we can reach without, till we rise above the tops of the highest mountains, which we have yet not done. We know the state of the air in all its regions to the top of Teneriffe, and therefore learn nothing from those who navigate a balloon below the clouds. The first experiment however was bold, and deserved applause and reward. But since it has been performed and its event is known, I had rather now find a medicine that can ease an asthma.

I am, Dear Sir, Your most humble Servant
Lichfield. Oct. 6. 1784   Sam: Johnson

To the Ladies at Stow-hill

Mr. Johnson sends his compliments to the Ladies at Stow-hill, of whom he would have taken a more formal leave, but that he was willing to spare a ceremony, which he hopes would have been no pleasure to them, and would have been painful to himself.

To Dr. Burney on coming home

Mr Johnson who came home last night, sends his respects to dear Doctor Burney, and all the dear Burneys little and great.
Nov. 17

To Lucy Porter: his Wife's Tomb

Dear Madam

I am very ill, and desire your prayers. I have sent Mr Green the epitaph, and a power to call on You for ten pounds.

I laid this summer a stone over Tetty in the chapel of Bromley in Kent. The Inscription is in Latin of which this is the English.

Here lie the remains of Elizabeth, descended from the ancient house of Jarvis at Peatling in Leicestershire; a Woman of beauty, elegance, ingenuity, and piety. Her first Husband was Henry Porter; her second, Samuel Johnson, who having loved her much, and lamented her long, laid this stone upon her.
She died in March. 1752.

That this is done, I thought it fit that You should know; what care will be taken of us, who can tell? May God pardon and bless us, for Jesus Christs sake. Amen.
I am, Madam, Your most humble Servant
Dec. 2. 1784   Sam: Johnson.

Johnson's Will

'IN THE NAME OF GOD. AMEN. I, SAMUEL JOHNSON, being in full possession of my faculties, but fearing this night may put an end to my life, do ordain this my last Will and Testament. I bequeath to GOD, a soul polluted with many sins, but I hope purified by JESUS CHRIST. I leave seven hundred and fifty pounds in the hands of Bennet Langton, Esq.: three hundred pounds in the hands of Mr. Barclay and Mr. Perkins, brewers; one hundred and fifty pounds in the hands of Dr. Percy, Bishop of Dromore; one thousand pounds, three *per cent.* annuities, in the publick funds; and one hundred pounds now lying by me in ready money: all these before-mentioned sums and property I leave, I say, to Sir Joshua Reynolds, Sir John Hawkins, and Dr. William Scott, of Doctors Commons, in trust, for the following uses:—That is to say, to pay to the representatives of the late William Innys, bookseller, in St. Paul's Church-yard, the sum of two hundred pounds; to Mrs. White, my female servant, one hundred pounds stock in the three *per cent.* annuities aforesaid. The rest of the aforesaid sums of money and property, together with my books, plate, and household furniture, I leave to the before-

mentioned Sir Joshua Reynolds, Sir John Hawkins, and Dr. William Scott, also in trust, to be applied, after paying my debts, to the use of Francis Barber, my man-servant, a negro, in such a manner as they shall judge most fit and available to his benefit. And I appoint the aforesaid Sir Joshua Reynolds, Sir John Hawkins, and Dr. William Scott, sole executors of this my last will and testament, hereby revoking all former wills and testaments whatever. In witness whereof I hereunto subscribe my name, and affix my seal, this eighth day of December, 1784   'SAM. JOHNSON, (L. S.)
    'Signed, sealed, published, declared, and delivered, by the said testator, as his last will and testament, in the presence of us, the word *two* being first inserted in the opposite page.

'GEORGE STRAHAN.
'JOHN DESMOULINS.'

    'By way of Codicil to my last Will and Testament, I, SAMUEL JOHNSON, give, devise, and bequeath, my messuage or tenement situate at Lichfield, in the county of Stafford, with the appurtenances, in the tenure or occupation of Mrs. Bond, of Lichfield aforesaid, or of Mr. Hinchman, her under-tenant, to my executors, in trust, to sell and dispose of the same; and the money arising from such sale I give and bequeath as follows, viz. to Thomas and Benjamin, the sons of Fisher Johnson, late of Leicester, and —— Whiting, daughter of Thomas Johnson, late of Coventry, and the grand-daughter of the said Thomas Johnson, one full and equal fourth part each; but in case there shall be more grand-daughters than one of the said Thomas Johnson, living at the time of my decease, I give and bequeath the part or share of that one to and equally between such grand-daughters. I give and beqeath to the Rev. Mr. Rogers, of Berkley, near Froom, in the county of Somerset, the sum of one hundred pounds, requesting him to apply the same towards the maintenance of Elizabeth Herne, a lunatick. I also give and bequeath to my god-children, the son and daughter of Mauritius Lowe, painter, each of them, one hundred pounds of my stock in the three *per cent.* consolidated annuities, to be applied and disposed of by and at the discretion of my Executors, in the education or settlement in the world of them my said legatees. Also I give and bequeath to Sir John Hawkins, one of my Executors, the Annales Ecclesiastici of Baronius, and Holinshed's and Stowe's Chronicles, and also an octavo Common Prayer-Book. To Bennet Langton, Esq. I give and bequeath my Polyglot Bible. To Sir Joshua Reynolds, my great French Dictionary, by Martiniere, and my own copy of my folio English Dictionary, of the last revision. To Dr. William Scott, one of my Executors, the Dictionnaire de Commerce, and Lectius's edition of the Greek poets. To Mr. Windham, Poetæ Græci Heroici per Henricum Stephanum. To the Rev. Mr. Strahan, vicar of Islington, in Middlesex, Mill's Greek Testament, Beza's Greek Testament, by Stephens, all my Latin Bibles, and my Greek Bible, by Wechelius. To Dr. Heberden, Dr. Brocklesby, Dr. Butter, and Mr. Cruikshank, the surgeon who attended me, Mr. Holder, my apothecary, Gerard Hamilton, Esq., Mrs. Gardiner, of Snow-hill, Mrs. Frances Reynolds, Mr. Hoole, and the Reverend Mr. Hoole, his son, each a book at their election, to keep as a token of remembrance. I also give and bequeath to Mr. John Desmoulins, two hundred pounds consolidated three *per cent.* annuities: and to Mr. Sastres, the Italian master, the sum of five pounds, to be laid out in books of piety for his own use. And whereas the said Bennet Langton hath agreed, in consideration of the sum of seven hundred and fifty pounds, mentioned in my Will to be in his hands, to grant and secure an annuity of seventy pounds payable during the life of me and my servant, Francis Barber, and the life of the survivor of us, to Mr. George Stubbs, in trust for us; my mind and will is, that in case of my decease before the said agreement shall be perfected, the said sum of seven hundred and fifty pounds, and the bond for securing the said sum, shall go to the said Francis Barber; and I hereby give and bequeath to him the same, in lieu of the bequest in his favour, contained in my said Will. And I hereby empower my Executors to deduct and retain all expences that shall or may be incurred in the execution of my said Will, or of this Codicil thereto, out of such estate and effects as I shall die possessed of. All the rest, residue, and remainder, of my estate and effects, I give and bequeath to my said Executors, in trust for the said Francis Barber, his Executors and Administrators. Witness my hand and seal, this ninth day of December, 1784.

'SAM. JOHNSON'
Boswell, *Life*

(DATE UNKNOWN)

Talking Jacobitism

Yet there is no doubt that at earlier periods he was wont often to exercise both his pleasantry and ingenuity in talking Jacobitism. My much respected friend, Dr. Douglas, now Bishop of Salisbury, has favoured me with the following admirable instance from his Lordship's own recollection. One day when dining at old Mr. Langton's where Miss Roberts, his niece, was one of the company, Johnson, with his usual complacent attention to the fair sex, took her by the hand and said, 'My dear, I hope you are a Jacobite.' Old Mr. Langton, who, though a high and steady Tory, was attached to the present Royal Family, seemed offended, and asked Johnson, with great warmth, what he could mean by putting such a question to his niece? 'Why, Sir, (said Johnson) I meant no offence to your niece, I meant her a great compliment. A Jacobite, Sir, believes in the divine right of Kings. He that believes in the divine right of Kings believes in a Divinity. A Jacobite believes in the divine right of Bishops. He that believes in the divine right of Bishops believes in the divine authority of the Christian religion. Therefore, Sir, a Jacobite is neither an Atheist nor a Deist. That cannot be said of a Whig; for *Whiggism is a negation of all principle.*'

Boswell, *Life, s.a.* 1763

Epitaph on Parnell

In his Life of PARNELL, I wonder that Johnson omitted to insert an Epitaph which he had long before composed for that amiable man, without ever writing it down, but which he was so good as, at my request, to dictate to me, by which means it has been preserved.

'*Hic requiescit* THOMAS PARNELL, *S. T. P.*
Qui sacerdos pariter et poeta,
Utrasque partes ita implevit,
Ut neque sacerdoti suavitas poetæ,
Nec poetæ sacerdotis sanctitas, deesset.'

Boswell, *Life, s.a.* 1781

The Stream at Lichfield

Errat adhuc vitreus per prata virentia rivus,
  Quo toties lavi membra tenella puer;
Hic delusa rudi frustrabar brachia motu,
  Dum docuit blanda voce natare pater.
Fecerunt rami latebras, tenebrisque diurnis
  Pendula secretas abdidit arbor aquas.
Nunc veteres duris periêre securibus umbræ,
  Longinquisque oculis nuda lavacra patent.
Lympha tamen cursus agit indefessa perennis,
  Tectaque qua fluxit, nunc et aperta fluit.
Quid ferat externi velox, quid deterat ætas,
  Tu quoque securus res age, Nise, tuas.

PRINTED IN
GREAT BRITAIN
AT THE
UNIVERSITY PRESS
OXFORD
BY
CHARLES BATEY
PRINTER
TO THE
UNIVERSITY